Testament to Ruthenian

HARVARD UKRAINIAN RESEARCH INSTITUTE

HARVARD SERIES IN UKRAINIAN STUDIES

Cambridge, Massachusetts

Testament to Ruthenian

A Linguistic Analysis of the Smotryc'kyj Variant

Stefan M. Pugh

Distributed by Harvard University Press
for the
Harvard Ukrainian Research Institute

Publication of this volume has been made possible by
John Halawaj, benefactor of Ukrainian studies
at Harvard University

ISBN 0-916458-75-X

This book has been printed on acid-free paper and bound to meet ANSI standard Z39.48.

The Ukrainian Research Institute of Harvard University was established in 1973. It supports research associates and visiting scholars who are engaged in projects concerned with all aspects of Ukrainian studies. The Institute also works in close cooperation with the Committee on Ukrainian Studies, which supervises and coordinates the teaching of Ukrainian history, language, and literature at Harvard University.

This book is dedicated to my parents,
William and Luise Pugh

Editorial Statement

The Harvard Series in Ukrainian Studies publishes original scholarship, archival research, and conference proceedings for the Ukrainian Research Institute of Harvard University. Within the Series, we endeavor to use place-names in a form which reflects the language of the current political jurisdiction of the place, for example, L′viv instead of Lwów or L′vov, and Mahilëŭ instead of Mohyliv or Mogilev. When a place-name refers to a historical province or region that does not have an exact equivalent among contemporary states, then the historical form is preferred, for example, Podolia when referring to the palatinate of the Polish-Lithuanian Commonwealth, but Podillja when referring to the geographic region in contemporary Ukraine.

The presentation of personal names defies such an easy formula. Many of those mentioned within the present volume were of Ruthenian ethnic origin, but were born into, and spent their active lives in, a Polish-speaking milieu within the Polish-Lithuanian Commonwealth. As a series dedicated to the encouragement and dissemination of Ukrainian studies, it is our mandate to promote a recognition of the Ruthenian element in the history of the Commonwealth. The term "Ruthenian" itself has varying meanings. At present, it often means simply "Ukrainian"; however, in the early-modern period it referred to a shared social, intellectual, and religious sphere that gave rise to modern Ukrainian and Belarusian culture, language, and identity. Since the Series is dedicated primarily to the Ukrainian part of this sphere, the names of all those considered Ruthenian are rendered in Ukrainian form, even though they may have been equally important to Belarusian history and culture.

Contents

Preface

Meletij Smotrycʹkyj (ca. 1578-1633) was a cleric, polemicist, and scholar of Slavonic who wrote in Polish and an East Slavic literary language known at the time as "ꙗзыкъ рꙋєькїй" 'Ruthenian', the predecessor of literary Ukrainian and Belarusian. It is the Ruthenian literary language that is the subject of this book.

When scanning a Ruthenian text—for instance, a text of Smotrycʹkyj—the reader's first reaction is, "This isn't Ukrainian, it isn't Belarusian—what is it?" Depending on the provenance of a given author, a Ruthenian text can indeed contain features identifiable as "Ukrainian" or as "Belarusian," and the presence of such features has led many scholars to claim such authors as either "Ukrainian" or "Belarusian." Comparison of Ruthenian texts shows, however, that their language is extremely similar, differing perhaps in degree (more Polonisms, fewer Slavonicisms, etc.) more than in essence. An analysis of the language of Smotrycʹkyj's texts has as its primary task the description of the language, the identification of its components—in short, finding an answer to the question, "what is it?" As Smotrycʹkyj's texts reflect one variant of Ruthenian, this study will also consider his variant in comparison with the language of some of his contemporaries; comparisons of this kind will lead to a better description of Ruthenian in general. The second purpose of the study is to evaluate the Smotrycʹkyj Variant of Ruthenian from the standpoint of modern Ukrainian and Belarusian: to what extent does Smotrycʹkyj's system foreshadow either or both modern systems, and how?

I would like to acknowledge here the assistance and advice given to me by a large number of people and institutions. The procurement of textual materials was made possible first of all by Ms. Oksana Procyk, at that time of the Harvard University Library, and secondly by Ms. I. F. Grigorʹeva of the International Exchange Section, Saltykov-Shchedrin State Library, St. Petersburg, who provided me with a microfilm copy of Kazanʹe, one of the texts analyzed here. Thanks to Professor Horace G. Lunt of Harvard University for his detailed critique of the manuscript, and to Professor Edna Andrews of Duke University for her advice and comments. I am especially grateful to Ms. Sandra Bostian for her help in checking the page and line references of a very large number of linguistic citations in this book. Finally, for her immense patience and endless encouragement during the writing and re-writing process, my heartfelt thanks to my wife, Barbara A. Fennell.

Abbreviations

A, acc	Accusative
Act	Active
Adj	Adjective
Adv	Adverb
Br	Belarusian
B-R	Belarusian-Ruthenian
CES	Common East Slavic
ChSl	Church Slavonic
Coll	Collective
Colloq	Colloquial
Cond	Conditional
CS	Common Slavic
CSBR	Contemporary Standard Belarusian
CSP	Contemporary Standard Polish
CSR	Contemporary Standard Russian
CSU	Contemporary Standard Ukrainian
Cz	Czech
D, dat	Dative
Fem, f	Feminine
FS	František Skaryna
Fut	Future
G, gen	Genitive
Grammatiki	*Grammatiki slavenskija pravilnoe syntagma*
Imp	Imperative
Inf	Infinitive
I, inst	Instrumental
IV	Ivan Vyšens'kyj (written corpus)
JU	*Jevanhelije učytelnoje*
Kaz	*Kazan'e. Na čestnyj pogreb . . . o. Leontija Karpoviča*
L, loc	Locative
Masc, m	Masculine
MS	Meletij Smotryc'kyj (written corpus)
Neut, n	Neuter
N, nom	Nominative
OCS	Old Church Slavonic
Part	Participle
Pass	Passive
PB	Pamvo Berynda (written corpus; *Leksykon*)
Pl	Plural
P–M	Pseudo-Meleško (written corpus)
Pol	Polish
Poss	Possessive
Pres	Present
Pret	Preterite
Rus, R	Russian
Sg	Singular
SinSlav	*Sinonima Slavenorosskaia*
Slk	Slovak
Sub	Substantive
SV	Smotryc'kyj variant
Ukr, U	Ukrainian
U-R	Ukrainian-Ruthenian
V, voc	Vocative

Citation of Forms

Three texts have been analyzed for the purposes of this study; forms from these texts are identified by page and line numbers following each example:

1) Roman numerals refer to the preface to *Grammatiki* (e.g., IIIa,1=page III recto, line 1; IIIb,1= page III verso, line 1); citations follow the numbering system of Horbatsch 1974, but forms are taken directly from the facsimile edition of Nimčuk 1979.

2) "K" followed by Arabic numerals refer to *Kazan'e* (K7a,1; K7b,1); forms are cited as they appear in Maslov's 1907 edition. The Maslov edition was checked by this author against a microfilm copy of the original to ensure the accuracy of the forms.

3) Arabic numerals without the designation "K" refer to page numbers in the 1987 edition of *Jevanhelije učitelnoe* (Harvard Library of Early Ukrainian Literature, Texts: vol. II); numbers are followed by "a" or "b," in reference to left and right columns, respectively, followed by line numbers (e.g. 59a,15). All textual lines on a page are counted, including text in smaller type, at the beginning of a passage as well as in the middle of the Ruthenian explication (in the middle this smaller type represents a repetition of a part of the opening reading). Chapter headings (e.g., on page 27, the first six lines of large type) and the phrase **выкладъ** . . . , which occurs at the beginning of every explication of biblical text (or just **выкладъ** in the middle), are not counted as lines. These are omitted from linguistic consideration in the study as well, as they are clearly differentiated from the text per se.

Testament to Ruthenian

Eastern Europe at the Time of Meletij Smotryc'kyj's Literary Activity (cir. 1620)

CHAPTER ONE

Smotryc'kyj and the Ruthenian Language

1.0 *Historical Notes.* The history of any language or family of languages is the product of the history of the peoples who speak those languages. Communities of the East Slavic linguistic family interacted with one another as well as with speakers of other languages, Slavic and non-Slavic. These contacts influenced the historical development of the Russian, Ukrainian, and Belarusian languages in different ways and to different degrees depending on the period and region in question. The evolution and areal distribution of linguistic features were also affected by changes in the political and spiritual structures that grew in the East Slavic world over a long period of time.

Broadly speaking, the major events which helped shape the East Slavic languages as they are spoken today include: 1) the Christianization of Rus′ in ca. 988 and the subsequent introduction of the Slavonic liturgy; 2) the invasion and rule of Kyivan Rus′ by the Tatars from the twelfth to the fifteenth centuries; 3) the domination of much of the present Ukraine and Belarus by Poland from the fifteenth to the eighteenth centuries; and 4) various later waves of West European influence in Russia proper during and after the time of Peter I. The first event mentioned was particularly important for the development of Russian. The periods of Tatar control and Polish hegemony were crucial for the development of many of the characteristics of present-day Ukrainian and Belarusian. The invasion of the Tatars from the East had little direct (that is, formal linguistic) influence on the development of the Ruthenian language; it had the practical effect, however, of separating the Ruthenian regions politically from those of Russian proper (some southern Russian lands were, of course, also ruled by the Tatars). Immediately following the period of Tatar rule, the Ruthenian lands came under increasing pressure from the West and Northwest, culminating in the political and cultural union of most Ruthenian regions with the Kingdom of Poland. Strong Polish—and via Polish also West European—influence on non-Russian East Slavic is most evident in the lexicon of the modern languages. Polish political and ecclesiastical domination also served to continue the relative political and cultural isolation of these languages from Russia proper: one of the results of this separation was the absence of a strong Slavonic component in the lexicon, which is characteristic of Russian. It was this period under Polish rule that led to the use of a shared literary language throughout the Ruthenian lands. This was the time during which Meletij Smotryc'kyj was active.

1.1 *Terminology*. Writers of the sixteenth and seventeenth centuries from Kyiv to Vilnius considered themselves to be members of one greater linguistic community. The word used to identify the lands and peoples of this community was ρꙋськїй,[1] and the literary language used by them was therefore known as ꙗзыкъ ρꙋськїй. In this study I use the term "Ruthenian" to correspond to ρꙋськїй, in reference to both people and language: "Ruthenian" is therefore to be understood as the uncodified literary language used by East Slavs inhabiting territories now known as "Ukraine" and "Belarus," from approximately the fourteenth century until into the eighteenth century.

Use of the term "Ruthenian" is part of a larger problem of nomenclature in East Slavic linguistics, beginning with "Old Russian." This is the name applied in much of the literature to what is more precisely Common East Slavic (CES), the language out of which all three modern languages arose. The very name "Old Russian" may be taken to imply, however, that only "Russian" is its direct descendant. An alternative to "Old Russian" and the more cumbersome "Common East Slavic" is "Rusian," a term that is based upon the name of the ancient state of Rus' (e.g., Pritsak 1981). There can be no opposition to this term on ethno-linguistic grounds, for it makes no distinction between "pre-Russian," "pre-Ukrainian," and "pre-Belarusian." In comparison with the misleading English formulation "Old Russian," the corresponding East Slavic terms are more successful: Rus древне-русский язык, Ukr давньоруська мова, and Br старажытнаруская

---

[1] Cyrillic words and phrases in the text that represent usages of Smotryc'kyj's period and have orthographic significance are set in a paleo-Cyrillic font that is patterned on a typeface used by East Slavic presses of Smotryc'kyj's time. All other Cyrillic phrases (modern or otherwise) are set in a contemporary typeface.

мова all indicate a stage in the language of Rus′ that precedes the oldest period of Russian (proper) by prefixing the element "ancient-" to *-rus-*. "Common East Slavic" is occasionally found in Slavic-language studies (e.g., Br агульнаўсходне-славянская мова in Jankowski 1977, 19), but is rare in English. Note the term "Old East Slavic" in Rudnyc′kyj 1966– . In this study I use the term *CES* in place of "Old Russian" to represent the earliest period of the East Slavic languages, and the latter term is taken to refer only to Old Russian proper, the oldest identifiable form of the *Russian* language.

Following the earliest period, we encounter difficulties in connection with the use of "Old" and "Middle" as stages of "Ukrainian" and "Belarusian": along with Rus старорусский язык, are Ukr староукраїнська мова and Br старабеларуская мова; in rare cases this period can also be referred to as "ancient-," for example, in старажытная беларуская пісьмовая мова "the Old (lit. 'ancient') Belarusian literary language" (Jankowski 1983, 46). The terms "Old Ukrainian" and "Old Belarusian" are used in reference to the language of the period we speak of as "Ruthenian." Plujšč (1971) speaks of the "Old Ukrainian literary language" as spanning the fourteenth to eighteenth centuries: 1) from the fourteenth century to the first half of the seventeenth, representing the time of the formation of the Ukrainian nationality, and 2) from the second half of the seventeenth century to the end of the eighteenth, representing the formation of the Ukrainian nation (народність vs. нація). Вахан′кой et al. (1970) use "Old Belarusian" in reference to the very same period. In other words, the modern languages are considered to have arisen out of older forms of "Ukrainian" and "Belarusian."

In Western writings these same periods are often referred to as "Middle Ukrainian" (e.g., Sysyn 1986b, 398, in reference to the L′viv Chronicle) and "Middle Belarusian" (e.g., McMillin 1980, 106–109, in reference to the Lithuanian chancellery language), and may be temporally equated with "Middle Russian." "Middle, Old Ukrainian" are differentiated from "Middle, Old Belarusian," implying the existence of different "languages" at the "Old" as well as the "Middle" stages. George Shevelov projects the term "Ukrainian" back even farther, including a Proto-Ukrainian period (1979, 31). With regard to the "Ruthenian" stage, Shevelov points out that the problem of nomenclature was most acute after the mid-seventeenth century, when the Ukrainian regions were incorporated into the Russian empire: a new name was needed (ibid., 30). The modern Ukrainian terminological system has found a solution to the problem: the term руський is sufficiently well differentiated from the Ukrainian designation for "Russian proper" (російський)[2] to avoid confusion: Jaremenko states that one of Smotryc'kyj's writings was written руською...книжною українсько-білоруською мовою "in the Ruthenian...[i.e.,] literary Ukrainian-Belarusian language" (1986, 61). For Belarusian, on the other hand, problems are certainly apparent: рускі cannot be used in reference to "Ruthenian" because it designates "Russian (proper)" in the modern language; hence the ease with which "Old Belarusian" is accepted in Belarusian-language treatises. Polish *ruski*, which is used in reference to the medieval Ruthenians and their language, is as acceptable as Ukr руський, as it is formally opposed to Pol *rosyjski* 'Russian (proper).' It is particularly difficult, therefore, if not impossible, to settle on a set of terms that is acceptable in Slavic and non-Slavic languages alike.

Some scholars writing in English avoid discussion of a "Ruthenian" language, preferring "Ukrainian" and "Belarusian" because the former is vague or ill-defined: Shevelov, for instance, states that use of руський before the mid-seventeenth century was ambiguous because it was used to describe "Ukrainians" as well as "Belarusians" (1979, 30). Others may avoid the term because they equate it with a dialect of "Ukrainian" (e.g., Carpatho-Ruthenian), or because some scholars choose to apply the term to Ukrainian in general (e.g., Bohdan Strumiński, Entwistle and Morison).[3] I choose to turn the perceived ambiguity of "руський" to advantage, interpreting its application to pre-Ukrainian and pre-Belarusian alike as a reflection of linguistic reality. In this I follow the lead of Henry Leeming in reestablishing the position of the term "Ruthenian" as one covering the literary language of both

---

2 Compare the Russian term российский "Russian" used in reference to Russia proper (not the language) in historical and political terminology, for example, in the republic name Российская Федерация.

3 Strumiński, for instance, states that the term "Ruthenian" refers to "Ukrainian-'Belarusian'" (second quotation marks his), while "White Ruthenian" specifically replaces "Belarusian"; use of this separate designation then causes the term "Ruthenian" to take on a primarily "Ukrainian" coloration, of which "White Ruthenian" could (incorrectly) be considered a subset (see Struminsky 1984, 7).

Ukrainian and Belarusian lands during the period in question, i.e., as the "language of Kyiv, Vil′no, and other centres of East Slavonic culture outside the dominion of Moscow from the 14th to the 17th century" (1968, 282). Other scholars support this position, for example, in reference to the chancellery language of Lithuanian Rus′: "Although clearly divergent from Muscovite Russian, the language is scarcely distinguishable from the written form used in the Ukraine" (Grimsted 1981, 447n4). Frank Sysyn refers to this language as "administrative Ruthenian," and as "middle Belarusian-Ukrainian" (1986a, 288). Paul Wexler's approach to the period might be called "early Ruthenian." It is much like that of the present work, referring to the regional variants as "pre-Belarusian" and "pre-Ukrainian" dialects, and to particular *features* as OBr, or "Old Belarusian"; in reference to the period spanning the fifteenth century to the present, however, he uses the term "Belorussian [Belarusian] language" (Wexler 1977).

In sum, this approach emphasizes the unity of the literary language while recognizing the existence of diversity among the varieties, or recensions, of written Ruthenian. In the event individual texts contain a significant number of features characteristic of Ukrainian and Belarusian *per se*, then we can identify them more closely as "Ukrainian-Ruthenian" (U-R) or as "Belarusian-Ruthenian" (B-R). On the basis of phonological features, I have previously referred to Smotryc′kyj as "Ukrainian-Ruthenian," and an author like Skaryna is correspondingly identified as "Belarusian-Ruthenian." We can also label the Lithuanian chancellery language as "Belarusian-Ruthenian." The differences between U-R and B-R regional variants can be very slight, however, and some texts may be open to a variety of interpretations. The language of Ivan Uževič represents an example of this phenomenon: Bilodid (1970) asserts that he was Ukrainian, and lists features that could lead to such an interpretation; Dingley (1972), however, shows that his language can more convincingly be interpreted as an example of the literary language of the Grand Duchy of Lithuania (in other words, B-R). Such a system of classification emphasizes the identity of the regional variants as members of one larger Ruthenian system, while still pointing out the connection between these variants and the modern codified Ukrainian and Belarusian languages.

1.2 *Smotryc'kyj. Ukrainian, Belarusian, or Both?* Meletij Smotryc'kyj was born ca. 1578, presumably in Smotryč, Podolia, the son of Herasym Smotryc'kyj. He attended the Orthodox school in Ostrih, Volhynia, before eventually moving to Vilnius.[4] Exact dates and the length of time spent in these regions are not known, but he probably lived only for a short while in Podolia, and is assumed to have arrived in Vilnius sometime before 1601; between 1601 and 1610 he made several trips to Germany in connection with his studies, after which he returned to Vilnius (Frick 1983, 13–16). Because the Podolian and Volhynian regions are considered ethnically and linguistically Ukrainian, modern Ukrainian linguistic studies consistently list his works as source material for the history of that language. Belarusian works which identify Smotryc'kyj's writings, and therefore the person, as Belarusian, do so on the basis of his long stay in Vilnius, a city historically considered part of Belarusian linguistic territory.

The objections of Ukrainian and Belarusian scholars that a particular "Ruthenian" author was in reality "Ukrainian" or "Belarusian" are not unreasonable: the linguistic systems of these authors are usually characterized by some feature or set of features that can be readily identified as "Ukrainian" and "Belarusian" based on the modern languages. But there need not and indeed really cannot be strict separation of sixteenth- and seventeenth-century writers from each other on the basis of modern geo-linguistic divisions. The differences which exist today between closely related literary languages frequently are the product of recent decisions made by the codifiers, and they often are necessarily arbitrary. With regard to modern Ukrainian, codification of the literary language in the first half of the nineteenth century was the result of mixing and reconciling the rather distinct eastern and western variants of the language. As for Belarusian, the process of codification took place even more recently, at the end of the nineteenth and beginning of the twentieth centuries. The variant that became the basis for the Belarusian standard language was chosen as much for its central geographical location as for fact that many features of this particular form of Belarusian were present in the variants of other regions. Between the linguistic entities representing the literary Ukrainian and

---

[4] Herasym Smotryc'kyj was himself a well-known polemicist and the first rector of the Ostrih School; he also played a prominent role in the publication of the Ostrih Bible of 1581 (Nimčuk 1979, 8–9).

Belarusian languages we can identify a large number of transitional speech areas, and, in effect, the whole of the Ukrainian-Belarusian region can be seen as a continuum of features or isoglosses. Without recourse to standardized Ukrainian and Belarusian, it would be difficult indeed to draw a definitive line between the two languages today.

When faced with a text lacking an overtly "Ukrainian" or "Belarusian" linguistic identity, it is not uncommon for scholars to emphasize the need to differentiate between the "Ukrainian" or "Belarusian" nationality of the author of that text on other than linguistic grounds. Compare the following two statements, Ukrainian and Belarusian, respectively:

> Але ця мова внаслідок спільного походження і спільного життя обох народностей в одній державі в XVI ст. не завжди виявляла специфічні риси української чи білоруської мови. Тому важко дослідити, хто був автором чи перекладачем якогось твору—українець чи білорус (Kernyc'kyj 1967, 3).

> But this [Ruthenian] language, as a result of the common origin and common life of both peoples in one state in the XVI century, did not always exhibit specific features of the Ukrainian or Belarusian language. Therefore it is difficult to determine who the author or translator of a particular work was—a Ukrainian or a Belarusian.[5]

> . . . нацыянальная прыналежнасць помнікаў звычайна вызначаецца па аднаму з трох паказчыкаў: нацыянальнасць аўтара, месца ўзнікнення помніка і моўны аналіз, хоць асобная даследчыкі па-рознаму ацэньваюць значенне такіх паказчыкаў. У гэтим даследаванні аўтары за аснову ўзялі тэрытарыяльны крытэрый (Bulyka et al., 1988, 6).

> . . . the national identity of monuments is usually determined by one of three factors: nationality [!] of the author, place of origin of the monument, and linguistic analysis, although individual researchers interpret the

---

5 This and all subsequent translations are my own unless otherwise noted.

> meaning of such factors in different ways. In this study the authors have taken the territorial criterion as the basis [for judgment].

These statements, especially the second, are circular: in order to describe a document as "Belarusian" or "Ukrainian" we have to determine the nationality of the author. It would be reasonable to expect the тэрытарыяльны крытэрый [territorial criterion] to consist of an author's place of birth and adolescence, rather than of his place of residence as an adult. If such a criterion can be loosely applied to cover the whole of his life, however, then Smotryc'kyj can indeed be claimed by modern Belarus as well as by Ukraine. One particularly important thrust of this study is that he, as a Ruthenian, does in fact belong to the literary, historical, linguistic, and cultural traditions of both modern nations. This argument is not new, for it is also made by Belarusians and Ukrainians: in the summary preceding the text of Jaremenko 1986 we read that Jaremenko's book analyzes the life and work of Meletij Smotryc'kyj, відомого українського і білоруського письменника-полеміста [the well-known Ukrainian and Belarusian writer-polemicist]. In spite of harmonious-sounding statements of this sort, the question of nationality nevertheless always seems to enter into the discussion: in the same sentence that contains this phrase, Smotryc'kyj is also described as having been "на передньому краї ідеологічної боротьби українського народу проти польско-шляхетського гноблення" [in the forefront of the ideological struggle of the Ukrainian nation/people against oppression by the Polish nobility] (ibid.). His writings are commonly cited as source material in Ukrainian as well as in Belarusian linguistic works: *Kazan'e* and *Hrammatiki* in the bibliographies of Bevzenko et al. 1978, Bulyka ed. 1982– , and Bulyka et al. 1988; *JU* in Aničenka 1969, Bevzenko 1978, Vynnyk et al. 1983, and Bulyka et al. 1988. In an article entitled "Starabelaruskaja litaraturnaja-pis'movaja mova" A. I. Žuraŭski states: "...на *бел.* мове было апублікавана некалькі казанняў . . . 'Казанне на пахаванне Лявонція Карповіча' Мялеція Сматрыцкага . . . " [in the *Belarusian* language were published several sermons . . . (such as)...'Sermon for the funeral of Leontij Karpovič' by Meletij Smotryc'kyj . . . "] (1988b, 508). The temptation to label the author as solely "Belarusian" or "Ukrainian" clearly could not be resisted by the authors of these studies.

In this study Smotryc'kyj will be considered first and foremost to be "Ruthenian." We shall approach the problem of the language of Smotryc'kyj without applying the terms "Ukrainian" and "Belarusian" to his language as a whole. That he is claimed as Ukrainian by Ukrainians and as Belarusian by Belarusians was another impetus for writing this book: does either nation have the right to claim Smotryc'kyj as its own? Do both?

1.3 *Smotryc'kyj and Language(s).* Smotryc'kyj has been the subject of a growing number of studies in recent years, in the West and in the former USSR; scholars have clearly been attracted by his role in the struggle between rival ideas (Catholic/Uniate vs. Orthodox, Latin vs. Slavonic) and nations (Poland vs. Ukraine-Belarus), and his appeals stretches from linguists to cultural historians. Among the large number of works devoted to Smotryc'kyj are general biographical and literary studies such as Solovij 1978, Frick 1983, Jaremenko 1986; Smotryc'kyj's collected works have been published as volumes 1 and 2 of the Harvard Library of Early Ukrainian Literature (1987). Volume 1 of the Harvard Library contains a fine bibliography of works relating to Smotryc'kyj compiled by David Frick.*

Smotryc'kyj is known to linguists/philologists primarily for his grammar of Slavonic (*Grammatiki*), by means of which he undertook to bring order and comprehensibility to a liturgical language that had long been unintelligible to listeners and misunderstood by readers. The writing of that book in reality had far greater consequences than those intended by the author: beyond making Slavonic intelligible, or at least more intelligible than it had been, Smotryc'kyj introduced a model for the construction of grammars (prescriptive rather than descriptive) of the East Slavic languages based on the classical Greek and Latin grammars. The grammatical model established by Smotryc'kyj for Slavonic was used by Lomonosov as late as the 1750s when he was writing his grammar of Russian; Lomonosov went so far as to use some of Smotryc'kyj's rules and grammatical paradigms verbatim (Nimčuk 1979, 104). The number of later editions of *Grammatiki*

---

* Shortly before *Testament to Ruthenian* went to press, the Harvard Series in Ukrainian Studies published David Frick's biography of Smotryc'kyj, *Meletij Smotryc'kyj* (Cambridge, Mass., 1995). The author of the present study was unable to utilize it at this late date.—*The Editors*

attests to the importance of this work: Moscow 1648 and 1721, Wallachia 1655 and 1755. *Grammatiki* not only described, but was composed in Slavonic, dubbed "Meletian Slavonic" by Shevelov (1979, 568). Several studies of Meletian Slavonic have appeared in recent years, most notably those by Horbatsch (1964, 1974) and Nimčuk (1979). Numerous Ruthenian and specifically Ukrainian features of Smotryc'kyj's own morphological system have been identified in the text of the grammar by Aničenka (1982, 126–27), Bacenko (1982, 155–57) and Horbatsch (1974, VII).

Smotryc'kyj's role in using Ruthenian (as opposed to Slavonic) is important for the cultural study of this period in general: "Smotryc'kyj and others saw a functional equivalence between Latin and Slavonic, on the one hand, and between Ruthenian and Polish, on the other" (Frick 1985, 50). Thus, he believed in the use of Slavonic as a language of learning, similar to the role of Latin in the West, but Smotryc'kyj's work as translator of *JU* shows that he also believed in a role for the written Ruthenian language: since biblical texts were impossible for lay people to understand, recourse to a vernacular-based language was imperative. In this respect Ivan Vyšens'kyj showed similar leanings, but he felt strongly that Ruthenian should be used not in the course of the liturgy but only afterwards, as an aid to understanding (Goldblatt 1991, 13). We shall call the literary Ruthenian language used in his texts the "Smotryc'kyj Variant" (SV), rather than appropriate Shevelov's "Meletian" as a label for his Ruthenian: "Meletian Slavonic" refers to the standard which Smotryc'kyj established for that language, a claim that cannot be made for the Ruthenian in which he wrote.

1.4 *The Polish Language and Bilingualism.* The role of Polish in the Ruthenian lands has been the subject of many studies, the most thorough of which still is Martel 1938. The status of Polish as a language of culture and power was not unlike that of Norman French in medieval England or of Russian in the former Soviet Union: to succeed in Ruthenian society, whether in academic, ecclesiastic, or governmental circles, learning Polish was of paramount importance. Lower levels of society were also affected, however, for Polish had become the *lingua franca* of the land: members of this society, and in particular its learned members, were necessarily bilingual. Such a linguistic situation has significant consequences for the language which is indigenous to a particular region, not the least of which is the frequent use of large numbers of lexemes in L1 (Ruthenian) taken from L2 (Polish).[6] As Shevelov points out, the overall character of these loans changed from one of governmental/administrative language to that of everyday life (1991, 237). We can compile impressive lists of Polish words ("Polonisms") in Ruthenian texts, written in Cyrillic and adapted to the Ruthenian morphological system, and treated as an integral part of "cultured" Ruthenian. Similar situations existed in the former Soviet Union, where the socio-political power structures corresponded to the Polish-Ruthenian relationship and yielded similar linguistic results. For example, in a recent Soviet dictionary of Udmurt (a Finno-Ugric language), there are an enormous number of Russian lexemes listed as Udmurt, for example, закон 'law,' салат 'salad,' обед 'noon meal,' and устной 'oral,' translated into Russian as закон, салат, обед, and устный.

The bilingualism of Ruthenian writers is particularly clear in the case of Smotryc'kyj, because he wrote many treatises in Polish: Smotryc'kyj the Ruthenian might therefore also be considered a "Polish" writer. Ruthenian texts in which there are many Polonisms can certainly be used as source material in the study of the history of Polish; W. Taszycki includes in his collection a Ruthenian text (no. 35) with a substantial number of Polonisms for that very purpose (1969, 147–49). The problem with this example in particular, and this is symptomatic of the problem of Ruthenian lexicon in general, is the identification of this text as "rusko-polski" ('Ruthenian-Polish'), i.e., as something of a *Mischsprache*. With reference to Smotryc'kyj in particular, Isačenko describes the preface to Smotryc'kyj's grammar of Slavonic as lexically and syntactically primarily Polish, but as morphologically East Slavic or Slavonic (1980, 311–12); he makes no mention of phonology. When couched in negative terms (e.g., the language is *not* pure Ruthenian or Polish), statements like these are not particularly useful. One must remember that the presence of Polish lexemes in Ruthenian texts does not imply that they are "extrasystemic"; in fact, Isačenko himself admits this by saying that it is not clear whether the Polish lexical elements

6 "L1" designates the primary language of the speaker—the speaker's "mother tongue." "L2" here refers to a secondary language that the speaker must learn in opposition to L1.

used by Smotryc'kyj were already elements of the "Ukrainian" and "Belarusian" languages (ibid.).[7]

Use of Polish lexical items does not in and of itself make a text "mixed" to the extent that it can no longer be called "Ruthenian." Polonisms are rather to be viewed as loan words that function as part of the system of the speaker's L1. One way to test the status of Polish loanwords in one particular text or author's language is by verifying their presence in texts by other authors of the same period: if such lexemes are present (and certainly if they are retained in CSU/CSBR) then they must be considered all the more part of the system. The Polish component of Smotryc'kyj's lexicon is generally found in the language of his contemporaries and therefore cannot be described as "non-Ruthenian." Individual forms can only be interpreted as occupying a place outside the Ruthenian system if they are not used by other writers or (in those rare instances) when they are accompanied by Polish morphological features.

1.5 *A Ruthenian "Standard"*? Every language that has a codified "standard" form is still characterized by variation. While such variation is most obvious in spoken language, which is relatively free of the constraints placed on written language, it is also observable in writing (prescriptivists refer to examples of this phenomenon as "mistakes"). Regional, stylistic, and social variation (or "choice") exists on every level of language: phonology, morphology, lexicon, syntax, and semantics. The spoken language of Kyiv naturally differed from the spoken East Slavic language of the Lithuanian Grand Duchy, but the supradialectal Ruthenian literary language used in both areas reflects two ends of a spectrum of regional variants. While the two regions clearly belong to the linguistic traditions of modern Ukrainian and Belarusian, we are still dealing with one shared literary language during the Ruthenian period.

Ruthenian is sometimes described in terms of a diglossic relationship: there is an opposition between the spoken "Ukrainian" and "Belarusian" languages on the one hand and the written, supranational

---

7 The author also overstates the role of Slavonic morphology in Smotryc'kyj's text: instead of правого (IIa,15) he cites this form as *pravaho*, in which -aho represents the Slavonic variant of the genitive singular non-feminine adjective desinence (1980, 311).

(or perhaps better, a "supradialectal") проста мова on the other (Uspenskij 1987, 260). Citing Berynda's terminology, Uspenskij distinguishes between руская речь, волынская речь, and литовская речь, that is, between (written) проста мова, (spoken) Ukrainian, and (spoken) Belarusian, respectively (ibid., 261). While such descriptions are superficially acceptable, objections remain. The most important of these is that Uspenskij's description of проста мова is that of a system in which features of the local (spoken) language do not occur; i.e., it is a language that is at best non-Russian East Slavic, making use of a number of universally understood lexical Polonisms. Linguistic analysis has shown, however, that some phonological and morphological features are reflected in Ruthenian texts which can only be described as "Ukrainian" (e.g., ѣ = [i] in Smotryc'kyj's *Kazan'e*: see chapter 2) or as "Belarusian," thus negating a crucial aspect of Uspenskij's definition of проста мова.[8] The fact that Berynda differentiates among three systems poses no problems or conflicts for the approach proposed in this study: руская, волынская, and литовская речи are simply interpreted here as representing written literary Ruthenian vs. specifically U-R and B-R, respectively. The term "Ruthenian vernacular standard" (Goldblatt 1991, 12) is extremely useful: the language is "Ruthenian" (not Ukrainian or Belarusian), it is based on (but not equal to) the living spoken language, and it has many of the attributes of a standard literary language, used and understood over a large territory.

A fresh approach to the study of this language is necessary: 1) texts from the entire Ruthenian area (disregarding those that are obviously Polish or Slavonic) ought to be described as "U-R" or "B-R" based primarily on phonological and morphological analyses; 2) the lexical

---

8 Uspenskij (1983) discusses the question of "bilingualism" vs. "diglossia" in the Ruthenian lands, but that study focuses on the nature of the relationship between Ruthenian and Slavonic. He concludes that the relationship is one of bilingualism (not diglossia), because 1) the spoken or less prestigious language has been codified (witness the appearance of the dictionary Синонима Славенороссская and Uževič's grammar) and 2) biblical passages had to be translated in order to be understood or explained, as exemplified by the appearance of parallel texts with identical content (1983, 84). One might argue with the application of the term "bilingualism" to this situation on the grounds that Slavonic was not a spoken language: a Catholic who can read the Latin Mass would not be described as "bilingual in Latin and Language X."

core of these texts ought to be recognized as "pan-Ruthenian," with some allowances for regional variation; and 3) additional subcategories of the terms "U-R and B-R" should be defined and differentiated on the basis of larger Polish and/or Slavonic lexical components. This last point is dependent upon the stylistic level or subject matter of a given text. Such a general approach would ensure equality of treatment for all manners of texts, would avoid misnomers, and would discourage the temptation to apply twentieth century designations to texts and authors to whom they do not apply. The purpose of the present analysis of Smotryc'kyj's language is two-fold. First, the description and explanation of the linguistic system(s) used in the composition of his texts. Second, the identification of individual features of "Ukrainian" and/or "Belarusian." As the seventeenth century represents the period immediately preceding the emergence of more clearly distinct Ukrainian and Belarusian linguistic communities, one of the tasks of the linguist is to identify unequivocal features of these nascent "national" languages in texts of this period. Ideally, to present as complete a picture as possible of the Ruthenian system, with all of its variant features and vacillations, it will be necessary to study the language of every available Ruthenian text and combine the resulting data in one "grammar," that is, in one database. Eventually, data from all texts that can be identified as "Ruthenian" ought to be brought together without regard for the origin of the author or their present identification as "Ukrainian" or "Belarusian." The broad and exhaustive compilation of the features of these texts will allow linguists to identify those phonological, morphological, and lexical features (allowing for regional and stylistic variation) which are "pan-Ruthenian." In a sense, this will represent the Ruthenian "standard" which was not codified by the Ruthenians themselves. A direct result of this effort would also be a clearer periodization of the history of the modern languages.

Several studies of the language of individual Ruthenian writers have already been published; it is hoped that this analysis of Smotryc'kyj's texts will, together with the previous studies, become part of the description of the "Ruthenian Vernacular Standard."

1.6 *The Texts.*

1. **Грамматїки славенскиѧ правилное сvнтаґма**, hereafter *Grammatiki*. (1618–19, Vievis). The preface to Smotryc'kyj's Slavonic grammar is extremely short, consisting of under 450 words; it is stylistically neutral (i.e., it lacks overt Slavonicisms), and therefore is of value in spite of its length. This text is available in Horbatsch 1974, and in facsimile form in Nimčuk 1979.

2. **Казанье. На честный погребъ ... ѿ. Леонтїѧ Карповича**, hereafter *Kazan'e*. (1620, Vilnius). This text is a sermon delivered on the occasion of the burial of the Archimandrite Leontij Karpovič, and as such presents a stylistic picture that differs substantially from that of *Grammatiki*; it contains approximately 9000 words. The primary difference is that this text contains many Slavonicisms, for example in Biblical quotations. This fact notwithstanding, it is a very valuable resource: it is a work meant for oral presentation/aural reception, and its language therefore represents a good example of (higher style) Ruthenian; learned Polonisms are present throughout the text. *Kazan'e* is reproduced in Maslov 1907.

3. **Єѵангелїе оучителное**, hereafter *JU* (1616, Vievis). This massive work became available to researchers in the West in 1987, when it was published as volume 2 of the Harvard Library of Early Ukrainian Literature (1987); it totals approximately 1100 MS pages, or about 120,000 words. *JU* is a Ruthenian translation of a Homiletic Gospel from the Slavonic and Greek and has been successfully ascribed to the hand of Smotryc'kyj (Frick 1983, 22–23). Jaremenko categorically states that *Kazan'e* is the only known work of Smotryc'kyj's that is written in Ruthenian ("руською мовою," cf. 1986, 61): the preface to his grammar and the text of *JU* are disregarded, the latter either because it is not an original composition or because its ascription to Smotryc'kyj was not known to the author.

1.6.1 *Register (Linguistic-Stylistic Level).*

The linguistic profile of *JU* is broadly similar to that of *Grammatiki*, as the role of Slavonicisms is minimal: this is an explanatory work, and therefore meant to be understood; this stands in marked contrast to *Kazan'e*, which is meant to be solemn and formal, and therefore needs to employ Slavonicisms. *JU* differs from the other two, however, with regard to the use and status of Polonisms in this work. Whereas *Kazan'e* tends to use Slavonicisms in order to achieve a higher stylistic level, *JU* uses larger numbers of *Polish* lexemes for the same purpose; this is evident in very well-defined contexts, viz. in the biblical passages that begin each new reading or chapter. It is important to recognize that these sections of text are not *explanations* of biblical quotations, because explanations clearly follow the "biblical" texts, and they are more heavily East Slavic than the biblical passages; the latter are also visually set apart from the corresponding explanations by appearing in smaller type. It is important to point out that both sets of passages can be described as "Ruthenian" (the biblical introductions are not written in Polish); both, as expected, are characterized by the presence of Polonisms, but the Polonisms represent a higher proportion of forms in the introductory passages.[9] This is not to say that Slavonicisms are completely absent from *JU*: a few rare passages in the body of this text, e.g., the Lord's Prayer, are cited in Slavonic because of their very nature. The use of marked forms, whether in the guise of Slavonicisms or of a high concentration of Polonisms, is therefore text- and context-specific.

1.7 *Scope of this Study.* Individual features of Smotryc'kyj's language have been noted in studies by the authors named above, and examples from *JU* are occasionally cited in historical studies of Ukrainian and Belarusian; I have analyzed *Grammatiki* and *Kazan'e* (Pugh 1984, 1985, 1986, 1987), but a more comprehensive study of his linguistic system was impossible before the appearance of *JU*. This text contains an immense amount of new information, and the picture of the Smotryc'kyj Variant that has emerged is consequently much more complete, and balanced, than it was when analyses were based primarily on *Kazan'e*. In the course of this study, SV is compared and contrasted as closely as possible with the language of his contemporaries, in particular with that of Vyšens'kyj (IV) and Berynda (PB); other sources, such as the language of *Синонима Славено-росская* (SinSlav), Pseudo-Meleško (P-M), Skaryna (FS), *Словник*

9 Cf. my article, "Polish Lexemes as Cultural-Stylistic Markers in Smotryc'kyj's *Jevanhelije Učitelnoje*," in the Henry Leeming Festschrift (forthcoming, Cracow).

староукраїнської мови (SSUM), and *Гістарычны слоўнік беларускай мовы* (HSBM) are also consulted.[10] Not all of these authors are coeval with Smotryc'kyj: the only ones one can describe as true "contemporaries" are Vyšens'kyj and Berynda; *Sinonima slaveno-rosskaja* may date from the late-seventeenth century, while Skaryna was active in the early part of the sixteenth century. Such a broad comparative scope is important for the formulation of a description of Ruthenian as a whole—it allows us to identify those elements that remain constant from early to late Ruthenian, and to highlight those features that are peculiar to the Ruthenian system at the apparent height of its heterogeneity, the late-sixteenth to mid-seventeenth century.

The present study is somewhat different from other descriptions of the Ruthenian language. Didiakin-Leeming 1969 is a straightforward description of Berynda's flectional system. The most comprehensive description of any one Ruthenian author's language to date is Gröschel 1972, but it is an analysis of Vyšens'kyj's Ruthenian in strictly etymological terms, identifying forms as "Ukrainian," "Belarusian," "(Church) Slavonic," and "Polish," with little regard for the systemic status of particular elements, especially Polonisms. The present study of Smotryc'kyj's written language is more concerned with identifying the nature of the Ruthenian system, whatever the origin of its constituent parts.

1.8 *The Linguistic Analysis. Phonology*. In chapter 2 I formulate a general phonological analysis of Smotryc'kyj's Ruthenian. It cannot pretend to reflect all of the characteristics of his spoken language,

---

[10] Синонима Славенороссская (see Nimčuk 1964) represents a reversal of Berynda's *Leksykon*, and as such is extremely valuable for studies of the Ruthenian language. It is difficult and time-consuming to confirm the presence of a particular form in that language on the basis of *Leksykon* alone. In addition, there is not always a one-to-one correspondence between the Slavonic-Ruthenian glosses of *Leksykon* and the Ruthenian-Slavonic glosses of Синонима Славенороссская (there are even occasional disagreements); comparison of entries in the two works therefore occasionally provides the reader with valuable new information.

In the text, page references following IV and PB refer to Gröschel 1972 and Didiakin-Leeming 1969 respectively, unless otherwise indicated. References to Skaryna (FS in the text) are taken from Aničenka's works (1977–1984). References to Berynda's *Leksykon* are from Nimčuk 1961.

because of orthographic constraints and the nature of the texts that have come down to us. Although it is consequently impossible to identify his phonological system as that of a clearly localized geographical area (such as Smotryč), many general and some regional features are identifiable.

1.8.1 *Morphology*. The analysis and description of a morphological system is essentially the construction of a descriptive grammar. Chapters 3 through 9 examine the language of Meletij Smotryc'kyj according to traditional morphological categories, viz. the substantive, adjective, pronoun, numeral, adverb, preposition, conjunction, particle, and verb. The order in which these categories are presented, as well as the order in which some subdivisions of these larger categories are described, is similar to—although not exactly the same as—the order of presentation in Gröschel 1972. The premeditated structural similarity of this work to Gröschel's will facilitate use of both works by readers interested in pursuing the comparison in greater depth. The actual analysis of the morphological component differs according to the properties of each category: because of the systemic nature of inflected categories, MS' inflectional morphology is compared with PB and IV.[11] The "lexical" nature of non-inflected categories requires that we broaden the scope of our comparison and include other sources (PB, IV, SinSlav, P-M, FS, SSUM, HSBM), especially in order to gauge the systemicity of various morpho-lexical Polonisms; cf. "Lexicon" below. The results of the analyses, with particular focus on "U-R" and "B-R" features, are summarized in chapter 10.

1.8.2 *Lexicon*. The lexicon of Smotryc'kyj's texts enters into the morphological analysis more by accident than by design: "lexicon" and

---

11 Didiakin-Leeming 1969 describes only Berynda's inflectional morphology. MS' system is therefore compared with that of PB by consulting SinSlav in search of Slavonic glosses for Ruthenian morphological forms; the Slavonic glosses are in turn looked up in Berynda's Leksykon, and the glosses for these headwords may or may not include those Ruthenian forms attested in MS. Note that I am presenting forms in IV in a paleo-Slavonic typeface, rather than the Latin transliteration presented by Gröschel 1972. This is to ease comparison of forms by the reader, but necessarily means a loss in graphic verity, although with no functional significance for the present study. See Gröschel (1972, 5–6; especially n.17).

"morphology" can merge in what may be considered traditionally morphological categories. In a category such as that of the numeral, for example, attention is focused on the shape of the lexical root as well as on the identity of the morphological desinence. In addition to the most "purely" morphological components, that is, those aspects dealing with inflectional morphology (substantive, adjective, pronoun, verb), there are significant morphological categories which may be thought of as "lexical" in nature (adverb, conjunction, preposition). Among the "most lexical" of the uninflected morphology is the adverb (with the exception of deadjectival forms, which can be said to have an adverbial *ending*), if we define "lexicon" in the strictest sense as a set of elements that does not consist of bound morphemes. The analysis of Smotryc'kyj's system reveals that these categories share a characteristic justifying their inclusion in one non-flectional mega-category: there is significant Polish influence in all of these classes, especially in comparison with inflectional morphology. Although the preposition ought to resist influences to which the adverb and conjunction may be open, by virtue of being the most purely "grammatical" and presumably closed class of the three, a sizable number of Polish elements is in evidence here as well.

As in the morphology of SV, the greatest part of the lexical component *per se* is best called "Ruthenian," i.e., most lexical elements used by Smotryc'kyj will be found in all variants of the Ruthenian language at that time. This is true regardless of the origin of the particular elements: Common Ruthenian (that is, forms which developed in and were shared by Ruthenian regional variants but not by Russian), Polish, or Latin/Greek forms. The many Polonisms found in MS reflect the norm for the period; by and large the same Polonisms are found in Berynda, Vyšens'kyj, and others. A study of Smotryc'kyj's lexicon should be part of the larger compilation of a Ruthenian lexicon, sensitive to the Ruthenian dialect continuum, from U-R in the south to B-R in the north. In fact, the language of MS is already part of the "B-R" dictionary, viz. *Гістарычны слоўнік беларускай мовы,* as it is of the planned "U-R" dictionary (*Словник української мови XVI–першої половини XVII ст.*); at the time of this writing, only *Kazan'e* and *Grammatiki* are listed in the bibliographies of the respective dictionaries, but it is to be hoped that *JU* will be included. All that remains is to combine these two dictionaries, and we will have a good basic dictionary of "Common Ruthenian."

1.8.3 *Syntax*. The component of Smotryc'kyj's language traditionally described as "syntax" is not given separate consideration here. Syntax necessarily occupies an important position in the morphological analysis, however, because the domains of morphology and syntax are intertwined in an inflecting language ("morphosyntax"). Whether we are discussing the use or distribution of certain case forms of substantives, adjectives and pronouns, or the occurrence of one or another preposition with particular cases, we are analyzing forms in and explaining them on the basis of context. Such a discussion of the combinability of forms traditionally belongs under the heading "syntax," but cannot be disregarded in a thorough morphological examination. The question of word order is not considered here .

CHAPTER TWO

Orthography and Phonology

2.0 *Orthography*. Many assumptions concerning the phonological makeup of Smotryc'kyj's Ruthenian have to be more or less tentative because they are based on analyses of the orthographic norms followed in the composition of his texts. Although we can certainly draw some conclusions about the language of Smotryc'kyj's writings, it is not often possible to describe with any degree of certainty what his spoken language sounded like. The phonetic values of letters can sometimes be deduced by a comparison of Ruthenian forms with modern East Slavic. First and foremost, however, it is necessary to describe his writing system and establish, by internal comparison of forms and paradigms, what the norms are. Especially valuable for the study of the phonetic makeup of the author of a text are occasional inconsistencies in the use of particular letters, that is, in environments where they are not expected on etymological grounds. Equally valuable are Polonisms (forms of Polish origin or Latin and Greek forms transmitted via Polish) which sometimes allow us to interpret sound values for particular graphemes with greater precision than is possible on the basis of East Slavic lexemes alone.

Below is the set of characters used in the three texts, with approximate phonetic values. In the event an orthographic variant is peculiar to only one or two of the texts, this is also indicated. Interpretations of the value of individual graphemes that are not obvious are found in the notes in the table and in the following discussion of individual features ("Phonology," 2.1).

Letter	*Sound (approx.)*	*Examples*	*Notes*
а	a	Авторъ	
б	b	бꙋдетъ	
в	v	ведлꙋгъ	
г	h	где	On this and the next two graphemes, see 2.111 below.
Ґ	g	Ґды	In *Kazan'e* and *Grammatiki.*
кг	g	кгды	In JU only.
д	d	длѧ	
е	e	ведлꙋгъ	Note the distinction of the grapheme "е" and the grapheme "є" (see next entry).
є	je, (C)'e	єго, єднакѡ єстесь неволничеє	Not in *Grammatiki.* є is used to distinguish "soft" from "hard" stems in certain plural desinences: Dpl младенцємъ. Cf. єго in *Grammatiki* but єго in *Kazan'e* and JU.
ѣ	i	нѣгде, ꙋставѣчне	See 2.1.2.1 below.
ж	ž	животъ	
з	z	Здравствꙋйте	
i	i,y	i, славенскимъ	See next entry and 2.1.2.2 below.
і, ї	i,y	Иерей, славенскїи, нехай	Of the three "i" letters и is most commonly used; і occurs in Biblical names and terms, while ї is often written before other vowels and before j, as well as in some borrowed lexemes, e.g., міліѡны.

			Cf. unstressed ї + V: нє́прїѧтєль; stressed і + V: прі́атєль.
к	k	кождый	
л	l	любо	
м	m	мимо	
н	n	новый	
о	o	особѣ	
п	p	пожитокъ	
ρ	r	Рꙋскїй	
с	s	смєрть	
т	t	той	
ꙋ, оу	u	бꙋдꙋтъ, оучитисѧ	Usually оу initially, elsewhere ꙋ but оу can also occur anywhere, e.g., root-initially after a prefix (наоучаєтъ), medially or finally (бєздоушноє, трꙋбоу).
ф	f	фарба	
х	x	хто	
ц	c	цнота	
ч	č	чинитъ	
ш	š	штобы	
щ	šč	що, Єщє	
ю	ju, (C)′u	южъ	See 2.0.1 and 2.0.3 below.
ѧ, ꙗ	ja, (C)′a	ꙗзыкъ, ꙗкъ; прирожєнѧ, крщєнїѧ	ꙗ initially, elsewhere ѧ; see 2.0.1 and 2.0.3.
ь	—	зась, скромность	Indicates palatalization of preceding consonant. See 2.0.2.
ы	y	который, оузычитъ	
ъ	--	часъ, ихъ; въскрєсъ	Indicates lack of palatalization in preceding (final) consonant;

			medially: in Slavonicisms; see 2.0.2.
ѡ	o	ѡтъ, ѡ, кождогѡ	Traditional environments in East Slavic texts; also finally in adverbs: ꙗкѡ, скорѡ, живѡ (in *Kaz* and *Gram*; -o is the rule in JU).
	u?	слѡвъ, смыслѡвъ	See 2.1.2.3 below
ѿ	ot	ѿца, prep. ѿ (=отъ)	
ѵ	i	Єгѵптѧне	In foreign borrowings (mainly via Greek).
	v	Єѵ҃гліє	In Greek borrowings (representing the Greek prefix ευ-)
ѳ	f	Виѳлеема	In Greek borrowings (representing Greek θ [theta]).

2.0.1 *Palatalization.* As an East Slavic language, Ruthenian had the consonantal phonemic opposition palatalized:non-palatalized. This is especially clear in word-final position, when the loss of a front jer vowel caused a preceding consonant to be left phonemically (no longer positionally) palatalized, as indicated by the use of the front jer-letter in this position in Ruthenian texts. The opposition did not affect all consonants; those lacking a palatalized counterpart are described synchronically as "unpaired": š, ž, k, g, x, c, č, and šč. Thus, cf. CES dьnь > Ukr день [den′], Br дзень [dz′en′], R. день [d′en′].

While the appearance of a front jer-letter in final position is the clearest reflection of consonantal palatalization in Ruthenian, the front vowel graphemes ѧ, ѣ, ю, and є also indicate that immediately preceding consonants are palatalized (but not ꙗ, which is found only initially). The grapheme и, does not, in my opinion, indicate palatalization because of the occasional confusion of ы and и in the texts (see 2.1.2.2 below). There is no evidence that the grapheme є indicates that preceding consonants are palatalized; paired consonants lost palatalization (hardened) before *e and e < strong *ь in the U-R region (cf. Ukr [den'] above), but not in the B-R region. The graphemes representing back vowels, viz. а, о, оу/ȣ, ы, ѡ indicate that preceding consonants are not palatalized (hard), as does the back jer ъ.

Notes. The labials can be palatalized before front vowels (въ церквѣ alongside церкви), but they are hardened word-finally (as in CSU/CSBR): любовъ, церковъ, кровъ < любовь, etc. Forms in MS' texts also indicate that labials are hard before [j], as in CSU: пъѧнства (532a,16) "drunkenness" (cf. Ukr/Br п'янство/ п'янства). See 2.1.1.9 on the presence of [r'] in MS' language.

2.02 *The jers.* All three texts use the jers sparingly. The front jer reflects palatalization in a preceding consonant (see 2.03 below), while the back jer indicates the lack of palatalization. In all three texts both jers can be replaced by a superscript grapheme: ̕ in Kaz, Gram, and in the introduction and "Biblical" passages of JU; and ʿ in the body of the text of JU. In all three texts these signs are used as space-saving devices; they are commonly used with the prepositions *z* and *v* as well as with some flectional and derivational morphemes, e.g.:

1. In the neuter nominal formant *-Сье (hereafter C=consonant, V=vowel): розознанѧ IIb; задивене K2b,1; голдованє 271a,21); but cf. одѣньє (278a,5). This is true of other forms which have the structure -CC-V in modern Ukrainian (e.g., 3rd declension feminine instrumental singular): помочю (K3b,11), but ночъю (463a,6); cf. Ukr ніччю

2. Between a consonantal ending and the particle -сѧ in reflexive/intransitive verbs (ставаетсѧ 94a,13 and K13a,2); cf. the use of ъ in Biblical quotations in Kaz: нероди́тъсѧ (K10a,15)

3. occasionally in past passive participles with the formant -nn-: for example, дш҃езбавенного (K14a,13 and K14b,9).

The use of these graphemes is particularly common at the end of the line in each text; given a final consonant (palatalized or not) a jer-letter is written if space allows, but ̕ or ʿ occurs if it does not: справедливост (94b,7), реч (94b,11), им (94b,12), бовѣм (94b,26), but беззаконникѡмъ (94b,6), неприѧтелемъ (94b,15), запожитокъ

(94b,18). Especially interesting in this regard are words continuing onto a following line in which the grapheme serves as a *de facto* hyphenating device; more often than not it does happen to occur where, historically, there was a jer:

1. Before the formant -*ьstvo: лакомꙿствомъ (271a,7–8), оубозꙿствомъ (271b,2–3), богатꙿствомъ (271b,6–7), лакомꙿство (271b,17–18).

2. Elsewhere (where posited etymologically): бж҃твенꙿного (271b,1–2), кривꙿдникови (271b,24–25), подꙿлеглыми (498a,7–8), боголюбꙿцами (498a,18–19), неподꙿдает сѧ (498a,25–26), скрѹшивꙿши (498b, 20–21), розꙿсвѣчаетъ (499b,23–24), мощꙿми (K8b,19), напочатꙿкѹ (K14b,18). (These last two examples do not occur line-finally in Maslov's edition of Kaz, but he has preserved their orthographic shape from the original document, in which they do.)

3. Rarely where not posited etymologically: банꙿкетѡвъ (K6a,10), мерꙿтвы (K11a,18: East Slavic *mьrtv-, OCS *mrьtv-); in the second example there seems to be contamination between the East Slavic form and the Slavonic.

In all of these environments the jer-replacement grapheme will not occur if the consonant after which it is expected is written *pod titlom* (see 2.0.4 below). We note that the lack of an expected front jer-letter does *not* necessarily reflect hardness word-medially, as doublets indicate: невольничаѧ but неволникѡве (38a,18–19; 20) '(having to do with) slaves; slaves.'

"Strong" jers were identified with full vowels, in East Slavic yielding ь>e, ъ>o, while "weak" jers are lost. One of the results of this phenomenon is the presence in Ruthenian (as in the modern Slavic languages) of morphophonemic vowel-zero alternations, especially apparent in the declension of substantives: ѡтецъ (<*отьць)– ѡтца, матка—матокъ (<*матъкъ), день («*дьнь) – днѧ, etc. The loss of the jers also contributed to the final rise of phonemic palatalization in East Slavic (see. 2.0.1 above).

2.0.3 *The Phoneme /j/.* The presence of the palatal glide /j/ is indicated in a variety of ways in Smotryc'kyj's texts. The clearest evidence of the presence of /j/ is the use of the grapheme й, which can only represent /j/; it occurs finally in the nominative singular masculine adjective (добрий), some substantival genitive plural forms (дней), and in the 2sg imperative of some verb types (читай); medially it is possible in a wide variety of lexemes (гойности, подойзрена, найти, etc.). This grapheme will always be preceded by a vowel-letter.

The occurrence of ѧ, ꙗ, ю, and є word-initially or following a vowel elsewhere in a word also reflects the presence of /j/: ꙗзыкъ (ja-), южъ (ju-), єстесь (je-); неволничеє (-je), котораѧ (-ja), которою (-ju). The sequence [jo-], present in CSU, cannot be identified as a result of Smotryc'kyj's spelling conventions, e.g., in the possessive pronoun єго, which corresponds to CSU його [johó] and CSBR яго [jahó]. There is likewise no obviously identifiable sequence [ji-], which exists in CSR and CSU, but not in CSBR. In a few environments in these works, however, I believe there is reason to posit it. In the genitive singular feminine adjective and pronoun we consistently find the spelling -он (vs. the dative/locative -ой): in *Grammatiki* it is written without any superscript accent marks, while in *Kazan'e* and JU we find the final -и with a grave accent (`). This is not an indication of stress, however, as other syllables usually carry stress as indicated by the use of the acute stress mark (cf. 2.0.4 below on the use of these diacritic marks): ко́ждоѝ (K14b,12), жа́дноѝ (63b,6); thus, this may very well reflect U-R [-oji]. (See also the discussion below in chapter 4, p. 94). The same feature is found in the nominative plural of adjectives, in which the standard spelling is -ыи, also with a grave accent over the final vowel (e.g., которыѝ [K8a,21]); as with the genitive feminine, the accent is not used in *Grammatiki*. It also occurs in the 3rd person singular feminine possessive pronoun, in all texts *with* the grave accent occurring alone to indicate final stress: еѝ (IVa,13); єѝ (K3b,10); cf. Ukr її [jijí], but Br яе [jajé].

2.0.4 *Accentuation and Indication of Place of Stress.* All three texts indicate the place of stress in almost every word and differences among the three are few.

Grammatiki. The place of stress is indicated by use of the *oksia,* or *acute* (´); word-final stressed vowels very rarely bear this diacritic, but the norm in this environment is the *varia*, or *grave* (`). Every initial or freestanding vowel (e.g., а 'and, but') is accompanied by a superscript ('), the *psili* or *spiritus lentis*. Stressed initial vowels have both (') and

(´) (=῎), a combination referred to as the *iso* accent.

Kazan'e. The patterns described in reference to *Grammatiki* hold for *Kazan'e* as well, except that final stressed vowels bear only the *grave*. There is one major difference, discussed in 2.0.3 above with reference to the presence of [j] before [i]: if there is an unstressed final и following another vowel, that и also occurs with the *grave* (ѝ). In other words this is a morphonological marker, because the phenomenon is limited to the morphological categories listed in 2.0.3. We thus are able to interpret the former ending as representing [-oi] or [-oji]. As I have noted, these final vowels occur without any diacritic in *Grammatiki*.

JU. The *acute* and *grave* accents are used to indicate place of stress and unstressed final post-vocalic и as in *Kazan'e*; *iso* is also commonly used over stressed initial vowels, as in *Kazan'e* and *Grammatiki*. The major difference setting JU apart from the other two texts is the general (but not complete) avoidance of *psili* with initial unstressed vowels, in favor of the *kamora* (̂). With the exception of those few forms using *psili*, all initial or lone vowels carry this diacritic: а̂, и̂. In such forms as а̂бы, а̂нѣ, а̂ле (alongside а̂ле́), ꙗ̂кобы the *kamora* also indicates the place of stress. While this pattern is the norm, occasionally we find *kamora* used elsewhere in the word to indicate stress in place of the *acute*: а̂за̂жъ (especially interesting because of two *kamoras* in the same form), до̂бромъ, понева̂жъ; note its occurrence in a few monosyllabic forms as well: ре̂клъ, ска̂рбъ, за̂съ, бы̂лъ, скро̂зь.

All three texts make use of the *pokrytie* containing a consonant letter belonging to the word underneath; this can take place in any type of word, regardless of its semantic field (e.g., быⷧ҇). In contrast, the *titlo* does not contain or cover any letters; it indicates an abbreviation of a word that is usually considered sacred: Бг҃а (*pro* Бога), etc.

2.0.4.1 *Stress Patterns*. It is beyond the scope of this study to describe the stress patterns of the language of MS' texts in a comprehensive fashion. As a general rule, the patterns observed reflect the East Slavic identity of this language, in some instances more specifically Ruthenian (or even U-R). Stress is mobile (well illustrated by the substantive and verb), unlike in Polish, which has fixed stress on the penultimate syllable. Stress is considered below in individual members of morphological categories that are subject to large-scale use (and borrowing or both) of Polish elements, especially the adverb (chapter 7) and conjunctions (chapter 8). Stress in these categories can follow the Polish pattern or not: when it does not, it can sometimes indicate a greater "Ruthenianization" of the individual form.

The phonological analysis of Smotryc'kyj's Ruthenian that follows in 2.1 is therefore limited to a consideration of its sound segments (consonants and vowels).

2.1 *Phonology. General Remarks.* The modern East Slavic languages share certain phonological traits which differentiate them from West Slavic (as represented by Polish elements in MS) and South Slavic (as represented by Slavonic elements in MS). The opposition of East to West to South are central to the determination of the linguistic and stylistic level of a given form or passage. As a function of individual lexical items, however, Slavonic and Polish phonological features cannot be treated as features of the Ruthenian vernacular standard (or RVS, cf. Goldblatt 1991), whereas lexemes can be so treated. The phonological part of this study first of all describes shared "Ukrainian-Belarusian," or "Common Ruthenian," features, and then identifies features that are specifically "Ukrainian" or "Belarusian." Phonological features that are clearly "Polish" do not occur outside of Polish lexemes, and are therefore not described separately. Although the phonological study of Smotryc'kyj's Ruthenian necessarily has to be based on what can be gleaned from the orthographic system used in his texts, a relatively reliable (even if not complete) description of the author's phonological system can be formulated. The value of individual graphemes must be interpreted by comparing their occurrence in Ruthenian forms within the three texts, in identifiable non-East Slavic forms, and in comparison with the expected reflexes in CSU and CSBR.

Thus, for example, some major traits that indicate East, West, and South Slavic differences are as follows: 1) The CS sequence TORT (= Consonant + Mid-Vowel + Liquid + Consonant), as in CS **moldъ*, yields CES TOROT *molodъ* but OCS TRAT *mladъ*, Pol. TROT *młod-* 'young' (see 2.1.1.6 below on the occurrence of these reflexes); this feature identifies the source or linguistic level of a given root containing this sequence. 2) On the other hand, the reflexes of CS *tj can mark the linguistic identity of a morpheme (e.g., the marker of the present active participle), as well as of a given lexeme: č = CES, šč = Slavonic (OCS št), c = Polish, e.g., in **tysętj-* '1000' > CES *tysjač-*, OCS *tysęšt-*, Pol *tysiąc-*. 3) In the MS texts East Slavic and Slavonic lexemes exhibit the East Slavic reflexes of CS jers and nasal vowels; the contextual environment or other concomitant phonological features can identify a form as lexically "Slavonic" vs. "East Slavic." Polish forms may or may not be more easily recognizable as "non-East Slavic": if a CS word-formational morpheme is common to both Polish and East Slavic, then the Polish reflex of this morpheme is replaced by the East Slavic variant, e.g., in -ek > -ok (< CS *-ъкъ). This process was common already in 14–15c U-R and is discussed in Humecka 1962. If, however, an element (especially a root) was not identifiable with a like element in East Slavic, then the Polish form tends to be rendered phonetically: in **ꙁвендꙋючого** (K18a,1) 'smelling' *-en-* reflects the Polish front nasal vowel ę before a stop, while in **контпливости** (K8a,17, 4 times; in JU e.g., 67a,9) 'doubt' *-on-* reflects the back nasal vowel ǫ; the corresponding East Slavic forms would have been *svjad- or *vutpliv- had they existed. *Note.* Polish ó [u] is rendered by omicron o (**ѡ**), presumably under the influence of spelling in Polish: the differentiation of [o] and [u] (mod. ó) is still rare in the 16/17c (Klemensiewicz et al. 1981, 96–97).

Within East Slavic the following major features, among others, can be discerned that separate CSU and CSBR from CSR, e.g.: 1) *g > [h], 2) loss of initial *jь- (> i- in CSR), 3) *v and *l > [w] finally and before other consonants. (Others features are examined in 2.1.1 below.) Phonologically, CSU and CSBR diverge from one another in several respects and most of the features commonly cited as examples of this divergence actually serve to separate CSU from CSR as well as from CSBR: 1) *ě > [i] in CSU, but > [e] in CSBR and CSR; 2) *y and *i coalesced in CSU, but remained separate in CSBR and CSR; 3) *o and *e in syllables closed by the loss of the jers were raised > [i] in CSU, but not in CSBR and CSR; and 4) voiced consonants are not automatically devoiced before voiced consonants, as they are in the other two languages. Two major phonological features that serve as markers of "Belarusianness" are *akanne-jakanne* (the non-differentiation of mid and low vowels outside of stress) and *cekanne-dzekanne* (the affricatization of *t', d' > c', dz'); of these *akanne* is shared with CSR and *jakanne* also occurs in Russian dialects, leaving *cekanne-dzekanne* as the only truly "Belarusian" phonological feature.

2.1.1 *Common Ruthenian. Ukrainian-Belarusian Features.*

2.1.1.1 *g > [h]. By the time of the writing of *Kazan'e* and *Grammatiki* there are two graphemes in use to differentiate the new fricative and the voiced velar stop: the old grapheme г (=old [g]) now represents the fricative, and a new grapheme ґ represents the stop [g]. Spirantization of the velar stop [g] cannot be identified on the basis of East Slavic lexemes alone, however, as г consistently occurs where it is etymologically expected: presumably a Ukrainian-Ruthenian would have pronounced ѕтрашного (K26a,4) as [strašnoho], but we cannot deduce that from such etymological spellings in MS. Rather, it is lexemes of Polish, Greek, and Latin origin which allow this Ruthenian feature to be most clearly noted in Smotryc'kyj's texts: compare, for example, гойности (K22b,5) 'generosity' < Pol *hojność* (Cyrillic г =[h]) with арґѹмента (IIIa,11) "arguments" (Cyrillic ґ =[g]). According to Nimčuk (1979, 34) the new grapheme was introduced by Smotryc'kyj himself. In JU the digraph кг is used to represent [g]: thus, кгды occurs hundreds of times in JU (e.g., 94b,27); the spelling кды is attested twice, in which we can assume that к represents voiced [g] before the following voiced stop [d], if the spelling is intentional and not a typographical error. Cf. other examples: нѣкгды (117b,8); фикговоє дєрєво (392a,1); срокгїй (292a,21), reflecting Pol. *srogi* rather than East Slavic строгий; фикгѹрѹючи (86a,7). The implication of this difference between JU and *Grammatiki-Kazan'e* is that in the 3 years between the former (1616) and the latter (1619/20) Smotryc'kyj appears to have decided that the difference in sound should be represented by different graphemes. The timing of the introduction of this graphic opposition is probably not coincidental, since it was subsequently used in a grammar. This in turn was the path by which the new orthographic feature was eventually disseminated throughout the Ruthenian lands.

2.1.1.2 Loss of initial *jь- is clearly reflected in all of MS' texts. The environment in which this is most immediately evident is the preposition/prefix з/з-, which represents the coalescence of *izъ 'from' and *sъ 'with, from' (compare these two prepositions in modern Russian: із and с), and the verb маю/мѣти 'to have' (cf. Russian *иметь,* Polish *mam, masz*); these forms are extremely common in all three texts, e.g., зноѕити 'endure' (K14a,11). The verb зчез-/счез-

'disappear' is also attested with initial з-/с- < *izъ-, in JU as well as in *Kazan'e*: счєзнєтъ (K24b,12) 3rd sg non-past, but зчєзла (339b,26) fem past. This feature is shared with Polish, thus it is particularly in evidence because of the many Polish lexemes in use in MS' Ruthenian. In biblical quotations or in lexemes with religious significance the traditional shape of the morpheme is the rule in *Kazan'e*: Исповѣдника (K24b,19–20) 'confessor' Gsg; in JU, on the other hand, this shape does not occur because of the nature of the text: it has few Slavonicisms and many Polonisms. No examples are found in the preface to *Grammatiki* either, for the same reason.

2.1.1.3 The alternation i-j. The grapheme и can alternate with й in initial position depending on the identity of the preceeding phone: и if it is a consonant, й if it is a vowel; this feature is characteristic of modern Ukrainian orthography (він іде 'he goes,' but вона йде 'she goes'). The alternation is present in JU, for instance in нєйдєтъ < нє идєтъ (75b,9) 'does not go,' once in *Kazan'e*: дбалє й остоpожнє (K21a,7–8) 'mindfully and carefully.' Although this feature is not orthographically reflected in literary Belarusian, it is noted as a feature of the spoken language and can therefore be included here as "common Ruthenian." Such forms as пойдємо (308a,6), пєpєйдємо (308a,8), обыйдємо (308a,7), in which initial *i*- of the verb 'to go' alternates with *j*- in the presence of a vocalic prefix, are also characteristic of CSR (пойти, перейти, etc.).

2.1.1.4 In MS there is much evidence of the hardening of the originally soft hushings and affricates /c′, č′, š′, ž′, šč′/. This is especially noticeable before the vowel phoneme /i/, which is sometimes written ы in this environment: живꙋчымъ (K19b,3) 'living,' ближшыми (K21b,4) 'closest,' pоскошы (94b,4) 'luxuries,' оужываннємъ (IVa,3) 'use.' Another indicator of this phenomenon is the occurrence of the grapheme о rather than etymological *e* following hushings (whether it is stressed or not): пpишолъ (30b,3) 'arrived,' понижонъ (28a,1) 'lowered,' лєжачой (K14b,21) 'lying,' слꙋжачомъ (107b,12) 'serving,' вєчоpъ (247b,22) 'evening,' and especially in the clearly U-R form чоловѣкови (200b,10) 'man'; cf. also the writing of back jer after hushings, e.g., ночъю (463a,6). In modern Ukrainian the spelling 'hushing + o' is the rule. In Belarusian the reflection of akanne in the orthographic system results in such forms as чаго, obscuring the fact that the underlying phoneme is /o/ (note that [o] reappears under stress). In the same language the phoneme /i/ is always represented by the back allophone [y] in such environments, e.g., чытаць 'read,' чысты 'clean'; in Ukrainian both phonemes /i/ and /y/ can occur in these positions.

The evidence regarding the dental affricate /c/ (ц) indicates that this consonant is hard, e.g., spellings such as ѡ҃цы (167b,26) 'fathers,' человѣцы (367b,5–6) 'people,' оучєницы (369b,9) 'disciples,' младєнцы (IIIa,6) 'children,' the use of back jer in ловєцъ (K27b,12) 'fishermen,' and vacillations between hard- and soft-stem endings such as Dsg ѡ҃цєви (36a,2), концови (97b,9). The traditional-etymological form of the nominative plural (*-ci,* but -цы in the examples above), e.g., грєшници (K13b,10) 'sinners,' occurs in *Kazan'e*. While there are no examples of an apparently soft [c'] in Kaz or Gram (in младєнцємъ [IVa,6] the desinence indicates dative plural as opposed to instrumental singular, not soft *-c'*), one interesting form is noted in JU: на томъ мѣєтцю (346b,18) 'at that place.' One example like this can certainly not be taken as conclusive evidence, but it is interesting nonetheless: if [c'] were indeed present in MS' language, this would have to be interpreted as a clearly Ukrainian feature—/c/ is present in Belarusian only as a result of the affrication of *t' (*c' > [c] in that language).

2.1.1.5 The reflexes of tensed jers (/_j under stress) are another point of division between Russian on the one hand, and Ukrainian-Belarusian on the other. In the former such jers are identified with strong jers, resulting in their identification with the full vowels /o/ and /e/ (R молодой 'young,' but Ukr молодий, Br малады). In JU there are many such forms, e.g., молодый (49a,9–10), verbs открыютсѧ (47b,14) 'they will close,' открыєтъ (48b,11) 'it will close,' омыємо (65a,7) 'we shall wash,' ѹмый (55a,9), отыймѹєтъ (264a,13), здыймѹєтъ (250a,2), взыйти (K 2b,6), and so forth. Note also обыйдємо (308a,7) noted above. While such spellings might just as easily be interpreted as representing orthographic tradition, comparison with other forms such as кріετсѧ (115a,27) 'will hide,' in which a marked Slavonic spelling occurs, indicate that they ought, in fact, to be interpreted as reflecting a feature of Ruthenian. The forms зишолъ (K 26b,21), зишло (K22b,16) probably do not reflect phonetic [i] (as in CSU зішол), but reflect the confusion of the letters и and ы characteristic of U-R texts (see below).

2.1.1.6 The CS sequences *TRъT/TRьT developed with the reflexes of strong jers in Russian proper. In Ruthenian, however, the jer was lost before being identified with strong jers, and a secondary vowel [y] developed in its place: Ukr слиза 'tear,' кривавий 'bloody,' but Rus. слеза, кровавый. Two examples of this phenomenon are found in MS, based on the same root: дрижачи (341b,20) 'trembling,' задрижѣмо (210a,19) 'let us tremble!' (cf. these forms also in the context of hardened *r′, see 2.122 below). One additional form might be cited as influenced by this phenomenon: чирвоное море (86b,10) 'the Red Sea,' чи҃вонитъ (193a,15–16) 'makes red,' but червоная (467a,10) 'red' fem, which reflects Pol. *czerwony*. The former variant is common in the Ruthenian period, and may represent a blending of CES червенъ and Old Polish *czyrwiony* (Shevelov 1979, 292); because červ-/čyrv- is ultimately derived from the TъRT sequence čьrv-, it is not inconceivable that the common occurrence of the phonetic shape čyrv- was influenced by the Ruthenian development of *TRьT > TRYT.

The following forms represent pure Polonisms: трвожит ся (344a,14) 'worry, be alarmed,' Pol. *trwożyć się;* зе лзами (405a,27) 'with tears' = Poli. *ze łzami* (cf. CSU слиза, but CSBR слязá=CSR слезá); з крви (53b,27) 'from [by means of] blood' (CSU кров, кривавий; CSBR кроў, крыві, крывавы).

2.1.1.7 Lexemes with the CS sequence *TORT yield TOROT (commonly referred to using the term 'pleophony' or the Russian term *polnoglasie*) throughout the East Slavic area. This phonetic shape is more common in CSU and CSBR than it is in CSR, because of the strong South Slavonic influence exerted during the formation of the standard Russian literary language: in the latter we often find the Slavonic reflex TRAT next to TOROT (compare also the Russian form полногласие with the Ukrainian повноголосся). Many examples of East Slavic (E) *polnoglasie* are attested in Smotryc'kyj's texts, fewer Slavonic (S), and occasional Polish (P) variants (especially common for some of the roots in question); a few examples:

E солодкимъ 'sweet,' солодкость 'sweetness' (both in 41a,4)
E сорому (155a,2) 'shame'; P сромотною (419a,11) < *sorm- 'shameful'

P млоденецъ (frequently, e.g., 267a,1/9–10; 268a,25) 'child'; S младенца (463a,13)
E вперeдъ (23 times, e.g., 11b,7) 'beforehand'; P вproдъ (139a,10)
E перѐ (202a,21) 'before' (prep.); P(S) прѐ (29a,22) [with regard to Polonisms versus Slavonicisms, see 8.1]; S пре҇де (K13a,12–13) 'before' (adv.)
E посередъ (248a,1) 'in the middle of'; S посре҇ (K7a,10); P посредкꙋ/посродкꙋ (132a,4; 409a,22 respectively)

Compare Ukr солодкий, сором, and Br салодкі, сорам with the corresponding Russian forms сладкий, срам. Although this feature is not specifically "common Ruthenian" vs. Russian (because Russian also has *polnoglasie*), we can cite it here because Russian texts from this period are characterized by a smaller number of such forms. Although not a *polnoglasie* form, we should note here the root *čelov-/*čьlov- 'man, person' attested in MS: чловеченство (467b,15) 'humanity, humankind,' which reflects Pol. *człowieczeństwo* (not Slavonic чловѣ-), vs. East Slavic человѣкѡ҇ (56b,9) and the specifically Ruthenian form чоловѣкови (200b,10; 236a,24): cf. Ukr чоловік, Br чалавек.

2.1.1.8 Only rarely do MS' texts reflect the labialization of etymological *v in the environment of a following consonant or zero and of *l in *TъLT sequences, phenomena characteristic of CSU and CSBR; the few forms that can be cited as evidence of these features occur only in JU:

> вподовжъ (86b,10) 'lengthwise' (<*v+po+dolž-). The SUM lists подовж/подовш as a "dialect" form and defines it as "уздовж" 'along'; cf. подолжи (also glossed as "уздовж") cited from the year 1488 in SSUM. In MS we also find etymological *l in the related form вдолжъ (456b,23) "along." This adverb is no longer current in modern literary Belarusian, but the related verb падоўжыць 'lengthen' and adjective падоўжны "lengthwise" are included in TSBM.
>
> ѹпередъ (201a,21; 280b,8; 542b,2) 'before, ahead of.' Cf. Ukr уперед/вперед and Br уперад, used as a preposition and as an adverb in the modern languages, as it is in MS. Compare the etymological spelling in впере҇ (451b,2; 505a,16). Note the

> environments in which these forms occur (resp.): after a final consonant, and twice clause-initially.
>
> ꙋвєсь (471a,2) 'all.' This spelling is found only once, following a final consonant (чєр͡є оуѵвєсь) next to hundreds of attestations of the etymological spelling весь (see chapter 5). SUM lists the variants весь, ввесь, увесь for CSU, while TSBM only gives the newer variant увесь; HSBM has all three variants.
>
> нашовши (3 times, e.g., 152b,17) 'having found,' from найти 'find.'
>
> The gerundial marker -вши is characteristic of vocalic stem-types (говори-вши), whereas -ши < -вши occurs with consonantal stem-types (thus, the expected form for найти, a consonantal stem, would be *нашед-ши). It appears in this instance that -d was no longer recognized as the root-final consonant in this verb, because it was lost in the forms of the l-preterite: -шед- + л > -шел (> -шол/-шов). In other words, this particular form is based on the masculine preterite. Final -л, now in the environment of the following consonant ш, was free to be represented by the grapheme в (no doubt influenced by the marker -вши used with vocalic stems). The fact that this form is attested three times in MS indicates that it is not merely an insignificant slip.

The first example cited from Smotryc'kyj's texts is worthy of note because misspellings of в for л are described by Michael Flier as "rare throughout the Middle Ukrainian period (15th to late 18th centuries), testimony to the strength of orthographic tradition" (1983, 101). The earliest textual reflections of this feature predate Smotryc'kyj by only a century, for instance in невдовже 'soon' (1489) and вовну 'wool' (1496; ibid., citing Shevelov 1979, 412). One would expect such a feature to be absent in the language of a man as orthographically traditional as Smotryc'kyj; the fact that невдовже and Smotryc'kyj's form вподовж are formed from the same root suggests that the orthographic shape довж may have been fairly common for *долж by 1600. Indeed, this same root is found in another early example cited by Shevelov: подовъжь 'along' (ibid.). From these examples we may posit the presence of [w] in MS' texts.

2.1.1.9 Horbatsch cites dispalatalized [r] < [ŕ] as an East Podolian, Volhynian, and Polissian Ukrainian feature in Smotryc'kyj's language. This trait appears to be present in MS' texts, but the orthographic evidence is not unambiguous. It must be considered in conjunction with the coalescence of /y/ and /i/ and in the context of Polonisms or lexemes shared by Polish and Ruthenian.

Thus, for instance: крыкꙋ (218a,5; 47b,21) 'shout' might represent Pol. *krzyk* or Ukr/Br крик/крык [kryk] (cf. Rus. крик [krik]); товарышемъ (e.g., 264a,15) 'comrade' may be Pol. towarzysz or UkrBr товариш/таварыш (cf. Rus. товарищ); лѣкара (232b,9) 'doctor' Gsg might reflect Pol. *lekarz, lekarza* or Ukr dialect лікар, лікара, (cf. standard лікар, лікаря), or Br лекар, лекара. See 2.1.2.2 below, in which more examples of ри/ры are cited.

Especially noteworthy are forms in which spellings alternate between hard and soft desinential variants: по морꙋ (78b,25) 'about the sea' but по морю (78b,29–30), cf. Pol. *na morzu* (note that in Polish *ŕ>[ž]); пастыра (240a,25) Gsg, but пастыреве (276a,21) Npl: although Pol. *pasterz* might be seen as a motivating factor for the first spelling, the fact that this term is present in East Slavic (with a different vowel preceding r) makes this unlikely. Cf. the paradigm of this lexeme in the body of *Grammatiki*: пастырь, пастырѧ, etc. Compare also звѣрата (409a,19) 'little animals': Dpl звѣрѧтомъ (409a,17), SSUM звѣрѧта; царъ-царю (119b,16;17) 'king, lord.' Cf. дворане (125b,26) 'courtiers,' but etymological ŕ in самарѧн- in the body of *Grammatiki*. SSUM and HSBM cite both variants дворѧ-, двора-; the former predominate.

Two forms are particularly telling: декабра (409b,23) 'December' Gsg, a lexeme absent from Polish, and when it occurs in modern East Slavic (today only in CSR) it has a soft final [-ŕ] (cf. SSUM and HSBM, in which most forms reflect the traditional palatalized -ŕ), and Отвороу . . . ꙋста мои (321a,25) 'I shall open my mouth,' next to expected отворю (367a,7). All of this evidence strongly suggests the presence of hardened [r], or at least vacillation between [ŕ] and [r], in his system: the latter phenomenon, illustrated by means of forms such as царъ-царю, is the rule in CSU (лікар-лікаря), while the former is present in CSBR (лекар-лекара) and the modern dialects spoken in the regions of Smotryc'kyj's youth (Podolia-Volhynia); the dispalatalization of *ŕ in these areas had certainly been completed by the 16c (Shevelov 1979, 637–38).

2.1.1.10 One final feature present in JU might be cited as characteristic of Ruthenian in general, viz. the occurrence of the cluster ždž in выєжджаючи (346b,23) 'leaving.' Of the two modern literary languages, this exact form is found only in CSU: виїжджати 'leave (by vehicle)'; cf. CSBR выязджаць. The form identified in Smotryc'kyj's language was widespread during the Ruthenian period (Ukrainian as well as Belarusian varieties), however, as indicated by its inclusion as a variant in HSBM.

2.1.1.11 Horbatsch 1974 also cites the Ukrainian and Belarusian dialectal confusion of [xv] and [f] as a feature occurring sporadically in *Grammatiki* (e.g., χворма, фала). No other examples of this phenomenon were noted in the texts studied.

2.1.2 *Features Characteristic of Ukrainian.*

2.1.2.1 *ě > [i]. Smotryc'kyj's orthographic system is by and large conservative and etymological with regard to the use of the grapheme ѣ. Environments in which this grapheme is expected, and does in fact occur, include the following:

-Roots: мѣєт- (K7a,16); человѣк- (100a,2); вѣр- (99b,4); євѣт- (131a,5); etc.
-As a thematic/suffixal vowel in verbs: вид-ѣ- (K10a,15; 113b,7); χот-ѣ- (192a,12); терп-ѣ- (226a,1); etc.
-Declension: (Lsg) Києв-ѣ (K2a,5); вѣр-ѣ (241b,20); трав-ѣ (245b,24); (Dsg) покор-ѣ (245b,24); єил-ѣ (K24a,19); etc. We also occasionally find the Lsg ending -є in place of ѣ, however: see chapter 3.
-Conjugation: (imperative) проє-ѣ-тє (K23a,16); чт-ѣ-мо (273b,24); etc.
-Comparative formant: пожитєчн-ѣйш- (K24a,9); ꙗєн-ѣйш- (514b,12); etc.

A rare instance of desinential -ѣ in place of -и is seen in въ црквѣ (42a,1) 'in the Church,' which ought to read *въ церкви (cf. матєри, заповѣди in the paradigms of *Grammatiki*). Where the lexicon is concerned, the pronunciation of *ě as [i] is not discernible in purely

East Slavic (let alone Slavonic) lexemes; the use of the grapheme ѣ (jat') in place of и in Polonisms as well as Latin or Greek lexemes is telling, on the other hand: ѹстав ѣчный 'constant' for Pol. *ustawiczny* (in JU we find both spellings ѹставѣчн- [37a,15] and ѹставичн- [222a,15]), незлѣчоныи (K28a,17) 'countless' for Pol. *niezliczony*. Other examples from *Kazan'e* include: довтѣпꙋ (K22a,14) 'joke' (Pol. *dowcip*); нѣґды (K18b,18) 'never' (Pol. *nigdy*); нѣжъ (K17a,3) 'than'; вѣншꙋетъ (K2a,11) 'wishes' (Pol. *winszować*); вѣхрячой (K24b,5) 'turbulent, unsettled' (Pol. *wichrzyć*); внѣвечъ (K11a,9) 'into nothing(ness)' (Pol. *wniwecz*); вылѣчати (K22b,17) 'enumerate' (Pol. *wyliczać*). Cf. also: мѣнꙋтꙋ (417b,19) 'minute' A sg, for [minutu], наєдѣнѣ (258a,8) 'alone,' for [najedini] (cf. PB наєдинѣ, modern Russian наедине). As MS' spelling of the last form cited is not etymological, ѣ could be explained either as representing [i] or as an instance of graphic anticipation; given the presence of the other forms listed here, the former interpretation seems more plausible.

Forms with the root *-cvit-* 'blossom, flower,' e.g., зацвѝши (224b,5) 'having blossomed' do not necessarily reflect i<ě, because they are based on the root variant *cvisti, also present in the language of the B-R language of FS (in which we would expect *cve- if from *cvě-); however, the presence of both root forms in MS' texts, for example, зацвѣтъ (121b,4), зацвитетъ (121b,3–4), suggest that -и- and -ѣ- could represent the same sound in his texts. One example of North Ukrainian or B-R e for *ě might be posited in the Gsgf adjectival form in вмѣсто оѹставичное роспꙋсты (332a,7) 'instead of constant licentiousness,' in which -oe < *oě (cf. chapter 4).

2.1.2.2 The coalescence of etymological *y and *i. The presence of this feature in Smotryc'kyj's language is posited on the basis of the confusion of the two graphemes, ы and и, traditionally used to represent these Common Slavic (and Early East Slavic) phonemes. Several examples of this confusion have been noted in the Slavonic text of *Grammatiki*, e.g., неясить—неясыть (Horbatsch 1974, VII). This feature is attested in the shorter texts, in spite of Smotryc'kyj's general awareness of etymology: крилами (K27b,15) 'wings' (for *kryl-), досить (K8b,7) and досыть (K17b,15; K20a,11) 'enough,' Вилни (K4a,9; K5b,13), the genitive singular of Вилна 'Vilnius,' тисяча (K27b,20) '1000' for тысяча (both variants of the last example are found in JU, e.g., тысѧчꙋ [301a,21] Asg, тисѧчій [306a,11] Gpl), плачучы (65a,25) 'crying' (for *плачучих, in which -их represents the norm), ѧкови (27b,5) 'of the kind,' мꙋдрими 'wise' Ipl, next to etymological мꙋдрыми (201b,10;11).

Forms such as плачучы can also reflect the hardening of previously palatal consonants, in this example after the affricate /č/. Given such morphological doublets as дѧкꙋючы (148b,23)—дрижачи (341b,20), however, we can assume both that č is hard and that the writer felt no real difference between ы and и. (The statement made above that ѣ and и could represent the same sound [i] is therefore lexeme-specific; it is also morpheme-specific, dependent on "hard" vs. "soft" stem-types.) Compare also the confusion of the graphemes ы and и in the following forms: зышолъ (49b,19) 'descended' and отишолъ (27b,11) 'departed': in the latter ы is the expected grapheme; cf. also зишолъ (K 26b,21), and зишло (K22b,16) The corresponding CSU forms reflect the development of *ъ > o > [i]: зішов, одійшов. Because the grapheme и in MS' texts does not necessarily represent phonetic [i], a spelling such as отишолъ can only be cited as an example of the confusion of the graphemes ы and и; it should not be interpreted as reflecting a purely Ukrainian form.

As noted above, the confusion of и/ы after ρ is also a double-edged problem: is this a reflection of the hardness of r or of the coalescence of *i and *y? Given that it appears that r is either hard or primarily hard (cf. the vacillations noted above), we can with confidence cite doublets containing both и and ы as evidence both of the coalescence of *i and *y and as evidence of the hardening of *ŕ: вρыхле (65b,17) 'quickly, shortly,' ρихлеѣй (K22b,13) 'faster,' ρыхлѣйшого (K17a,13) 'fastest'; кρилъсѧ (117b,29) 'hid himself,' but откρыютсѧ [47b,14] 'they will open [themselves])', закρито (115b,3) 'closed'; кρыкꙋ (218a,5; 47b,21) 'shout,' кρикнꙋли (225b,8) 'they shouted'; ρыбы (207b,12) 'fish,' ρиболωве (206a,4) 'fishermen.'

2.1.2.3 *o and *e in syllables closed by the loss of the jers. By the time of Smotryc'kyj the vowels in question have certainly reached the stage [u], possibly even [ü], on the way to modern [i] (cf. Ukr стіл-стола; see Žovtobrjux et al. 1979, 275). Smotryc'kyj, here strictly adhering to traditional etymological spellings, almost never reflects this contemporary phonetic realization by using the graphemes ꙋ or ю. In many instances Greek omega (ѡ) appears in environments where we posit phonetic [u]: the Gpl desinence -ѡв (in CSU > -ів), and in forms with zero-endings in which a root vowel was raised. Cf. животѡвъ (K14a,7) 'lives,' шкѡлъ (IIIa,3) 'schools' (cf. Ukr шкіл), нѡ҇ (489b,15) 'night' (cf. Ukr ніч), and so forth. Many of these spellings are mere conventions, as evidenced by the nominal paradigms set up in Smotryc'kyj's Slavonic grammar: nouns with a root-vowel -o- are written with omega in the genitive plural, which has the practical purpose of differentiating the latter from the nominative singular of masculine nouns (домъ: Gpl дѡмъ or домѡвъ); this solution does not work for nouns of the type нѡч, however, as this is the nominative singular, or for neuters like слово-слѡвъ, as there is no other zero-form to which it is opposed. The realities of U-R provide a sound-based stimulus for this practice (modern слів, домів, ніч < Ruthenian [sluv, domuv, nuč]). I have found two examples of the use of the grapheme ȣ (=[u]) in such an environment, reflecting phonetic [u]: хȣть (245a,14; 52a,14) 'want, desire' < *хоть; cf. Ukr хіть-хоті. The fact that it occurs twice indicates that this is not merely a slip or error; the use of this grapheme instead of omega may reflect the desire to differentiate this form from the conjunction хоть (chapter 8): note that omega does represent [o] in many traditional environments (see 2.0 *Orthography*).

The orthography of U-R documents before as well as after Smotryc'kyj further supports an interpretation of the omega grapheme representing [u], e.g., Львѡв 'L'viv' (Haljatovs'kyj, "Sermon to Warriors in Times of War," 1671), у Сѡчавѣ 'in Sučava' (U-R document written in Moldavia, 1460: *Українські грамоти XV ст.*, 110–14). The practice of writing omega certainly did not begin or end with Smotryc'kyj—Shevelov (1979, 320) states that omega probably represented a diphthongal sound [uo] in syllables closed by the loss of the jers as early as the fourteenth century. Its use in the same environment was a common convention circa 1600; Smotryc'kyj attempted to regularize it in his grammar and Ruthenian texts. However, his orthographic system is not consistent, and omega is occasionally used in place of omicron in open syllables: вѡды (27a,13), слѡва (34a,20), цнѡты (33b,5), etc. These latter spellings can be explained as analogical to its occurrence in the same lexemes in closed syllables, and ѡ should only tentatively be interpreted as [u].

Apart from the front variant genitive plural desinence *-ev, written -ѡвъ in hardened soft stems in Smotryc'kyj's texts (e.g., отщепенцѡвъ K24b,11; слꙋхачѡвъ 49b,17), only one example of the raising of *e is found: межи камѣемъ (478b,23) 'among the rocks'; cf. CSU каміння, CSBR каменне. The remarkable thing in this example is the reflection of the development of *e to [i], as reflected here by the use of the grapheme ѣ. Although the grapheme е is still the rule in earlier U-R, e.g., каменье (1429, SSUM), in other forms of the root камен- 'stone' an early use of ѣ is found, cf. the adjective камѣнои (1468, SSUM). MS' spelling here must therefore be interpreted to represent [kamin-], rather than as an isolated slip.

Finally, the adverbial forms ѿсюль 'hence' and покꙋль 'until' (408b,12–13) do not show *e > ['u] and *o > [u]. Rather, these represent morphological variants (cf. chapter 7).

2.1.2.4 The retention of voiced consonants before voiceless consonants may be indicated in a number of examples: хꙋдозства (IVa,5) 'art,' ближшыми (21b,4) 'closest,' бозского (40a,3–4) 'of God'; убо́ствѣ (49b,20) 'poverty,' моу́кїй (49a,9) 'pertaining to man,' до мозкꙋ (257a,19) 'to the brain,' зпочаткꙋ (462a,7–8) "from the beginning,' зтрꙋдна (198a,26) 'with difficulty.' The form сприкра (224a,10) 'disagreeably,' with apparent devoicing, may represent Pol. *z przykra,* in which z is devoiced. Note the form дожчь (37b,6) 'rain': retention of voice may be reflected here (dž before č), but Shevelov believes that this actually represents phonetic [doždž] (1979, 483). Other forms of the word, e.g., the instrumental plural джджами (105a,20), lend support to this interpretation, but the phonetic shape [ždžami] may reflect or be influenced by the corresponding Polish form: cf. Pol. *deszcz-dżdżu.*

2.1.2.5 Horbatsch (1974, VII) cites several additional Ukrainian dialect features as present in Smotryc'kyj's language on the basis of spelling errors in *Grammatiki:* 1) the North Ukrainian non-differentiation of *e and *ě, warned against by the author himself (e.g., изменяютъ-премѣненꙋ, целбꙋ, ценю, бегꙋ, грехъ, тѣлеса); 2) the non-differentiation of *e and *ę, likewise characteristic of North Ukrainian (e.g., кладезь, игляно); and 3) the West Polissian pronunciation [žj'a] (e.g., in жятель). The first of these features also occasionally appears in JU, in some roots (єсти [29b,22] 'eat' *pro* *ѣсти) and in some substantival desinences, which may reflect features of B-R or Polish (see chapter 3).

2.1.3 *Features of Belarusian.* It is not possible to point convincingly to forms occurring in any of the three texts which reflect purely Belarusian phonological features; a few instances of the use of є in place of ѣ in inflectional morphology (which can also be North Ukrainian) are noted in chapter 3. If *cekanne/dzekanne*, the most obviously Belarusian (non-Ukrainian and non-Russian) phonological feature, was part of Smotryc'kyj's speech, then clearly the force of traditional (etymological) spelling outweighed the influence of his speech in his orthography.

There are no forms in which etymological *o is replaced by the grapheme a, the clearest reflection of *akanne,* a feature Belarusian shares with central and southern Russian. One example of the reverse phenomenon (that is, writing o for *a) might at first glance be cited as possible evidence of the presence of this feature in MS: the etymological stem of the verb пєчолꙋючи (350b,8) "being mindful" is *pečal- . With the stress on the verbal suffix *-uj-* the writer might seem to be "correcting" the spelling of the unstressed preceding syllable in order to avoid what he thinks is a reflection of a feature of the spoken language; this would then be considered a case of hypercorrection. Comparison of numerous modern Ukrainian and Belarusian, as well as Ruthenian, sources, appears to support such an interpretation, because all of the forms cited show the vowel a: Ukr печалувати, PB пєчалꙋю (in which stress is on ú, the same as in MS), FS пєчаловатисѧ, and Turaw Belarusian dialect печаль (CSBR appears to have lost many forms with this root). The form attested in MS' language probably does not reflect East Slavic печал-, however, but Old Polish *pieczoł-:* in Old Polish *pieczał-* and *pieczoł-* were in competition; the former is older, and was therefore used in marked environments such as biblical texts, while the latter represents an innovation (Brückner 1927,407).

A similar instance involving a Polish lexeme is цаловáлъ (35b,19) 'kissed,' which might be taken to reflect Br цалаваць, цалую. This form occurs in an opening biblical passage in JU, however, and reflects Pol. *całować;* cf. the expected East Slavic form цѣлꙋєтъ (42b,26). Another example (but carrying stress) of this Polish reflex of *ě is цалꙋю ночь (303a,18–19) 'all night.'

We may also note in this regard the form ходотáй (K25b,2) 'intercessor.' Given Rus ходáтай, Br хадáйнік, Bulg ходатáй, the second o could be interpreted as a hypercorrect spelling for etymological *a (cf. also OCS *xodatajь*). The form occurs three times in Kaz (all spelled the same way), however, and is present in this form in the body of his Slavonic grammar and in Berynda's *Leksykon*; rather than indicating *akanne*, then, it appears that this is an instance of the Ruthenian lexicalization of the hypercorrect spelling.

In sum, on phonological grounds Smotryc'kyj's Ruthenian can be described as "Ukrainian-Ruthenian." This does not, however, preclude the presence of B-R elements in other (morphological) components of the language as this study will show in later chapters.

2.1.4 *Miscellanea.* Occasionally there are forms attested in Smotryc'kyj's texts that give us hints regarding the pronunciation of individual items—these do not generally play a role in the narrower identification of his literary language as either U-R or B-R, but are of interest all the same.

Assimilations/Dissimilations. Whereas voiced consonants can remain voiced before voiceless consonants (as seen in 2.1.2.4), assimilation of voicing also can take place: **про̑ба** (499a,8), **про̑бы** (500a,27) 'request' (s>z/_b); cf. the etymological spelling of modern East Slavic просьба. Assimilation of place of articulation: **хꙋдозство** (IVa,5) < *xudož-ьstva, **бозскими** (K2a,15) < *bož-ьskimi, **моу̑скїй** (49a,9) < *muž-ьskij, **ꙋбо̑ствѣ** (49b,20) < *ubož-ьstvě (these examples were cited above with reference to the retention of voiced *z* before *s*); **ближшими** (K21b,4; 204a,25) < *bliz-ьšimi (note the next step of dissimilational > Ukr ближчий), **навышшого** (K19b,5) < *navys-ьšogo.

Consonant Cluster Simplification. **позно** (59b,13) 'late' < *pozdьn- reflects a tendency common to East Slavic (Ukr пізно, Br позна) and West Slavic (Pol. *później*); cf. the traditional spelling of CSR поздний, but pronounciation [poz'n'ij]. NB: a form like **срокг-** 'strict,' does not reflect the simplification of str-> sr-, but is a Polish lexeme (CSU строгий, CSP *srogi*).

2.1.5 *Conclusion. Smotryc'kyj's Phonological System.* From the study of the orthographic representation of forms in Smotryc'kyj's texts we can postulate the following tentative phonological structure of his (literary) Ruthenian language.

VOWELS:				
	i*		y*	u
	e		o	
		a		

**NB: i< *ě; y< *i/*y*

CONSONANTS:	Labials		Dentals (Alveolars)		Palatals	Velars	
Obstruents:							
Stops	p	b	t	d		k	g
	*p′	*b′	t′	d′			
Spirants	**f	v	s	z		x	
	*f′	v′	s′	z′		h	
			š	ž			
Affricates			c	č			
				šč			

**Not word-finally.*
***In borrowings:* фѣкгȣра, фȣндаментъ.

Sonorants:					
Nasals	m	*m′	n	n′	
Liquids			r	(r′ ?)	
			l	l′	
Glides	[w]				j

*Not word-finally.

CHAPTER THREE

The Substantive

3.0 Within the language of MS the substantive is the inflectional category that is the most varied and dynamic. It is characterized by a state of flux and variation, which is created by the vigorous competition of declensional systems.[1] Often there is no apparent contextual motivation for the use of one inflectional ending over another in Smotryc'kyj's texts—the use of competing desinences is, in such instances, evolutionary within the process of moving from a declensional system based on stem-types to one based on gender classification. In some grammatical categories, whether it is a particular declensional type or a set of uninflected forms such as the conjunction or adverb, it is possible to identify the presence of both U-R and B-R variants, again apparently not contextually determined but simply co-existing.

The desinence itself is of primary importance in any analysis of inflected forms, because it best reflects whether or not a particular lexeme is functioning as part of the native grammatical (morphological) system. This is true for lexemes inherited from the ancestral language, in this case Common East Slavic, as well as for those borrowed at a later stage from another language, such as Polish. This study of Smotryc'kyj's morphological system takes into account morphemes of all linguistic categories and includes elements which can be identified as Church Slavonic and Polish, in addition to the great majority of forms which are "Ruthenian" (Common Ruthenian as well as more specifically U-R and B-R). Attested Church Slavonic endings are included for the sake of completeness, as well as for comparison with those present in the language of Vyšens'kyj and Berynda—nonetheless,

---

1 The resultant competition and vacillation between forms within certain declensional systems in MS is still seen today in modern CSU and CSBR declensional systems.

these are certainly not to be considered living forms in Smotryc'kyj's own system.

The substantive in Smotryc'kyj's Ruthenian is described according to the declensional systems of CSU and CSBR, that is, with standard divisions into I, II, III, and IV declensions. The I declension can be labelled "non-neuter"—it consists of nouns that are primarily feminine but includes a number of masculines; they are recognized in the Nsg by the desinence -*a* (Cyrillic -а, -ѧ: бесѣда, волѧ), where a preceding consonant can be either hard or soft. The II declension is "non-feminine," and combines masculine nouns with the Nsg marker -# (zero: гнѣвъ, день) with neuter nouns identified by the Nsg desinences -о/-є (слово, мѣстцє); they are treated together because their paradigms are identical, with the exception of the N/Asg. The III declension consists of only feminine nouns, marked by the presence of a final palatalized consonant in the Nsg, or by a hardened hushing (смерть, речъ). The IV declension comprises the smallest number of nouns, all of which are neuter. These nouns are characterized by the presence of final -*a* (-а, -ѧ: отроча, имѧ) in the Nsg. I will make occasional reference to the Indo-European stem-type designations (for example, "ja-stems") when this is of use in describing the fate of a particular grammatical desinence.

Each declension is presented below in tabular form, together with lists of examples and remarks in which particular points of importance are examined in more detail; forms that are unambiguous (e.g., nominative singulars; vocatives in -*o*, and -*e*) are not discussed. The tables combine "hard" stems with "soft" and "mixed" declensional types, as the endings are frequently identical (they likewise are treated together in grammars of the modern languages); the "mixed" types consist of originally soft-stem nouns in which the stem-final consonants have hardened (e.g., hushings: дѹша), whereas "soft" stems have stem-final palatalized consonants (землѧ). The desinences listed in the tables below are cited according to the phonological interpretations of Smotryc'kyj's orthography discussed in chapter 2. Thus, for example, ѣ clearly indicates [i]; if both и and ы represent a particular desinence, then phonetic [y] may be posited as the sound represented, although [i] cannot be excluded as a possibility.

3.1 *Declension in the Singular.*

3.1.1 *Declension I. Non-neuter.*

N	-a	розмова (K7a,15) 'discourse,' потреба (79a,11) 'need,' дорога (271b,4) 'road,' волѧ (K7a,14) 'will,' землѧ (47b,1) 'land,' темница (48a,13) 'prison'
A	-u	ласкȣ (111b,18) 'grace,' оборонѹ (K3b,20) 'defense,' вѣрȣ (111a,19) 'belief,' волю (K5b,16), дȣшȣ (K11a,2) 'soul,' землю (49b,19)
G	-y, -i	владзы (157b,6) 'power,' воды (K10a,15) 'water,' матки (K7a,9) 'mother,' воли (K2b,8), дȣшѣ (450b,18), землѣ (464a,6), обѣтницы (K26a,6) 'promise,' волѣ (223b,9)
L	-i, -y, -e	бесѣдѣ (K7a,4) 'discourse,' дорозѣ (31b,2) 'way, road,' наȣце (460a,20) 'learning,' надѣи (IIIa,16) 'hope,' тр҃цы (68b,23) 'Trinity,' земли (47b,2), темницы (47a,5), дш҃ѣ (211b,25)
D	-i, -y, -e	силѣ (K24a,19) 'power,' наȣце (454b,13), воли (K6b,10)
I	-oju, -eju	охотою (198a,3) 'willingness,' ѹтѣхою (K6a,7) 'delight,' землею (K24b,5), неволницею (268a,2) 'slave,' лакомцою (268b,10) 'greedy person'
V	-o, -e	глȣбино (K2b,2) 'depth,' цорко (117a,16) 'daughter,' оборонцо (K27b,14) 'defender, protector,' братїе (K23a,16) 'brothers/brotherhood,' дш҃е (354a,7)

3.1.1.1 1) The basic genitive desinence in stems with hard (or hardened) consonants is -ы, -и after velars. The desinence -ѣ in stems with palatalized consonants and hushings reflects phonetic [-i], as in CSU. In the same stems we also find -и, but this must be interpreted as an archaizing feature: after the rise of phonemic palatalization and the coalescence of *y and *i in early East Slavic, the Gsg desinence -и appears with soft stem nouns, corresponding to the hard stem ending -ы. Thus, whereas CES paradigms have the N-G pairs жена-жены 'wife' and волѧ-волѣ "will," these two paradigms were unified along the pattern of the hard stems, yielding жена-жены and волѧ-воли, which is still the case in CSR. This is commonly found in U-R territory, as evidenced, for example, by the substantial list of attested forms in SSUM. During this older period (XIVth century) -ѣ is to be interpreted as representing the etymological (CES) desinence, whereas its occurrence in the early XVII century represents an innovation, with -ѣ reflecting [i]; see also Gröschel (1972, 107) on the value of jat' as [i] in IV.[2] Smotryc'kyj's texts provide evidence for this interpretation: we find only genitive -и (e.g., воли) in *Kazan'e*, while -ѣ is used as a rule in JU; the former document is generally more conservative. A clear example of the status of these endings is their occurrence with the same lexeme: до овча̑нѣ (433b,30) 'to the sheep-fold,' but до вышней нб҃ной овчарни (437a,7) 'to the sheep-fold of [highest] heaven.' The ending -и in the latter is clearly contextually determined. We can, however, also find -ѣ in environments where one might otherwise expect -и, that is, in contexts of a religious nature: бж҃твенной єго овчарнѣ (438b,16) 'his divine sheep-fold.' The implication is that this desinence [i] is primary.

Only one instance of ChS *-ja* (< CS front nasal vowel *ę) is found in MS' texts: отъ землѧ (K13a,19) 'from the earth.' This and other Church Slavonic morphological features occur in biblical quotations or similarly marked environments.

2) The great majority of hard stem locative forms have the ending -ѣ, as expected. The desinence -е, possibly reflecting the Polish or B-R variant, is not uncommon: бесѣдѣ (K7a,4), наѹцѣ (K20b,4), but въ ласце (K7b,20; 211a,19) 'in grace,' въ наѹце (460a,20); cf. Br ў ласцэ, P w łasce. The doublet seen here (наѹцѣ-наѹце) from two different texts does not appear to imply any stylistic differentiation, since the desinence -е is also attested in *Kazan'e*. Although lexical Polonisms

---

2 Thus in Volhynia, Kiev, and Černihiv: с литовскоѣ землѣ 'from Lithuanian territory' (1301) is CES, but земли (1359) is an early innovation (Bevzenko 1978, 75).

abound, it is better to interpret such forms as influenced by B-R because of where Smotryc'kyj lived and worked; it is highly unlikely that desinential Polonisms would find their way into his texts and only accidental that the desinence in question is the same in Polish and B-R. More such forms are attested in the II declension (see 3.1.2.1.1 below). The same is true in the dative: although most nouns end in -ѣ, the desinence -е is also infrequently attested, e.g., наѹце (454b,13).

3) Velars are mutated in the dative and locative cases. This is a feature of CSU, CSBR, and Polish that has been lost to CSR: на дорозѣ (31b,2) 'on the way/road.'

Remarks. The nouns of this declension correspond in all case forms to those occurring in CSU and CSBR. The spellings of these desinences conform to general East Slavic norms.

For all intents and purposes, there are no differences between this declensional type in MS, IV, and PB. All of the desinences found in MS are attested in the others. Didiakin-Leeming identifies the jat' of the Gsg in soft stem nouns as a relic of the "Old Russian" declensional system, but notes that it may be used interchangeably with the grapheme и in some lexemes (дѹшѣ-дѹши); this statement appears to imply a phonetic value [i] for jat', but the author does not make the point explicitly (1969, 45). I do not agree that jat' in this instance is a "relic," for the reasons outlined above. I believe that the use by Smotryc'kyj of the grapheme -и for the Dsg, and in the vast majority of instances for the Lsg, in palatalized and hushing stems can be explained by the desire to keep these case forms formally distinct from the genitive; the CES paradigm may have supported this practice: G волѣ, D/L воли. We find -ѣ in the locative of дѹша 'soul,' (e.g., 211b,24; 212a,24; 214a,12). It may be that the occurrence of this desinence is a function of the lexeme in this instance.

3.1.2 Declension II: Non-feminine

3.1.2.1 Masculine

N -#	животъ (K9b,16) 'life,' ѹчитель (K20a,18) 'teacher,' плачъ (K6a,7) 'lament'

A	-#, -a	дрꙋга (K3b,2) 'friend,' жаль (K6a,13) 'lament,' оучителѧ (K6b,21), камень (28,11) 'stone'
G	-a, -u	гнѣва (76b,24) 'wrath,' гнѣвꙋ (448b,19), оучителѧ (7,20), мꙋжа (3a,9) 'man,' мирꙋ (26a,3) 'world,' жалю (6,16), днѧ (47b,24) 'day,' огнѧ (48a,9) 'flame'
L	-i, -u, -e	свѣтѣ (K8b,1) 'world,' Виѳлеемѣ (459a,2) 'Bethlehem,' Виѳлееме (459a,9), жалю (K6a,5), мꙋжꙋ (K18a,12), збавителѣ (406a,15) 'Savior,' раи (60b,2) 'paradise,' покою (75a,14) 'peace,' камени (K17a,17)
D	-u, -ovi, -evi	Бг҃ꙋ (K6b,20) 'God,' Бг҃ови (K11b,20), сослꙋжителю (K2a,5) 'one who does a good turn,' мꙋжꙋ (K17a,11), концови (97b,9) 'end,' огню (48a,25), дневи (K9b,20)
I	-om, -em	совѣтомъ (K3a,24) 'advice,' ꙋчителемъ (K19b,20), днемъ (132b,15)
V	-e, -u, (-i)	Бж҃е (K5a,1) 'God,' сынꙋ (44b,23) 'son,' ꙋчителю (K24a,12), оучителе (IIa,10), богачꙋ (356b,13), Гд҃и (K27a,3) 'Lord'

1. In the genitive case two variant desinences are found, *-a* and *-u*. The latter, from the old u-stems, has become widespread in Ukrainian, Belarusian, and Polish, but not in Russian. Doublets containing the two desinences can sometimes occur as a function of context: розꙋмꙋ (IIb,14; K8a,20) 'reason,' but ChS разꙋма бж҃їѧ (K2b,2) 'the Reason of God.' In the case of гнѣва (76b,24) – гнѣвꙋ (448b,19; 465a,2–3) 'anger, wrath,' the former occurs in the phrase гнѣва Гн҃ѧ 'the wrath of the Lord,' while the latter either occur alone (465a,2–3) or in the phrase гнѣвꙋ кролевского. The form гнѣва is therefore to be interpreted as the marked variant, the form гнѣвꙋ as "native": cf. CSU гнів-гніву, CSBR гнеў-гневу. The variants до Iеⷬ҇лима – до

Iєр̃лимꙋ 'to Jerusalem' are not as clearly distinguishable on the basis of context; at best, the context in which the form with the ending *-a* is found might be termed "slightly more marked": Хс̃ Гдь пон̃ѧти до Iєр̃лима входилъ (119a,12–13); in biblical passages: до Iєрꙋсалима (177a,12), з Iєр̃лима (206a, 16–17). Cf. кгды шолъ Хс̃ до Iєр̃лимꙋ (107a,12–13; 177b,24–25); this form could be considered "unmarked" by virtue of the narrative character of the passage; we note, however, that CSU and CSBR have generalized *-a* with this lexeme. Doublets are also found with no apparent differences in contextual motivation, as in the case of до ада (477a,8–9) and до адꙋ (414a,8). The desinence *-u* (-ꙋ/-оу, -ю) is also common among substantives with stem-final palatalized consonants and hardened hushings and affricates, again as in the modern languages: звычаю (K3b,5) 'custom, habit,' жалю (K6a,16) 'lament,' плачꙋ (47b,20) 'lament,' овоцꙋ (278b,3) 'fruit.' As is the case among hard stem nouns, we occasionally find one and the same lexeme with both desinences, e.g., in покоѧ (126b,27) and покою (41b,6) 'peace.' Contextual interpretation does not allow us to identify either of these forms as more or less marked; the same two variants are used in *Kazan'e*, once each, again with no apparent difference in stylistic level (K2a,8; K25b,9). The occurrence of both variants in this more conservative text appears to indicate that they are truly in free variation. Evidence of such morphological doublets from earlier texts shows that Smotryc'kyj's forms merely continue and expand upon a tendency that was at least two centuries old: cf. дома 1433/домꙋ, 1386–1418; до Виѳлеѡма 1556–1561/до вифлеѡмꙋ XVI (Samijlenko 1964, 116).

Very broadly speaking, the distribution of *-a* and *-u* desinences follows one particular pattern that had become common in Ruthenian in the 16th and 17th centuries. The former generally occurs with nouns denoting animate beings, the latter with inanimate nouns (Kedajtene 1985, 131). Although their distribution is more complex in the modern languages, generally animate nouns still have the Gsg *-a* in CSU (робітника, учителя, товариша, but лісу, оркестру, холоду, обіду, Дунаю) and CSBR (каня, воўка, брата, лася, but пяску, народу, звычаю). Thus in JU: Бг̃а, ап̃ла, дїавола, Матѳеѧ, Адама, бѣса, баранка, чл̃вѣка, помочника, Пана; домꙋ, гнѣвꙋ, всходꙋ, початкꙋ, голосꙋ, столꙋ, часꙋ. Of course there are others with *-a*, as in the modern languages, that do not denote animate beings: закона, народа, обѣда, сꙋда, живота, поста; of these, only the last two have *-a* in CSU (where живіт now means 'stomach'), while CSBR still has закона, народа/народу, суда, жывата ('stomach'), паста. Kedajtene points out that the *-u* desinence is especially common in time expressions and in phrases indicating motion toward or to a place; both phenomena are reflected in Smotryc'kyj's Ruthenian: e.g., часꙋ оного, at the beginning of every biblical passage (versus от того часа), часꙋ зимы (155b,26) 'during winter,' нынешнего часꙋ (155b,5;14) 'at this time,' теперешнего часꙋ (115b,2–3), часꙋ теперешнего (155b,12) 'at this time,' and such phrases as до домꙋ, до Єрс҃лимꙋ; Kedajtene cites as examples (i.a.) часꙋ оного, до домꙋ, and до Рымꙋ (1985, 132).

2. Animate nouns in the accusative case are identical in form to the genitive in *-a* (but not in *-u*), while inanimates have the same form as the nominative, according to the well-known Slavic pattern.

3. The most common locative singular desinences are -ѣ and -ꙋ; their occurrence is not limited to original o-stem and u-stem nouns (respectively): мирѣ (K4a,6) 'world,' в҆ тыдню (144b,12) 'in a week.' Most conspicuous are nouns ending in a velar consonant, because the use of the desinence -ꙋ avoids the consonant alternation required by the presence of ѣ: compare, for example, в҆ . . . бѣгꙋ (K9b,4) 'in the course . . . ,' на початкꙋ (K25b,5) 'in the beginning,' о Богꙋ (155a,26) 'about God,' and so forth. Many forms such as чл҃вцѣ (K10a,3) 'person, man' and в҆ вѣцѣ (211a,27) 'age, time,' in which there is an alternation, are also found in MS; the lexeme вѣкъ frequently occurs with the desinence -ꙋ in such phrases as в вѣкꙋ ономꙋ (114a,24; 114b,5) 'in that age,' в҆ теперешне҃ вѣкꙋ (115b,23–4) 'in this age,' в пришло҃ вѣкꙋ (115b,24–25) 'in a future age.' Palatalization of velars in the locative and dative singular is characteristic of CSU and CSBR (but not Russian), as in U фабрика-фабриці, Br рука-руцэ; such forms in a Ruthenian text should therefore not be interpreted as archaisms or Slavonicisms. Both -ѣ and -ꙋ may occur with the same lexeme, in the following example with some stylistic differentiation: в҆ Богꙋ кохаючамсѧ (386b,9) 'being pleased with God' versus the marked environment в҆ Бозѣ збавители мое҃ (440a,14) 'in God my Savior.' The desinence -ꙋ can occur with the same lexeme to express two different cases, in which case (morpho)phonemic stress serves to keep them separate: L плачꙋ́ (124a,25–26)—G пла́чꙋ (47b,20), L домꙋ́ (39a,20)—G до́мꙋ (31a,18). In other instances there can be no difference in place of stress

because of the nature of the stem: L о поко́ю (75a,14)—G поко́ю (41b,6). This last example also is holotypical with regard to stress for the class of masculine nouns whose stem ends in -vowel + jot—the desinence cannot be stressed here in MS' system.

The frequent occurrence of Lsg -ꙋ has been ascribed in part to the influence of the dative: for example, a preposition such as по can govern either case (in addition to the A) in U-R and B-R, as it can in Polish (among others, see Kedajtene 1985, 135). This is still the case in CSBR, but not CSU, in which it only governs the L and A[3]. In sum, the great frequency with which L -ꙋ occurs in MS with nouns of this declension can be explained as the result of the influence of a) Polish in general, b) Polish with regard to velar stems in particular, in order to avoid consonant alternations (compare modern Pol *bogu*), and c) interaction on the morpho-syntactic level (D-L).

In the locative of soft-stem substantives -и is also frequently found in MS' texts: в̔ огни (227a,26) 'in flame,' в̔ раи (60b,2) 'in paradise,' камєни (K17a,17) 'stone,' о вєликомъ . . . Короли По̑скомъ (500a,21–22) 'about the great Polish king,' о Ѿци (188b,22) 'about the Father,' дни (132b,2) 'day,' в̔ Бозн збавитєли мо̑є (440a,14) 'in God my Redeemer.' The ending -и is a remnant of the old jo-stem and i-stem declensions; under the influence of the hard stems this was eventually replaced by -ѣ, which became -i in Ukrainian (cf. при ко(н)ци, въ кораблн [1596], but also въ кораблѣ [1642], as cited by Bevzenko et al. [1978, 99]). The desinences -i, -y, and -еві are found in CSU soft-stem nouns, while only -i occurs in CSBR; in Belarusian dialects, however, there is great variation depending on the region in question: the endings -e, -ы/-i, -y, and -ові/-еві are all attested (Blinava and Mjacel'skaja 1980, 73–75). Дни and камени are historically consonant stems, in which the old G/Lsg desinence was *-e;* this ending is attested in IV, but not in PB.

[3] Gröschel believes that the -u/-ju desinences are taken from the dative singular (1972, 103), while Bevzenko et al. assert that the source of the desinences was the Old Russian u-stem locative singular (1978, 98). As Gröschel points out, the influence of Polish must also be taken into consideration in this instance (ibid.). Žytecʹkyj states in no uncertain terms that 'мѣстцꙋ' in the phrase на ко̑дом мѣстцꙋ is a Polish form (1889, 50n2).

Finally, the desinence *-e* is also attested, for example, in о прєзацном празницє (411a,27) 'about [this] most worthy festival' and в҆ Виѳлеемє (459a,9) 'in Bethlehem.' It is very common with the lexeme вѣк 'age, time' in such constructions as в пришлом вѣцє (434a,20) 'in the future (time),' allowing us to assume that its use (at least with this lexeme) is a regular feature rather than the product of random selection. The locative desinence for this lexeme is *-u* in modern Polish; in Old Polish, however, both desinences *-u* and *-e* were used (e.g., *języku-języce;* Vaillant II, 1, 124); although one could argue that this is a morphological Polonism, a stronger case can be made for the influence of B-R, as was the case with other *-e* desinences (e.g., L/Df discussed above). We note that doublets with the desinences *-e* and *-ě* also occur in this case, e.g., with the lexeme "Bethlehem": the form with *-ě* occurs in the beginning of the narrative of a biblical passage (459a,2), whereas the desinence *-e* occurs later in the same passage, in which speakers are being quoted; the context in which these two forms occur appears to indicate that *-ě* represents a stylistically higher variant (etymological spelling), whereas *-e* might be identified as less marked. Two occurrences of *-e* in IV are explained by Gröschel as orthographic variations influenced by the norms of the Belarusian Chancellery language; however, he does not rule out the possibility that they reflect the northern Ukrainian change of *ě > [e] (1972, 95). A distinction of this kind is unnecessary, since the north Ukrainian feature is part of a phenomenon that includes Belarusian: the reflex of [e] < *ě appears over an area that includes both modern Belarusian and also north Ukrainian territory. In this case, as above in MS, this ending in IV clearly is B-R. One form in *-i* (законі) is attested in IV, which Gröschel explains as a reflection of the Ukrainian development *ě > [i] (ibid.).

4. In the dative of II declension substantives there are also two variant endings, *-ovi/-evi* and *-u/-ju* (historically from the u-stem and o-stem declensions, respectively): сѹдови (K6b,16) 'judgement,' мирови (K18b,9) 'world,' свѣтови (499b,9) 'world,' концови (97b,9) 'end,' огню (48a,25) 'fire,' отцєви (36a,2) 'father,' милосєрдїю (175b,17) 'mercy,' постѹ (60b,7) 'fast,' створитєлєви (37b,23) 'Creator,' чл҃вѣкови (38a,7) 'person.' Doublets are frequently found in this case as well, in the case of Бг҃ѹ-Бг҃ви (404a,4–404a,7; also K6b,20–K11b,20) with no apparent stylistic differentiation; based on the much greater frequency of the former desinence (e.g., on pages 403a-b: 8

times -ꙋ, 0 times -ови) we can identify *-u* as the preferred ending with this lexeme: there is also a vast preponderance of the same ending in Old Ruthenian as seen in SSUM. Another doublet of this kind is свѣтꙋ—свѣтови: it is difficult to discern a difference of level in the two phrases всемꙋ свѣтꙋ свѣтили (71a,9)—покой всемꙋ свѣтови (499b,9). There are occasional indications of Smotryc'kyj's preference for one variant over the other, e.g., in the following: латвѣй бовѣм єстъ велбꙋдови . . . (379a,14) 'it is easier for a camel . . . ' occurs in a biblical passage, which is subsequently explained as лацнѣйшаѧ єстъ речъ велбꙋдꙋ . . . (383a,28–29). Here it is clear that the author prefers the -ꙋ variant, whereas the -ови desinence is marked as "higher" style, perhaps as a feature of Polish since it occurs in a biblical text. The lexeme велбꙋдъ reflects Old Polish *wielbąd*, cf. modern Polish *wielbłąd:* Smotryc'kyj goes on to explain that this word is to be understood as велблюд (383b,3–4). In general, 17th-century Ruthenian saw the use of *-ovi* extended to animate nouns, in addition to its retention among originally u-stem nouns (e.g., домъ; Kedajtene 1985, 133–34): in MS we do find *-ovi* with animates as well as with inanimates. This desinence is common in CSU; it is known in B-R as well as in modern Belarusian dialects, but *-u* was generalized in CSBR (as in CSR); the common occurrence of -ови in MS can be interpreted as a U-R feature, one that is certainly supported by, if not affected by, the presence of the same desinence in Polish.

5. In the vocative we find the variants *-e* and *-u/-ju* in MS. The former accounts for the vast majority of hard-stem vocatives in his texts. Use of both endings with one and the same lexeme does occur only with the lexeme сынъ 'son': сынꙋ (44b,23) and сыне (36a,7). In this particular lexeme the forms in *-u* outnumber those in *-e* (7:2), reflecting the status of сынъ as an old u-stem noun; both forms may occur in the context of biblical passages, so it is not possible to assign one or the other to a particular stylistic level on this basis alone. The same situation occurs in IV—Gröschel points out that both forms are found in CSU, сину in the literary language and сине in southwest Ukrainian (1972, 97). Among soft-stem nouns the same two desinences are found (*-u/-ju* is preferred, 27 times): Леонтїе (K25b,8) 'Leontij,' оучителе (IIa,10), but учителю (K24a,12) 'teacher,' Хе Црю (526b,10–11); the use of -е in JU is restricted to ѿче, according to tradition. With soft-stem nouns, for example, вчитель, *-u* (therefore, вчителю) is the rule in CSU, as it is

in Polish and CSBR; this particular lexeme is no longer extant in Belarusian. The fact that the form оучителю is found in OB suggests that the form оучителе in *Grammatiki* occurs only by analogy with the hard-stem ending.

In the event the desinence -ꙋ is used to express more than one case with the same lexeme, stress can again function to differentiate the two forms: бога́чꙋ (V; 356b,13)—ѐ богачꙋ́ (L; 357a,3–4).

6. The substantive господь 'Lord' has a mixed declenesion in MS' texts, as it did in OCS and CES. This substantive only occurs in its abbreviated form: N гдь҃ (K8a,14), V гдн҃ (K27a,3), I гдемъ҃ (K10b,4) reflect desinences from the old i-stem declension; G гда҃ (e.g., K12b,11; 58b,1), and D гдꙋ҃ (K25a,3) reflect old o-stem desinences, while D гдеви҃ (K10b,7; K10b,8) exhibits the front variant of the old u-stem morpheme *-ovi*. In the locative form гдѣ҃ (K12a,12) the final jat′ represents either the o-stem desinence or phonetic [-i] of the i-stem declension.

3.1.2.1.1 *Remarks.* The forms of the masculine second declension are in complete agreement with those second declension forms found in the language of PB. The few differences present in IV are noted above. A proliferation of endings characterizes this declension as a whole more than any other, in the singular as well as in the plural (but note the locative singular of II declension neuters in 3.1.2.2). If we approach this second declension synchronically, it becomes apparent that individual case morphemes often have two or even three different morpho-syntactic functions—representing more than one case each. Among hard and soft/mixed stems, as described above, the morpheme *-u* can be a marker of the genitive, dative, locative, and vocative cases. By the same token, particular cases can be expressed by two or even three different endings, sometimes (but not always) contextually or lexically determined.

In the following hard stem substantives it is common to find two different endings for the same case (the first example illustrates an extreme instance of three variants). The CSU, CSBR and Polish forms are supplied next to MS' Ruthenian examples for purposes of comparison.

	MS	CSU	CSBR	CSP
a.	к вѣцѣ			
	к веце			
	к вѣкꙋ	віку	веку	*wieku*
‘in the time/age’ (locative)				
b.	о Богꙋ			*Bogu*
	о Бозѣ	Бозі	Бозе	
‘about God’ (locative)				
	к Богꙋ			*Bogu**
	к Бозѣ	Бозі	Бозе	
‘in God’ (locative)				
c.	к дꙋхꙋ		духу	*duchu*
	к дꙋсѣ	дусі		
‘in (the) spirit’ (locative)				
d.	гнѣва			
	гнѣвꙋ	гніву	гневу	*gniewu*
‘anger’ (genitive)				
e.	до Єр҇лима	Єрусаліма	Ерусаліма	
	до Єр҇лимꙋ		(now Nsgf. *Jerozolima*)	
	‘to Jerusalem’ (genitive)			
f.	до ада	——	——	——
	до адꙋ	——	——	——
‘to hell’ (genitive)				
g.	к гробѣ	гробі	(гробе)	*grobie*
	к гробꙋ			
‘in the grave’ (locative)				
h.	сынꙋ	сину	(сыну)	*synu*
	сыне	(*dial.* сине)		
‘Son’ (vocative)				

In examples a., b., and c. the occurrence of VELAR + DESINENCE (front vowel or non-u) causes the alternations /k, h, x/ > /c, z, s/ (historically the "second velar palatalization"). We note that in all three instances Polish has opted for the u-desinence, that is, the one that does not trigger the alternation; the u-stem desinence was generalized only for BR дух. Compare CSR о Боге, в духе, в веке, which illustrate the loss of this alternation; the u-stem веку is still found in one specific phrase: на своем веку 'in his time,' in which final stress serves to differentiate this form from the Dsg. The masculine noun Jerusalim is no longer extant in CSP; the feminine substantive Jerozolima is based on the Greek variant of the name. The lexeme ад is no longer extant in any of these modern languages; it is historically a Greek borrowing, declined in OCS with u-stem endings. Sometimes the choice of ending appears to be determined by the particular preposition or idiom: часꙋ оного 'at that time' always occurs as a unit (cf. CSU того часу), but от того часа 'from that time (on)'; likewise in мовлю Бг҃ви 'I say to God,' but always к Бг҃ꙋ 'to God.'

As shown in examples cited earlier, the same ending can also represent different cases in the same lexeme, with or without difference in the place of stress. The choice of case ending is not necessarily determined by the particular substantival paradigm; in other words, nouns with a genitive in *-a* will not automatically have a dative desinence *-u,* or those with G *-u* cannot be expected to have D *-ovi:* e.g., G свѣта (68a,9) 'world,' but D свѣтови (499b,9). The interaction of the two axes—same ending but different meaning, and same meaning but different endings—graphically illustrates an important point: change in the phonological component of language that modifies the equilibrium of the system can provide an impetus for futher alteration to reestablish equilibrium; so, too, with change in the morphological component. In the first illustration (below) the two forms of the lexeme pokoj- 'peace' above the line represent the "ideal" system, assuming only one ending for each case per lexeme; the element below the line upsets the equilibrium, interacting with both elements which make up the ideal:

1. G покоꙗ—L покою
G покою

G покою interferes by expressing the same case meaning as покоꙗ and by expressing a case meaning different from L покою. The modern Polish system has in fact one and the same form pokoju for both cases, that is, syncretism has resulted in the loss of formal differentiation between these case forms. In the CSU and CSBR systems, on the other hand, equilibrium has been reestablished by limiting the desinence *-u* to the expression of the genitive case (in this example); the locative is now expressed by the desinence *-i* in both languages. The patterns are substantially more complex when there is interference on a broader scale, such as we see with the lexeme Бог 'God.' In this instance, there are 2 cases, 3 endings, and 4 attested combinations:

2. (a) D Богꙋ—(b) D Богови
(c) L Бозѣ- (d) L Богꙋ

Here there are three possible systems of equilibrium: (a-c), (b-d), and (b-c); there are also 3 directions of interference or competition: (a-d), (a-b), and (c-d). Various solutions to this Ruthenian system are reflected in the modern languages:

	Ukrainian	*Belarusian*	*Polish*
D	Богу-Богови	D Богу	D *Bogu*
L	Бозі	L Бозе	L *Bogu*

The L form Богу is no longer current in CSU, so it cannot interfere with D Богу; both dative forms could therefore theoretically remain in the system. Hrinčenko's dictionary of 1907–1909 lists Богу as the first variant in the dative, but the recent Academy dictionary (SUM) cites Богови first: the system has shifted in favor of the latter, accepting Богу for the most part in frozen expressions such as слава Богу 'thank God' (which is supported by the same phrase in Russian). The CSBR system has also avoided ambiguity by generalizing Богу in the dative (i.e., a-c in MS' system), while Polish has undergone syncretism.

3.1.2.2 *Neuter*

N	-o, -e	розлꙋчене (K9b,18) 'separation,' воскресеніє (113b,2–3) 'resurrection,' тѣло (115b,22) 'body,' писмо (118b,23) 'writing(s)'
A	-o, -e	слово (113b,22), чꙋдо (114b,26) 'miracle,' ѡчекиване (K5b,17) 'patience,' отпꙋщеніє (70a,15–16) 'absolution'
G	-a, (-ese)	слова (IIb,7) 'word,' добра (K11a,6) 'good,' чꙋда (113a,7), мѣстца (K6a,20) 'place'
L	-i, -y, -e, -u (-esi)	хꙋдозствѣ (IVa,13) 'art,' днꙋ (86b,10) 'bottom,' чꙋдѣ (113a,11), ѡтпочиненю (K15a,15) 'rest,' мѣстцю (346b,18), мѣстцы (500b,12)
D	-u, (-esi)	злꙋ (K11a,11) 'evil,' насѣню (K12a,11) 'seed'
I	-om, -em	правомъ (K16a,7) 'right,' чꙋдомъ (113a,29), ѿцемъ (K7b,2) 'father'

1. A clear distinction exists between native Ruthenian and Slavonic stems, especially noticeable among deverbal nouns: the former are marked by stem-final [-n′-], the latter by [-nij-]. The desinences are the same in both sets of forms, e.g., N/Asg збавеньє (206b,20) 'salvation'—воскресеніє (113b,2–3) 'resurrection'; Gsg оуслꙋханѧ (211b,13–14) 'listening'—распѧтїѧ (K23a,14) 'crucifiction,' etc.

2. The nouns of the etymological s-stems had completely adapted to the non-feminine hard stem declensional paradigm by the 16th century (slovo, slova, etc.). Four times the old s-stem forms occur in MS' texts; twice in *Kazan'e* in quotations from the Bible: G нбсе (K13a,14; 2 Cor 12:2) 'heaven,' and D словеси (K12a,6; Psalm 119? The reference here is unclear, possibly verse 35 or 133) 'word.' In JU: L на нбсѣ (51a,17), на нбси (474a,1) 'in heaven'; note that the latter, with the traditional CES ending, occurs in the Lord's Prayer (marked), while the

former clearly reflects U-R [-i]. The desinence *-esi* is attested in IV, but not in PB (Gröschel 1972, 114; Didiakin-Leeming 1969, 39–40).

3. The overwhelming majority of hard stem forms have the L desinence *-ě*; as expected, this is also found to be true in IV and PB. In addition to this ending, *-u* occurs 3 times: по днꙋ морскомъ (86b,11) 'along the sea bottom,' на ложкꙋ (183a,13) 'on a bed,' в҆ мѣстечкꙋ (464b,3) 'in the small town'; the last two can be explained as morphological Polonisms based on Pol *łóżko, miasteczko,* but по днꙋ is an anomaly: this could be a dative (the expected L is *-ě*), but the form of the attributive adjective indicates that it is indeed locative. The desinence *-e* is found only once in жидовстве (430a,11) 'Jewish nation'; it is found in IV only in the phrase въ христианстве 'in Christianity,' that is, also with the suffix *-stv*o, but as it occurs only once in MS it is most likely a slip influenced by B-R orthography.

The soft-stem nouns in MS' texts reflect greater variation in the locative, but variation primarily in spelling rather than in the number of different desinences. In MS the endings attested are *-i, -u, -y,* and *-ě.* Of these the last is rarest, occurring only once in морѣ (253b,2) 'sea'; the latter probably represents Ukrainian [i]. The desinence *-i* is found 27 times in MS: въ лици (K22a,6) 'face,' на мѣстци (7 times, e.g., K7b,22) 'place,' на мори (10 times, e.g., 140a,27) 'sea,' etc.; this is the etymological jo-stem ending, spelled as it was in CES. The spelling -ы (25 times) either reflects the Ukrainian change *i > [y], which is retained in this declension in southwest Ukrainian, or the hardness of [c]; thus, for example, along with seven occurrences of мѣстци there are 17 of мѣстцы (e.g., 93b,1), cf. ср҃цы (3 times, e.g., 58a,11). In the spelling -ии we unquestionably are dealing with a feature of Slavonic, and it is found 74 times: благочестїи (K5b,5) 'piety,' прощении (46a,1) 'forgiveness,' and others.

The desinence *-u/-ju* is the most frequently occurring ending; the largest group of forms occurring with is that of the deverbal nouns with stem-final *-n'-*, e.g., позволан҃ю (57b,12) 'permission,' нарꙋган҃ю (49b,21) 'derision' and a few with -t'-, e.g., принѧтю (K10a,20) 'acceptance.' The spelling -ꙋ occurs 19 times, primarily in the forms мѣстцꙋ (7 times, e.g., K7a,6) 'place' and ср҃цꙋ (8 times, e.g., 108b,30) 'heart'; cf. ср҃цы, мѣстцы, мѣстци above. Compare also морю (78b,29) 'sea,' next to морꙋ (78b,24), again evidence of vacillation between hard and palatalized [-r'-], and повѣтрю (5 times, e.g., 174a,25) 'wind.' The form

мѣстцю (346b,18) is interesting because it appears to reflect the palatalized affricate [c′], as we have in CSU; this form should probably be treated as an aberration from the norm, however: the same form occurs with hard [c] (**мѣстцꙋ**) 5 times, reflecting the southwest Ukrainian pronunciation. The form **в҆ милосердїю** (53b,8) 'in mercy' represents a Slavonicism, and may, in Gröschel's opinion, reflect a contamination of *-ii* and *-'u* (1972, 103).

Among the modern languages, in the locative case CSU has the desinences *-i* (possibly the Ukrainian reflex of *ě from the old o- stem declension), *-u*/*-ju* (the old u-stem locative), and *-evi* (the old u-stem dative singular); in southwest Ukrainian, however, the reflex of the CES jo-stem desinence *-i* (> [y]) is still extant (Žylko 1966, 182). In CSBR the ending is uniformly *-i* (жыцці 'life,' полі 'field'), while *-e*, *-y*/*-i*, *-u*, and *-ovi*/*-evi* are found in the dialects, as they are with masculine substantives.

3.12.2.1 Remarks: The hard stem substantives of this declension are straightforward, while the soft paradigm is much more complex. This is the case in the language of all three Ruthenians. There are no substantial differences between the attested forms of this declension in MS and IV, except that more variant spellings are found in the former. In general PB also agrees with MS; the primary difference is the presence in the language of the former of thirty deverbal nominatives with the desinence *-ja*, as in CSU, where MS and IV have *-'e* (<*- je). Lengthened *-nn-* characteristic of these forms in CSU and CSBR is not found in MS; although the force of etymological spelling may have played a role here, the lack of gemination can be interpreted as a (West) U-R feature since it is not present in this dialect area. There are also two instrumental forms with the desinence *-jam* attested in PB, the origin of which is unclear. Finally, the s-stem dative desinence *-esi* is not found in PB (39–40).

The distinction "native" versus "Slavonic" in this paradigm is artificial and usually lexeme-dependent: the larger "context," or the lexeme's occurrence in a passage of continuous text, often has little or nothing to do with determining the choice of ending. Thus, for instance, we may find the native form next to the Slavonic form in the same sentence or phrase: **многого милосердиꙗ и помилова҃ꙗ** (439b,9–10) 'much mercy and forgiveness'; **перед смертью и въскресенїемъ**

(194a,4-5) 'before death and resurrection.' In these particular examples the choice of morpheme is determined by the identity of the lexeme; this is true of all MS' texts. A contrast can be drawn between MS and IV with regard to the use of Slavonic morphemes. In the language of the latter, Slavonic forms are by far in the majority, because there are so many jo-stem deverbal abstract nouns (Gröschel 1972, 103). In MS, on the other hand, the native forms vastly outnumber the Slavonic, e.g., in the genitive by approximately 5:1 (1263 in *-ja* : 258 in *-ia*) in JU alone. This work was, after all, meant as an explanation of the gospels, and was intended for consumption by other than the clergy alone. Vyšens'kyj in turn was consciously trying to use Church Slavonic in the same way that Latin was used in the West.

The possibilities for the occurrence of doublets among substantives of this type are more restricted than they are among the masculines. The only possible areas of interference and overlap between two different cases are in fact forms with the ending *-u* (-ю, -їю) of the dative and locative cases; instances involving the Slavonic variant are virtually excluded because of the substantially smaller number of forms occurring with this ending. One Ruthenian doublet is D подѧкова̑ю (133b,5)—L в̓ подѧкованью (403b,21) 'thanks.' Within the locative case it is, as we have seen, possible for one lexeme to occur with more than one desinence, e.g., in (по) морꙋ/морю—(по) мори (337a,1) 'sea'; the forms мѣстци/мѣстцы—мѣстцꙋ/мѣстцю 'place' represent the most extreme example of morphological and orthographic variation: cf. CSU місці, CSBR месцы, CSP *miejscu.* The majority of forms cited for the fourteenth and fifteenth centuries in SSUM have the desinence *-i*; this desinence (and its variant *-y*) represent the Ruthenian and later Ukrainian-Belarusian norm. Pressure from other soft-stem forms, including masculines, and especially the influence of Polish, account for the common occurrence of the ending *-u* with such lexemes. The situation is similar in IV, e.g., the lexeme *měsc-* occurs only once with *-i,* but 3 times with *-u*; cf. CSP *miejscu, sercu.*

3.1.3 *Declension III: Feminine*

NA -#	радость (K5b,20) 'joy,' рєчъ (K3b, 11) 'thing,' цєрковъ (K2b,18) 'church,' моцъ (135b,15) 'power,' памѧ̑ (183b,26) 'memory'

G	-i	смєрти (K3a,22; 135a,26) 'death,' цєркви (IIIa,20), оуфности (184a,24) 'trust'
L	-i	старости (K2b,14) 'old age,' цєркви (K24a,8), цєрквѣ (42a,1), проповѣди (71a,14) 'sermon,' радости (184a,1)
D	-i	плоти (K10b,20) 'flesh'
I	-ju, (-iju)	помочю (K3b,11) 'help,' мыслїю (K2b,5) 'thought,' роскошєю (371a,5) 'luxury,' оуфностью (183b,6)

1. The nouns of this declension include old feminine i-stems and long u-stems; in the N/Asg the front jer (ь) is the marker of the zero (#) ending after palatalized consonants, while back jer (ъ) occurs after consonants which have dispalatalized: памѧть (K3b,10) 'memory,' but ночъ (K10a,1) 'night,' цєрковъ (K2b,18) 'church.'

2. The substantive мати 'mother' is declined according to the expected East Slavic paradigm (G матєри, etc.). In the accusative we find the form матєръ (381b,13) in a biblical passage, but it is not necessarily a Slavonicism: чти ѿца твоєго и матєръ твою 'honor thy father and thy mother.' The CSU form is матір < матер, making a strict distinction between Slavonic versus U-R impossible in this instance. In Belarusian this form has the accusative маці in the literary language, while the dialects also reflect the forms маты, матеры (Blinava and Mjacel'skaja 1980, 80). Just as common as *maty*, however, is the Polish form *matka*, which is still present in CSBR (alongside маці: TSBM) and, as a rare or dialect variant, in Ukrainian (SUM).

3. The Ruthenian instrumental desinence *-ju* occurs 367 times; the Slavonic variant *-iju* (69 times) is found in biblical contexts and in lexemes the use of which is restricted to contexts of a religious nature: compare смєртю (e.g., K10a,4) 'death,' but смєртїю (K10a,7) used in a biblical passage, and бл҃гтїю (e.g., K2a,1) 'grace.' Next to the expected form роскошъю (152b,7–8) 'luxury,' we find one occasion in which the I declension desinence is used with this lexeme: роскошєю (371a,5). This unexpected form may be interpreted as marked (*pro* роскошїю?), as indicated by the citation from JU: тыми трома покꙋшєнми и Хрⷭ҇а Гдⷭ҇а

бѣсъ кѹснл҇: роскошею . . . (371a,4–5) 'with these three temptations the devil tempted Christ the Lord: with luxury. . . .' In CSU and CSBR the corresponding form is *-ju*, for example, Ukr повістю, сіллю, Br соллю, радасцю.

4. The different linguistic levels represented by *Kazan'e* on the one hand, and by JU on the other, are clearly shown in the instrumental case forms of the old long u-stem lexemes: only the Slavonic desinence *-iju* occurs in the former (e.g., кровїю [K20b,22]), while both endings are in evidence in the latter (*-ju* 350 times, e.g., церковю [P2 III,167], but only 60 attestations of *-iju*). Among old long u-stems in addition to G *-i* we also find the old u-stem desinence *-e* twice: церкве (K7b,15) and крове (K25a,12) 'blood'; both of these are used in *Kazan'e*. In the locative we find -ě as well as *-i*, but only the latter (traditional) variant in *Kazan'e*: в҇ цр҇квѣ (42a,1) 'in the church'; this ending appears to occur by analogy with hard stem I declension feminines, since the lexeme is feminine and the final consonant (at least in the N/A) is hardened.

3.1.3.1 *Remarks.* In addition to the lexemes present in MS, the language of IV also exhibits the old r-stem noun дшчер (p.113) 'daughter'; this lexeme is not present in MS, as he generally uses the newer derivation дочка (e.g., 232b,17), or, in marked contexts, the Polish variant цорка (e.g., цорко 117a,16). The desinences found in MS generally agree with IV; in the latter Gröschel also identifies G *-e* among i-stems (where MS has *-i*) and N *-y* among u-stems (where MS has #). All the feminine III declension desinences found in PB agree with MS (1972, 43–48).

Apart from the two isolated examples of genitives in *-e*, a clear distinction of Slavonic versus Ruthenian levels is only apparent in the instrumental case (as described above). Here, as in the neuters discussed earlier, sharp contextual divisions are not possible; rather the use of one or the other ending is dependent on the particular lexeme or context. Thus we can find both desinences in the same sentence or phrase, such as in мѹдростью, покорою, и любовїю (410b,5) 'with wisdom, humility, and love'; compare also the occurrence of Ruthenian *-ju* alongside the Church Slavonic neuter ending *-iem* in перѐ҇ . . . смертью и въскресенїемъ (194a,4–5) 'before death and resurrection.' Distinctions between the two endings in one lexeme are also possible: смертью (65b,17) in an unmarked context, but смертїю

(71a,22) when spoken by the prophet Ezekiel. Twice the Polish variant Gsg крви (*pro* крови) is used in JU (e.g., 62b,13).

3.1.4 *Declension IV: Neuter*

The IV declension substantives are characterized by consonantal suffixes as they are in the modern languages, and are amply represented in MS. Here I combine the old "n-stems" and "t-stems" into one group because their declensions are identical. Most of these substantives can be characterized as "Ruthenian" forms, and only those identified as (ChS) belong to the archaic or Slavonic stylistic-linguistic level. All the forms found are based on the following lexemes: имѧ 'name,' дитѧ 'child,' отроча 'child' (ChS), жребѧ-жеребѧ 'young mare,' кнѧжа 'young prince,' знамѧ (67a,19) 'sign,' рамѧ 'shoulder' (ChS), быдлѧ 'young cattle,' сѣмѧ 'seed,' пламѧ 'flame' (ChS), овча 'sheep' (ChS), козлѧ 'goat' (ChS). Some of these, although described as 'Slavonic/archaic,' may still be found in modern Ukrainian dialects (e.g., рамя, SUM, but not in TSBM) or are characterized simply as 'rare' (e.g., козля, SUM).

NA	имѧ (74 times, e.g., 67b,17), дитѧ (4 times, e.g., 168a,5), отроча (12 times, e.g., 464b,7), кнѧжа (5 times, e.g., 379a,1), племѧ (496a,26), жребѧ (2 times, e.g., 120a,15)-жеребѧ (120b,10), знамѧ (67a,19), рамѧ (444a,16)
G	имени (36 times, e.g., 57b,13), дитѧти (255b,28), отрочати (5 times, e.g., 441a,23), кнѧжати (237b,14), быдлѧти (352b,14), пламени (447a,3), сѣмени (196a,19), овчати (429a,15); имене (K5a,1), козлѧти (36a,4)
L	дитѧти (461b,19), отрочати (459a,15), жребѧти (120a,18)
D	————

I		именемъ (25 times, e.g., 112a,9), княжатемъ (3 times, e.g., 158a,26), рамененмъ (440a,18), овчатомъ (201b,14)

The dative forms of this declension are conspicuous by their absence in MS. The Slavonic G имене (K5a,1) is attested in a prayer at the beginning of the main body of Smotryc'kyj's sermon (cf. G козляте in OB); the remaining forms (G and other cases) are still current with those lexemes surviving in CSU (жереб'я-жереб'яти) and CSBR (жарабя/жарабё-жарабяці). Apart from имя, the only other members of this declension identified in *Kazan'e* are отроча and рамя (the latter in the plural: see below). Worthy of note among the many forms listed above are the pair жребя-жеребя: East Slavic *polnoglasie* is exhibited in the latter (жребя could be described either as Polish *źrebię* or as a variant of Slavonic жрѣбя). In овчатомъ the desinence is that of the second declension; instrumental forms in *-om* are known in the modern southwestern dialects, and this one example in MS may therefore represent a living form in his language. Forms of the type именем occur in CSU next to variants with the newer ending, as in им'ям (Bevzenko et al. 1978, 118–23); іменем is the form used in CSBR. The G и́мени is usually stressed on the first syllable, but one example is found with final stress (168b,7), possibly as a stylistical marking device: для и̂мени́ є̂го. Alongside отроча we also find the derived feminine I declension отрочатко (e.g., 465b,23).

The number of forms of this declensional type attested in MS is far greater than that identified in either of the other Ruthenians. This is easily explained by the subject matter and size of the texts: the JU explains the stories of the Bible, in which the young (people as well as animals) often play a large role. In IV Gröschel finds only N имя, G имени, and I именем (1972, 114). In PB the following are identified: N племя (37); G времене, имене, племене, next to the newer forms имени, времени, and пле(мени) (38); and I именем, семене(м) (39).

3.2 *Declension in the Plural*

3.2.1 *Declension I: Non-Neuter*

N	-y, -i	молитвы (K15b,1) 'prayers,' справы (122b,1) 'affairs,' дȣшѣ (466b,28) 'souls'
A	-y, -i	рȣки (K12a,2) 'hands,' ноздри (K12a,2) 'nostrils,' велможи (K17a,20) 'magnates,' дȣшѣ (116a,9; 208b,16)
G	-#, -ij	потребъ (K8a15) 'needs,' дȣшъ (116a,5), вѡдъ (117b,13) 'waters,' цнѡтъ (124b,23) 'virtues,' земель (K20b,8) 'lands,' притчїй (IIIa,6) 'proverbs'
L	-ax	рȣкахъ (K28a,10), темницахъ (K17b,17) 'prisons,' мȣкахъ (121b,24) 'torments'
D	-am	бесѣдамъ (K5b,6) 'discourses,' дȣшамъ (K14a,15; 129b,9), ногамъ (287a,2) 'feet,' церквамъ (186a,13) 'churches'
I	-amy	силами (K14b,4) 'strengths,' кȣплями (K20a,12) 'transactions,' цнѡтами (124b,13), працами (115b,17) 'deeds'

1. This declension is straightforward. Only in the N/A of soft-stem nouns do we find different graphemes representing the ending *-y/-i*: -ы/-и represent the inherited CES orthographic variants, while -ѣ reflects Ruthenian [i]. In *Kazan'e*, the more archaizing of MS' texts, we find only the former, e.g., д҃ши (K11a,20) 'souls,' овцы (K20b,6) 'sheep,' границы (K18a,6) 'borders'; cf. GSPS Npl юноши. Compare: дȣшѣ (466b,28; 208b,16; 116a,5) 'souls.'

2. The expected genitive desinence in this declension is -# (zero). Among soft stems this results in a palatalized consonant in final position, orthographically rendered as 'consonant plus soft sign' (front

jer): землль. In this form, as in others with stem-final consonant clusters, a vowel is inserted in the presence of the Gpl #-morpheme: матѡ҇к (442,12) 'mothers.' The Gpl of forms with a root vowel *o* reflect the alternation Nsg о > Gpl ѡ, possibly indicating a change in vowel quality; as described in 2.123, the vowel occurring in closed syllables may have been [u] (which ultimately > [i] in CSU): вѡдъ, цнѡтъ, осѡбъ (K22b,6), шкѡлъ (IIIa,3), etc.

In some lexemes the desinence is *-ij* (e.g., in притчїй 'proverbs'), which is characteristic of the old i-stem declension (see 3.23 below). As we have seen with other case morphemes in previous declensions, the use of this desinence is widespread and a function of the lexeme in question; it cannot be explained merely as being an "error," for the same lexeme cited here is found with the i-stem desinence (albeit *-ej* rather than *-ij*) in IV (135).

3.2.1.1 *Remarks*. In the declension of nouns from the old a- and ja-stems we find no differences between MS and IV in the oblique cases (Gröschel 1972, 138); in the direct cases, however, Gröschel identifies a number of desinences not present in MS. Nominative: endings in *-a* are Slavonic < *-ę; forms in *-ove/-eve* denote masculine persons (e.g., владикове), the use of which the author ascribes to Polish influence (135). Accusative: again *-a* < *-ę (so identifiable as Slavonic); the masculine (II declension) genitive plural desinence *-ov* occurs with nouns referring to masculine persons. There is complete agreement between the forms of this declension in PB and MS (49), and overall the paradigm conforms to norms still characteristic of CSU and CSBR.

3.2.2 *Declension II: Non-Feminine*

3.2.2.1 *Masculine*

N -y/-i, -e,
-ove/-ωve/-eve — стаиы (K9b,14) 'states, conditions,' сѹсѣдове (K3a,6) 'neighbors,' дворане (125b,26) courtiers, ст҃ители (K23a,20) 'priests,' богачѣ (53b,21) 'rich men,' ѿ҃цы (167b,26) 'fathers,' люде (K12b,12) 'people,' родичѡве (207b,29) 'parents,' мѹжеве (181b,12) 'men'

A	-y/-i, -ωv/-ev, -e, -ej, -ij	дрꙋги (K7b,2) 'friends,' грѣхи (K6a,3) 'sins,' оученикѡвъ (52b,6) 'pupils,' людий (381b,18), прїателей (267b,4) friends, пастырєвъ (71b,20) 'pastors,' царѣ (K17a,20) 'kings,' мешканцѡвъ (157b,27) 'inhabitants,' людє (293b,25)
G	-ωv/-ev, -ej, -ij, -#	животѡвъ (K14a,7) 'lives,' родичѡвъ (K15b,18), людий (K15a,11), мꙋжевъ (162a,12), гостей (54a,19) 'guests,' Иерихонѧнъ (395a,21–22) 'inhabitants of Jericho,' болєв (219b,15) 'pains'
L	-ax, -ex, -ox/-ωx, -ix	страха́х (K17a,14–15) 'fears,' здроѧхъ (20b,13) 'sources,' мꙋжахъ (K3b,19), днєхъ (35b,5), домѣхъ (501a,13) 'houses,' образѡхъ (67b,24) 'images,' домохъ (67a,22–23)
D	-ωm/-em	Хрїстїѧнѡмъ (K22a,12) 'Christians,' младенцємъ (IVa,6) 'youths,' слꙋхачѡмъ (K5a,6) 'listeners,' людємъ (30a,41)
I	-amy, -mi, -y	голосами (K3a,26) 'voices,' часы (123a,6) 'times,' слꙋхачами (K6b,3), днѧми (133b,13) 'days,' конми 128b,7) 'horses,' с҃ны (K16a,8) 'sons,' оучителми (209a,20), кролми (238a,16) 'kings,' непрїателми (213b,7–8) 'enemies,' болми (215a,6), болѧми (152a,13) 'pains'

1. In many unmarked contexts the hard stem nominative desinence is the old o-stem accusative plural *-y* (*-i* after velars): совѣты (K6b,4) 'advice,' роки (K17a,6) 'years.' In biblical passages or similar contexts the Slavonic desinence *-i* may be found; stem-final velars mutate in the presence of this desinence: раби (K26b,3) 'slaves,' Херꙋвими (K23b,10) 'cherubim,' грѣси (K10b,17) 'sins,' грѣшници (K13b,10)

'sinners,' дрꙋзи (428a,12) 'friends'; cf. the unmutated velar in Apl дрꙋги cited above, reflecting *y, as in GSPS N пророци—A пророки 'prophets.' Note the forms оучєницы (434a,10) 'pupils' < оучєници, and чєловѣцы (367b,5–6) < *чєловѣци, in which final *-y* reflects the hardened affricate /c/. Among soft-stem forms *-i* is the basic nominative desinence in *Kazan'e*, while -ѣ (=[i]) is commonly found in JU, e.g., in оучитєлѣ (283a,10) 'teachers,' приатєлѣ (208a,1) 'friends,' ногтѣ (348a,9) '(finger)nails' (cf. other similar distributions of /ě/ and /i/ above, e.g., genitive singular of soft stem I declension substantives). The desinence *-y* occurs after hardened /c/, as noted above: младєнцы (IIIb,6) 'youths, children,' ѿцы (167b,26) 'fathers.'

The desinence *-ove* is extremely common in MS' texts; it occurs primarily with substantives denoting human beings, but it is also used with other types of nouns: сꙋсѣдовє (K3a,6) 'neighbors,' сынѡвє (107a,17–18) 'sons,' жолнѣрѡвє (125b,25) 'soldiers,' but сꙋдовє (K2b,3; Rom 11:33) 'judgements,' народѡвє (29a,24) 'peoples.' Cf. the soft-stem variant *-eve* in ꙋчитєлєвє (K23a,20; 352a,12) 'teachers,' злодѣєвє (40b,15) 'criminals,' оучнєвє (249a,6) 'pupils'; the hard-stem variant -ѡve may occur after hushings that have hardened: родичѡвє (207b,29) 'parents.' The rise of *-ove* as a marker of the nominative plural for animate substantives was characteristic of all Ruthenian variants (Bulyka et al. 1988, 67), but it is no longer productive in the modern East Slavic literary languages. Although many of the forms could be interpreted as Polonisms (жолнѣрѡвє [above], панѡвє [74b,21] 'lords') the common use of this desinence in present-day southwest CSU and the hundreds of attestations in MS allow for its interpretation as a feature of Smotryc'kyj's Ruthenian.

The originally i-stem nominative plural desinence *-e* is found in людє (72 times, e.g., K12b,12) 'people'; Slavonic *-ie* occurs only 5 times, in all instances in biblical contexts: пꙋтїє (K2b,3; Rom 11:33) 'ways,' людїє (K26b,13: a reference to the Wisdom of Solomon; 3 times in JU, e.g., 146a,15) 'people.' The ending *-e* is also found once in спо͠слꙋхачє (K7a,18) 'fellow listeners,' probably a Polish form: cf. Pol Npl *słuchacze* 'listeners.' The ending *-e* is also characteristic of substantives formed with the formant *-jan-* denoting groups of people, as it is in GSPS: хрїстїанє (57b,13) 'Christians,' дворанє (125b,26) 'people of the court,' and the like. Once this desinence is found with another substantival type, viz. the noun 'soldier': жолнѣрє (301b,13).

The desinence *-e* might reflect the Polish plural morpheme, but it occurs very early in U-R with this lexeme (1389 SSUM; cf. HSBM, in which it is cited as a late form, viz. from the 17th century); ѣ in MS represents [i]: SSUM жолниръ, жолнере, CSU жовнір. In люде we see the same phenomenon: it might represent Pol *ludzie,* but this form is found in U-R as early as 1422 (SSUM). Polish may have influenced the increased use of люде over люди, but it is without doubt firmly entrenched as a U-R variant.

2. In the accusative the desinence for inanimate substantives is *-y*, with the variant *-i* after velars: дωмы (211a,10) 'houses,' нарωды (249a,4) 'peoples,' but грѣхи (K6a,3) 'sins.' The genitive desinence spelling -ωв is frequently found in the accusative of animate nouns in JU, e.g., in оученикωвъ (52b,6) 'pupils,' but it is not found in *Kazan'e*. Sometimes, however, the old accusative ending *-y* is still found in such substantives, as in сыны (52b,4; K16a,8) 'sons'; this ought to be interpreted as reflecting a higher style or level of language. Compare the animate accusatives (e.g., мѹченики (174a,22) 'martyrs' and перⷣе человѣки (544a,27) 'before the people'), in which the desinential variant *-i* (*pro* *y) occurs after velars. We also find the nominative and accusative sharing the desinence *-y* in the same lexeme: N сыны (488b,7)—A сыны (52b,4); the original nominative-accusative opposition is retained in N Агг҃ли (174b,1)—A Агг҃лы (174a,22) 'angels'; cf. дрѹги-дрѹзи cited above. Once accusative *-y* is found with a substantive with the formant *-jan-*: Самарѧны (489b,3) 'Samaritans'; this can only be interpreted as a Slavonicism (in place of **Samarjan*), as this is the form given in GSPS: A римлѧны. Cf. the animate Apl рⷨилѧ҃ (276a,14) 'Romans.'

In the lexeme люд- 'people' the nominative desinence *-e* occurs in the accusative 3 times (e.g., 293b,25); cf. SSUM, in which it is also cited in one early (1457) example as the accusative, alongside *-i*, *-ej*, *-ii*, *-y*.

Among soft-stem substances the desinence *-i* is the rule in *Kazan'e* (e.g., псалтыри). This desinence is found only 5 times in all of JU, and every attested form occurs in a prepositional phrase: на люди (5 times, e.g., 82b,10) '[upon] people'; the phrase implies motion. In these instances it is evidently the preposition which allows the old ending to be retained, since these phrases were probably regarded as units. Note that the phrasal stress falls on на́. According to Kernyc'kyj, both *-i* and *-ě* are used in the accusative plural in the sixteenth century (Kernyc'kyj 1967, 61). The second of these is occasionally found in MS with animate substantives in place of the genitive-accusative desinence: царѣ (K17a,20) 'kings' in *Kazan'e*, лихвѧрѣ (264b,11–12) 'usurers,' among others, in JU. As was the case with hard stem substantives, the genitive desinences are never found for the accusative in *Kazan'e*. In JU, however, they are extremely common, e.g., пастырєвъ (71b,20), мєщканцѡвъ (157b,27).

3. The predominant hard-stem genitive desinence is -ωv, from the old u-stem desinence *-ov*: грѣхѡвъ (34a,12) 'sins,' сынѡвъ (37a,1) 'sons,' пожиткѡвъ (34b,19) 'profits,' etc. It is possible on the basis of textual evidence that omega in the desinence -ωv (as in the dative -ωm) has a phonetic value approximating tense [o] or [u]; the attested forms in *-uv* in the texts of IV lend credence to this theory. Next to hundreds of forms with the spelling -ωv, the spelling with omicron (-ов) occurs only 6 times.The Slavonic ending # (zero) is clearly identifiable only once, in гл҃ъ (IVa,18) 'verbs.' In ловєцъ (K27b,12) 'fishermen,' the grapheme є appears to indicate phonetic [lovjec]; in fact its use reflects the convention used by Smotryc'kyj in his Slavonic grammar to differentiate such a form from an otherwise identical Nsg (cf. Nsg отєцъ- Gpl отєцъ). It is presumably because of context (note that this form is found in *Kazan'e*) that the Slavonic form was chosen, rather than *ловцѡвъ. I assume that the Nsg of ловєцъ is ловєцъ, not ловца as in Pol *łowca* (the former is used in U-R texts, cf. SSUM); if it were the latter, of course, this noun would have to be labeled a II declension form. Finally, nouns containing the formant *-jan-* have the expected #-ending, e.g., in Иєрихонѧнъ (395a,21–22) 'inhabitants of Jericho.'

Among soft-stem substantives we find the spellings -ѡвъ/-євъ and and -єй/-ий. The spelling -ѡвъ occurs frequently (46 times) after hardened hushings and the affricate /c/: родичѡвъ (K15b,18) 'parents,' ѿщєпєнцѡв (K24b,11) 'apostates,' мѹжѡвъ (156b,7) 'men.' The variant *-ev* is attested slightly more often (60 times), for example, in ѡбычаєвъ (K21a,10) 'customs, habits,' мѹжєвъ (162a,12), ѿцєвъ (171b,24) 'fathers,' among others. Note that the lexeme боль 'pain' is a masculine noun, as it is in CSU/CSBR: G болєв (219b,15). The i-stem desinence *-ej* is numerically as common as *-ev*, e.g., in мѣсѧцєй

(K2b,22) 'months' (cf. CSU місяців), гостей (54a,19) 'guests.' This desinence occurs with nouns of numerous old stem types, and was evidently in competition with the ending *-ev*, as well as with *-ij*. The latter may be interpreted as a feature of southwestern CSU, since in the rest of the East Slavic area this desinence is *-ej*. The desinence *-ij* (>*-yj*) is still found in modern western Ukrainian (Kernyc'kyj 57). Although *-ij* is also the Slavonic ending, because it is found in words of Polish as well as of East Slavic origin we can assume that this was a living form to Smotryc'kyj. This desinence is most frequently attested in the form людїй (133 times) 'people' (next to людей 3 times), but also occurs 19 times with other lexemes, e.g., in добродѣтелїй (36b,4) 'virtue.' In the accusative case 43 out of 44 occurrences of this morpheme occur in the form людий.

There is one example of a genitive plural desinence *-i*, used in неприятели (49a,22) 'enemies.' This is one of six possible genitive forms used in U-R with this particular lexeme (SSUM); the ending *-i* could variously be interpreted as a contracted i-stem ending (-ii > -i), as a formation analogical to jo-stems such as N край, G краи, or as a feature of Old Polish. According to the dictionary of Old Polish *nieprzyjacieli* was in use in the XV century (SSP V:221).

4. The standard locative ending among hard-stem substantives is *-ax*, e.g., страхах (K17a,14) 'fears'; *-ex* is found 2 times, while *-ox* occurs 3 times (the spelling -ωхъ 1 time), and *-ěx* 9 times. The form *-ex* occurs once in a biblical passage in *Kazan'e*: члвцехъ (K2b,24) 'people' (this is the form used in OB, Luke 1:25), and it occurs once in JU: ѱалмехъ (255a,21) 'Psalms.' *-ex* should be interpreted as an orthographic variant of the o-stem desinence *-ěx*, that is, under the influence of B-R (or North U-R) orthographic conventions; this is especially clear in the first of the two examples, because the mutation of /k/ > /c/ was conditioned by a following *ě. Locatives in *-ox* (< *-ъхъ) are found in western U-R from the 16th century, and are still widespread in this Ukrainian dialect region (Bevzenko et al. 1978, 111); in MS: образωхъ (67b,24) 'images, icons,' сынох (494b,13) 'sons,' and домохъ (67a,22–23) 'houses.' The old o-stem desinence *-ěx* is found with numerous lexemes: престолѣхъ (407a,20) 'thrones,' домѣхъ (501a,13), грωбѣхъ (226b,23) 'graves,' часѣхъ (351b,21) 'times,' разѣхъ

(343b,6; 233a,8) ‘occasions,’ and дарѣхъ (3 times, e.g., 448a,3) ‘gifts.’

Among soft stems there is a difference between *Kazan'e* and JU. Only *-ax* is attested in *Kazan'e*, e.g., in здроах (K20b,13) ‘sources, springs.’ In JU there are 10 occurrences of this desinence, e.g., днѧ҃х (49b,29) ‘days,’ палацахъ (54a,20) ‘palaces’; however, there are also 27 substantives with the ending *-ex*, e.g., днехъ (35b,5), людехъ (20 times, e.g., 72b,8), тѣнехъ (163b,10) ‘shadows.’ In comparison, only one such form is found in IV (129). The number of attestations of this desinence in MS is significant enough to warrant their consideration as more than an aberration: it is still widespread in southwest Ukrainian dialects, suggesting that its use in JU reflects a feature of MS’ system. The fact that IV was northern Ukrainian-Ruthenian most likely explains the (almost total) absence of the desinence from his texts.

5. The dative desinence among hard-stem substantives is -ωm in the vast majority of attested forms (viz. 190 times as opposed to only 9 occurrences of *-om*), e.g., in сынѡ҃ (137a,10) ‘sons’; cf. оученикомъ (134b,10). The variant -ωмъ also occurs after the hardened affricates /c/ and /č/: слꙋхачωмъ (K5a,6) ‘listeners,’ лакомцωмъ (62a,23) ‘greedy people’; elsewhere among soft-stems the ending is *-em:* людемъ (59 times with this lexeme out of a total of 67 occurrences, e.g., 30a,14), приятелемъ (248a,30) ‘friends.’ The a-stem ending *-am*/*-jam*, characteristic of modern East Slavic, is not yet in evidence in Smotryc'kyj’s texts. The forms used by Smotryc'kyj were certainly current in his time, however: the desinences *-om* (*-um*, *-im*) and *-em* (*-jum, -im*) are still found in many Ukrainian dialects (Bevzenko et al. 1978, 107); stressed *–óm* is also still current in southwest Belarusian (Blinava and Mjacel'skaja 1980, 82–83).

6. The instrumental desinence *-ami* is the norm in MS and in all modern East Slavic languages: братами (52b,6) ‘brothers,’ сынами (127a,1) ‘sons,’ голосами (K3a,26) ‘voices.’ Alongside this desinence we find a competing ending *-y*, representing the original o-stem form that was supplanted by *-ami*. In *Kazan'e* it occurs only once, in a biblical passage: єп҃копы (K20b,21) ‘bishops, overseers.’ This ending is found an additional 10 times in JU, but all of its occurrences cannot be dismissed as Slavonicisms, regardless of the nature of the one attested

form in *Kazan'e*. Instead, it is possible to interpret this ending as Ruthenian, the use of which is dependent on phrasal context: **вѣчными часы** (7 times, e.g., 123a,6) '(for) eternal times/ages,' as well as **иншими разы** (457a,9) '(at) other times' (but **тыми разами** [457a,11]). In other words, *-y* can occur as long as an accompanying form is clearly marked as 'instrumental' (for example, with the ending *-ami*). Only once does this desinence occur outside of such units: **з Самаряны** (160b,1) 'with Samaritans.' The interpretation of this ending as a reflection of MS' native system is supported by the use of similar phraseological constructions in some modern southwest Ukrainian dialects, e.g., Galician and Lemkian давными часы (Bevzenko et al. 1978, 109). Although such forms are now limited to the westernmost of the southwestern Ukrainian dialects, it is probable that they were in wider use, over greater geographical regions, in Smotryc'kyj's time. The same patterns are seen in examples cited by Bulyka et al. (1979) for B-R: со всеми сны, с тыми то короли, з листы своими, великими голосы, and всеми домы; only one example does not fit the pattern (with the preposition s; see p. 83). The ending *-y* also occurs slightly more frequently in IV than *-ami* (53 times:46 times, respectively; pages 126–27), indicating that *-y* was current in U-R. This desinence is even more common with neuter substantives (see 3.2.2.2 below).

Among soft-stem nouns we also find competing desinences: *-mi* versus *-ami*. The former occurs more frequently than the latter (82 times and 45 times, respectively), but more than half of all occurrences of *-mi* are with **люд-** 'people,' a lexeme that is frequently anomalous (as we see throughout this study). As in other cases and among hard-stem instrumentals, there are morphological doublets: cf. **оучителями** (99b,16–17), **оучителми** (70b,15) 'teachers.' Other forms in *-mi* include **мѹжми** (70b,14) 'men,' **конми** (128b,7) 'horses,' **пастыми** (436a,16) 'shepherds,' **люми** (e.g., 53a,21), etc. Compare **товаришами** (303b,4) 'comrades, friends,' **днями** (133b,13) 'days.' The number of forms in *-mi* outnumbers those in *-ami* by 11:7 in IV, almost exactly the ratio found in MS' texts, indicating that MS and IV represent typical 16th-17th century U-R patterns. Gröschel suggests that Polish influence is partly responsible for this in IV (1972, 128), and the same can be said for MS. The distribution of the two desinences, e.g., in **оучителми** (4 times)—**оучителями** (8 times) indicates that *-ami* is on the way to becoming the norm (at least for some lexemes), while Polish influence and developments in the Ruthenian dialects serve to reinforce the place of *-mi* in the system. In present-day southwest dialects the desinence *-mi* is still more widely used than in other dialects. Compare also CSU кіньми 'horses,' гістьми 'guests,' людьми 'people,' and CSBR конямі/коньмі (both accepted), людзьмі; the first and last of these examples are found in MS. The extent to which *-mi* occurs in Ruthenian texts (in many of the same lexemes in MS and IV), together with its current distribution, allow us to identify this morpheme as 'Ruthenian.'

3.2.2.1.1 *Remarks*. The desinences listed above from MS' texts are in overall agreement with those found in IV, differing only in some details. Thus, in both we find the desinences of the old a-stem used in the locative case, becoming prevalent in the instrumental as well, but not yet occurring in the dative (IV, 138). The desinences used in IV which do not occur in MS are only found among the hard stems: G *-ox* and I *-mi*; the soft/mixed stem declension is for all intents and purposes exactly the same. All of the attested forms in PB occur in MS (PB 27–34).

This declensional type (particularly among soft/mixed stem substantives) is clearly characterized by the same phenomenon as in the singular: a proliferation of desinences invariably provides that one substantive may occur with more than one desinence in a given case, and one desinence may function as the marker of more than one case. Instances of the latter are comparatively rare, as in the example сыны N (488b,7) and A (K16a,8). The former is amply represented, however:

N	агг҃лѡве—агг҃ли	'angels'
	сынѡве—сыны	'sons'
	жолнѣре—жолнѣреве	'soldiers'
	мȣжѣ—мȣжеве	'men'
	оучителѣ—оучителеве	'teachers'
G	днев҄ъ—дний—дней	'days'
	мȣжѡвъ—мȣжевъ—мȣжей	
	пѣнязевъ—пѣнязей	'money'
	(не)прїателевъ—прїателей	'friends (enemies)'
I	товаришами—товаришми	'comrades'

	оучителѧми—оучителми	
	(не)пріателѧми—пріателми	
L	днѧхъ—днехъ	
	домохъ—домѣхъ	'houses'

Some word-formational formants appear to play a role in determining whether a particular form is more or less liable to occur with two different desinences; this is true of the formants *-tel'* and *-děj,* expressing 'one who performs action X.' Examples with the former show, however, that such lexemes do not necessarily occur predictably with one more frequently than with the other: cf. оучителѧми—оучителми 'teachers' (8 times versus 3 times respectively) but (не)пріателѧми—(не)пріателми (5 times versus 6 times respectively). Some forms occur frequently enough to show which desinence was favored: (не)пріѧтелевъ (5 times)—(не)пріѧтелей (20 times); the former has become generalized for soft stem substantives of this type in CSU (-ів) and CSBR (-яў), but the latter was clearly still viable in Ruthenian. Examples of competing forms with the formant -děj are few, and therefore indicate only that competition between forms exists, without favoring one over another: I казнодѣѧми (461a,4) 'preachers' and злодѣйми (435b,27) 'criminals.'

In spite of the large number of desinences used with the soft-stem substantives, we must not overestimate the importance of some of them, as they are often bound to anomalous lexemes such as люд-. In the genitive, for example, the ending *-ij* is primarily found in the form людій 'people' (133 times, only 19 times with other lexemes). The same lexeme is widely attested in other cases as well: of 79 instances of instrumentals in *-mi*, людми accounts for 42; of 29 instances of locatives in *-ex*, людехъ accounts for 20. Although the root люд- is commonly used to express 'people,' note the occurrence of the competing genitival constructions зъ людій (381b,18)—зъ человѣкωвъ (381a,25).

3.2.2.2 *Neuter*

NA	-a	слова (K8a,2; 114b,6) 'words,' тѣла (114b,19–20) 'bodies,' преслѣдованѧ (K15b,2) 'persecutions,' ровенїѧ (K11b,10) 'quarrels,' мѣстца (K19b,13) 'places'

G	-#, -ij	лѣтъ (IIIb,6) 'years,' словъ (113b,26), ѡко͠ченїй (IIb,9) 'endings, desinences'
L	-ax, -ex, (-ix)	мѣстахъ (K2b,15) 'towns,' оустѣхъ (171b,23) 'mouth,' дѣѧнїѧх (K13a,18) 'acts,' оуваженѧхъ (K14b,10) 'considerations,' реченїихъ (IIb,5) 'phrases, sentences'
D	-am, -om	словамъ (K7a,2), склоненїѧмъ (IIIb,15) 'declensions'
I	-ami, -y, -mi	богатствы (K12b,12) 'riches,' крилами (K27b,15) 'wings,' оуваженми (K14b,23–K15a,1), деревами (121a,8) 'trees'

1. As in the modern Slavic languages, the accusative ending in Ruthenian is the same as the nominative. The genitive of hard stems is -# (zero) throughout: лѣтъ (IIIb,6) 'years'; деревъ (121a,9) 'trees.' All but two soft-stem forms have the vocalic desinence *-ij*; these soft stems are derived substantives formed by means of the suffix *- ьj-(e), e.g., приказанїй (125a,22) 'commandments,' and поколѣнїй (489a,23) 'tribes.' The zero-endings are found in поль (148b,24) 'fields' and мѣстцъ (355b,21) 'places.' The former has a parallel in CSU: поле 'field' has two possible genitives, viz. піль and полів. The latter is reflected in CSU, viz. місць (with simplification of -stc- > -sc). We do not find a #-ending for the first in CSBR, but it is possible for the second: поле-палёў, but месца-месц/месцаў.

2. In the locative case the a-stem desinence *-ax* is the rule among hard and soft stems, e.g., слѡвахъ (43a,4) 'words,' мѣстах (392a,231) 'places, cities,' мешка͠ѧхъ (121b,3) 'dwellings,' мѣстцахъ (80a,4) 'places'; cf. Slavonic дѣѧнїахъ (351b,7) 'acts.' The ending *-ex* occurs twice: лѣтехъ (280a,9,26) 'years,' and воротѣͯ (172a,18) 'gate(s),' and twice, in the same lexeme, the old o-stem ending *-ěx:* в оустѣхъ (479a,20; 171b,23) 'in the mouth(s).' The latter occurs in references to biblical passages; it is possible to interpret both of these spellings as

'Slavonic,' as GSPS gives both as possible locative plurals for the second declension.
3. In the dative case the original o-stem ending *-om* occurs once in *Kazan'e* and once (written -ѡмъ) in JU, while the desinence *-am* (from the a-stems) is found a total of 8 times in all texts: оустомъ (K12a,5) 'mouth,' but оустам (190a,21), єлѡвамъ (K7a,2; 299a,10). Cf. the soft stem єклонєнїамъ (IIIb,15) 'declensions.'

4. In the instrumental there is strong competition between the old o-stem desinence *-y* (attested 48 times) and the a-stem ending *-ami* (attested only 37 times): богатєтвы (K12b,12) 'riches,' лѣты (K16a,14) 'years,' єловы (K22a,11) 'words,' добры (K23b,16) 'goods,' дѣлы (105b,18) 'things, affairs,' but єловами (K3b,12; 38b,24) 'words,' добрами (403b,18). Soft-stem instrumentals occur with the desinence *-mi* (on dual *-ima* see 3.3 below), reflecting the old i-stem or consonant-stem ending; this desinence is seen 4 times in MS in оуважєнми (K14b,23–K15a,1) 'considerations,' приказа҃ми (2 times, e.g., 358a,3) 'orders,' покꙋшє҃ми (371a,4) 'temptations.' Several nouns also retain the consonantal or i-stem desinence *-mi* in CSU and CSBR, e.g., Ukr кіньми 'horses,' Br коньмі.

The desinence *-y* can occur in any environment or text, and therefore is not perceived as an archaism; what is striking is the extent to which this desinence is retained among neuter nouns, as compared with masculines (see above). One obvious reason for this is the fact that there is no ambiguity involved: *-y* does not express any other case form in the neuter, in contrast with the masculine where it also serves as the nominative or accusative plural. The pattern of occurrence noted with masculine substantives is in much greater evidence among the neuters: when the neuter substantive occurs with a modifier or other substantive in which the case marker is clearly instrumental (that is, *-ami* with substantives, *-ymi*/*-imi* with modifiers), then the desinence *-y* is likely to be used. Note the following examples:

> тыми єлѡвы (352a,21; 361b,9)
> прикрыми лѣка҃єтвы (148a,26)
> дѡбры євоими (356a,12)
> мнѡгими родами и лѣты (452b,7–8)
> вшєлакими добры (361a,4–5)

писмы своими (351b,28)
блюзнѣрствы геретицкими (69a,19)
оучинками, и слωвы и всѣми . . . (70b,5)
добрыми дѣлы (105b,18)
земскими панствы (95a,15)
которыми словы (103b,13–14)
мꙋдростю и преложенствы (542b,13)
титꙋлами и достоенствы (542b,14–15)
словы и приповестми (36b,13–14)
всѣми свѧты (123b,15)
трωма лѣты (177a,26)

In a phrase such as словами его (38b,24) 'in his words,' the desinence *-ami* is necessitated by the lack of any case marker in the third person singular possessive pronoun. One of MS' forms most likely reflects a Polish original: прⷣекилкома лѣты (K16a,13–14) is reminiscent of the Polish construction przed laty 'years ago' (the instrumental of Pol *lato* is otherwise *latami*). The rule—or perhaps better "tendency"—is broken in several examples, e.g., in словами добрыми (522a,27) 'with good words,' and своими чꙋдами (149a,8) 'by means of his wonders/ miracles,' among others; such examples may be taken to indicate the increasing preference for the a-stem desinence. True exceptions to the rule (that is, use of *-y* alone) are few in number: небⷥепеченствы обложена (121a,16) 'surrounded by dangers,' богатствы оплываетъ (542b,20) '(is) laden with riches.' All substantives with the formant *-stvo* have the instrumental *-y*, not *-ami*; the lack of a competing (non-instrumental) morpheme *-y* and the agentive nature of the constructions together make it extremely unlikely that a listener would interpret such forms as anything but instrumental.

Bevzenko et al. (1978) offer more attestations of the pattern noted here: whereas a large number of their examples of instrumental *-y*/*-i* involve the presence of other clearly instrumental markers, those with the ending *-ami* are cited most often alone or with prepositions (108–109). The continued use and vitality of the ending *-y* in and around 1600 is apparent also in IV, in which this desinence occurs 10 times, as opposed to only 3 examples of the a-stem desinence *-ami* (132). The co-occurrence of two different desinences in the same phrase is paralleled in CSU, in which the dative endings *-u* and *-ovi* co-occur in situations of apposition; in fact, the dative desinences of two substantives in apposition *must* differ: братові Степану or брату Степанові '(to) brother Stepan' (note that both combinations are possible). Compare the same dative construction in MS: нєприѧтєлєви дїѧволꙋ (206a,24–206b,1) '(to) the enemy, thedevil.'

3.2.2.2.1 *Remarks*. The neuter declension is much like that of masculine substantives, except that the influence of the a-stems is now seen in the dative (something not seen in the masculines) in addition to the instrumental and locative. The most interesting points to note concern the use of the instrumental desinences, hard as well as soft/mixed stems. Among the former, there is still a true competition between rival endings, but contextual evidence supplies guidelines for their occurrence. In the soft/mixed stems the a-stem ending is conspicuous by its absence. The desinences used in IV but not occurring in MS are: in the soft stems G *-ej*, in the hard stems L *-ox*; I *-mi* and L *-ěx* are not found in IV (138). The plural forms in the neuter paradigms of PB agree with those cited above for MS with only one exception: PB only has *-om* in the dative of hard-stem substantives (42–43), where MS has *-am* as the basic variant.

3.2.3 *Declension III: Feminine*

NA	-i, -y	кличи (K11b,12) 'shouts,' моцы (31b,5) 'strengths'
G	-ij, -ej	печалїй (K12b,20) 'sadnesses,' частєй (67a,26) 'parts'
L	-ax, -ex	костєхъ (K24b,4) 'bones,' пожадливостѧⷯ (54a,2–3) 'desires'
D	-am, -em	справєдливостєм (K27a,14) 'righteousnesses,' пожадливостѧмъ (K18b,11)
I	-ami, -mi	страстми (18a,13–14) 'passions,' мыслѧми (78a,3) 'thoughts'

1. As in the neuter, III declension feminine substantives do not differentiate the nominative from the accusative cases. In the genitive case there are two competing desinences *-ij* and *-ej*, which can occur with the same lexeme: рєчїй (K9a,15) (the rule) and рєчєй (273a,16) 'things.' The latter desinence is used only 13 times, all instances of which occur in JU, while the former is attested 316 times in all three texts; *-ej* is the rule in CSU for this declension, while CSBR admits both *-ej* and *-(j)aw*. On strictly formal grounds, it is possible to identify *-ij* as Slavonic, but its wide use by MS suggests instead that it be identified as southwest U-R, since it is still currently widespread in this Ukrainian dialect region (see Bevzenko et al. 1978, 117); the few *-ej-* genitives that occur in MS are most likely the result of north U-R or B-R influence.

2. In the locative of soft-stem substantives we find two desinences in competition in MS: forms in *-ax* outnumber those with *-ex* (< *-ьхъ) by 82:31, or ca. 72.6%:27.4%. Thus, for example, двєрєхъ (363b,6) 'doors,' частєхъ (306a,21) 'parts,' but рєчахъ (162a,20) 'matters, things,' злостѧхъ (83b,9) 'evils.' Both desinences may occur with the same lexeme: злостѧх́—злостєх́ (45a,7); in this particular case, however, choice of morpheme appears to be determined by the lexeme: злостѧх occurs once, while злостєх́ is attested 6 times. The distribution of these two desinences between *Kazan'e* and JU is noteworthy (they are not attested in *Grammatiki*): in the former *-ex* and *-ax* occur 5 times and 2 times, respectively, while they are found 26 times and 80 times, respectively, in JU. The generally more traditional/archaic character of *Kazan'e* does not allow the spread of the a/ja-stem ending *-ax* in this stem-type to be reflected as clearly as it is in JU.

3. The dative desinence *-em* is the East Slavic reflex of CS *-ьmъ, originally the i-stem desinence; it occurs 2 times, once in *Kazan'e* and once in JU: справєдливостєм (K27a,14) 'righteousnesses,' заповѣдємъ (447b,11) 'commandments.' The ja- stem desinence *-am*, current in the modern East Slavic languages, is the rule (31 times): e.g., in пожадливостѧⷨ (K18b,11; 45a,6) 'desires,' роскошамъ (40a,12) 'luxuries,' мыслѧмъ (286b,4) 'thoughts.'

4. There also are two competing endings in the instrumental case, viz. *-mi* (the old i-stem desinence) and *-ami* (the old a-/ja-stem desinence). Whereas the a-/ja-stem forms clearly predominate in the locative, instrumental forms with the desinence *-ami* outnumber those with *-mi* by the small margin of 78:59, or 56.9%:43.1%; parallelling the distribution of the locative forms, *Kazan'e* yields *-mi* 5 times, *-ami* 2 times, again not reflecting the spread of the old a-stem desinence to this stem-type as much as JU (they are not attested in *Grammatiki*). As with the locative, both endings may occur with the same lexeme; note the following doublets: мысльми (402a,21) and мыслѧми (78a,3) 'thoughts,' пѣсньми (469b,27) and пѣснѧми (468a,24) 'songs.' The lexeme злость again shows that choice of morpheme is not always random: злостми (e.g., 124a,3) 'evils' is found 17 times.

3.2.3.1 *Remarks*. This declension is characterized by the (as yet incomplete) adoption of a-stem desinences in the plural; that the process is incomplete is reflected by competition between old and new desinences, as is the case in the other declensional paradigms examined to this point. Here the rival endings are clearly those of the i-stems (e.g., L *-ex*, I *-mi*) and the a-/ja-stems (L *-ax*, I *-ami*). The i-stem desinences *-ex* and *-mi* are still in evidence in modern Ukrainian dialects (Bevzenko et al. 1978, 118), so it is reasonable to interpret their presence in MS' texts (to some degree at least) as a reflection of synchronic reality, rather than merely of an archaic system. The data from MS are particularly interesting in comparison with IV: there is overall agreement between the two in the locative (although differing in scale, with only 4 forms in *-ex* and 2 in *-ax* in IV), but in the instrumental the new desinence -(j)ami is not in evidence in the language of the latter. This may indicate an earlier adoption of the ja-stem desinence in the more southerly U-R regions (as represented by MS) than in the northwestern regions (as represented by IV). Kernyc'kyj does not mention possible periodization (1967, 99); Bevzenko et al. do state that the expanded use of the ja-stem endings *-jami*/ *-ami* took place from the XVI–XVII centuries, but they do not discuss the question of geographic distribution (1978, 118). With the exception of the instrumental ending *-(j)ami,* all of the desinences found in MS are also attested in IV (128) and PB (50–51).

3.2.4 *IV Declension: Neuter*

A large number of consonant-stem substantives is found in MS, primarily from the old n- and nt- declensional types. Of the s-stems, Ruthenian нєбо 'sky, heaven' commonly reflects the s-marker in the plural, as in CSU and CSBR:

N-A	нєбєса (47a,33)
G	нєбєсъ (413b,2)
L	нєбєсєх (200b,3)

Cf. CSU небо, Npl небеса, but CSBR неба, Npl нябёсы. The genitive очєсъ (K12b,7) 'eyes' is attested one time in a biblical passage; the corresponding southwest U-R очий follows the biblical verse (K12b,9). Many substantives of the old consonantal stem-types have, by the time of MS, come to be identified with mainstream second declension neuters; thus, the (originally) s-stem substantives слово 'word' and чꙋдо 'wonder' now generate such forms as G словъ (in place of earlier словєсъ) and N чꙋда (in place of чꙋдєса). The following occur with the old s-marker in IV: A нєбєса, G словєс, and I словєси (134); cf. from PB: G нєбєс, тєлєс, and чꙋдєс (42).

The following n-stem substantives are attested in the plural in MS:

imja 'name; noun (gramm.)':	N-A	имєна (328b,3)
	G	имєн (328a,29)
	I	имєны (437a,5)
sěmja 'seed':	N-A	сѣмєна (242b,1)
ramja 'shoulder':	N-A	рамєна (96b,3–4)
	I	рамєнами (K27b,14).

Today the lexeme рам'я is described in SUM as a dialect form (CSU плече), while it is not cited in TSBM. We note that two different forms of the instrumental are attested with these substantives, as is the case among II declension neuters: *-y*, *-ami*. In IV only one form of this type is attested, viz. N имєна (133); Didiakin-Leeming cites the following forms from PB: N-A имєна (1969, 41), G врємєн (42), and L имєнєх, имєнох (43).

Nouns of the old nt-type are numerous in MS:

N	кнѧжата (12 times, e.g., 109a,19) 'young princes'
	внȣчата (519a,12) 'little grandchildren'
	звѣрата . . . и быдлѧта (409a,19) 'young wild animals and young cattle'
	овчата (430a,25) 'lambs'
	ѩгнѧта (73b,6) 'lambs'
A	отрочата (466a,25–26) 'children'
	кȣрчата (546a,15) 'young chickens'
G	кнѧжат (5 times, e.g., 197a,12)
	отрочаⷮ близнѧтъ (453b,17–18) 'young twins' (lit. 'children-twins')
	пташатъ (375b,9) 'young birds'
L	кнѧжатахъ (499a,9)
	быдлѧтахъ (179b,2)
D	кнѧжатамъ (528b,9)
	звѣрѧтомъ . . . быдлѧтомъ (409a,17)

This declension follows the general patterns established among II declension neuters described above: a-stem endings are evident especially in the locative, while both a-stem and o-stem endings are used in the dative. Judging by the frequency with which these substantives occur, all of them ought to be considered viable Ruthenian forms (that is, including Polonisms such as кнѧжата), rather than be subdivided into Ruthenianisms ('Ukrainianisms' and/or 'Belarusianisms') and Polonisms. In comparison with MS, the number of nt-stems used in the texts of IV and PB is rather small because of the different nature of their respective texts. All three forms cited for IV are identified by Gröschel as Polonisms: кнѩжата and нєбожата/нєбожѩта < Pol *książęta, niebożęta,* respectively (1972, 134); Didiakin-Leeming cites NA звєрѩта, щєнѩта, лєвнѩта, and G звєрѩт, зєрнѩт (1969, 41–42).

Finally, the standard word for "children" must be included here because it was originally a 'nt-stem' дитѧ. It is clearly still considered neuter, as we see that there is no differentiation between the nominative and the accusative:

N	дѣти (6 times, e.g., 167b,19)
A	дѣти (2 times, 546a,14 and 548a,15)
G	дѣтїй (204a,10; 10 times)/дѣтєй (1 time 300a,12)
L	дѣтєхъ (3 times, e.g., 232b,26)
D	дѣтємъ (3 times, 232b,26; 167b,26; IVa,6)
I	дѣтми (6 times, e.g., 58b,7)

3.3 *The Dual*

The dual was no longer a productive category in the Ruthenian period; it is nevertheless occasionally encountered in individual lexemes, especially those representing naturally occurring pairs such as "eyes," "ears," "legs," among others.Such forms were "inherently" dual. The forms очи 'eyes' and оушн 'ears' belong to this group of words; although they may by this stage be considered soft-stem II declension neuter (*plural*) substantives, their forms can be listed here because half of the attested forms are in fact duals:

ѡчи	(74b,26) N *dual* of око
ѹши	(503b,14) N *dual* of оухо
ѡчїй	(82a,15) G *plural* of око (i-stem desinence)
оушѹ	(440a,10) L *dual* of оухо
ѡчах	(274a,13) L *plural* of око (a-stem desinence)
очѡмъ	(487b,1; 511a,9) D *plural* of око (o-stem desinence)

and

ѡчамъ (241b,18) D *plural* of око (a-stem desinence)
очима (22 times, e.g., 72b,6) I *dual* of око

In CSU очі 'eyes' and плечі 'shoulders' still have the old dual instrumentals очима, плечима, while уші 'ears' has two acceptable forms in the instrumental, viz. the old dual form ушима and the a-stem plural form вухами. CSBR, on the other hand, has only the a-stem forms вачамі, плячамі, and вушамі.

For the rest, if the dual were still a viable category, we should expect to find dual forms in the presence of the number "2" and the word "both"; in fact, there is only one clearly dual form in such an environment: 32 лѣтѣ (446b,12) '32 years.' All other forms occurring with '2' or 'both' are identifiable as nominative plurals; this is a reflection of Ruthenian and/or Polish usage, which require the nominative plural after 2 (as well as 3 and 4).[4]

4 Klemensiewicz, et al., cite Polish *dwa braty* as an example of an incorrect ending attested for the dual number in the 16th century in place of correct *brata* (1981, 310); judging by the competition of declensional forms at the time, however, браты fits the pattern seen in Smotryc'kyj above, i.e., it could also be interpreted as a nominative plural.

CHAPTER FOUR

The Adjective

4.0 The adjectival system found in MS' texts reflects no significant departures from the CSU and CSBR systems, or from those of his Ruthenian contemporaries. The comparative and superlative forms are morphologically the most complex adjectival forms, consequently the greatest part of the chapter is devoted to them. The format adopted in the discussion of the substantive is followed for the adjective.

4.1 *The Short Form*

By the 16th century the short form adjective was primarily used in predicative constructions; the most common case forms found are therefore those of the nominative, singular and plural (Kernyc'kyj 1967, 103). The short forms are common in Smotryc'kyj's language, but they are less frequent than the long forms. The most widely attested forms are the nominative singular of all three genders, the accusative singular feminine, and the nominative plural. By this period the occurrence of a short form adjective in any oblique case is very rare; only one example of a genitive form is identified in MS (see below).

Examples

Nsgm	чєстєнъ (K15b,8) 'honorable,' милъ (K23a,20) 'fine,' нєбєзъчадєнъ (K26b,20) 'not childless,' здоровъ (147b,16) 'healthy,' страшєⷩ҇ (47a,24) 'terrible,' слѣпъ (166b,7) 'blind'
Nsgn	бⷧ҇го (K4a,1) 'blessed'
Nsgf	смꙋтна (K14a,2) 'sorrowful,' слѣпа (K19b,12) 'blind,' прироⷣна (K18b,15) 'natural'
Asgf	нєпразднꙋ (K2b,19) 'not empty,' чєстнꙋ (K4a,6) 'honorable,' вѣчнꙋ (K3b,10) 'eternal,' однообразнꙋ (481b,10) 'monotonous'

Npl	бе̑чинни (K11b,12) 'disorderly,' покорни 'humble,' скромни 'modest' (both 50a,19), слаби (514b,27) 'weak,' чисты (202a,14) 'clean,' збавителевы слѡва (100a,8) 'the Saviour's words'
Gsgm	единосȣщна (185a,23) 'consubstantial' [1]

In the nominative singular of all genders the short forms are used only predicatively, as expected. Attributive short form adjectives are marked in relation to the long forms, and may occur in contexts of a religious/biblical nature. Thus, for instance, from *Kazan'e*: . . . ѹтробȣ рожена непраздн ношȣ, lit. ' . . . I carry a womb of birth [which is] not empty.'; and . . . ѹбїйства, пїанства, безчинни кличи, и подобнаѧ симъ. ' . . . murders, drunkenness[es], disorderly shouts, and the like (lit. things similar to these).' All of the accusative forms are by definition attributive. The one example of a non-direct case form cited above is clearly marked as Slavonic on several levels, viz. syntactically (attributive oblique case), semantically, and phonologically (*jedino-* instead of *odno-*, *-šč-* instead of *-č*): не признава абовѣ̑ злочестивый сей Ха̑ Спса нашего единосȣщна (185a,22–23) 'for this impious (person) did not recognize Christ our consubstantial Savior.'

The number of short forms attested in PB is likewise not very large, and again they are found primarily among the non-direct cases: nominative singular of all genders and nominative plural neuter; two oblique case forms are attested: genitive and locative singular neuter (66–67). In contrast, they occur in substantial numbers in IV, making up an almost complete paradigm. In addition to those identified in MS, Gröschel cites the Gsgn, Dsgm, Asgm and Asgn, Lsgn, Vsg and Vplm, Vsgf, Npln and Nplf, and Aplm and Apln (1972, 141). This comparative wealth of forms comes as no particular surprise, as it is indicative of the artificially archaic character of Vyšens'kyj's language resulting from his attempts to write in an elevated style (i.e., with Slavonic as a model); this is evident throughout our study, but particularly in this morphological category. The most noticeable feature

---

1 The possessive adjectives with the suffix *-ov/-ev,* such as Гдвы (K10b,9) 'of the Lord,' have only nominal short forms, and are therefore not considered here.

of the short form adjective common to all three Ruthenians is the complete lack of short form oblique case forms in the plural.

4.2.0 *The Long Form : Singular*

Case	Non-Feminine (Masculine	Neuter)	Feminine
N	-yj, -ij	-oe, -ee	-aja (-aa)
A	-yj, -ij	-oe, -ee	-uju
G	-oho, -eho (-aho)	-oho, -eho (-aho)	-oi, -ei (-oe)
L	-om, -em	-om, -em	-oj
D	-omu, -emu	-omu, -emu	-oj, -ej
I	-ym, -im	-ym, -im	-oju, -eju

Examples

N/A — *m:* притомный (K23a,15–16) 'conscious,' Славенскїй (IIIa,4) 'Slavonic,' великїй (39a,14) 'great,' остатний (58a,23)/ ост҇анїй (39b,27) 'last'

n: смꙋтное (K3a,27) 'sad,' чꙋдовное (250a,8) 'wondrous'

N — *f:* внꙋтрнаѧ (K11a,1) 'inner,' законнаѧ (515b,10) 'of the Law'

A — *f:* ѿцевскꙋю (K3b,24) 'paternal,' невымовнꙋю (515a,2) 'inexpressible,' теперешнюю (36b,16) '(of the) present (time)'

G — *non-fem:* дꙋховногѡ (K26b,14) 'spiritual,' щасливого (123a,22) 'happy,' нынешнего (472a,15) and теперешнего (K6a,16) '(of the)

present (time),' ст҃аго (K5a,1) 'holy,' вышнѧго (441b,12–13) 'highest'
f: вѣчнои (53a,26) 'eternal,' доброи (50b,10) 'good,' Б҃жеи (39a,6) 'of God'

L *non-fem:* Славенском (IIa,6) 'Slavonic,' б҃жтвеномъ (261b,1) 'divine,' послѣднемъ (K8b,14) 'last'
f: звыклой (IIIa,12) 'common,' дѹховной (K7a,4) 'spiritual'

D *non-fem:* Киевскомѹ (K2a,3) 'Kyivan,' правдивомѹ (123a,25) 'just,' вышнемѹ (73a,22) 'high(est)'
f: превѣчной (K6b,15) 'eternal,' хрїстианской (257a,23) 'Christian'

I *non-fem:* готовымъ (K22b,21) 'prepared,' великимъ (181a,1) 'great'
f: похвалною (K15a,12) 'praiseworthy,' ѿчею (K10a,19) 'of the Father'

4.2.0.1 The N/A masculine and the I non-feminine desinences spelled -ый and -ым have the variant spellings -їй/-ний and -им (respectively) after velar and hushing consonants; cf. вѣчный (K13b,2) 'eternal,' короткїй (K9a,10) 'short,' божїй (K11a,17) 'of God,' and готовымъ (K22b,21) 'prepared,' великимъ (181a,1) 'great.' In other environments the same spellings indicate palatalization in the preceding consonant (as in остатний/-їй above).

4.2.0.2 The nominative-accusative neuter -*oje*, nominative feminine -*aja*, and accusative feminine -*uju* were contracted in CSU to -*e*, -*a*, and -*u*, respectively, but the long forms are retained in CSBR. The appearance, by the mid-sixteenth century, of these "new" short forms in U-R probably supported the use of the short forms noted above, especially forms such as the attributive accusative feminines in -*u*. The latter, which I characterized as "marked" above, may then have been "doubly marked": some as Slavonicisms, others as newer features of the spoken language. It is an accident that the old and the new should be phonetically identical, and care should be taken before all such forms are identified as belonging to the Slavonic component of a given writer's language.

4.2.0.3 The Slavonic non-feminine genitive desinence -ago is found only 5 times, in references to the Bible or other similarly marked contexts, as in the prayer which opens Smotryc'kyj's sermon: ѻади имєнє твоєгѡ ст҃агѡ (K5a,1) 'for the sake of your holy name' (note the Slavonic genitive form имєнє as well), лѹкаваго (474a,5) 'the devil [evil one],' and вышнѧго Бг҃а Ѿца (441b,12–13) 'of the highest God the Father.' The Slavonic feminine nominative desinence -aa is found once in MS, in a present active participle: всємогѹщаа (266b,20) 'omnipotent.'

4.2.0.4 In the genitive singular feminine the formant *-oi* is completely regular in MS, and it appears to correspond to CSU *-oji* (phonetic [oji]) < CES *-oě (cf. Bevzenko et al. 1978, 201); *-oě is not attested. Given the frequent use of *-ě* for [i] in some roots as well as in substantival declension, the regular use in this morpheme of the grapheme y for what is probably phonetic [i] is exceptional and worthy of note; the phonetic value of this grapheme must therefore be morpheme-sensitive. The final vowel -i is accompanied by the grave accent (-ѝ), reflecting [-i] (or possibly even [-ji]), and opposing it to the D-L *-j* (-й); in these forms stress is indicated by the presence of an acute accent elsewhere in the word. As noted in 2.0.2 and 2.0.4, a grave accent mark over a final vowel can indicate stress in all forms *except* the Gsgf adjectival desinence. Additional examples of this form: ми́лоѝ (50b,30) 'dear,' лѣ́воѝ (54b,9) 'left,' правоѝ (62b,11) 'right, correct,' ти́хоѝ (55b,3) 'quiet,' ѻ̂ста́тнеѝ (48a,7) 'final,' and so forth.

The spelling -oe (also < *-oě) in IV reflects the influence of North U-R or B-R orthographic practice (Gröschel 1972, 149); one example of this orthographic feature has been identified in MS' texts among adjectives: вмѣсто оустави́чное ѻоспѹсты (332a,7) 'instead of continual dissolute living.'

4.2.0.5 All other oblique case forms correspond to those of CSU, while most also correspond to those of CSBR. Thus, the CSU feminine dative-locative is *-ij* < *-oj*, whereas MS reflects etymological *-oj*. The standard locative non-feminine in CSU is the old dative desinence

-*omu*, but -*im* < *-om is still found in dialects and is the form used by MS (Bevzenko et al. 1978, 199); in CSBR this desinence is -*ym*, the same as that of the instrumental case.

4.2.0.6 The adjective божїй 'of the Lord' is found with hard as well as with soft stem desinences, most of which are the same as the CSU and CSBR long form desinences; the attested forms are: божїй (Nm), божєє (Nn), божꙋю (Af), божого (Gm), божєи (Gf), божой (Lf), божимъ (In), and божєю (If). Slavonic forms are occasionally used: Божїѧ (K10a,15–16; John 3:5) Gn, Б҃жїєю (K2a,2; K2a,6) If; the latter, as well as the Nsg божїй, are the forms given in GSPS.

4.2.1 *Remarks*. The hard-stem adjectival declension in MS is in overall agreement with that of IV, but it reflects less variation than the latter. In IV several additional forms are found: in the masculine, L -*um* (< *-om), -*em, -ěm*; in the neuter, D -*om*; in the feminine, G -*yja, -oj, -oe*, and L -*ej, -ěj* (146). Of these, -*yja* is obviously of Slavonic origin (< *-yję); Gröschel interprets -*em*, -*ej*, and -*ěj* as being Slavonicisms, but considers dative -*om* to be nothing more than an error (1972, 148).[2] In PB, the forms of the masculine and neuter correspond exactly to MS (68–71); in the feminine PB agrees with IV with respect to the dative desinences (D -*oj* and -*ěj*) but is identical to MS in the remaining cases (71–73).

Soft/mixed stem adjectives are few in number in the language of all three Ruthenians. In IV one case form not found in MS is attested: Lf -*ej/-oj*. The following variants of the desinences attested in MS are used by IV: G non-fem -*jago* (e.g., also in вышнѧго), -*ogo, -ago,* L non-fem -*om*; Gf -*ee/-ej/-oj*. The desinence -*ej* could be explained as a contraction of -*eji* (as -*oj* would be from -*oji* < *-oě), although Gröschel believes Polish influence is partly responsible for this spelling (1972, 149, 157). Didiakin-Leeming cites the following forms as occurring in PB: Nm -*ij*, Nn -*ee*, G non-fem -*ego*, Gf -*ej*, Af -*juju*, and Lf -*juj*. The

2 In view of the adoption of the old dative desinence -omu to express locative meaning, it might be possible to interpret this simply as an example of the reverse phenomenon (i.e., the use of the old locative desinence for the dative): this might serve as an indication that the system was vacillating during the period in question.

last desinence reflects the Ukrainian development *-'oj* > *-'uj* (1969, 68–73).

One remark with regard to spelling innovation versus etymological spelling is called for here. It would appear that the Gsgf grapheme -ои represents phonetic [o(j)i], clearly reflecting the development of *ě>[i] in the sequence *-oě. On the other hand, DLsgf -ой represents the traditional spelling of this morpheme, although the vowel *o was certainly raised by the time of Smotryc'kyj; it was probably not yet raised all the way to [i] (cf. CSU), however, whereas *ě had doubtless already evolved into this high front vowel.

4.3.0 *Plural*

N	-yi, -ii (-yja, -aja)	бл҃гочестивыи (K5a,12) 'pious,' грѣшныи (37b,4) 'sinful,' справедливыи 37b,4) 'just,' ст҃ыи (36b,8) 'holy, saints,' ближнїи (57a,3) 'neighbors'
A	-yi, -ii -yx, -ix	мертвыи (K11a,19–20) 'dead,' недостатниⷯ (52b,7) 'deprived,' добрыхъ, злыхъ (37b,5–6) 'good, evil'
G	-yx, -ix	безꙋмныⷯ (K6a,11) 'crazy,' лю҃скиⷯ (39b,11) 'of people,' вѣчныⷯ (89a,8) 'eternal,' ближниⷯ (53b,8)
L	-yx, -ix	Апл҃киⷯ (K13a,18) 'Apostolic,' бѣлыⷯ (181b,9) 'white,' бж҃ихъ (K21a,5) 'divine'
D	-ym, -im	лживымъ (K13b,15) 'lying, mendacious,' справедливымъ (36a,14), бѣсовскимъ (262b,14) 'diabolical,' бж҃имъ (K3a,4), нищымъ (K22b,5–6) 'poor'
I	-ymi, -imi	добрыми (K27b,3; 122b,19) 'good,' бж҃ими (K16b,13), блⷤ҇ними (69a,22)

4.3.0.1 In hard-stem forms desinences beginning with -i- rather than -y- occur after velar consonants: G высокихъ (K26b,8) 'high'; spellings such as N Православнїи (K11b,1) 'Orthodox' reflect Slavonic orthographic practice, as exemplified in GSPS: С҃тіи 'Saints, holy' (Npl).

4.3.0.2 One accusative masculine form occurs with the Slavonic desinence -*yja* (< *-yję) in a biblical passage: гнѣвъ Бж҃їй на сн҃ы непокоривыѧ (K12a,22–23; Col 3:6) 'the wrath of God onto unruly sons.' Three other forms have the Slavonic desinence -*aja*, twice in the nominative neuter: дѣѧнїѧ плотскаа (K12a,15) 'carnal acts,' и подобнаѧ симъ (K11b,12) 'and the like'; and once in the accusative neuter: во многаѧ лѣта (K4a,5) 'for many years.' Of these neuter adjectival forms, the first two occur in quotations from the Bible (Rom 8:12–13 and Gal 5:19–21, respectively), while the last is used in a prayer closing the preface to MS' sermon.

4.3.0.3 All plural desinences are the same as those found in CSU and CSBR, with the exception of the nominative: in CSU the originally long desinence underwent contraction > -*i* (cf. the singular above), while the desinence in CSBR is -ыя.

4.3.1 *Remarks*. The declension of hard stem adjectives is identical in MS and PB: all of the desinences in the table above occur in PB (73–75). The same is true of IV for all except the nominative-accusative cases, in which several variants occur that are not attested in MS: *-ye/-ie, -ia, -aa, -ija*. The first of these variants are the CES accusative plural desinences, often found in seventeenth century Ruthenian for the nominative as well as the accusative, while the rest are Slavonic (151). Bevzenko et al. view the rise of *-yi/-ii* as the result of a fusion or contamination of the nominative desinence -*ü* and accusative *-ye* (1978, 182).

In the language of IV Gröschel finds only 20 soft stem long forms, with the following desinences: G -*ix*, D -*im*, Am -*iix*, An -*jaa*, I -*imi/ -ymi,* and L -*ix* (1972, 158). The two accusative desinences cited represent Slavonic elements. The language of IV also reflects the use of the genitive desinence(s) *-yx/-ix* in the accusative of adjectives modifying animate nouns (ibid.). The attested desinences of PB do not include any exceptional forms: N -*ii,* G -*ix,* D -*ym* (большымъ: compare ницымъ in MS), and I -*imi* (73–75).

4.4.0 *The Formation of the Comparative and Superlative Degrees*

The comparatives and superlatives are the morphologically most complex of the adjectival forms; these Ruthenian categories are also characterized by actively competing formants, requiring careful analysis.

4.4.1 *The Comparative*

The comparative degree of the adjective is formed by means of the suffixes *-š-* and *-ějš-*, in MS as well as in IV (159) and PB (75); both suffixes are inherited from Old Russian and are still in use in the modern East Slavic languages. In CSU the comparative suffix *-iš-* is a contraction of the older form *-ějš-* (where -ěj- > -ij- > -i-), while CSBR still exhibits the uncontracted suffix *-ejš-* (Hurski 1962, 135; Bevzenko et al. 1978, 213). Comparatives with these two formants can be used attributively as well as predicatively and are declined as soft stem adjectives; 4.4.1.1–4.4.1.2 below are devoted to those forms with attributive function.

4.4.1.1 Comparatives with the formant *-š-* are the most frequently found forms in MS, occurring 432 times: 1 time in *Grammatiki*, 15 times in *Kazan'e*, and 416 times in JU: e.g., **слабш-** (60b,14) 'weaker,' **твердш-** (K17a,16) 'harder,' **ближш-** (204a,25) 'closer,' **знаменитш-** (IVa,11) 'better known,' **шкодливш-** (K11a,4) 'more harmful,' **старш-** (35b,26) 'older,' etc. These may also occur with short adjectival endings: **болша** (210b,15) 'greater' and **знаменитша** (337a,13–14) 'well-known.' The comparative forms of **добрый** 'good,' **злый** 'bad,' **великий** 'large,' and **малый** 'small' are, respectively,

> **лѣпш-** , 13 times, found today in southwest U, CSBR, and Polish; (K26a,17)
>
> **горш-** 20 times, today in CSU, CSBR, and Polish; (K11a,3)

and

плохш- 2 times, retained in Belarusian dialects; (179b,9)[3]
болш- 112 times, today in CSU, CSBR, and CSR; (K23b,11)
менш- 21 times, today in CSU, CSBR, and CSR; (47a,11)

The phonetic shape of this formant is not affected by single root-final consonants, so various complex consonant clusters may be found in these forms: горячш- (88a,12) 'more burning, hotter,' легш- (150a,17) 'easier,' богатш- (110a,25) 'richer,' and so forth. Velar stops may assimilate to the following hushing *-š-*: мнωжш- (57b,24) 'greater, more' < *mnog-, срѡ̃ш- (53b,25) 'stricter' < *srog-, оубожш- (73b,13) 'poorer' < *ubog-, etc. Dental spirants may or may not assimilate: вышш- (109a,5) 'higher' < *vys-, ближш- (204a,25) 'closer' < *bliz-, but ни̑ш- (179b,9) 'lower,' next to нижш- (K17a,3). In CSU this formant *-š-* sometimes dissimilates from a preceding consonant, e.g., *нижшии > нижчии. On the formation of comparatives with root-final consonant clusters see 4.4.1.2 (below). Isolated comparatives with the formant *-š-* may function as superlatives; these are examined in 4.4.2 below.

4.4.1.2 The formant *-ějš-* occurs in comparative forms a total of 182 times, some of which may also function as superlatives, much as they do in Russian today (see 3.4.2 below): 1 time in *Grammatiki*, 8 times in *Kazan'e*, 173 times in JU; as examples of the comparatives we may cite: пожитечнѣйш- (K24a,9) 'more useful,' силнѣйш- (182b,26–27) 'stronger,' рыхлѣйш- (K17a,13) 'faster, quicker,' ꙗснѣйш- (514b,12) 'clearer,' etc. Note the following forms with short adjectival endings: єсли не бꙋдетъ обфитнѣйша справедливость ваша нѣжъ . . . (32b,12–13) 'if your righteousness is not more abundant than . . . '; вѣрнѣйша и певнѣйша въскресенїа Хв҃а таемница . . . (138a,22–23) 'the secret is truer and more certain than the resurrection of Christ.'

The choice of formants *-š-* versus *-ějš-* in CES was not dictated by the phonetic shape of the root; by the time of the writing of MS' texts,

---

[3]This form is still attested, albeit phonetically altered, in some CSBR dialects: cf. плошей (where x > 0) cited in *Turaŭski Sloŭnik* (1985, 4:62). (Minsk, 1985).

however, *-š-* had become the favored formant. The variant *-ějš-* appears as often as it does in MS because it is required by the phonetic shape of the adjectival root: in the presence of a final consonant cluster, the vocalic desinence *-ějš-* was suffixed instead of the consonantal *-š-*. This is especially true and apparent for derived adjectives formed with the suffix *-ьn- appended to a preceding root-final consonant; in fact, of the 64 different stems found with the formant *-ějš-* in MS, fully 48 have this suffix (темн- 'dark,' вѣрн- 'true,' ѧсн- 'clear,' etc.). Most of the remaining adjectives end with the consonant clusters *tl, tv, dl, lž, st, pl:* for example, in свѣтлѣйш- (514b,12) 'brighter,' теплѣ̀ш- (203a,21–22) 'warmer.' Such strict phonetic conditioning is not present in CSBR, in which *-ejš-* is the most common comparative formant (*-š-* is unproductive, as in Russian); *-š-* is still widely used in CSU, frequently undergoing assimilation or dissimilation from final root consonants (cf. нижчий above). The phonetic conditioning that requires the suffix *-ějš-* in MS is characteristic of Polish as well, e.g., *czarny-czarniejszy, rosły-rosłejszy;* this can either be described as an areal feature encompassing southwest East Slavic and Polish (more research would be needed to confirm this, especially in modern dialects) or as a possible instance of Polish influence.

A comparison of the distribution of *-š-* versus *-ějš-* among the three texts shows: *Grammatiki* is not informative, as it is too short (1:1); in *Kazan'e* we find the ratio 15:8 (or 65.2:34.8%); in JU it is 416:173 (or 70.6:29.4%). The two formants are numerically distributed evenly, even in two texts that are stylistically quite different. The numerical preponderance of the suffix *-š-* in the formation of comparatives is deceptive, because the proportion of *-š-* forms to *-ějš-* forms (432:182, or approximately 70.4:29.6%) does not correspond to the proportion of the number of roots found with the two suffixes. The roots occurring with *-š-* are among the most common in the language (болш- 'larger,' for example, is found 112 times in JU alone), while the use of the suffix *-ějš-* is required by many roots by virtue of their phonological structure; consequently, we find that *-š-* is used with only 43 different roots, while *-ějš-* occurs with 65 different roots.

4.4.2.0 *The Superlative*

It is possible for the comparative adjective itself to express the superlative degree. This phenomenon is rare, however, and is for all intents and purposes limited to very specific lexemes commonly used to express such basic distinctions as "large," "small," "old," "young." These forms contain the comparative formant *-š-*, which is now unproductive in CSU, CSBR, and CSR; examples of this type are noted in all three modern languages, as in CSU старший 'older' (attributive and predicative, next to predicative старіший). In many instances these forms have been lexicalized as adjectives with very specialized functions: CSBR старшы выкладчык, малодшы лейтэнант 'senior instructor, second lieutenant'; CSU молодший, старший лейтенант 'second, first lieutenant.' This phenomenon is only occasionally noted in MS' texts, and may be illustrated by such examples as то єстъ першеє и болшеє приказа̑нє (282b,8) 'that is the first and greatest commandment' and старшїй сынъ (35b,26) 'the eldest son.'

The suffix *-ějš-* can likewise occasionally give an adjective the expressive force of the superlative. The interpretation of a particular form as "superlative" as opposed to "comparative" can be a function of purely formal features (i.e. phonetic shape of the root) as well as of the semantic characteristics of the particular adjective and, naturally, context. Particularly important in this regard is the presence or absence of an adverb expressing "than": when it is present, the form is clearly comparative, while its absence signals a possible superlative usage. Thus: чекаетъ и оная надъ Херувимωвъ честнѣйшая и на̑ Серафимωвъ славнѣйшая ... оутѣха (K23b,11–13) 'that joy/serenity awaits [that is] more honored than the Cherubim and more glorious than the Seraphim'; the same formulation is found in JU: честнѣйшую на̑ Херувими, и славнѣйшую над Серафимы (411b,22–23). In the following, two "comparatives" stand without any object of comparison, and can in this instance be interpreted as superlatives:

> Срожшимъ абовѣмъ теперъ ωкрутный душъ лю̑скихъ Пожирца быти захочетъ: хитрѣйшымъ лукавый Пекелникъ напротивъ намъ в тисячо прехирныхъ своихъ Мустерїахъ ставитися замыслитъ (K27b,4–7).

There is also a formal aspect to this question: those roots attested in MS in which there is *no* stem-final consonant cluster but which occur with the suffix *-ějš-* (in other words, those that would not theoretically *require* the formant *-ějš-* in the comparative) may be most open to interpretation as superlatives. These forms are also subject to lexicaliztion as new positive adjectives with limited function: за нашєго старѣйшого началника цєрковного Патрїархꙋ Константїнопол͏єкого (501b,26–27) 'and for our ecclesiastical Superior [lit. senior] the Patriarch of Constantinople'; compare the similar semantic expression of *staršij* 'senior' in the modern East Slavic languages discussed above.

The use of historically comparative forms (e.g., *starš-* or *starějš-*) with superlative meaning is an entirely secondary development, however: the most common markers of the superlative are prefixes, which are *not* used in the formation of comparatives. There are three prefixes in use in the Ruthenian period, two of which are purely Ruthenian (на- and най-), while the third is Slavonic (прє-). The first two differ from the third in the way they are used to form superlatives: the Ruthenian prefixes may not occur with adjectives in the positive degree, requiring the presence of one of the two comparative markers, *-š-* or *-ějš-*; the Slavonic marker прє- can only be affixed to adjectives in the positive degree.

4.4.2.1 The superlative formation *na-* + *comparative* adjective occurs 97 times, e.g., in: набыстрѣйш- (K22a,16) 'fastest,' напростореш- (K22a,15) 'most spacious,' навышш- (29a,25) 'highest,' наболш- (K27b,17) 'greatest,' нагѡ҃ш- (76b,8–9) 'worst,' напобожнѣйш- (K19b,10) 'most pious,' etc. The distribution of *na-* among the three texts is as follows: *Grammatiki* 0 times, *Kazan'e* 12 times, JU 85 times; *na-* is frequently stressed in such forms.

If the number of *na-*superlatives formed with *-š-* is compared to those with *-ějš-*, we find that the proportion is very similar to that of comparatives: *-š-* to *-ějš-* is 70.4:29.6%, while *na-* + *-š-* to *na-* + *-ějš-* is almost exactly the same, at 68:29 or 70.1:29.9%. These statistics simply confirm the numerical distribution of the two comparative formants in Smotryc'kyj's language. Morphological doublets can also occur, as they do among comparatives: насвѧтш- (297b,21) and наст҃ѣйш- (159a,27) 'holiest.' In this particular instance there is a contextual differentiation of level, with the latter variant (used in a statement addressed to Jesus Christ) representing the higher level. Note that the root does not end in a consonant cluster, so that the formant *-ějš-* is not required on formal grounds; the marked form also occurs with an abbreviated root, a device seen frequently and mentioned in 2.0.4. Cf. also the following rare lexical doublet: нагѡ̑ш- (76b,8–9) and наплоχш- (329a,24) 'worst.' No forms with the marker на- are identified in IV (165), while they appear to be quite common in PB (75–76). IV seems to have avoided *na-* in favor of another prefix with greater lexical prestige, viz. прє- (see 4.4.2.3 below); it is probably not a question of linguistic geography, as на- was common throughout U-R as well as B-R and therefore certainly known to IV.

4.4.2.2 All 6 *naj-* + *comparative* forms in MS are found in JU. Only 2 such forms occur in IV (ibid.), while *naj-* is as common as *na-* in PB (ibid.). MS' texts provide the following: найболш- (213a,18) 'biggest,' найвышш- (308b,12) 'highest,' найзнаменитш- (467a,17) 'most significant, important,' найсрожш- (252b,14) 'cruelest, strictest,' найѡбфитш- (193b,17) 'most abundant,' and найменш- (245b,22) 'least, smallest.'

There is disagreement among scholars as to the identity of the prefixes *na-* and *naj-*. The prefix *naj-* is used in CSU, CSBR, and CSP, and is considered to be a general Slavic superlative marker (cf. also Czech nej-, Slovak *naj-*); it is described in ESSJ/P as a reinforced form of the original marker *na-* (II:433). With regard to *na-*, Łesiów treats *na-* forms in Ruthenian as Polonisms (347) because *na-* is well attested in Old Polish; Gröschel agrees with this assessment, while Leeming believes the use of both *na-* and *naj-* may be ascribed to Polish influence (1968, 288). Bevzenko et al. say that the use of *naj-/na-* is not the result of Polish influence (1978, 214–15), while Bulyka et al. only say that the prefix *naj-* was often found in 'Belarusian' without *-j-* (1979, 174). If we assume a Common Slavic origin for *naj-* (note its use in OCS), then it would appear that *naj-* and *na-* must have coexisted for a long period of time. The frequent use of *na-* in Old Polish and in (U- and B-) Ruthenian simply shows, then, that this original superlative marker was retained with some success by the contiguous Polish and Ruthenian languages: its continued use represents an areal feature encompassing parts of West Slavic and Ruthenian. Only later did this marker give way completely to the compound *naj-* in all of the languages involved; *na-* is not found in CSU, CSBR, or CSP.

4.4.2.3 The Slavonic superlative formation *pre- + positive adjective* occurs 110 times, e.g., прєст҃- (K5a,2) 'most holy, holiest,' прєчист- (159b,2) 'most pure, purest,' etc. Two attribute forms made up of *pre-* + comparative are found, on the pattern of *na-* + comparative: прєчєстнѣйшємꙋ (K2a,1) 'most honorable,' and прєвєлєбнѣйшємꙋ (K2a,1) 'most reverend' (both in *Kazan'e*). Of the 110 attestations, 75 occur in JU, 35 in *Kazan'e*; none are used in *Grammatiki*.

Gröschel contends that this form of the superlative cannot be classified as peculiarly "Slavonic," suggesting instead that it be interpreted as an element of educated speech (1972, 166). MS offers support for this assertion, because in *Kazan'e,* a document consciously written in a high ("educated") style, прє- is used with a lexeme of *Polish* origin, in addition to the expected Slavonic lexemes: прєвєлєбнѣйшємꙋ г҃днꙋ (K2a,1) 'most worthy Lord,' < Pol. wielebny, occurring in the opening line of the text; cf. *pre + zacny* cited by Gröschel (ibid.). 13 forms with this prefix are attested in IV; this figure appears to be high when compared with the number of forms with *na-* (2) and *naj-* (0), but once again it makes sense in the context of Vyšensʹkyj's written system, which is generally characterized by an educated/Slavonic tenor. Only one such superlative is cited for PB by Didiakin-Leeming, who identifies it as a Slavonicism (ibid.).

4.4.2.4 *An Overview of Superlative Formation*

The most noticeble differences among MS's texts, as we have seen, do not concern the relative distribution of the comparativizing suffixes *-š-* and *-ějš-*, but of the prefixes used in the formation of the superlative. A short overview of their distribution (and in comparison with PB and IV) will allow for a better understanding of their relative standing in his language:

	na-			***naj-***			***pre-***	
Gram	*Kaz*	*JU*	*Gram*	*Kaz*	*JU*	*Gram*	*Kaz*	*JU*
0	12	85	0	0	6	0	35	75
Totals:		**97**			**6**			**110**
(IV:		**0**			**2**			**13**)
(PB:		**7**			**25**			**1**)

pre-: This prefix is clearly meant to reflect an "educated/ sophisticated" stylistic level, whether or not one chooses to label it as "Slavonic." It predominates in IV, in keeping with the general character of his writing style, whereas is almost non-existent in PB. Its distribution in MS is misleading: although a large proportion of these superlatives occur in JU (68.2%), it is significant that so high a proportion (in relative terms: 31.8%) should occur in a text as short as *Kazan'e*, while so few forms (again in relative terms) are used in one as long as JU. The conclusion to be drawn from this is that the character conveyed by the former text is overall one of high style, while *pre-* superlatives occur in JU only where they are appropriate.

naj-: As the least common prefix in MS (2.8%), *naj-* might be characterized as stylistically representing the "lowest" level; its complete absence from *Kazan'e* would support this assumption. The fact that it is the most commonly found superlative prefix in PB also lends support to such an evaluation, as Berynda's material can be described as stylistically the most neutral of the writings of all three authors. This method of forming superlatives is now the norm in CSU and CSBR: we can assume, then, that use of *naj-* was increasing during this Ruthenian period, and that those authors writing in a higher style tended to prefer *pre-* and *na-*: note that it is also the least common prefix in the texts of IV.

na-: The distribution of this prefix is not very difficult to interpret, as *pre-* is used to mark a higher style of language: where a neutral superlative is needed, *na-* is the prefix of choice for MS. 87.6% of MS' forms occur in JU, but the fact that *na-* is not rare in *Kazan'e* indicates that it does not reflect the least sophisticated stylistic level; more significantly, of all superlatives in JU (166), a stylistically more neutral text, forms with *na-* make up the majority (albeit by a slim margin: 51.2%).

4.4.3.0 *Methods of Comparison and Intensification*

4.4.3.1 Comparative constructions in the East and West Slavic languages commonly consist of the elements compared and a conjunction (the latter can by origin be a preposition, adverb, or pronoun); conjunctionless constructions are also found, in which case the element to which something is compared occurs in the genitive case. The following are the forms attested in Smotryc'kyj's texts, together with those used in the modern languages:

	niž	*ot*	*nad*	*jak*	*čim*	*za*	*Genitive*
Smotryc'kyj	**ниж**	**от**	**над**	——	——	——	Gen
CSBR	ніж	——	——	як	чым	за	——
CSU	ніж	від	над	як	——	за	——
Polish	*niż*	*od*	——	——	——	——	——
Slovak	*než*	*od*	*(nad)*	*ako*	——	——	——
Russian	——	——	——	——	чем	——	Gen

Of these, *niž, jak*, and *čim* govern the nominative of the object of comparison (they may also occur with prepositional phrases); *nad* and *za* occur with the accusative case, and *ot* governs the genitive. The most simplified system is that which is found in modern Russian (only two methods of comparison), while the modern CSU system appears to be the most complex (with five methods). Smotryc'kyj's language represents the middle ground, with four ways to compare elements. The conjunctionless comparative construction "X is ADJ-er than Y" is made up of the comparative form of the adjective + the genitive of Y, the object to which X is compared: **вышше всѣхъ нбсъ** (414a,3) 'which is higher than all the heavens.' This construction is current only in CSR and represents an archaic/Slavonic feature in MS' texts (and note the same construction in OCS). The use of the prepositions *nad* 'over, above' (with the accusative case) and *ot* (with the genitive case) as conjunctions 'than' is common in comparative constructions. Some textual evidence suggests that *nad* is a marked element in this function, as in: Хс҃ болшїй єстъ на҄ Іѡанна (502b,8) 'Christ is greater than John.' In the first part of the following example, however, we find *nad* juxtaposed to *ot* in a complex series of comparisons that do *not* seem to indicate that *nad* is in any way marked:

> И та҄к знаменитшими и зацнѣйшими сѹтъ на҄ посполитыи ꙗрмарки и торги, и на҄ вшелѧкѹю сєгосвѣтнюю кѹплю, ꙗк҄ зацнѣйшаѧ єстъ дѹша ѿ тѣла, и ꙗкъ знамени҃шеє єстъ нб҃о ѿ землн, и ꙗкъ роскошнѣйшїй є҆ст҄ животъ пришлый, вѣчный, завжды трвающїй, ѿ сєгосвѣтнего житїа марного, дочасного, и врыхлѣ оминаючого (494a,2–9).

The widespread use of *niž* in comparative constructions in West and East Slavic (with the notable exception of Russian) suggests that it be treated as an areal phenomenon. Because the occurrence of *ot* (*од, від*) in such constructions is limited in the East Slavic area to CSU, the rise of this feature in CSU can be ascribed to Polish influence; the currency of this construction in CSU requires, however, that its presence in Smotryc'kyj's texts be described as a U-R feature rather than as a Polonism. The use of *nad* is more limited still, found today only in CSU and marginally in Slovak: this feature ought to be interpreted as a geographically limited areal phenomenon, encompassing only CSU and Slovak: at one time use of *nad* was likely generalized for both comparative and superlative constructions in Slovak, but in the face of competing conjunctions it lost ground in the comparative. Didiakin-Leeming identifies an analytic superlative construction using *nad* in PB: на(д) всеҳ силнейший (1969, 75–76); *ot, nad* and *niž* are discussed at greater length in 8.1 and 8.2.

4.4.3.2 The pronoun *što* 'what' may be used as an intensifier with the comparative degree, expressing the sense "even more X": што горшого (151a,10–11) '[what is] even worse.' The instrumental of the pronoun *to* is also used as an intensifying element, in this instance to express "all the more X": **тым знаменитша была сила** (337a,13–14) 'all the more significant was (the) strength'; this construction is still current in CSU and CSBR. *Тym* may also occur with adverbs, specifically with adverbialized comparative forms (cf. 6.5).

The pronoun *ščo/što* may also be prefixed to superlative forms as intensifying elements, in order to express "as X as possible," for instance in: **щонапростѣшїй** (369a,28) 'as simple as possible,' **што назацнѣйшїи** (467a,25–26) 'as honorable as possible.'[4] This construction was known in U-R as early as the fifteenth century, as in the form **штонайлепшій** (SSUM: 1492); it also occurs in CSU, CSBR, and Polish (with що-, што-, and co-, respectively; also U як-), limited to use with adverbialized superlatives. Such adverbial forms are attested in MS as well, but only the adverb як- 'how, as' (not *ščo/što*) is prefixed to superlatives. In the modern languages these adverbialized superlatives are formed with *naj-* superlatives, whereas in MS they occur only with *na-* superlatives (see 6.6).

---

4 The spellings **што** and **що** may or may not be purposely differentiated in these two examples. In the first example cited, the CSU form *що* is directly linked (graphically) to the superlative adjective, while *што* is not in the second one: this may indicate that the lexeme with *što* is perceived to be "not as native" as the lexeme with *ščo* (note that the stem *zacn-* is purely West Slavic).

CHAPTER FIVE

The Pronoun

5.0 There is very little variation in the category of pronoun beyond the purely orthographic. The forms of variation that are present and require comment are lexical (choice of lexeme) and phonetic in nature. These phenomena primarily are represented in such subcategories as indefinite, qualitative, relative, and distributive pronouns. Other subcategories (personal, reflexive, possessive pronouns) are extremely homogeneous, not only across the East Slavic languages but across all three branches of the Slavic family. The main form of differentiation in such homogeneous groups is the establishment of opposing linguistic/stylistic levels, in this case "Ruthenian" versus "Slavonic." Because of the great number of forms attested, the format established for the study of the substantives will not be followed here, that is, examples of each case and each number are not supplied outside of the tables; specific examples will be cited only when the precise identity of a form is in doubt or when particular features are worthy of special mention.

5.1 *The Personal and Reflexive Pronouns*

5.1.1 The first, second, and reflexive pronominal forms follow the same declensional pattern:

Case	*2sg*	*2sg*	*Reflexive*
N	ꙗ	ты	———
	азъ		
A	мене	тебе	себе
	мѧ	тѧ	сѧ
G	мене	тебе	себе
L	мнѣ	тобѣ	собѣ
D	мнѣ	тобѣ	собѣ
		тебѣ	себѣ
	ми	ти	
I	мною	тобою	собою

Nominative. The Slavonic 1sg form азъ occurs twice in *Kazan'e*, both times in citations from the Bible (K13a,5; Song of Songs 5:2). It occurs in JU when required by the style or level, for example, in a quotation attributed to Jesus Christ. The unmarked Ruthenian form ѧ is the same in all East Slavic languages, as is the 2sg pronoun ты. The reflexive pronoun by definition cannot have a nominative form.

Genitive. These forms are identical to CSU мене, тебе, себе; allowing for the orthographic reflection of Belarusian *jakanne* and *cekanne*, they can also represent Belarusian мяне, цябе, сябе. Almost all examples of these genitives are used in conjunction with prepositions in MS. The normally final stress of these forms is then retracted to the first syllable: тєбє́ but до тє́бє (K8a,8). This phenomenon is characteristic of CSU but not of CSBR.

Accusative. Мєнє, тєбє, сєбє are identical to the genitive forms, as they are in CSU and CSBR. Retraction of stress after prepositions is also seen in this case: на мє́нє (K8b,15). The corresponding enclitics мѧ, тѧ, сѧ are not limited to marked contexts, and thus may not be interpreted strictly as Slavonicisms. These forms are no longer used in CSU, but do still exist in the southwestern dialects (Žylko 1966, 184–85). The reflexive сѧ is used in MS' texts primarily as a suffixal particle attached to verbal forms, as it is in the modern East Slavic languages, but it may also be placed before the verb (сѧ молилъ [27b,3] 'he prayed') or be graphically attached to forms preceding the verb (такъсѧ стало [K6b,21–22] 'thus it happened'). Of particular interest is the use of suffixal *-sja* with nouns derived from verbs which have this suffix: cf. розлꙋченєсѧ (K11a,5) 'separation.' All of these phenomena must be viewed as influenced by Polish, in which the particle *się* is unbound; it is also used with deverbal nouns in that language. Gröschel counts 74 attestations of *sja* placed before the verb, 40 after the verb in IV (1972, 295), while Didiakin-Leeming states that *sja* may occur before or after the main verb (1969, 113). This use of the reflexive enclitic/particle *sja* is one (presumably Polish) morpho-syntactic feature that was clearly the norm in Ruthenian of this period.

Dative. In the 1sg only the Slavonic/Common East Slavic form мнѣ and the enclitic ми are attested in MS. The former is still current in some southwest Ukrainian dialects (e.g., Volhynian, where *мьнě > *mni*), while CSU has мені, apparently a contamination of the old genitive and dative forms; cf. CSBR and Russian мне < *mьně. 2sg тобѣ reflects the native Ruthenian pronoun, which is also the modern literary form: CES *tobě > Ukr тобі, Br табе; cf. also Polish *tobie*. The Slavonic variant тебѣ is only found in marked environments, for instance in a passage addressed to God (512b,24). In the reflexive pronoun both Slavonic себѣ and Ruthenian собѣ are attested (cf. Ukr собі, Br сабе, and Pol *sobie*) while the reflexive enclitic *си is not found. The form себѣ only occurs in biblical citations or otherwise marked contexts. The 1sg enclitic ми occurs more frequently than 2sg ти, reflecting the fact that the former was still widely used in the 16th century, while the latter was losing currency a century before that (Kernycʹkyj 125–26). These enclitics are still current in modern southwest Ukrainian (Žylko 1966, 184–85).

Instrumental. All the instrumental forms attested are identical to those used in CSU. While they can also occur in CSBR, the forms мной, etc., are more common (see Krivicki, et al., 1978, 158).

Locative. The locative forms occurring in MS' texts are the same as those used in the dative, except that the Slavonic variants are not found. The 1sg locative мені in literary and dialect Ukrainian is the same as the dative; here MS' form мнѣ agrees with CSBR мне.

Remarks. With the exception of an occasional unattested form, the three Ruthenian sources are in agreement; in addition to the forms cited above PB also exhibits the dative form мнѣ in the 1sg (IV: 167; PB: 56–58).

5.1.2 All of the 1pl and 2pl personal pronouns are used in MS' texts:

N	мы	вы
A	насъ	васъ
G	насъ	васъ
L	насъ	васъ
D	намъ	вамъ
I	нами	вами

These forms are inherited essentially unchanged from CES, and occur in these forms in the modern East Slavic languages; the same forms are used in the texts of IV (170) and PB; 1pl locative and 2pl locative and instrumental are not documented for the latter (58–59).

5.1.3 The forms of the third person singular personal pronouns attested in MS are the following:

Case	*Masculine*	*Neuter*	*Feminine*
N	онъ	——	она
A	єго	є, єго	єи
	нєго, -нь	нє	ню
G	єго	єго	єи
	нєго	нєго	нєи
L	нєм	нєм	нєй
D	ємꙋ	ємꙋ	єй
	нємꙋ	нємꙋ	
I	нимъ	нимъ	єю
			нєю

Nominative. The traditional CES masculine and feminine nominative forms онъ and она correspond to the prothesized CSU forms він, вона (but not to CSBR ён, яна). Neuter оно does not occur.

Accusative. After prepositions governing the accusative as well as the non-direct cases, the third person pronouns are characterized by initial n-; this is characteristic of CSU but not of CSBR. The marked forms є, -нь, нє, and ню are each attested once: e.g., вонь (< prep. *vo* + *nь*) in the biblical citation da всѧкъ видѧй Сн҃а, и верꙋѧй вонь (K13b,4) 'and everyone seeing the Son and believing in him.' Є is attested as the object of a verb and is therefore found without initial *n*-. The A/G єго and єи are clearly Ruthenian (as opposed to 'Slavonic'); the latter reflects the same phenomenon noted in the long-form adjectival declension, as with the purely U-R phonetic shape [jeji] < *eě, an intermediate stage on the way to CSU її [jiji].

Oblique Cases. In the instrumental non-feminine and the locative of all genders only forms with initial *n*- are attested. The feminine instrumental form єю reflects the traditional spelling of early Slavic texts, Slavonic and CES—this form is accordingly only found in marked environments (such as biblical passages). Instrumental нєю may occur in prepositionless constructions as well as with prepositions (e.g., K22a,10 'by means of it,' in reference to a noun of feminine gender), cf. єю (K10a,4); CSU has only нею while Belarusian has only ею (or ёю), indicating that this form in MS ought to be identified as U-R: note that it is present even in the heavily Slavonic *Kazan'e*.

The orthographic shape of the non-feminine genitive, accusative, dative, and locative forms in MS do not show evidence of the 14th century change of *je-* > *jo-* characteristic of Ukrainian (його, йому, ньому); neither do the feminine dative, instrumental, and locative forms reflect the same change characteristic of Belarusian (ёй). Although the old forms його, него are still found in southwest Ukrainian, specifically in the Podolian and Dniester dialects, MS' orthography in this instance should be interpreted as traditional CES/Slavonic): Cyrillic orthographic practices hindered the reflection of this change until the 17th century, and it is unlikely for Smotryc'kyj to have adopted this innovation at the beginning of that century (Shevelov 1979, 647–48; Kernyc'kyj 1967, 127; Žylko 1966, 184–85). The CSU non-feminine locative form is ньому or нім; the latter corresponds to MS' нємъ (where [*e] > [i] in a closed syllable in CSU). In Belarusian the form is ім, again without initial *n-*.

5.1.3.1 *Remarks*. There are few differences between MS' pronominal forms and those of IV and PB. The latter two agree completely with MS in the non-feminine. In the feminine IV exhibits G-A єє, which apparently reflects the Belarusian-Ruthenian spelling of old *eě (cf. U-R єи), as well as the old accusative g (cf. MS Єю above; Gröschel 1972, 169, 171). The differences between MS and PB are also confined to the feminine: forms not found in MS include Slavonic Єѧ and ю, the same feminine accusative attested in IV. Of particular interest in PB are two feminine forms which exhibit the typically Ukrainian change of [e] > ['u] (intermediate stage of e > [i]) in closed syllables: D юй and L к нюй (58–59).

5.1.4 *Plural*. The 3pl paradigm for the most part reflects the forms found in CSU and CSBR:

N	они (Ukr вони, Br яни)
A	нхъ/нихъ (Ukr їх/них, Br ix)
G	нхъ/нихъ (Ukr їх/них, Br ix)
L	нихъ (Ukr них, Br ix)
D	нмъ/нимъ (Ukr їм, Br ім)
I	ними (Ukr ними, Br імі)

As in the singular paradigm, only the unprefixed forms (without *n*-) occur in CSBR when 3pl pronouns follow prepositions, in contrast to Ukrainian and Russian; in this respect, then, MS' forms may more specifically be labelled U-R. The forms of the plural attested in IV (171) and PB (59) agree with those used in MS' texts.

5.2 *The Demonstrative Pronoun.*

Four demonstrative pronouns are commonly used by Smotryc'kyj: той 'that,' сей 'this,' оный 'that,' овый 'this (in close proximity to the speaker).' With the exception of сей, these are declined as hard-stem long-form adjectives; сей is declined as a soft-stem adjective.

5.2.1 той

Case	*Masculine*	*Neuter*	*Feminine*
N	той	тоє	таѧ
A	тотъ, той, того	тоє	тѹю
G	того	того	тои
L	томъ	томъ	той
D	томѹ	томѹ	той
I	тымъ	тымъ	тою

East Slavic тотъ arose as a result of the reduplication of the CES pronoun тъ; it is still current in CSR. In Ukrainian and Belarusian, however, the form той came about as a combination of *тъ* + the third singular (masculine) pronoun *jь : the change *tъjь > той took place after the loss of the jers. In the nominative only this newer form is attested in Smotryc'kyj's language; in the accusative, however, both той (e.g., K10a,2) and the older form тотъ are found; the latter frequently occurs in the frozen expression на/под(ъ) тот(ъ) час(ъ) (e.g., K17b,11) 'at that time.' Once we find the variant тӑтотъ (383b,15), which is probably best described as a Polonism (compare CSP *tamten* 'that'); this pronoun is attested as early as 1459 in U-R (SSUM).

The neuter form *toe* underwent contraction > те in CSU, the same process that is noted in the adjectival paradigm, while CSBR retains the uncontracted form тое; only the latter form is used in MS. The non-feminine locative томъ reflects one of the possible forms used in CSU, viz. тім (tom > tim after the loss of the jers); the CSU form competing with тім is identical to the dative, with the exception of the place of stress: D тому́, L то́му (cf. Br тым). Instrumental тымъ in MS is present in CSU and CSBR, and may have arisen by analogy with CES *sim* 'this' (cf. CES *těm*; Kernyc'kyj 1967, 139). In the feminine, N тая and A тую may be identified as "pan-Ruthenian," because they occur in U-R and B-R texts (Svjažynski 1988, 145); they are identical to the CSBR forms, while the Ukrainian forms have undergone contraction to та and ту. G тои and I тою, on the other hand, correspond more specifically to CSU тої and тою, which exist alongside the variants тієї, тією (respectively); cf. CSBR G той (тае), I той (тою).

In the plural only four forms are attested in Smotryc'kyj's texts: A тыи, G тыхъ, I тыми, and L тыхъ. All but the accusative form cited are found in CSU and CSBR; N/A тыи is characteristic of sixteenth-century U-R, but it later underwent contraction > Ukr ті (Kernyc'kyj 1967 also cites тые for this period, 140; also note the corresponding Belarusian form тыя, where *-ja* < *-e* reflects *jakanne*).

As with the declension of adjectives, the singular paradigms for той are virtually the same in the language of all three Ruthenians. The differences that may be noted for IV are his use of the feminine genitive forms тоя, тое, and той, all of which agree with the long-form adjectival paradigm in his language (173; note also the adjective, 146). In PB and IV both тот and той are found in the non-feminine, indicating that the two forms were current in U-R at this time. In PB instrumental тѣм reflects CES *těmъ;* in the feminine PB has the Slavonic spelling таа next to тая in the nominative, genitive тое (and тои), but no instrumental form (59–60). Only three plurals are found in PB: N тыи, I тыми, and G тых (61), the same forms (minus one case) as in MS. In contrast, IV exhibits an almost complete paradigm in the plural, lacking only the dative plural neuter and instrumental plural feminine (173); all of the forms occurring in MS and PB are also found in IV.

5.2.2 сєй

Case	*Masc*	*Neut*	*Fem*	*Plur*
N	сєй	сєє	сѧѧ	сии
			сiѧ	
A	сєй	сєє	сюю	
	сєсь		сiю	
	сєго			
G	сєго	сєго	сєи	сихъ
L	сємъ	сємъ	сєй	сихъ
D	сємꙋ	сємꙋ	сєй	симъ
I	——	——	сєю	сими

In the nominative singular masculine the only form attested is сєй, a well-known and widespread form in seventeenth-century Ruthenian. Сей is still marginally present in Ukrainian, although it is considered archaic in the literary language, in which the primary form of this pronoun is цей; it has been lost in CSBR and CSR: cf. Br гэты, Rus этот. In the accusative we find сєй as well, but сєсь is used in the expression по̑ сєсь ча̑ (e.g., K27a,16) 'at this time'; сєсь may therefore be considered an archaism frozen in this expression, just as тотъ appears to be (see above). The etymological development of these two forms is the same: сєй represents the combination of the elements *сь + *jь (cf. toj), while сєсь resulted from the reduplication of *сь. The neuter nominative-accusative is uncontracted сєє; but again cf. CSU це. Two forms each are encountered in the nominative and accusative feminine: uncontracted Ruthenian сѧѧ, сюю, and Slavonic сiѧ, сiю; the latter are used in biblical passages and otherwise marked environments (e.g., K13b,3; John 6:40). Сiю also occurs in IV and is described by Gröschel as a "learned" form ("*gelehrte* Form," 1972, 177); its use in MS supports its identification as "Slavonic." All other attested forms in the singular reflect the expected Ruthenian paradigm. An almost complete plural paradigm is attested in MS' texts; only the accusative case is not represented.

The singular forms of this pronoun attested in IV, but not occurring in MS, are I masc симъ, N-A neut се, сїе; in the plural only N сїи, G-A сихъ, and A neut сїѧ are found in IV, fewer forms than in MS (176). The situation in PB is similar to IV: the same singular forms lacking in MS are attested in PB (I masc симъ and N-A neut сие); in the feminine, however, far fewer forms are found, viz. only N сiѧ and L сей. The plural paradigm of PB is exactly the same as that in MS, including the lack of an accusative form.

It is relatively easy to assign singular forms of this pronoun to one of two linguistic-stylistic levels based on purely formal (that is, phonological, graphemic) criteria: among masculines, сесь is used in a limited way and is therefore marked (versus сей); among feminines, those with the stem *si*- rather than *s'*- are Slavonicisms (сiѧ versus сѧѧ, etc.). In the plural, however, this distinction cannot be made strictly on such formal grounds: forms such as сии belong to both levels: their frequent occcurrence in unmarked as well as in biblical passages (сии in K13b,10; симъ in K11b,12) is evidence of their dual status in the system.

5.2.3 овый

Case	*Masculine*	*Neuter*	*Feminine*
N	овый	овое	оваѧ
	овъ	ово	———
			оваа
A	=N or G	= A	овꙋю
G	ового	ового	овои
L	овомъ	овомъ	овой
D	овомꙋ	овомꙋ	овой
I	овымъ	овымъ	овою

The declension of овый (< *овъ + *jь) follows the paradigm of той given in 5.2.1. This pronoun is rare in sixteenth- and seventeenth-century U-R: Gröschel regards it as either a dialectal feature or as a Polonism in Vyšensʹkyj's language (1972, 178–79). Овый is not cited in

SSUM. Bulyka et al. do not mention овый with regard to B-R, and the fact that it is not cited in the dictionary of Skaryna's language indicates that this pronoun was lost in B-R areas at a rather early date (see 1990, 110–20). As in Vyšens'kyj's case, this pronoun is either a feature of Smotryc'kyj's dialect or a reflection of the Polish pronoun ów with U-R desinences. In MS we note the use of short as well as long forms in the masculine and neuter; in the nominative feminine there is one example of the Slavonic variant spelling оваа. In the plural there are only two morphological forms: N овыи (e.g., K20b,18; cf. тыи above), N овыи (432a,11) and A animate ѡвыхъ (30b,18).

In IV this pronoun occurs only a few times: N sg masc овъ, D sg masc овомꙋ, and D pl овымъ (178). Didiakin-Leeming cites only the N-A neut овоє for PB (1969, 60).

5.2.4 оный

Case	*Masculine*	*Neuter*	*Feminine*	*Plural*
N	оный	оноє	онаѧ	оныи
A	онъ	оноє	онꙋю	——
	оного			
G	оного	оного	онои	оныхъ
L	ономъ	ономъ	——	оныхъ
D	ономꙋ	ономꙋ	——	——
I	онымъ	онымъ	оною	——

The pronoun оный (< *onъ + *jь) is well attested in U-R texts while it is comparatively rare in B-R writings (Kernyc'kyj 137–40, Bulyka et al. 1990, 118, respectively); this pronoun is cited (2 occurrences) in the dictionary of Skaryna's language. Of particular interest here is the masculine short form он(ъ), because, as with тотъ and сесь above, it is only attested in time expressions: **вонже день** (K10a,6; Genesis 2:17), **на онъ часъ** (e.g., K17a,10) 'at that time'; such expressions can be compared with **часꙋ оного** (e.g., 184b,11) 'at that time,' which frequently marks the beginning of a new biblical reading in JU. The use of this form in MS and its rarity in Ruthenian in general allow it to be interpreted as "Slavonic," while the three preceding pronouns can be described as "Ruthenian." In IV two forms occur which are not found in MS: Gsgf **оное** and Dsgf **оной** (the former reflects B-R or North U-R orthography); in the plural only G-A **оныхъ** is found (178). The number of forms attested in PB is smaller still, and all but two forms are identical to those in MS; those that are not are I non-fem **онемъ** and N fem **онаа** (of which the latter reflects Slavonic orthography). As in IV, only G/A **оныхъ** is attested in the plural (61). Neither *ovyj nor *onyj are attested in CSU and CSBR; *ów* is current in CSP.

5.3 *The Possessive Pronoun*

5.3.1 The 1sg, 2sg, and reflexive possessive pronouns **мой**, **твой**, **свой** are declined as soft-stem long adjectives (cf. 4.22); as they decline in the same way, the forms of **мой** only are given here (exeptional forms are supplied when necessary, however):

Case	*Masculine*	*Neuter*	*Feminine*	*Plural*
N	**мой**	**мое**	**моѧ**	**мои**
A	= N or G	**мое**	**мою**	**мои** (2x **моѧ**)
G	**моего**	**моего**	**моеи**	**моихъ**
L	**моемъ**	**моемъ**	**моей**	**моихъ**
D	**моемꙋ**	**моемꙋ**	**моей**	**моимъ** (1x **своима**)
I	**моимъ**	**моимъ**	**моею**	**моими**

Singular. The traditional spellings encountered in Smotryc'kyj's language are the rule in 16th- to 17th-century Ruthenian; again with the exception of the genitive singular feminine, they do not reflect particularly Ukrainian or Belarusian phonological characteristics (as was encountered in the long-form (soft) adjectival declension). Nevertheless, many of them are still identical to the corresponding CSU and CSBR forms. In two forms CSU departs substantially from this earlier norm: in the genitive non-feminine the desinence *-ojeho* was contracted > *-oho* (e.g., мого), and the locative non-feminine is now the same as the dative (viz. MS моємъ, etc., but Ukr моему, etc.). The traditional locative desinences are still found in the southwest Ukrainian dialects, as are the uncontracted forms of the genitive, where the corresponding forms may be мойого, твойого, etc. (Žylko 1966, 185); Gröschel, citing Bevzenko et al., states that мойего, etc., are still found in southwest Ukrainian while мойого, etc., occur in the southeast dialects (1972, 179, 182). Thus MS could reflect either the traditional CES paradigm or southwest U-R. Changes have also taken place in the Belarusian system: the genitive and dative non-feminine forms also exhibit contraction, but here [j] is retained while the following vowel is lost (майго, майму). As in Ukrainian, there is a shift in the Belarusian locative non-feminine, but in CSBR it has the same form as the masculine instrumental: маім. Finally, feminine genitive and instrumental маёй differs from MS and CSU in that the final vowels (*-i* and *-u,* respectively) were lost; instrumental маёю may also occur as a variant form.

The singular forms used by IV are identical to MS in every case but the genitive feminine. The desinences used in this case form are the same as those found in IV's declension of long-form adjectives: твоєє, своєє, своєѧ. As with the adjectives, the spelling -єє reflects B-R orthography, while -єѧ is Slavonic (180). In the non-feminine the forms found in PB are identical to those used in MS' texts; in the feminine the following differences may be noted: N твоа (next to моѧ), and G моєа/моєѧ (62).

Plural. All of the forms of the plural are traditional and represent the norm for Ruthenian texts of this period. With the exception of the nominative, they also correspond to the CSU and CSBR paradigms: Ukr мої, моїх, моїм, моїмі, моїх; Br мае (< моѣ), маіх, маім, маімі, маіх. Note the retention of intervocalic [j] before [i] in Ukrainian, whereas it has been lost in CSBR. Only three forms in MS require special comment: Apln моѧ (K12a,6), Aplf моѧ (< *moję: K12a,6), and Idln своима (K13a,19) are all Slavonic forms occurring in biblical passages.

The forms found in MS and IV are virtually identical; in the latter the Slavonic accusative plural -оѧ is attested as it is in MS. The only differences are orthographic in nature: in the accusative plural feminine the variant своє (< *svoě*) occurs, which Gröschel again explains as a feature of Belarusian (B-R) orthography (1972, 181–82). Few of the plurals are attested in PB, but those that are agree with MS' paradigm (62).

5.3.2 The declensions of the 1pl and 2pl possessive pronouns нашъ and вашъ are identical; we need therefore cite only one of these, viz. нашъ:

Case	*Masculine*	*Neuter*	*Feminine*	*Plural*
N	нашъ	нашє	наша	наши, нашѣ
A	=N or G	нашє	нашȣ	(ваша, m.)
G	нашєго	нашєго	нашєи	нашихъ
L	нашємъ	нашємъ	нашєй	нашихъ
D	нашємȣ	нашємȣ	нашєй	нашимъ
I	нашимъ	нашимъ	нашєю	нашими

The possessive pronouns cited are all expected Ruthenian forms; all of them occur in CSU and CSBR, albeit with modifications such as [e] > [o] in Ukr нашого and *jakanne* in Br нашага. The etymological spellings (нашєго rather than нашого) stand in constrast to the adjectival paradigms, in which the newer spellings -ого are indeed found following hushings (нанижшогѡ [K19b,5] 'lowest') as they are in other types of pronouns (иншомȣ [193b,5] 'other'). The variant spellings in MS of the nominative plural наши and нашѣ reflect different stylistic levels: the former represents the older standard and is used in *Kazan'e*, while the latter exhibits the newer U-R use of jat' for the phoneme [i] and is used in JU. The same phenomenon was noted earlier in the soft-stem substantival declensions. Only one clearly Slavonic form is attested, Aplm ваша < *vašę (K12a,20), used in a biblical citation Оумєртвитє оуды ваша . . . (Col. 3:5); cf. the paradigm of нашъ in GSPS, in which the Aplm is нашѧ.

With the sole exception of U-R нашѣ, all of the forms cited here are found in IV. As is the case with the long-form adjective and other pronominal paradigms, IV exhibits several variants in the genitive feminine, including Slavonic *-eja* and B-R *-ee*. In addition, next to etymological spellings such as нашєго (= MS) IV also reflects the change [e] > [o] in these forms: нашого, нашомȣ, etc. (183). All the forms of the plural are expected; in addition to the forms attested in MS Gröschel also finds two instances of Slavonic forms, viz. наша, ваша . The forms attested in PB are identical to those of MS; MS and PB share the nominative plural form нашѣ which differentiates their paradigm from that of IV. Didiakin-Leeming explains this form as a reflection of the confusion of the soft stem case-endings, viz. the nominative plural feminine and the accusative plural masculine, in Berynda's *Leksykon* (1969, 62–63); while this explanation provides a paradigmatic source of jat', the underlying motivation must still be seen as the widespread use of this grapheme to represent phonetic [i] in soft and mixed declensions.

The genitive forms of the third person singular and plural personal pronouns are used as the corresponding third person possessive pronouns in MS, as they are in all East Slavic languages, and they are invariable in form: non-fem єго, fem єи, pl нхъ (all genders).

5.4 *The Interrogative Pronoun.*

5.4.1 што, що, кто, хто. The Ruthenian forms што 'what' and хто 'who' are widely used in Smotryc'kyj's texts, as they are in IV and PB. These pronominal forms are extremely versatile and occur in many different functions, but their function as interrogatives is primary; all other uses of these forms are examined in subsequent sections.

The use of the nominative CES/Slavonic form кто 'who' in MS is limited to contexts of a biblical nature; significantly, it only occurs in *Kazan'e*. Thus: ктобо разꙋмѣ ꙋмъ гс̃днь (K2b,3) 'for who (has) understood the reason of God,' but juxtaposed to this marked form is the immediately following phrase хто з насъ . . . (K2b,4) 'who of us . . . ,' in reference to the congregation listening to the sermon. The form што (< *čьto) 'what' is the rule in all texts; in JU, however, next to што Smotryc'kyj twice uses the purely Ukrainian form що (e.g., 389b,18), as do IV and PB (it also is used once in a superlative construction: щонапростѣшїи 369a,28). Unlike MS, these authors also use the traditional-etymological spelling что (IV: 186–89; PB: 63–64). Cf. CSU що, CSBR што.

The forms attested in MS are: N-A што/що, G чого, L чомъ, D чомꙋ/чемꙋ, I чимъ (note the occurrence of variant spellings in the dative, the former representing the newer convention, the latter representing traditional orthography). N кто/хто, G кого, L комъ, D комꙋ, I кимъ.

The backing of e to o in the pronoun што (e.g., чого < *čego) is reflected in the language of all three Ruthenians. The dative of што/що may be used as the interrogative 'why' (e.g., in 196b,14), as it is in CSU and CSBR.

5.4.1.1 The negative pronouns corresponding to "what" and "who" are н[i]што, н[i]що, н[i]кто, and н[i]хто. The negative prefix *ni-* in these three forms is spelled according to traditional orthography, while all unmarked Ruthenian forms in MS reflect phonetic [ni-] by means of the spelling нѣ-: e.g., нѣхто. "No-one": the marked CES/Slavonic никто is only found 3 times, in biblical passages cited in *Kazan'e* (никтоже K10b,6; K10b,7; and K20a,11). "Nothing": нѣшто is the rule, Ukrainian нѣщо occurs once. Initial *ni-* ([ni]) is the norm in CSU and CSBR, although the prefixal elements used in these languages ultimately derive from two different sources: Ukr ні- < *ně-, Br ні- < *ni-; in other words, the CSU form (as well as that of MS) represents an innovation, while CSBR has retained the CES prefix unchanged. The Ukrainian reflex of *ni- is still seen in some modern southwest Ukrainian dialects, e.g., in the form ныч 'nothing' (Bojkian, Lemkian: Kernyc'kyj 1967, 135). The contrast of marked versus Ruthenian levels in MS is parallelled in IV, where forms with ни- are interpreted by Gröschel as Slavonic, while those with нѣ- are seen as native (1972, 189). In MS as well as in PB the negative forms with нѣ- are differentiated from indefinites with the same prefix by the place of stress, e.g., MS нѣчо́го (K3a,23) 'nothing,' but нѣ́што (K7b,3) 'something' (in PB: 64; see 5.6.2 on indefinite pronouns in MS).

The declensional paradigms of -хто and -што/-що are the same as those attested in the positive. When prepositions are used with the negative pronouns the prepositions must occur between the negative prefix and the pronoun: L нѣвчомъ (K6b,18) 'in nothing,' A нѣнащо (396b,3) 'not for (any)thing,' A нѣна̂кого (74a,25) 'not over/than anyone,' etc. The preposition на conditions the shift of stress away from one-syllable pronominal forms onto the preposition. This phenomenon is found in CSR and CSP, but is not present in CSU and CSBR (Rus за́ руку 'by the hand,' but Ukr за ру́ку, Br за ру́ку), it ought to be interpreted as a morphophonemic Polonism.

5.4.2 **Который**. The pronominal form который is declined like a hard stem long form adjective. It is attested several times as the interrogative pronoun "which?" in Smotryc'kyj's language, although it is more frequently used as a relative pronoun (see below); this use of который is found in IV as well (190). The following is an example from Smotryc'kyj's texts: тєды запыталн єго, который то єстъ чєловѣкъ што тобѣ рєклъ, возми постѣль свою и ходи (147b,21–22) 'then they asked him, "who is that man who said to you 'take your bed and go'?"' The dual function of this pronoun in MS and IV reflects its status in CSU, in which котрий functions as an interrogative and as a relative pronoun; CSBR каторы occurs as an interrogative but not as a relative (які is used in this function instead). The interrogative function of который still survives in CSR, most significantly in a few common phrases such as который час? 'what time is it?' Skaryna's B-R который is defined as 'тоє, што ꙗкі' 'the same as jaki,' indicating that its dual function was widespread in East Slavic. Only later did the relative function emerge as primary in CSBR, while CSU retains the older dual system. The difference in stylistic levels between *Kazan'e* and JU is again apparent with regard to this form, since it only occurs as an interrogative in the latter; this also indicates that the interrogative use of который may be viewed as an innovation to be avoided in texts that are stylistically conservative. Didiakin-Leeming mentions который only in the context of relative pronouns in PB (1969, 63; see 5.5.2 below).

5.4.3 чїй/чєй. The possessive-interrogative 'whose' is attested 6 times, only in JU: the basic variant in the nominative singular masculine is чїй (5 times, e.g., 67b,14). This form is Ruthenian (cf. чїй in SSUM), although in a different text or marked context it could be interpreted as Slavonic; it is retained in CSU and CSBR as чий/чый, Polish czyj. The variant чєй occurs once (282b,15), exhibiting the reflex of a strong front jer (cf. Ruthenian *-yj* versus *-ej* in the genitive plural of substantives, 3.2.2.1); this is the form current in CSR. Forms with vocalic desinences are stressed on the first vowel of the desinence: Asgn чїѐ (67b,17), Asgf чїю̀ (436b,7), Gsgf чї́ѐн (436b,6), Isgm чї́нмъ (286b,9); stress is not marked in Gsg non-feminine (negative) нѣчїєго (395a,2). Cf. CSU чий, чия, чиє, CSBR чый, чыя, чые. For PB Didiakin-Leeming cites чїй, чїєго (1969, 61), while only one form is cited by Gröschel for IV: Lsgm чїємъ (1972, 190).

5.5 *The Relative Pronoun*

5.5.1 што/що and кто/хто. These pronouns sometimes function as relative pronouns in Smotryc'kyj's texts, and have the same case forms as the corresponding interrogatives. They can occur with or without an antecedent: што сѧ и стало (438a,17) 'which is also what happened'; а Бгу даси тоє што нє єстъ, чого єщє и самъ нємаєшъ (95b,3–4) 'and give to God that which is not, that which you yourself do not yet have'; о чомъ и самъ оучєникωвъ своихъ оувѣдомилъ (51b,3–4) 'about which he himself informed his students'; хто нєрозумѣлъ (515b,18–19) 'he who did not understand'; we note also that the Ukrainian variant що occurs two times in this function (e.g., 449a,23–24). The use of што and кто (and variants thereof) in a relative function is not mentioned by Didiakin-Leeming (1969, 63–64); Gröschel cites 10 instances of the use of these pronouns as relatives in IV, some of which occur in constructions found also in MS, e.g., што сѧ стало (1972, 191).

5.5.2 который. This form is frequently used as a relative pronoun, as it is in IV and PB: знаєтє и вы Православныи . . . , которы͡м онъ былъ оучитєлємъ (K19b,18–20) 'and you Orthodox, for whom he was a teacher, know . . . '; compare also той который (e.g., 527a,13–14) 'he who' with хто above. The purely Ukrainian form котрый is attested in the language of the other two Ruthenians, as well as in SinSlav, whereas it is lacking in the texts of MS. According to Kernyc'kyj 1967, который was still more widely used than котрый in the sixteenth century (150). Here, then, Smotryc'kyj's language is traditional, while that of Vyšens'kyj and Berynda can be considered more innovative. The form used by MS is retained in CSBR (каторы) and CSR (который).

5.5.3 ижє, ѩжє, єжє. In addition to the common Ruthenian relatives, a few Slavonic relatives are attested in MS: Nsgm Ѿчє наш ижє єси на нбсєхъ (235a,19–20) 'Our father who art in heaven,' Gsgm нєгожє (K4a,1), Lsgn внємжє (K20b,20), Asgf южє (K20b,22). All but one occur in *Kazan'e*, while ижє in JU is used in the opening passage of the

Lord's prayer. These Slavonic forms are also attested in IV (191) and PB; in the former they are relatively numerous (39 times, in biblical citations and similarly marked contexts), while they are rare in PB (2 times).

The form ижъ, possibly representing a shortened form of иже, can also function as a relative (only masculine): грѣшный, ижъ земныхъ марностій шукаетъ (359a,17–18) 'the sinner who seeks earthly vanities.' This relative is formally identical to the *conjunction* иж(ъ) which expresses 'that' or 'so that' (chapter 8). The possible use of ижъ as a relative is explainable as an instance of parallelism with the conjunction što, which also has the same phonetic shape as the relative што (cf. above). Since ижъ is formally distinct from иже (etc.), and because it is used outside of biblical passages, this form should not be interpreted as a Slavonicism: the relative ижъ is cited in SSUM, therefore it can be labelled "Ruthenian."

MS and IV share one more marked relative pronoun, that is єликъ 'as much as'; in MS the form Npl єлици (K10a,16) is used in the sense 'those people who' in a biblical passage: єлици ... во Ха Іса крестихомся ... 'all [we] who have been baptized into Christ Jesus ... ' (Rom 6:3).

5.6 *The Indefinite Pronoun.* A pronominal form that expresses such overtly indefinite concepts as "some," "any," "-ever," or that is used as a quantifier of an inexact number ("many") or undefined subject ("other"), may be referred to as an indefinite pronoun. All pronominal forms which occur with long-form hard or soft adjectival desinences are declined accordingly.

5.6.1 што/що and кто/хто. The versatility of these pronouns, which we have already seen as interrogatives and relatives, also extends to the category of indefinites: without formal modification they can express "something" and "someone" (respectively). The most common use of such indefinites is in clauses which are introduced by conjunctions such as "if" and "when": а єсли хто достоєство ѿ Стго Дха принятое не ведлугъ пристойности обходитъ ... (443b,15–16) 'a if someone does not observe (value) virtue received from the Holy Spirit as he should [lit. according to propriety] ... '; кгды хто шукаєт собѣ пожитку ... (510a,18–19) 'if someone seeks for himself profit.' An interesting construction often used by Smotryc'kyj is a combination of хто functioning as a relative (as discussed above) followed by што or хто functioning as an indefinite: бо хто кого любитъ . . . (129a,7) 'for [he] who loves someone . . . '; бо хто што любитъ . . . (270b,11) 'for [he] who loves something . . . .' The form хто only occurs once in this manner in *Kazan'e* (K19b,7) and once in the preface to *Grammatiki* (IVa,4); што is not used as an indefinite pronoun in those works. Consequently, the use of these pronouns as indefinites ought perhaps to be considered stylistically neutral, or least as closer to the spoken norm than to the higher stylistic level of *Kazan'e*. On the basis of data from the modern languages, the use of што/що and кто/хто as indefinites in MS indicates the influence of spoken Ruthenian: in Ukrainian as well as in Belarusian the indefinite function of these pronouns is described as "colloquial" in SUM and TSBM, respectively. This indefinite usage is also found in IV (192–93), but is not mentioned with regard to PB (see 63–64).

5.6.2 *Prefixal ně- and suffixal -s'.* A common means of forming indefinite pronouns is the prefixation of stressed *ně-* to a variety of pronominal forms:

- нѣ́што 'something' (7 times, e.g., K7b,3 and 58b,17);
- нѣ́хто 'someone' (3 times, e.g., 112a,9);
- нѣ́котор- 'some, some kind (of)' (99 times, e.g., K9b,14 and 35b,1);
- нѣ́як- 'some, some kind (of)' (49 times, e.g., K19b,1 and 58b,26–27).

The prefix *ně-* is inherited from Common Slavic; it is not reflected in CSU as an indefinite marker, while it is retained as such in CSBR, as it is in CSR. These forms are differentiated from the graphically identical negative pronouns by the place of stress: all of the forms are stressed on the prefix *ně-,* while the corresponding negative pronouns have their stress on the root (нѣхто́, etc.). Such forms are also found in PB (65) and IV (for example, 193), and are also attested in SinSlav (нѣкоторый, нѣкій). It is reasonable, then, to identify them as a pan-Ruthenian feature, which later lost its currency in the southern Ruthenian (> CSU) regions. Of the forms listed above, Gröschel only identifies the forms нѣ́который and нѣ́кій in the language of IV, both of which are also found in SinSlav (нѣшто and нѣхто are simply labelled “negatives,” as stress is not indicated in his texts: 1972, 192). Didiakin-Leeming does discuss this issue, and identifies нѣшто and нѣхто as indefinite pronouns when the stress is on the prefix (“na partykule”), as negatives when it is on the root (“na zaimku”; 1969, 64).

Another indefinite construction reflected in MS’ texts, although not nearly as productive as the use of the prefixal particle *ně-,* is the suffixation of *-s′* ‘this,’ historically the old demonstrative pronoun *сь, to the same pronominal forms:

> штось ‘something’ (4 times, e.g., K26a,17 and 164b,5);
> ꙗкійсь ‘some, some kind (of)’ (392b,5).

The formant is still found in CSU (якийсь, котрийсь), in CSBR (штось, хтось; although more common are штосці, хтосці) and in CSP (*coś* ‘something,’ *ktoś* ‘someone’). The presence of the indefinite suffix -s′ in all three languages, and lack thereof in CSR, suggest a case of borrowing from Polish by Ruthenian. This suffix is not attested in PB (65; see below), and it is not mentioned as a feature of the language of IV. Of particular interest are the numerous forms attested in MS’ texts in which the formants *ně-* and *-s′* co-occur:

> нѣ́што҇с ‘something’ (K23a,2 and 93a,6);
> нѣ́хтось ‘someone’ (344a,5);
> нѣ́ꙗкійсь ‘some, some kind (of)’ (5 times, e.g., нѣ́ꙗкаꙗ҇ [fem] 392b,6);
> нѣ́которыйсь ‘some, some kind (of)’ (нѣ́которомоу҇: 164b,6).

The stressed prefix may be required because of interference from the phonetically and graphically identical 2sg suffix -сь, which can be suffixed to non-verbal as well as to verbal forms: далесь (36a,4) ‘you gave/have given,’ тысь мнѣ . . . не далъ (44b,15–16) ‘you did not give to me.’ Context is crucial, because the 2sg element -сь can be suffixed to pronouns preceding the verb just as easily as to any other form. A form that outwardly appears to be an indefinite pronoun can thus turn out to be a mere “carrier” in a verbal construction: чогось не взялъ (241a,6) ‘which you did not take,’ которыхесь ми далъ (189a,30) ‘which you gave to me’; in the latter the connecting vowel *-e-* does indicate the verbal status of this formant, however. The same construction is seen in the form нѣꙗкаꙗсь, cited by Didiakin-Leeming for the language of PB (1969, 65).

In terms of the status of these two formants in relation to each other, we can say that *nĕ-* is clearly widespread (and unmarked), while *-s'* is rarer (and therefore marked). Indefinite pronouns occurring with both elements fall somewhere in the middle of this hierarchy: consequently they are found more often in MS than are forms containing only the suffix *-s'*. With regard to the modern languages, it bears repeating that *both* formants are current in CSBR, while only *-s'* is found in CSU; the geo-linguistic position of Belarusian vis-à-vis Russian and Ukrainian allows for the conclusion that the Belarusian linguistic region represents a transitional territory between the areas of *nĕ-* and *-s'*-dominance (North and South East Slavic, respectively). In this particular respect Smotryc'kyj's language is closer to CSBR than it is to CSU.

5.6.3 -колвек. The suffix -колвекъ (Pol *-kolwiek*) is without doubt part of the system reflected in MS' texts, but is clearly a Polonism. Indefinite pronouns are found 186 times with this formant, including three times in *Kazan'e* and one time in *Grammatiki*:

> хтоколвекъ 'whoever' (24 times, e.g., K2b,20);
> которыйколвекъ 'whatever, whichever' (24 times, e.g., 82b,26–27);
> ꙗкійколвекъ 'whatever, whichever' (21 times, e.g., 54a,5);
> штоколвекъ 'whatever' (e.g., 31b,21; note also the Ukrainian form щоколвекъ, 230b,21).

Such forms are also present in PB, e.g., ꙗкоеколвек (65), but are not extant in IV. In these indefinites the pronominal root is declined and *-kolvek* is simply treated as any other immutable formant, as is *-s'*: вчомъколвекъ (64a,20) 'in what- or whichever'; other elements may also be inserted between the two parts: штобысѧколвекъ (106a,27) 'whatsoever.' The latter construction in particular is reminiscent of patterns typical of Polish; this structure has already been mentioned above with regard to the reflexive particle *-sja*.

The Polish origin of the formant *-kolvek* is clear, not least because it is no longer found in the modern East Slavic languages: cf. CSP *cokolwiek,* Slvk *čokol'vek,* but Cz *cokoli* 'whatever.' The extreme frequency with which it occurs in the written language of some Ruthenians (in this case MS) allows it to be interpreted as a feature of

Ruthenian at that time, if only because of intensive Polish-Ruthenian language contact. Its subsequent loss in the Ruthenian regions is probably the result of the competition between the numerous formants used for the construction of indefinite pronouns. We note that the retention of *-s'* as well as *-kolwiek* in Polish is justified by a difference in degree; the former expresses "some, any," while the latter is used for intensified forms of the kind "whatsoever": *coś* 'something, anything,' but *cokolwiek* 'anything, what(so)ever.'

5.6.4 *Other Indefinite Pronouns*.

5.6.4.1 ин-. иншій. This pronoun is made up of the pronoun *инъ 'other' and the comparative suffix *-š-:* it expresses "other, another, different." It is attested hundreds of times in MS' texts, as it is in IV, PB (65), as well as in SinSlav and P-M. This pronoun can justifiably be described as a vital part of the Ruthenian system, and it also is found in CSU and CSBR. Leeming identifies *inšyj* in *Aleksandryja*, and considers it to be a Polonism (1968, 290). By itself this form is used to express the meaning "other," as we see in иншїи . . . способы (K15a,3) 'other manners/kinds.' When contrasted with одинъ and дрȣгий, the sense imparted is that of "still other": одны . . . , дрȣгїи . . . , а иншїи . . . (278b,19–20) 'some . . . , others . . . , and still others . . . .' The phrases иншее што (343a,17), иншого чого (374b,10) consist of two indefinite pronouns, and can be translated as 'anything else.'

The unsuffixed form иный is attested only 10 times (e.g., 66b,7) and can be considered marked in comparison with иншый, for numerical as well as contextual reasons; this form is not attested in IV (193) but does occur frequently in PB (60–61). The marked status of иный is confirmed by its distribution among the modern East Slavic languages: it is not found in Ukrainian or Belarusian, whereas it is retained in Russian (иной), a language which exhibits a much greater degree of Slavonic influence than do the other two languages.

Инакшый. Another indefinite containing the root *in- is инакшый 'another,' consisting of *inak-* 'other' (cf. OCS *inakъ*) and the comparative suffix *-š-*. It occurs most frequently in the phrase инакшимъ способомъ (312a,6) 'in another/different manner.' It is found 6 times in MS and is attested in PB (61), but it is not cited by Gröschel. This pronoun still occurs in CSU (інакший) and CSBR (інакшы) as a variant of інший and іншы, respectively. The unsuffixed form инакъ functions as an adverb in Smotryc'kyj's language (e.g., 295a,26), and is examined in chapter 7.

5.6.4.2 мног- is translated as 'many' or 'much,' depending on whether it occurs in the plural or the singular. In the singular the most common form is the neuter много, a pronominal form that can also function adverbially; in the plural, when it does not modify a substantive, this pronoun expresses "many people": многїи (K11a,18). The extent to which *mnoh-* is used by MS (hundreds of attestations) indicates that the form was very common in the Ruthenian period. It is attested in IV (194) and is found in Berynda's *Leksykon*, in compound Slavonic headwords as well as in Ruthenian definitions. Мног- is current in modern Russian, but is not found in CSBR. In CSU this form is characterized as "archaic" (SUM), the preferred form being багато 'much.' The present-day distribution of мног- is similar to that of иный, but the former should not be interpreted as a Slavonicism on this basis—its wide occurrence in Ruthenian precludes this interpretation. It is most clearly the case that мног- was commonly used in earlier East Slavic (from CES to Ruthenian), becoming increasingly limited in its use, until finally common use is limited to CSR proper: just as that language preserves many Slavonic elements, it also preserves other archaic (CES) elements which have been lost to CSBR and CSU. This pronoun is attested with a Slavonic desinence in the set phrase многаѧ лѣта (K4a,5) 'many years'; the latter occurs in a prayer closing the preface to *Kazan'e,* and stands in contrast to the Ruthenian version лѣта многїи (K2a,11) 'many years' in the same text.

5.6.4.3 The form прочїй 'further, other' is a Slavonicism. In MS it only occurs 2 times, both in *Kazan'e*, as a way of introducing a prayer or biblical citation in *Kazan'e*: прочєє: бг҃а, от нєгожє всѧко даѧнїє бл҃го . . . (K4a,1–2) '(and) further: [of] God, from him every [act of] giving is blessed . . . .' Gröschel also assigns this form to the Slavonic level, and cites Berynda's use of such living forms as позостаалий, остатєчний (etc.: 1972, 195) in its definition. The characterization of прочїй as a Slavonicism is also supported by its occurrence in the text of GSPS (82, 186, 189 of Horbatsch 1974) and absence from JU. This form is foreign to CSU and CSBR; as in the case of other Slavonic or archaic CES pronouns, modern Russian preserves прочий.

5.6.4.4 жадєнъ 'none' occurs 187 times, 9 times in *Kazan'e* and 178 times in JU: жаднои (48a,16) Gsgf, жаднымъ (K19a,11) Isgm; when this form occurs without a substantival complement in the plural, it is commonly used to refer to people, as is мног-. The phonetic shape of this pronoun is the same as that which is found in CSP and CSBR (żadny, жадны respectively); cf. CSU жодний. Rudnyc'kyj is of the opinion that this form ultimately comes from Polish (EDUL II:381), as does Leeming (1968, 290); given the presence of other Polish elements in this morphological category, there is no reason to disagree with this view. This pronoun is also attested in IV (ibid.), FS, and SinSlav, but is not mentioned as occurring in PB.

5.7 *Other Pronominal Forms.*

5.7.1 The forms такїй 'such, this kind,' and ꙗкїй 'what kind of, that' derive from the qualitative-demonstrative pronouns *takъ* and *jakъ,* and both are present in CSU and CSBR: Ukr такий, який, Br такі, які. Ꙗкїй appeared later than такїй, as is illustrated by the number of forms cited in SSUM (one form of the former, many of the latter). These forms are very common in MS, occurring 82 times and 130 times, respectively; both of these pronouns also occur in IV (196) and in PB (59–61). All forms of такїй in MS are end-stressed, as are most examples of ꙗкїй; this is also the case in the modern languages. In the latter form we do find several instances of penultimate stress (in this case, intial stress) which may be ascribed to Polish influence.

The pronouns таковый and ꙗковый express the same meanings as такїй and ꙗкїй above, but reflect the combination of *takъ/jakъ* and the formant *-ov-*. Whereas такїй and ꙗкїй are evidently both widely used in Ruthenian, differences in the distribution of these two derivative forms are clearly evident. The more common of the two is таковый, which is identified in MS' texts 104 times, 99 times in JU and 5 times in *Kazan'e*: 77 of these (or 74%) have penultimate stress on the Polish pattern, including all 5 in *Kazan'e,* while the remainder have Ruthenian final stress (cf. такїй above). The corresponding short forms таковъ, такова, таково are attested 7 times. This pronoun is common in IV

(197–98) as well as in PB (60–61), but is no longer extant in CSU or CSBR. *Takowy* is still extant in Polish. The present-day distribution of this pronoun and the stress statistic indicate that this form is a Polonism, but one that was clearly part of the Ruthenian system.

Ꙗковый is comparatively rare in MS, occurring 17 times only in JU; both final and penultimate stress patterns are found with this pronoun, as they are with ꙗкїй, but this time the Ruthenian stress pattern predominates; the short forms ꙗковъ (etc.) are used 6 times. Таковъ and ꙗковъ can occur juxtaposed in the same utterance expressing approximately 'in the [same] way . . . that': жебы люде знали и вѣрили ижъ ты ѿцъ мой и Бг҃ъ таковъже єстесь, ꙗковъ и ꙗ єдинородный Сн҃ъ твой и Бг҃ъ єстемъ (187b,9–12) 'so that people know and believe that you are my Father and God in the same way that I am your only-begotten Son and God.' Ꙗковъ is found in PB (*Leksykon* 52, cited by Gröschel 1972, 197), one short form ꙗковъ and каковъ (equals ꙗковъ) are attested in IV; it is not cited in SSUM. It is not present in CSBR, CSP (cf. OP *jakowykolwiek:* Reczek), or CSU as a pronoun, but two adverbial forms based on this pronoun are still present in CSU: яковось, 'somehow,' and the interrogative яково used to express 'what is X like?'; the latter is described as 'archaic' in SUM. The CSU forms and MS' stress patterns indicate that this pronoun ought to be considered U-R.

5.7.2 вшелякий 'any, each' is a Polonism: compare Ukr всілякий, Br усялякі, Pol *wszelaki*. It is extremely common in the texts of MS (for example, 58a,13), occurring 375 times, including nine forms in *Kazan'e* and one in *Grammatiki*. This pronoun is found once in IV (p. 196), and occurs in PB's *Leksykon* under the Slavonic headword всячески: вшеляким способо҇; the adverb вшеляко is found in SinSlav and the pronoun вшелякий in SSUM, however (SSUM: in texts dating from 1389 and 1438). There can be no doubt that вшелякїй was part of the Ruthenian system: its (near) absence from IV may be ascribed to the generally Slavonic character of the language of his texts.

5.7.3 The pronominal-prepositional construction што за (e.g., K17b,18) 'what kind of' most likely came to East Slavic via Polish *co za*, which in turn calques German *was für (ein)?* 'what kind of (a)?' This expression is still current in the modern East Slavic languages.

5.7.4 The long form distributive pronoun всѧкій 'each, any' was relatively common in the Ruthenian period, and it is still used in all three modern East Slavic languages: Ukr всякий, Br усякі, R всякий. In MS only 4 examples of this pronoun occur, all in JU (e.g., L всѧкомъ 82b,3); it is also found in IV (195–96) and PB (60–61). Short forms such as всѧк҆ and всѧко are attested 5 times, but they are marked as Slavonicisms. Of these, 2 are used in JU, 3 of them occur in *Kazan'e*, in a biblical passage and a prayer: всѧко даѧнїе бл҃го (K4a,1) 'every [act of] giving is blessed,' and да всѧкъ видѧй с҃на . . . (K13b,4) 'so that each/anyone seeing [His] Son . . . .' The relative status of the long and short forms is clearly reflected in PB's *Leksykon*, where the (Slavonic) headword въсѧкъ is defined as (Ruthenian) всѧкїй.

The Slavonic derivative всѧческїй 'all, every kind of' is attested in the same prayer cited above: всѧческое . . . попранїе (K4a,3–4) 'every [manner of] destruction'; note the headwords въсѧческаа, въсѧчески in *Leksykon*. As with other archaisms and Slavonicisms, this form is current in CSR but lacking in CSU and CSBR.

5.7.5 The distributive pronoun кождый 'every' is extremely common in MS, and represents the norm in his language. A parallel form каждый is also attested, but it occurs only 3 times next to hundreds of attestations of кождый: the latter is found in modern Ukrainian dialects, while the former is used in CSP (*każdy*) and CSR (cf. CSU кожний < *koždьn-, CSBR кожны). The variant каждый is not attested in *Kazan'e*, and can be considered a Polonism. All forms of кождый/каждый are inflected according to the hard stem long adjective paradigm, with the exception of the dative non-feminine form коемꙋждо, in which the first element is declined; the form is Slavonic, and occurs in a biblical citation: єдиномꙋ коемꙋждо насъ дадесѧ бл҃дть (K10a,22–23) 'to each one of us grace was given' (Ephesians 4:7). Both каждый and кождый are attested in PB (60; кождый is found in *Leksykon* under the Slavonic headword кождо), as they are in IV: Gröschel attributes the former to Polish influence (1972, 198–99).

Another distributive pronoun in MS' texts is што 'every,' patterned after the Polish construction. Thus, in the same sentence next to the phrase на кождꙋю годинꙋ и мѣнꙋтꙋ 'every hour and minute' we find што день 'every day' (417b,19–20). This construction is not mentioned with regard to IV or PB, and is still extant in CSU (e.g., що день).

5.7.6 The totalizing pronoun весь 'all' occurs in the singular as follows:

Case	*Masculine*	*Neuter*	*Feminine*
N	весь ȣвесь	все	——
A	весь	все	всю всюю
G	всего	всего	всеи всеѧ
L	всемъ	всемъ	——
D	всемȣ	всемȣ	——
I	——	——	всею

In the sixteenth-seventeenth centuries the non-feminine desinences had not yet replaced desinence-initial *-e-* with *-o-* (*vs-e̲ho* etc.: Kernyc'kyj 147–48); cf. such CSU (and southeast Ukrainian dialect) forms as the 3rd person singular possessive pronoun *joho* < *jeho*. Most of these forms are widely used in Ruthenian, but we note the following :

Gsgf всеи is the (by now) expected U-R form derived from CES *vьseě (cf. previously discussed pronominal as well as adjectival paradigms). CSU has the form всієї, while two forms are current in CSBR, viz. усёй (preferred) and усяе.

Gsgf всеѧ is a Slavonicism: Митрополитȣ . . . всеѧ Рѡссїи (K2a,3–4) 'metropolitan . . . of all Russia.'

Asgf всюю (134a,19) is found next to the expected form всю and must be explained as analogical to the accusative feminine of the soft-stem adjectival paradigm, in which -юю represents the CES and later CSR and CSBR long form ending. The form всю is now standard in all three East Slavic languages.

Nsgm оувесь (Ee III,73) has been described in 2.1.1.8. It occurs only once, and is the same as the CSU and CSBR forms; весь reflects the CES norm, and is retained in modern Russian.

Of the remaining forms, Nsgn все and Lm/n всемъ are still current in CSU, orthographically represented by все/усе and всім, respectively: Ukr всім < *vsem is an acceptable variant next to the newer form всьому. CSBR has усё and усім; Lm/n усім is not to be identified with Ukr усім, however, because they have different origins: here L усім is identical to I усім (the result of syncretism between these two case forms).

The singular paradigm of this pronoun present in the language of IV and PB is virtually identical to the paradigm attested in MS. Several examples with initial u- are also found in IV (N-A оувсе; 200) as well as PB; both ȣвесь and ввесь occur in the latter (63).

The plural paradigm is as follows:

N всѣ, вси

A всѣ, вси, вся

G всѣхъ

L всѣхъ

D всѣмъ

I всѣми

Smotryc'kyj's plural paradigm is essentially the CES paradigm; only the nominative and accusative need comment. One Slavonic form is used in a biblical quotation in *Kazan'e*: A pl вся (K10b,11; 2 Cor 5:15). N всѣ (e.g., K13a,22) and N/A вси (N in 286a,6; A in 409b,7) both existed in the CES paradigm, but the former was feminine while the latter was masculine (there is, of course, no gender distinction in the plural in Ruthenian). The use of both forms in MS' texts appears to indicate that his N/A plural was U-R [vsi], not B-R [vse].

The plural forms of this pronoun in PB and IV are for all intents and purposes identical to those found in MS' texts; the only differences are the use of (genitive) всѣх for the animate accusative in PB and IV, and the lack of the graphic variant вси in PB (IV: 200; PB: 63).

5.7.7 The isolative pronoun самъ 'oneself, alone' is end-stressed in the oblique case forms in the singular and throughout the plural; several forms do occur with initial stress (Nsgn, Nplm, Isgn), but they are forms of самый 'the very,' which is characterized by initial stress (=CSU cáмий, CSBR cáмы). The differentiation of forms by stress alone has led to interference in CSU, in which end-stressed самúй is a variant of сам, but occurs less frequently than сам. The forms attested in MS are the following:

Case	*Masculine*	*Neuter*	*Feminine*
N	самъ	само	——
A	——	——	самѹю
G	——	——	——
L	самомъ	самомъ	——
D	самомѹ	самомѹ	——
I	самымъ	самымъ	самою

One spelling of a dative non-feminine form is apparently a typographical error: самонмѹ (K20a,1). MS' locative non-feminine самомъ is still reflected in CSU самім as a variant of standard самому (cf. *vsim* above); the other forms are the same as in the modern language. In this respect MS is U-R, as the CSBR locative non-feminine singular is самім, which is again the instrumental form. The usual CSBR instrumental feminine is самой, although самою is also found; in the accusative feminine both саму and самую occur (in CSU only саму). Only a few forms are attested in the plural: N сами (K9a,10), G самыхъ (K13a,3), D самымъ (K13a,4; K20a,15). The stress pattern of MS' plural forms is the same as that of CSBR, that is root-stressed in the nominative (end-stressed in CSU), end-stressed in the oblique cases. There are no formal differences between the paradigms of MS, IV, and PB.

CHAPTER SIX

The Numeral

6.1 *The Cardinal Numeral*

6.1.1 All forms of East Slavic одинъ are attested in the singular, and are identical to those found in CSU; this numeral is declined according to the pronominal paradigm described in chapter 5:

Case	*Masculine*	*Neuter*	*Feminine*
N	одинъ	одно	одна
A	одинъ/одного	одно	одну
G	одного	одного	однои
L	одномъ	одномъ	одной
D	одному	одному	одной
I	однымъ	однымъ	одною

Most of these forms are also present in CSBR; the exceptions are the locative masculine (Br адным), genitive feminine (адной or аднае), and instrumental feminine (адной or адною). The plural forms of одинъ are used to express the indefinite quantifier "some" in MS. This is the practice in the modern East Slavic languages. The attested forms are N одны/одни, G одныхъ, and I одными—all of these forms are used in CSU and CSBR.

The Slavonic variant has initial *je-* and no mobile vowel, in contrast to East Slavic одинъ; the forms attested in MS (6 in *Kazan'e*, 3 in JU) are Nmsg єдинъ, Nsgf єдина, Gsgm/n єдиного, Gsgf єдинои, Dsgm/n єдиному; the Slavonic genitive non-feminine desinence -аго is used once in a biblical quotation (K13a,19). The four forms єдно (Nsgn), єдна (Nsgf), єдномъ (Lsgm/n), and єднымъ (Isgm/n) are all attested in JU, and can be identified either as Polish or southwest U-R, since they have initial є- and a mobile vowel: cf. Pol. *jeden, jedno, jedna*.

East Slavic одинъ and Slavonic єдинъ differ contextually, and often semantically: whereas the former simply represents the (unmarked) numeral "1" or "only," the Slavonic variant usually expresses "the one and only" or "sole," and most of the 9 examples of this numeral occur in biblical contexts. Compare, for example, єдинъ оный Богъ (K25b,2) 'that one and only God,' and єдинъ дх҃ъ (40b,3) 'the one (and only) spirit,' with до одного зъ свѧщеннонноковъ (K23a,1) 'to one of the holy monks.' Thus, although the form likely to be used to express the unmarked meaning "one" is одинъ, it does not necessarily have to be so: cf. єдн҃и ѿ дрꙋгого (203b,18) 'one from another.' It is important to note that єдиный, declined as an adjective, is still used in CSU (and CSR) to express "the only"; a similar form is found in CSBR, but it is derived from East Slavic *odin*-: адзіны.

The declension of один/єдин in IV agrees with the attested forms in MS, as does the use of єдин meaning 'only.' Gröschel does not indicate whether the Slavonic form may be translated as 'the one and only' (1972, 202). The same numeral in PB occurs only 4 times with East Slavic initial o-, all instances of which decline as they do in MS and IV; there are, however, 9 attestations of initial *e*- (or *je*-), of which 4 can be classified as Slavonicisms of the type єдин; the other 5, e.g., єден, єднымъ, are characterized by Didiakin-Leeming as Polonisms (1969, 86–87), citing Kuraszkiewicz (1954, 72). Gröschel is of the opinion that instrumental єднымъ is a Polonism (ibid.). These forms were certainly vital members of both the U-R and B-R systems (cf. SSUM, HSBM, and PB), but are clearly not the preferred variant for MS, as forms of одинъ (etc.) are attested hundreds of times, in all texts. For MS, then, they should also be treated as Polonisms rather than as southwest U-R.

6.1.2 A complete paradigm of два 'two' occurs in MS:

Case	*Masculine*	*Neuter*	*Feminine*
N	два	два	двѣ
A	два/двохъ/двѡхъ	два	двѣ

All Genders

G	двохъ/двωхъ
L	двохъ/двωхъ
D	двомъ/двωмъ
I	двома/двωма

The forms of два are essentially the same as those used in CSU and CSBR. The parallel forms with the vowels о and ω are interesting in light of corresponding modern forms, if ω represents phonetic [u] (see chapter 2): consequently G/L [dvox]-[dvux], D [dvom]-[dvum], and I [dvoma]-[dvuma], the CSU and CSBR forms (respectively), may all be reflected in Smotryc'kyj's texts. For the instrumental of два IV uses the form двєма, which Gröschel describes as a Ukrainian dialect form (1972, 203); in PB we find the same instrumental form as in MS, viz. двома. Other forms of два in IV are: D двом, A два and двє (ibid.); in PB: Nm два, Nf/n двє, G двою and newer двохъ (87–88).

6.1.3 A complete paradigm is also present for "three":

All Genders

N	три
A	три
G	трωхъ
L	трєхъ, трωхъ
D	трωмъ
I	трωма

Of MS' two locative variants, the form трωхъ is more common (4 times versus 2 times трєхъ); cf. modern southwest Ukrainian трох. Both трєх and трох were current in sixteenth-century U-R (Kernyc'kyj 1967, 161), while G трєхъ (< CES trьxъ) was preferred in earlier U-R, and is the only form attested in the locative (SSUM). As traditional трєхъ is the prescribed form in *Grammatiki*, it can be described as Meletian Slavonic; it is also plausible, however, that its continued use in 16th-century U-R was supported by the existence of Pol *trzech*. G/L трωхъ can be explained as arising by analogy to двохъ; likewise, I трωма likely developed by anology to двома (Bevzenko et al. 1978, 227). MS' genitive, dative, and locative forms appear to be closer to the CSBR system than they are to the CSU (the CSU paradigm is characterized by palatalized [ŕ], where CSBR has [r]), but these forms were the norm in U-R as well as in B-R. Три and трєхъ are attested in IV (203), while the forms три and трохъ occur in PB (88).

6.1.4 Two competing root forms are found for the numeral 'four' in MS, чот- and чт-, both of which are common in the Ruthenian period. The former is current in CSU and CSBR, while the root *št-* (< *čt-*) is still found in the Carpathian Ukraine (Bevzenko et al., ibid.): CSU чотири, CSBR чатыры, but CSP *cztery*. In MS' texts the form чот- is clearly preferred—it is found 15 times, while the southwest Ukrainian/Polish form чт- occurs 8 times:

All genders

N/A	чотыры/чотыри	N/A	чтыри
G	чотырωхъ/чотырохъ	G	чтырωхъ/чтырохъ
		D	чтырємъ

With the exception of D чтырємъ (447a,6), the declensional morphemes of these forms agree with those attested with два and три. The root of чтырємъ reflects southwest Ukrainian/Polish, while the desinence is the expected reflex of CES *(četyr)ьmъ;* the CES desinences are prescribed by Smotryćkyj in GSPS (e.g., чєтырєхъ). Since context offers no help in in determining the level to which this desinence belongs, it can only be identified as "traditional East Slavic." Only the form чотыри is attested in IV; in PB, on the other hand, we find чєтыри, чтыри, чтыры, in addition to L чтырохъ (88).

6.1.5 The numerals 5–19 are declined as III declension feminine substantives, as they are in the modern East Slavic languages. The attested N/A forms are:

пѧть '5'
шєсть '6'

сємъ ‘7’ (note final hard *-m*)

осмъ ‘8’ (note final hard *-m)*

дєвѧть ‘9’

дєсѧть ‘10’

один(н)аⷣцать ‘11’

дванаⷣцать ‘12’

чотырнаⷣцать ‘14’

пѧтнаⷣцать ‘15’

осмнаⷣцать ‘18’

One clearly Slavonic form is used in *Kazan'e*, G чєтыⷬ҇надєсѧти (K13a,12) ‘14’ reflects the older root spelling чєт- (*pro* чот-) and the uncontracted на+дєсѧти- (*pro* надцать). For all other cases with the exception of the instrumental the desinence is *-i,* and it occurs with all the numerals listed above. Only two instrumental forms are attested in MS—пѧтма ‘5’ exhibits the dual ending seen above in двома and трома; сєдми ‘7’ reflects the CES Ipl desinence. Пѧтма has the same form as the CSU instrumental form (п’ятьма, alongside п’ятьома), as opposed to CSBR пяццю, CSR пятью, in which the desinence is that of the i- stem instrumental singular. Gröschel cites only пѧть, пѧти, and шєсть in IV (1972, 204), while a relative wealth of forms is attested in PB: пѧти, пѧтми, шєсть, шєсти, сєдмъ/сѣмъ, сє(д)ми, осмъ/осмь, осми. Didiakin-Leeming considers пѧтми and сє(д)ми to be characteristically southwest Ukrainian innovations (1969, 89); note the presence of the latter in MS as well.

6.1.6 Multiples of 10 and 100 are equally numerous in MS; the following forms are attested in his texts:

тридцать, -и ‘30’

чотырдєсѧтъ, -и ‘40’

пѧтдєсѧтъ ‘50’

шєстдєсѧтъ ‘60’

сємдєсѧтъ, сємидєсѧти ‘70’

осмдєсѧтъ ‘80’

сто ‘100’

триста '300'

пѧтисотъ (G) '500'

девѧтисотъ (L) '900'

All of these forms can be considered general Ruthenian. Kernyc'kyj (1967, 177–78) identifies чотырдесѧтъ as characteristic of sixteenth-century Galician (U-R), whereas the Volhynian and Dniester dialects (i.e., Smotryc'kyj's dialects) used the later form сорок instead. The old compound form чотырдесѧтъ was also the norm in the B-R of Smotryc'kyj's day (Bulyka et al. 1988, 142), as it was earlier during the time of Skaryna (but with the traditional spelling четырдесѧтъ), and is retained in CSP (*czterdzieść*); MS' form exhibits either B-R or Polish influence. In all modern East Slavic languages the form сорок (CSBR сорак) is the norm.

Ruthenian compound numerals under 100 are formed by simple addition, that is, by means of the conjunction и 'and' (cf. Bulyka et al. 1988, 143; Kernyc'kyj 1967, 168–69); thus in MS: чотырдесѧтъ и девѧть '49,' осмдесѧтъ и чотыри '84.' The conjunction does not occur between multiples of 100 and 10 in MS: сто пѧтдесѧти '150.' None of the modern East Slavic languages (or Polish) use the conjunction in the formation of compound numerals. In the texts of IV Gröschel finds only сто '100' and Slavonic тридесѧт '30' (1972, 204), while more are identified in PB: два(д)цѧ(т) '20,' L тридцѧти '30,' девѧтьдесѧть '90,' and пѧ(т)со(тъ) '500' (1969, 90); in the first two of these forms we note the presence of palatalized [c'], a U-R feature not reflected in Smotryc'kyj's language.

6.1.7 The numeral 1000 is frequently attested in MS; its forms are those of a soft stem I declension substantive. In the singular we find only the forms now current in CSU and CSBR: N тисѧча, G тисѧчи, A тисѧчꙋ. In the plural a few i-stem desinences are attested: next to the newer genitive plural тысѧч (2 times), there are 11 occurrences of тисѧчїй and 3 of тысѧчей (these forms are found following other numerals such as пѧть '5' and десѧть '10,' and the indefinite много 'many'); in addition to 6 occurrences of the instrumental plural тисѧчами, there are 4 of the i-stem тисѧчми. The variant spellings ти- and ты- reflect the coalescence of *i and *y in Ukrainian: etymologically the vowel was *y (cf. OCS тысѫщи, тысѧщти). In IV only two forms are found: тисеча, in which the northern Ukrainian feature *ę > [e] is reflected, and Slavonic тисѧщи (203–204); this numeral is not attested in PB. On the basis of these data, it is possible to say that MS' system of cardinal numerals is closer to that of PB than that of IV.

6.2 The Collective Numeral

The collective numerals are well represented in Smotryc'kyj's texts, especially in comparison with Vyšens'kyj and Berynda.

6.2.1 The following are historically neuters, generalized to refer to groups (of any gender) of the number in question:

- двое 'a group of 2' (6 times): чирвоное море . . . ѹдаривши, на двое роздѣлилъ (86b,9–10) 'having struck the Red Sea, divided it into two [parts]'; the instrumental form is also attested: межи двоимъ . . . злымъ (532b,7) 'between two evils.'
- трое 'a group of 3': все трое подъ справѹ розѹмови поданое (61b,4–5) 'all three [things] subjected to reason.'
- четверо 'a group of 4': четверо ѡвчатъ за одно ѿдати (397b,3–4) 'to give up [a group of] four sheep [in exchange] for one.'
- семеро 'a group of 7': а онъ тобѣ всемеро болшъ ѿдасть (73a,23) 'and he will give to you sevenfold more.'
- двана̂дцатеро 'a group of 12,' or 'the 12': одинъ народъ естъ Израилскїий, на двана̂дцатеро з одного коренѧ розрослый (453b,2–3) 'the Israelite people is one, out of one root grown into [a group] of twelve.'

6.2.2 **Оба**. The forms of оба 'both' in Smotryc'kyj's texts can be divided into three groups which are formally and functionally different: оба and newer обадва; singular adjectival forms; plural adjectival forms. Most of these forms are prescribed by MS in GSPS. The forms for the singular adjectival forms are found in his "singular" paradigm of обой; the plural forms from the "plural" paradigm. Note that обѣма is the prescribed D/Idf form.

оба and newer обадва:

NA	обадва (7 times), обѣдвѣ (4 times)
GL	обохъ (8 times)
D	обомъ (4 times)
I	обѣма (1 time)

singular adjectival forms:

NA	обоє (8 times)
G	обоєго (2 times)

plural adjectival forms:

NA	обои (2 times)
G	обоихъ (8 times)
D	обоимъ (2 times)
I	обоими (1 time)

Of those forms not already mentioned above, the most easily recognizable forms are those which developed through a fusion of "both" and "two": оба-два, обѣ-двѣ (with agreement of case-number-gender markings). These do not exactly reflect the CSU or CSBR forms, however, the constituent parts of the compounds are expected CES forms (оба, два, обѣ, двѣ) and the model was known in early U-R (cf. SSUM) and in Polish. The forms in the оба and newer обадва paradigm represent the largest number of forms of the three types, and are structurally the same as the commonly occurring forms in U-R of the 16th century, that is, обыдва, обыдви in the direct cases and обохъ, etc. in the non-direct cases (Kernyc'kyj 1967, 169). Обохъ and обомъ reflect the paradigms of the cardinals '2,' '3,' and '4.'

6.2.2.1 Given this degree of formal differentiation, it is worth examining the forms in question in context, as follows:

Masculine or Common Gender (Plural)

N обои (2 times, *JU*; 286a,20–24): пытали Са҃дꙋкеєѡве . . . пытали и фарисеєѡве . . . : обои є пѡ̑стѹпныхъ своихъ мыслѧхъ обличены зостали 'the Saducees asked . . . , and the Pharisees asked . . . : both [groups] remained convinced of their perfidious thoughts.' Here the numeral is used alone, expressing "2 previously mentioned groups of people."

N обадва — (7 times, *JU*; 143a,18–19): обадва до гробѹ внесли и положили 'the two [of them] took [Jesus] to the grave and laid him [in it].' This form is also used alone, here in reference to Joseph and Nicodemus, and expresses "the two of them" (previously mentioned individuals).

G обоего — (2 times, *JU* and *Kazan'e*; 333a,26–7); до обоего . . . живота 'to both forms/kinds of life' (i.e., the here and now versus the eternal). обоего, a singular form, refers to two kinds of the same thing, and the complement животъ is necessary.

G обо́ихъ/-и́хъ — (8 times, *JU*; 276b,4–5); который злѹчилъ ро̑зно стоѧчих҆, а з҆ обоихъ одно ѹчинил '[he] who joined those standing apart, and out of them made one.' This form parallels обои above, in which we speak of "two groups" of people. On the basis of context alone it is not possible to determine whether or not the two different stresses are meaningful; it appears that they are in free variation.

G/L ѡбохъ/обѡхъ — (8 times, *JU* and *Kazan'e*; K12b,5 and K3b,24); ѡ ѡбох҆ сихъ животахъ 'about both of these lives,' and до ѡбохъ насъ 'to/towards both [the two] of us.' These constructions parallel обадва by expressing "both/the two of X"; they are used with complements, animate as well as inanimate.

D ѡбомъ — (4 times, *JU*; 257a,2–4); ѡбом҆ тєды загрозил Гдь, бѣсови . . . , а лѭнатикови 'God then threatened both [of them], the Devil . . . and the madman . . . .' Here it appears as though no complement is needed, except possibly for clarification; обомъ is used in the same way that обохъ is above: "both (of them)," here in reference to "persons."

D ѡбо́нимъ/обо́нимъ (3 times; *JU*; 327b,21–23); для тогожъ и цнѡты и злѡсти прекладаетъ и ознаймуетъ, ѡбонимъ свою заплату и нагороду покладаючи 'That is why he explains and makes known both virtue and evil, bestowing his recompense and reward on both of them.' Обонимъ refers to two things, in this case "virtue" and "evil"; in form and function this parallels the use of обонихъ above, occurring with the adjectival long form desinence. There is no apparent contextual contrast between end-stressed and penultimate-stress forms.

I обо́ними (1 time, *Kazan'e*; K9a,10); обоними вашими смыслами 'with the thoughts of both (groups).' Judging by previous examples with this long form referring to two groups this is preferable to interpreting the phrase as referring to "two thoughts."

I обѣма (1 time, JU; 416b,21–24); Двѣ речи злыи былы, которыи рожай людскїй былы опановалы, роскошъ, и смутокъ: тыми обѣма налѣганъ Гдь, незвытяженъ зосталъ 'There were two evil things which had mastered the human race, luxury and sadness: the Lord (being) pressed by those two (things), he remained unconquered.' Reference is to "both/the two" things (fem), previously mentioned; this example can be compared with обохъ and обомъ above.

6.2.2.2 *Neuter*

N/A обоє (8 times, JU; 236a,4–5); обоє теды тоє, о чомъ ихъ запыталъ 'both things, then, about which he asked them.' Grammatically neuter singular, this form may be interpreted as referring to two parts or sides of one question; in form and function this can be compared with обоєго above.

6.2.2.3 *Feminine*

N/A обѣдвѣ (4 times, JU; 283b,8–10); межи и҃шими мнѡгими сектами Жидѡ҃скими были немаль перⷣнѣйшїй двѣ, фарисейскаѧ и Саⷣдꙋкейскаѧ, обѣдвѣ однако Хв҃и протн҃ыи. 'Among the many other Jewish sects two were ['almost'] foremost, the Pharisean and the Sadducean, both equally repugnant to Christ.' Here again, the form обѣдвѣ is used in reference to two previously mentioned entities (this time groups, not individuals), and therefore definite, in contrast to the preceding indefinite двѣ.

6.2.2.4 Compare the following overview of the paradigms as used in the modern languages and CES:

	U	*Br*	*CES*	
			Masc	*Neut/Fem*
N-A	обидва (M/N)	óба/абодва	оба	обѣ
	обидві (F)	абóе		
	обоє			
G	обидвох	абóдвух	обою	
	обох	абаíх		
L	обох	абаíх		
D	обом	абаíм	обѣма	
I	обома	абаíмі	обѣма	

Polish

	Masc/pers	*Masc/non-pers+obj*	*Fem*
N	*obaj*	*oba*	*obie*
A	=G	=N	=N
G	*obu*	*obu*	*obu*
L	*obu*	*obu*	*obu*
D	*obu*	*obu*	*obu*
I	*obu,oboma,obiema*		
N	*obadwaj*	*obadwa*	*obydwie*
	obydwaj	*obydwa*	*obiedwie*
	[arch: o*badwa, obydwa*]		
A	=G	=N	=N
G	*obydwu*	------>	
	obydwóch	------> [arch: *obudwu, obudwóch*]	
L	*obydwu*	------>	
	obydwóch	------> [arch: *obudwu, obudwóch*]	
D	*obydwu*	------>	
	obydwom	------>	
I	*obydwoma*	------>	*obydwiema*

Polish has witnessed the most far-reaching development of all these languages, maintaining two wholly separate paradigms. The two sets of forms are differentiated by their use with substantives (*obaj* X etc. 'both X' etc.) or without such complements (*obadwaj* etc. 'both' or 'both of them'). The distinction between the forms обоє-обидва in CSU are not so clear: обидва appears to be used primarily without a complement, i.e., as "both of them," but not exclusively; with a complement обидва occurs mostly in frozen, set expressions, such as в обидва кінці 'round trip.' There is no separate form *oba/obaj as in Polish, but the form обоє is specifically used when referring to two persons (already mentioned) of different genders: обоє, і брат і сестра 'the [group of] two, the brother as well as the sister.' In CSBR both forms оба and the variant абодва are used without a complement, and are therefore unmarked; the use of абое in reference to two people of different genders is the same as in CSU, but this form is in addition applied to neuter substantives denoting animate beings: абое дзеці 'both children.'

As mentioned above, the long form adjectives are prescribed by GSPS; the use of plural desinences has long been attested, and these are still the norm in the oblique cases in CSR and CSBR. N обои is no longer used, and was common in 16th and 17th century Russian texts (Bogusławski 1966, 137–38). MS' forms, with the exception of the instrumental, generally correspond to those of CSU rather than of CSBR. Обоими is identical to the CSBR form except in the place of stress, as it follows GSPS; the occurrence of this form in *Kazan'e* rather than in JU also reflects its marked status in Smotryc'kyj's system (compare also the CSR form, with the same spelling and place of stress as MS' version). The use of singular adjectival endings is not mentioned by Kernyc'kyj 1967, Bulyka et al. 1988, or Bogusławski 1966; the archaic and learned status of these forms is evidenced by their presence in the B-R texts of Skaryna: обоє (злоє) and обоєго (ногьлавїѧ).

Collectives of the type двоє (etc.) are apparently not attested in the works of IV and PB. Оба 'both' only occurs in the instrumental form обєма in IV (cf. also двєма; 203), while several forms are attested in PB: G/L обоχъ (=MS), Am обєχъ, and Af обє (90).

6.3 *The Ordinal Numeral (Declined as Adjectives)*

6.3.1 *First.* Two competing roots, перв- and перш-, express "first" in MS. Their distribution among the texts is stylistically and contextually determined: in *Kazan'e* only the former are found (12 times), while both forms are present in JU. Neither form occurs in the preface to *Grammatiki*. The distribution of the two forms in JU reflects their status in MS' language: перв- occurs 26 times in JU, while перш- occurs a total of 101 times. In this text первый is limited to contexts of a biblical or otherwise specifically religious nature: первый чл҃вкъ А҆да́мъ (325a,21) 'Adam, the first man,' первоє свѧто (148b,14) 'the first feast day/holy day,' etc. Twice we find the form напєрш- (28a,16) 'the very first,' in which the superlative prefix на- occurs with the unmarked Ruthenian variant.

The ordinal пєрв- (< CES *pьrv-*) is found in the texts of all three Ruthenians, but is in the process of being supplanted by the newer formation пєршний (< *perv-* + comparative suffix *-š-* + adjective ending). Note that the corresponding Polish form is *pierwszy*, in which the consonant cluster *-vš-* was not simplified to *-š-* as it was in Ruthenian. Gröschel identifies the following forms of "first" in IV: пръвый, пєрвый, пєршний, and пръвѣйшний. The first and last of these are easily described as belonging to the Slavonic level (the last he calls "pseudo-Slavonic"), while пєршний is the new Ruthenian form. Gröschel does not relegate пєрвый to the status of a Slavonicism as пєршний was not in common use until the second half of the sixteenth century (1972, 205). It seems to me, however, that if the latter was indeed in common use at this time (and it appears that it was) then пєрвый necessarily must represent the marked (Slavonic/traditional) member of the opposition пєрвый-пєршний. The contextual distribution of these two forms in MS support such an assertion. As for PB, the first three forms cited for IV are also attested in his language (91).

6.3.2 *Second.* As in the expression of "first," there are two competing forms (втор- and дрꙋг-) expressing "second," of which the former is contextually marked as belonging to an elevated style of writing—as a Slavonicism. Only this form is used in *Kazan'e* (2 times), for instance in a biblical citation (K13b,16), while both втор- and дрꙋг- are used in JU (neither is attested in *Grammatiki*); the latter is the form now used in CSU and CSBR, as well as in Polish (drugi). The use of this doublet in JU parallels the case of пєрв-/пєрш- described above, since дрꙋг- may occur in all environments, while втор- is generally limited to marked environments such as второго своєго приєтѧ (292b,27–28) '(of) His Second Coming,' and in chapter headings in JU (as is пєрв-). The distribution alone of дрꙋг-/втор- in JU is not as indicative of the relative status of these forms, as it is in the case of пєрв-/пєрш-. The forms with дрꙋг- are found 11 times, versus 15 attestations of the marked втор-: in this instance context alone is critical. Finally, although дрꙋг- is commonly used to mean "second," depending on context this form may also express "other"; thus, if дрꙋг- is preceded by одинъ '1' rather than by пєрш- 'first,' it can only be interpreted as expressing "other" (e.g., 403a,22).

In IV вторый is the only form found for "second," while дрѹгий expresses only "other." Gröschel does not treat вторый as a Slavonicism, because it is used by IV in "volkssprachlichem Kontext" (contexts [in which] the spoken language [is used]); he cites similar data from Kernycʹkyj to support this assertion (1972, 205). In Berynda's *Leksykon*, however, второє is listed as a Slavonic headword, and is glossed as дрѹгоє; in SinSlav дрѹгій is the headword, glossed as Slavonic вторый. The use of дрѹг- in MS and the Slavonic coloration of вторый in PB and SinSlav suggest two possibilities: 1) IV mirrors a slightly earlier phase in the competition between the two forms, since by the teens of the 17th century there has been a definite shift in favor of дрѹгий in U-R; or 2) the shift took place slightly earlier in southwest U-R than in more northerly dialects, i.e., the replacement of вторый by дрѹгий took place in a South-to-North direction, coming to an end before reaching the territory of the present-day central Russian dialects. With respect to both of these possibilities (which do not necessarily contradict one another) MS and PB reflect the more advanced state of development in the southern dialects, while IV would reflect the situation in the north.

6.3.3 *Ordinals 3–10.* The ordinals from "third" to "tenth" are all represented in MS, with a variety of adjectival desinences:

трєт- '3rd' (the only soft-stem form, e.g., G трєтєго 65b,9)
чєтвєрт- '4th'
пѧт- '5th'
шєст-/шост- '6th'
сєм- '7th'
осм- '8th'
дєвѧт- '9th'
дєсѧт- '10th'

One Slavonic desinence is found in *Kazan'e*: G non-fem трєтїѧгѡ (K13a,14). These ordinals can be described as generally East Slavic; various regular phonetic features characteristic of the modern languages are not reflected (cekanne/dzekanne третий > Br трэці, prothetic v-

осмый > восмый, etc.) An exception is "6th": in **шєст**- (4 times), **шост**- (3 times) the former reflects the CES vowel, while the latter exhibits Ukr/Br [e] > [o] after hushings. In IV only **трєтий**, **чєтвєртый** and **пѧтый** are attested. The feminine form **трєтıа** is found in IV and PB (cf. **трєтѧа** in MS), in Gröschel's opinion reflecting the influence of Bulgarian orthography (1972, 205). The language of PB exhibits a greater number of these ordinals than IV: **трєт**-, **чєтвєрт**-, **пѧт**-, **шєст**-, **сєдм-/сєм-** (91).

6.3.4 *Other Ordinals.* Ordinals above "10" are relatively rare in Ruthenian texts. They are completely ignored in Bulyka et al. (1988, 127–44) and are only cursorily discussed in Kernyc'kyj 1967 (no ordinals of multiples of ten are mentioned by the latter: 176–77). In Smotryc'kyj's Ruthenian ordinals of multiples of ten can be formed with or without the suffix *-n-:*

одинадцат- '11th'
трь҇ıца҇н- '30th'
чотырдєсѧтн- '40th'
пѧтдєсѧт- '50th'
шєстдєсѧтн- '60th'

Forms with the suffix *-n-* are not cited in SSUM, and are not present in CSU or CSBR. They are not attested in the texts of IV or SinSlav, but one such form is used by PB (see below). Sreznevskij's *Materialy* cites forms with and without the suffix: **триდєсѧтьный** '30th' (III:994); but **чєтырдєсѧтый** '40th' (III:1514), **шєстьдєсѧтый** '60th' (III:1591). The basis for such forms clearly existed in CES, and they ought to be interpreted as archaisms in Smotryc'kyj's texts. No ordinal numerals above '10' are attested in the texts of IV; in PB, however, several do occur: **тринадєсѧт**- '13th,' **пѧтьнадєсѧт**- '15th,' **пѧтдєсѧтн**- '50th,' **сєдмдєсѧт**- '70th,' **тысѧ(ч)ны(й)** '1000th' (91).

6.4 *Other Numerical Formations*

6.41 Two examples of the numeral **дєсѧтокъ** 'a group of ten' are attested in Smotryc'kyj's texts; this substantive was common in U-R (SSUM for the early period) and B-R (HSBM): **три дєсѧтки**

(326a,23) '3 groups of 10,' and шєсть дєсѧткѡвъ (326a,25) '6 groups of 10' (see 6.4.2.1 below for the contexts in which these and following forms occur). This form is still current in the modern languages (U десяток, B дзесятак).

6.4.2 Smotryc'kyj frequently (12 times) uses the term двоѧкїй 'two-sided; of two varieties': двоѧкїй єстъ чл҃къ, двоѧкоє єстъ єго освѣчєнїє (95b,23–24) 'man is two-sided, two-sided is his education [*lit.* "illumination"].' Once the form троѧкїй is attested: троѧкїй конєцъ (82b,15) 'a three-sided end [end of three kinds].' This formation can be considered native Ruthenian: it is still found in all three East Slavic languages; троѧкїй is also present in SinSlav.

6.4.2.1 Very similar in form to двоѧкїй and троѧкїй is a set of numerical forms characterized by a formant *-rak-* in place of *-jak-:* these forms are patterned after corresponding collective numerals. All but one are based on numerals including and larger than "10." Some function adjectivally while others are formally adverbs:

чворако (4 times) 'occurring in 4 kinds/forms; 4-fold' (adverb). Here it is not difficult to identify Polish *čv-* (cf. Pol *czwarty* 'fourth'): the Polish collective *czworo* serves as a model for this form, and CSP also retains the form *czworaki*. In addition, the neuter adjective чворакоє (397b,5) 'the fourfold' is attested once.

дєсѧтєрако (1 time) 'occurring in 10 kinds; 10-sided' (adverb): this is clearly based on the corresponding East Slavic collective numeral (дєсѧтєр-), but it is in Polish rather than in East Slavic that this form is still current: *dziesięcioraki*. It is cited in HSBM as occurring twice in the 17th century.

тридцаторакїй (2 times) 'of 30 kinds; 30-sided': the corresponding collective is present in CSP and in CSU, viz. trzydzieścioro and тридцятеро.

шєстдєсѧторакїй (2 times) 'of 60 kinds; 60-sided'; formed in the same manner as the preceding.

сторакїй (2 times) 'of 100 kinds; 100-sided' is of special interest because the sequence *-or-* is not based on the collective, for the vowel is part of the stem: here we might posit an analogical formation *sto* + *orak* > сторак-, with deletion of the first of the vocalic elements.

тысѧчорако (1 time) 'of 1000 kinds; 1000-sided' (adverb): in this form the hardened stem-final affricate *č* allows the occurrence of *-orak-* (for an earlier variant *-erak-).

6.4.2.2 The existence of the modern Polish forms *czworaki* and *dziesięcioraki* offers support for identifying this entire class of numerical formations in Smotryc'kyj's language as "Polish" in origin. The frequent use of these forms nevertheless allows the reader to treat them as part of the Ruthenian system, and specifically late Ruthenian, since they are not present in SSUM; the presence of десѧтерако in HSBM (the volumes in which the others might be contained have not yet appeared) indicates that they are general Ruthenian and not specifically U-R.

6.4.2.3 Examples: 1) А вставши Закхей рекл҄ къ Гдꙋ, ото половицꙋ маетностїй моихъ, Пане, даю ѹбогимъ, а єслимъ кого вчомъ скривдилъ, ѿдаю чворако (392a,7–9) 'And rising Zakxei said to the Lord, Oh Lord, behold I give half of my belongings to the poor, and if I have done wrong to anyone, I shall give fourfold.' 2) трицатоoракїй овоцъ, вѣрꙋ, мовѧтъ, значитъ, бо три десѧтки, Трцꙋ Бжскихъ особъ выражаютъ. Шестдесѧторакїй овоцъ ... шесть цнотъ єѵглскихъ выражаютъ ... сторакїй овоцъ значитъ, мовѧтъ, досконалость (326a,22–326b,2) 'Fruit of thirty kinds (thirty-fold) means faith, they say, for three tens represent the Trinity of divine persons. Fruit of sixty kinds (sixty-fold) represents the six Apostolic virtues. And fruit of 100 kinds means, they say, perfection.'

6.4.3 The forms трицатокротный (326a,16–17) 'occurring 30 times; 30-fold,' шестдесѧтокротныи (326a,10) 'occurring 60 times; 60-fold,' стокротныи (326a,2) 'occurring 100 times; 100-fold,' all contain the formant крот 'time, instance,' and can be compared with the adverbial form частокроть 'frequently' cited in chapter 7. Gröschel describes the compound двакрот in IV as "Multiplikationsadverb" and labels it a Polonism because of *krot* (< *kroć*; 1972, 203). An equivalent to these forms is found in CSU, except that the vowel *a* is found in place of o: CSU стократний (this is the only one of the three forms cited in SUM). Consequently the adjectival formations attested in MS may be treated as Polonisms; the parallelism between this group of forms and that described in 6.4.2.1 (i.e., including the numerals '30,' '60,' and '100') is not coincidental, as they all occur in the context of the same subject matter: the compounds with кροт occur in descending order (100-60-30), followed by the compounds with -ορак- in ascending order (30-60-100).

CHAPTER SEVEN

The Adverb

7.0 The morphological class of the "adverb" includes a vast number of forms which must be treated as members of two distinct subcategories: those described according to their lexical source (for example, deadjectival adverbs) and those described according to their function or semantic expression (for example, adverbs of time, place, etc.). There is overall agreement between MS and IV with regard to the formation and use of deadjectival adverbs. Only a few examples are provided, since this is a morphological and not a lexical study (7.1 below). All other adverbial forms are listed and described individually.[1]

7.1 *The Deadjectival Adverb*

The CES ending in deadjectival adverbs was *-o* for hard stems and *-e* for soft stems. By the 16th-17th centuries *-e* is regularly found in adverbs formed from originally hard-stem adjectives; *-e* adverbs were most widely used in Ruthenian texts during the seventeenth century, after which *-o* again predominated (CSU; CSBR -a, reflecting *akanne*). Hard-stem adverbs in *-e* are still found in the southwest Ukrainian (especially Carpathian) dialects, while the literary language has very few such forms: for example, literary добре 'well,' зле 'badly.'

In Smotryc'kyj's texts there is a preponderance of forms with *-e*, a total of 1,066 forms versus 805 adverbs in *-o*. The ending *-e* is clearly productive in MS, and in Ruthenian in general, because it can occur with lexemes of East Slavic, Slavonic, as well as of Polish origin. It is therefore a stylistically unmarked, neutral, common Ruthenian feature. Bevzenko et al. state that the forms in *-e* never predominated in the

---

[1] The language of Pamva Berynda is included in this study insofar as information can be culled from his *Leksykon*. The reader is reminded that Diadiakin-Leeming's work focuses on the inflectional categories of his morphology.

(U-)R period (ibid.), while Bezpal'ko states that they did (cited by Gröschel 1972, 308). Judging by data from MS' texts, as well as by B-R data, it appears that this ending did in fact predominate in the seventeenth century (Kramko 1988, 293). In contrast to MS, the ending *-o* predominates in the texts of IV, occurring 128 times versus 96 forms with *-e*. This preference for *-o*, while not overwhelming, is nevertheless substantial. Although *-e* tended to predominate in 17th-century Ruthenian, IV is proof that this does not translate into absolute dominance in the texts of every writer. It is possible that *-o* was more important in IV's native dialect, or that the influence of Polish played a greater role in the language of MS and others. It is generally agreed that the widespread use of the desinence *-e* in U-R and B-R can be ascribed to Polish influence (Gröschel 1972, 307–310; Kramko ibid.).

7.1.1 *Adverbs with the ending -e.* A few examples suffice to demonstrate that this desinence is productive with lexemes of any provenance: рєчивистє (485b,24) 'in fact, really,' запєвнє (K8b,4) 'surely,' дбалє (K21a,8) 'mindfully, carefully' (clearly Polonisms: CSP *rzeczywiście, zapewne, dbale*), вдѧчнє (K14a,20) 'thankfully,' значнє (30a,24) 'considerably,' вѣрнє (K3b,13) 'faithfully,' истотнє (K19a,9) 'essentially,' щасливє (K27a,20) 'happily,' ѡткрытє (161a,30) 'openly' (< past passive participle ѡткрытый), мꙋдрє (28a,25) 'wisely,' злє (38a,1) 'badly,' добрє (38a,5) 'well.' This last example is in formal opposition to добрѣ (K20a,16), in which the ending -ѣ is marked as a Slavonicism; this lone example of -ѣ occurs in a biblical quotation (1 Tim 5:17). We note also the occurrence of the desinence *-e* with Slavonic lexemes such as блг҃одарнє (K14a,10) 'gratefully,' and бєврємєнє (K20b,3) 'in an untimely fashion.' Three forms worthy of note are:

далєцє (8 times, e.g., 294a,25) '(so) far . . . ' < *dalek-*
вєлицє (2 times, e.g., 318b,27) 'greatly' < *velik-*
высоцє (9 times, e.g., 287b,11) 'highly' < *vysok-*

These are best explained as reflecting original velar + *ě, resulting in the mutation of the stem-final velar *k* > *c*; the spelling thus reflects B-R or Polish rather than U-R.

7.1.2 *Adverbs with the ending -o.* The originally hard-stem ending *-o* is graphically -ѡ in *Kazan'e* and in the preface as well as the body of *Grammatiki*, whereas it is simply -о in JU; this difference is orthographic only, and was discussed in 2.0.3. Examples: долго (29b,16) 'long,' частѡ (K11a,16) 'often,' скоро (44b,19) 'soon,' легкѡ (K14b,1) 'easily,' близко (30a,27) 'near,' прїемно (76b,2) 'pleasing,' лацнѡ (K2b,11) 'easily,' моцнѡ (K17a,17) 'strongly, firmly.' Occasionally a lexeme is attested with both endings, for example, бѣднѡ (K14a,19) and бѣдне (K17a,8) 'poorly,' нерοвнѡ (K19a,16) 'by far, considerably; unequalled' and ровне (K12a,7) 'equally.' In these examples context plays no apparent role in stipulating the use of one or the other desinence.

7.1.2.1 *Adverbial forms with the suffix -sk-.* Adverbs from adjectives with the suffix *-sk-* are occasionally formed by means of the marker *-o*, presumably by analogy with other hard-stem adverbs (see above).[2] These forms are not uncommon in the Ruthenian period, and the following are attested in MS' language:

братерско (307b,14)	'in a fraternal/brotherly manner'
бозско (317a,5–6)	'as, in the manner of God'
царско (300b,23)	'as a king, in a kingly fashion'
непрїятелско (397a,1–2)	'in inimical fashion'
ѿцовско (255a,13)	'as a father'
пастырзско (255a,12–13)	'in a pastoral fashion, as a pastor'
властелско (2 x, e.g., 118a,14)	'as a lord'

All of these are cited by Kramko as adverbs that are commonly found in B-R; бозско is cited in HSBM, but the only example given is this one from JU. Note that Kramko describes this adverbial form as characteristic of Smotryc'kyj's *Kazan'e* (1988, 298)—it is only attested in JU, however. While such a detail might ordinarily be overlooked, the interpretation of the status of this feature in Ruthenian is directly affected: if adverbs in *-sk-o* are are characteristic of *Kazan'e* they can be assigned to a higher, literary style. If they are characteristic of JU they

2 These adverbial forms are listed together because of the presence of the formant *-o*. All other adverbs formed from adjectives in *-skij* are cited according to their meanings and functions.

ought to be treated as elements that are more widely used and understood by the Ruthenian public. For Vyšens'kyj's texts Gröschel only cites one such form, viz. мирєко; all other adverbs based on forms with the suffix *-sk-* have the adverbial ending *-i*, which Gröschel describes as the old non-feminine instrumental plural of short form adjectives (e.g., мирєки; 1972, 311). Ruthenian *-sk-o* is no longer current in the modern languages: in CSBR we find the marker -скі, e.g., братэрскі (cf. IV), in CSU по-Х-ськи, e.g., по-братерськи, in CSP *po X-sku,* e.g., *po bratersku;* this last formation is also attested in MS (cf. 7.4.1 below).

7.2 *Adverbs of Time and Place*

This category contains such a large number of adverbial forms that it must be subdivided into: 1) prefixal formations, 2) forms containing the common roots -єл-/-ол-, -ѹд-, -огд- (including prefixed adverbs with these roots), 3) adverbs with the suffix -дє, and 4) others. This last grouping includes all of the most commonly used adverbs of time and place, for example, 'here,' 'now,' 'today,' etc. Further subdivisions, such as, a separate group for adverbial constructions containing the prefix нѣ-, were avoided, because some of these forms contain roots subsumed under group 2 (7.2.2 below).

7.2.1 *Prefixal Formations*

вдолжъ (456b,23) 'along, lengthwise' is common Ruthenian, and is attested in FS (note the secondary polnoglasie form вдолож in SSUM); вдолж is extant in CSU and CSBR, but is lacking in CSR (cf. CSR вдоль).

вкоро́тцє (19 times, e.g., K18b,20) 'in short, briefly' [< preposition въ 'in' + коротцє 'short'] is a Ruthenian polnoglasie variant of Pol *wkrótce*, and is used in JU and *Kazan'e*. The Polish form expresses 'soon, presently,' a meaning which does not agree with the Ruthenian version (e.g., in вкоротцє рєкши 'briefly stated [*lit.* stating]'); CSR вкратце agrees semantically, and represents the Slavonic variant (cf. OCS въ кратъцѣ). The form attested in MS is cited by

Kramko as a Polonism phonetically adapted to the Ruthenian system (1988, 295); вкоротце is not found in the language of IV, SinSlav, PB, FS, nor is it present in CSU and CSBR.

внꙋтръ (1 time: 344b,12) 'inside,' used in MS with a verb of motion; it is found in IV, FS, and CSBR (but not in CSU; cf. CSP *wewnątrz*). See 8.1 on the *preposition* внꙋтр; also звнꙋтра below.

впереⷣ (23 times, e.g., 11b,7; оуперед 201a,20) 'beforehand, earlier, ahead of time; ahead' [< preposition въ + передъ preposition 'before']. This adverb functions as an adverb of time as well as of place: впереⷣ нѣшто розмовилъ (K7b,3) 'he said something beforehand/earlier'; . . . которыи южъ давно впереⷣ бѣгꙋтъ (111b,6–7) '[those] who have already long (since) been running ahead'; and впереⷣ видячи (511a,1–2) 'seeing ahead.' In CSU this adverb is considered rare, the standard form is наперед; наперад is also found in CSBR, and appears to occur somewhat more frequently than уперад. In both modern languages, however, уперед/уперад is used in reference to time as well as to space, as it is in MS. Since вперед is attested in MS, IV, P-M, and Sin-Slav, it can be described as native Ruthenian; one example of the Polonism впроⷣ occurs in MS (139a,10), as well as in *Aleksandryja* (Leeming 1968, 302).

вподовжъ (86b,9) 'lengthwise' [< preposition въ + preposition по + adverb должъ < *dolg* 'long'] is found once, in a description of Moses parting the Red Sea with his staff: чирвоное море вподовжъ оꙋдаривши 'striking the Red Sea lengthwise.' This adverb is still attested in CSU, and is defined in SUM as 'уздовж'; it is not found in CSBR, but this one particular example from JU is included in the HSBM. It is not attested in the other Ruthenian sources consulted.

впродъ See впередъ above.

врихлѣ/врыхлѣ/врыхле (8 times, e.g.64b,17) 'quickly, shortly' appears to be a Polonism that is no longer extant in CSP. It also is not extant in CSU or CSBR. *Wrychle* is cited in Reczek 1968 as an Old Polish form, and it is also included in HSBM: we note that the variants врихле, врыхле, and врихлѣ listed in the latter are almost exactly the variants present in MS. The final vowel etymologically is *-ě: the variant *-e* can be explained either as a reflection of the Polish form or as the B-R reflex of *ě. (The latter is more likely, based on Old Polish.) This form is not attested in IV, nor is it in PB (but cf. скоро, glossed as рыхлѡ, борзѡ).

вслѣдъ (260a,16) 'after (space), following' [< въ + слѣдъ 'path, track'] is extant in CSU and CSBR as an adverb and as a preposition (on the preposition вслѣдъ in MS see 8.1); this form is not attested in FS, IV, or SS, nor is it cited in SSUM (but cf. IV наслѣди, 303).

вспакъ (302a,24) 'back(wards)' is a Polonism. It is now extant only in CSP; in addition to occurring in MS' texts, this form is attested in SinSlav but lacking elsewhere.

допо́зна (249b,17) 'until late' is general Ruthenian, but the place of stress suggests U-R rather than the B-R variant. Compare CSU допі́зна, CSPR дапазна́; Kramko cites this form from JU in his study of the B-R adverb (1988, 296–97).

заразъ (120 times, e.g., 33b,26) 'immediately, right away' [< preposition за 'for' + разъ 'time'] is extant in CSU, CSBR, and CSP. Richhardt considers the form to be a Polonism (1957, 113), and Gröschel agrees on the basis of the initial stress which characterizes the lexeme with this meaning in the modern East Slavic languages. In MS all examples but one have intial stress; the lone instance of final ('Ruthenian') stress is found in *Grammatiki* (IIIb,17). A variant with final stress is also extant in CSU and CSBR, but the meaning is slightly different, expressing 'at one time, simultaneously'; the one form attested with final stress in MS is semantically identical to за́разъ. The end-stressed CSU/CSBR form thus does not seem to reflect an earlier distinction. We might be tempted to interpret this one example as evidence of the higher level of 'Ruthenianness' of the form зара́зъ, but in view of the large number of attestations of за́разъ, one single form with final stress can only be treated as an exception to the rule. The currency of the form with initial stress in the modern languages and in the language of MS' contemporaries (SinSlav, P-M, PB: as a gloss for абиє) reflects its status in the Ruthenian system.

затым (5 times, e.g., 63b,19) 'then' [preposition za 'after' + instrumental of то 'that'] is common in East Slavic: it is attested in CSBR, CSU (described as 'colloquial' in SUM), CSR (затем), FS, and SSUM.

з҄ верхꙋ (391a,27) 'on/from the top' is extant in CSU, CSBR, and CSP. In MS this adverbial construction is written separately, following the Polish model, while it is written as one form in the modern languages. Зверхꙋ is attested in FS, SinSlav, and is cited by Kramko.

з҄ внꙋтра (2 times, e.g., 391a,26) 'on/from the inside' is not present in IV, SinSlav, SSUM, or FS, but does occur as a gloss for възнꙋтрꙋдꙋ in PB; there is no such adverb in CSU, but знутры is extant in CSBR.

здалека (13 times, only in JU, e.g., 42b,17) 'from afar' [< preposition зъ 'from' + далека, the short form G non-fem of *dalek-* 'distant']. Forms of this type are quite common in MS' texts, especially in JU. Gröschel identifies this formation as Polish, whereas the construction по + dative can be identified as native U-R (1972, 312); regardless of the ultimate origin of this construction, it is clearly productive in Ruthenian. Здалека is in Kramko's list of commonly occurring adverbs of this type in (B-)R (1988, 296), and is also found in FS; it is not attested in SinSlav. Among the modern languages, the identical form is extant in CSU (but different stress: зда́лека), but здалёк/здалёку in CSBR. CSP preserves the origin of the adverb by keeping the preposition orthographically separate from the adjective: *z daleka.*

здáвна (4 times, in *Kazan'e* and JU, e.g., K5b,5) 'long since' [< зъ + давна, 'previous, (of) long ago']. This particular form is cited as B-R by Kramko; it occurs in U-R texts as early as the fourteenth century (SSUM), appears in the language of FS, and is extant in CSU and CSBR (здаўна) as well as in CSP (*z dawna*); cf. CSR издавна with the older element *iz-*. In this instance place of stress indicates that the form is U-R. The CSBR variant has final stress, while initial stress is characteristic of the CSU form. Здавна is not attested in IV.

знадворѧ (2 times, e.g., 257b,14) 'from without' (see next form).

знꙋтра (4 times, e.g., 257b,13) 'from within' and the preceeding from are not attested in modern or Ruthenian sources, but appear to be formed according to the familiar pattern зъ + G (здавна, etc.). That they are not unknown in Ruthenian is clear from Kramko's study, in which these two forms are specifically cited as native (B-)R constructions (1988, 301); forms very similar to them are also still current in CSU (знадвору) and CSBR (знадворку, знутры).

зпочаткꙋ (462a,7–8) 'from the beginning, at first' is extant in CSBR and CSU, CSP (*z początku*), SinSlav, and Kramko, but not in IV.

зрѣ҇ка (2 times, only in JU, e.g., 382a,12) 'rarely, sometimes' is found in this form in CSU (cf. зрідка but CSBR зредку), SinSlav, and Kramko, but is lacking in IV; the older form изредка is extant in Russian but cited as rare for CSU (SUM).

назадъ (4 times) 'back' [< на + задъ 'back, rear'], as in назадъ вернꙋтисѧ неможетъ (K19a,12) 'cannot return [back],' is general Slavic.

наконецъ (10 times in *Kazan'e* and JU, e.g., K9b,8) 'finally, in the end' [< preposition на + конецъ 'end'], is not found in CSU, CSBR, CSP, the lexica of PB or SinSlav, or in SSUM, and is not listed by Gröschel as occurring in IV; it does occur in Russian. While it may not be possible simply to assign this lexeme to the Slavonic level, its distribution in the modern languages and the fact that it was not used in Ruthenian indicate that наконецъ belonged at the very least to a relatively high style; note, for example, the occurrence of this form in наконецъ єдиноро̑ныѝ єи Сн҃ъ, Гд҃ь твой . . . (K23b,14) 'finally her only-begotten son, your Lord . . . ,' in which the other lexemes are certainly marked by their phonetic shape (e.g., *jedin-*) as well as by their occurrence in a religious (and formulaic) context.

напєрє̂ (2 times in JU, 75b,19–20 and 429b,18) 'in the first place, first' is widely used in East Slavic: CSU наперед, CSBR наперад, FS, SSUM, and IV. Kramko identifies this adverb as a borrowing from Polish (CSP *naprzód*). In MS one form is unstressed (напєрє̂ 75b,19–20), while the other carries stress on на́-. In the two-syllable Polish form *naprzód* the prefix is stressed, thus MS' form reflects Polish stress, as well as the replacement of Polish *-przód* by East Slavic -пєрєд. The Polonizing form напродъ is attested twice in *Kazan'e* (K9b,5 and K15b,12): the use of this form without rendering *-przód* as -пєрєд is another reflection of the higher style of this text.

напєрєдѣ (100b,18) 'before (place), ahead (time)' is common Ruthenian: CSU напереді, CSBR наперадзе; it is present in FS, but is lacking in SS, SSUM, and IV.

напотомъ (18 times, e.g., 167b,10–11) 'afterwards' [< preposition на + preposition по + locative of то 'that']. Although this form is not attested in the modern languages (CSU, CSBR, CSP) it was evidently quite common in the Ruthenian period: it is attested in SinSlav (на потим), FS, and PB (under тажє), and is cited in SSUM. It is not attested in IV (but cf. потомъ below).

напродъ *See* напєрєдъ above.

натыхъмѣстъ (32 times, e.g., 80a,15; only in JU) ‘immediately, at once’ is a Polonism that was common in Ruthenian texts as of the end of the sixteenth century (Kramko 1988, 304): cf. CSP *natychmiast*. The late appearance of this form in Ruthenian is reflected in its absence in SSUM and FS; натыхъмѣстъ is also not attested in SinSlav or in IV.

одаль (321b,22) ‘from afar’ is not attested in any of the Ruthenian sources consulted, nor is it extant in CSU or CSBR. The form is extant in Ukrainian dialects, however, suggesting that it be treated as a dialect feature present in MS’ language.

оподаль (2 times, e.g., 27b,9) ‘nearby’ [< о + по + даль ‘distance’] is present in modern Polish and as a dialect form in Ukrainian, but lacking in CSBR, FS, IV, and SSUM; it is attested in SinSlav.

переⷣтымъ (e.g., 334a,12) ‘formerly, before’ [< preposition передъ ‘before’ + instrumental of то ‘that’] is extremely common in JU, but does not occur in *Kazan'e*; this form reflects Pol *przedtem,* which expresses the same meaning. Analogous forms do not occur in CSU or CSBR. This form is not cited for IV and is not included in SinSlav, but does occur in P-M.

поⷣчасъ (2 times, e.g., 29b,1) ‘in the meantime, meanwhile’ [< preposition подъ + часъ ‘time’] is extant in CSBR, but not in CSU or CSP. It is not attested in the language of Smotryc'kyj’s contemporaries, FS, or in SSUM. This form is more often used as a preposition in MS (cf. 8.1).

поннѣ (2 times, e.g., K4a,4) ‘at this time, up to now’ [< preposition по ‘after, about’ + adverb нынѣ]. (See нынѣ below). Gröschel states that this formation is characteristic neither of CSU nor of Slavonic, and that it therefore gives the impression of belonging to the vernacular (1972, 321). This adverb is lacking in CSBR, as it is in the language of other Ruthenians, but is cited for CSR as “obsolete” (Oxford Russian-English Dictionary); the latter fact and its occurrence in

Kazan'e rather than in JU suggests that MS used понн҃ѣ as an element of higher style.

потомъ (92 times, e.g., K15b,12) 'then, afterwards' [< по 'after' + locative of то 'that'] is general Slavic: cf. CSU потім, CSBR потым, CSP *potem*. All of these forms are attested in U-R documents of the fourteenth-fifteenth centuries, according to SSUM; потомъ is CES (> CSU potim), while CSBR потым reflects the later Belarusian locative non-feminine form of той. Stress is final in MS, but penultimate stress in the CSU and CSBR forms may indicate the influence of Polish. Note also CSR потóм.

7.2.1.1 A comparison of the distribution of adverbs with a prefixed з- (including also adverbs of manner здробна, злегка, зособна, and зтрѹдна noted in 8.4 below) reveals that they were not common in Old Ruthenian (only зособна, is cited in SSUM), and that they were frequently used in the Ruthenian period (all are cited by Kramko). On the basis of these few examples it appears that this construction should be termed U-R rather than B-R. Only two of the forms are retained in CSBR, whereas five are found in CSU; since only three occur in Polish, one cannot describe the entire category as typical specifically of that language.

7.2.2 *Commonly Occurring Roots:* -ел-/-ол-, -ѹд-, -огд-

всюды (31 times, only in JU, e.g., 66a,14) 'everywhere' is common Ruthenian, and is found in CSU and CSBR. Its status as an unmarked feature of the Ruthenian language is reinforced by the occurrence of всюды as a definition of Slavonic везде in PB (see above); in SinSlav we accordingly find всюды defined as весде. Kramko states that всюды is used more frequently in (B-)R than the older variant везде, while всюдѹ is identified with the Slavonic literary tradition (1988, 278–79); the latter is the variant attested in language of FS' texts, while neither occurs in IV.

доко́ль (432a,15) 'whither, to where?' [<preposition до 'to' + коль] is a native Ruthenian element, retained in Ukrainian dialects as до́кіль (for literary доки: SUM) and in CSBR as даку́ль. Compare отколь/оттоль below. The place of stress in MS agrees with the CSBR rather than with the CSU. In this and similar forms, the final palatalized consonant *-l'* is a contraction of *-l[i],* which ultimately goes back to *-lě* (cf. доколѣ in OB). This form does occur in SinSlav (докȣль) and in FS (доколє), but it is not found in IV.

иногды (47 times, e.g., 62b,4; K21b,10) 'sometimes, at times.' The ending -ы allows for an interpretation of this form as one that was current in Ruthenian: cf. Slavonic иногда 'on one occasion,' CSU иногда 'sometimes.' In CSU the form іноді does occur ([g] > [h] > ø, final ě > [i]), but it is commonly supplanted by інколи. The lexeme иногды does not occur in IV, but is cited in SSUM. Although it is not found in CSBR, according to Kramko it was widely used in (B-)R (1988, 289). This adverb and the marked variant иногда are both present in the language of FS.

инȣды (434b,20) 'elsewhere.' This is a Ruthenian form that corresponds to the Slavonicism инȣдȣ; it is attested in early Ruthenian texts (SSUM, FS), but is less common in the Ruthenian period of Smotryc'kyj. This adverb is not attested in IV or SS.

коли (e.g., 47a,6–7) 'when' was originally an adverb, but may function either as an adverb or as a conjunction (see chapter 8); use of коли in MS in this latter function is more frequent than as an adverb. Although it is occasionally difficult to make an absolute distinction between these two functions, there are clear examples of its adverbial function, for instance in the passage колижєсмо тѧ видѣли лакнȣчого, и накормили? (47a,6–7) 'when did we see you hungering and [did we] feed [you]?' The same adverbial use is documented in P-M, e.g., in text no. 29 (Struminsky 1984, 34), while in IV it apparently only serves as a conjunction (348). Note also SinSlav **коли** '**єгда, когда**,' and Berynda's *Leksykon* **єгда** which is glossed as '**Ґды, когда, коли**.' Both functions are retained in CSU коли and CSBR колі.

кꙋда́ (1 time: 544a,24) 'whither, to which place' can be identified as Slavonic in opposition to Ruthenian **кꙋды** (cf. final *-a* in **иногда**); the Ruthenian form is also attested once in MS (38a,4), and is retained in CSU as well as in CSBR. Gröschel refers to **кꙋда́** in IV as a 'Ukrainian' element corresponding to Slavonic **камо** (1972, 317); both forms are lacking in PB, but he defines Slavonic **камѡ** as '**гдє**.' The marked status of **кꙋда́** in MS is supported by its presence in modern Russian as well as by its phonetic shape. Ruthenian **кꙋды** also occurs once in the complex form **кꙋдыко̑вєк** (29b,27–30a,1) 'to whichever place.'

кꙋды *See* **кꙋда́** above.

мимо (350a,11) 'past' occurs primarily as a preposition in the texts of MS (see 8.1), but it is also used once in an adverbial function: **шли мимо** 'they walked past/by.' This dual function is retained in CSBR and CSU. Gröschel does not mention this form with respect to IV.

нєкогда (K20a,4–5) 'never' [< negative particle **нє** + **когда** 'when'] is a Slavonic form which is attested only once, in *Kazan'e*, in a quotation from the book of Exodus (19:24?): **да нєкогда ѿ҇стꙋпитъ ѿ҇ нихъ Гдь҇** 'lest the Lord leave them.' Compare **нѣколи** below, and the indefinite form **нєкогда** 'once' in IV (316); **нєкогда** is the form used in OB.

нѣко́ли (74 times, e.g., 193b,18; once in *Kazan'e*) 'never' [< **нѣ** + **коль**] is the common Ruthenian form, and corresponds to CSU ніколи/CSBR ніколі. Compare this adverb with the following form, which differs from **нѣко́ли** only in the place of stress. This adverb is present in P-M.

нѣ́коли (244a,18) meaning 'once' is also attested but once. Just as the stressed particle **нѣ́-** is instrumental in the formation of indefinite pronouns, it also forms an indefinite adverb of time in opposition to the negative adverb нѣко́ли (above). Compare CSU ні́коли which expresses the lack of time ('there is no time' = CSR не́когда); in CSBR this meaning is present as well, but in that language ні́колі can also express 'once,' 'sometimes.' Gröschel distinguishes Slavonic нѣколи 'sometimes' from 'Ukrainian' нѣколи 'never' (in which ně- replaces *ni-: 1972, 317) based on meaning alone (his forms from IV do not reflect place of stress).

нѣѿко́ль (3 times, e.g., 226a,5; only in JU) 'not from anywhere, from nowhere' [< нѣ + preposition ot 'from' + коль] reflects the native Ruthenian pattern "negative + preposition + interrogative." It is not present in IV. This form is essentially preserved in CSU and CSBR, with some expected phonetic changes: CSU нівідкіля (in which the final vowel is retained under stress), Br. ніадкуль; the place of stress in MS may be considered 'B-R.' Cf. отколь below. Note, on the spelling of the preposition '*ot,*' see 8.1.

ѿколь (28, e.g., 127a,13) 'whence' [< от 'from' + коль] is common Ruthenian. Compare CSU відкіль, відкіля, CSBR адкуль; CSU відколи is defined as 'since when,' with reference to time. Compare also IV отколѧ (p. 317), and MS оттоль below. In SinSlav ѿколь, ѿколѧ is glossed as ѿкꙋдꙋ 'whence'; Berynda's *Leksykon* glosses Slavonic ѿкꙋдꙋ as ѿкꙋль, ѿколѧ, reflecting elements of Ukrainian as well as of Belarusian. The final palatalized consonant -l′ < -li is described by Gröschel as a feature of the vernacular ("volkssprachlich," ibid.).

ѿсель (5 times, only in JU, e.g., 176b,6) 'hence, from here' [< от + сель 'this place'] corresponds to CSU відсіль, відсіля 'from here,' CSBR адсюль (next to адгэтуль). This particular form is not mentioned by Gröschel. An interesting dichotomy is presented by the evidence provided by SSUM and FS: in both of these sources the vowel-final form is attested (отселѣ and отселе, respectively), but the former functions as an adverb of time, while the latter agrees with MS, CSU, and CSBR as an adverb of place. In FS it also appears to be marked as belonging to a higher stylistic level, while the presence of відсіль, адсюль in CSU and CSBR, as well as the lack of a marked context in MS, preclude such an interpretation for the form in Ruthenian. See ѿсюль below.

ѿсюль (2 times, only in JU, e.g., 408b,12) 'hence, from here' must be interpreted as another form of ѿсель: it can be explained as reflecting either the Ukrainian development of [e] > [ju] in closed syllables (which eventually developed further to [i]: відсіль) or as the B-R variant. CSBR retained the form attested in MS, appearing to reflect an intermediate stage of the Ukrainian development *e > [i]. Shevelov treats such forms as phonologically independent variants when he writes (in reference to відтіль, відкіль): "[forms with the vowel i] may have been U[krainian] substitutes for B[ela]r[usian] u forms . . . widely used in the M[iddle] U[krainian] and especially in the E[arly] MU period" (1979, 610). Very interesting in this regard is the attestation of this form vis-à-vis ѿсель (above): whereas it is attested in SSUM and FS, ѿсюль is not. If ѿсюль does indeed reflect a phonetic change (rather than a substitution for ѿсель), then the Ruthenian of SSUM is too early for the reflection of this change, and Skaryna's written language generally conforms to more traditional spelling norms. Further evidence that ѿсель and ѿсюль are in fact variants of the same form is provided by SinSlav, in which the latter is attested while the former is not: ѿсюль is defined as 'отзде, отсюдꙋ' 'from here.' ѿсюль is not attested in IV.

ѿтамъто̂ (3 times, only in JU, e.g., 206a,7) 'thence, from there' is a variant of ѿтоль (see below) which appeared in 16th- to 17th-century Ruthenian under the influence of Polish (Kramko 1988, 283). The example cited here occurs in a biblical passage in MS, supporting its identity as a Polonism. It is lacking in IV and SinSlav.

ѿтоль (35 times, e.g., 62a,20) 'thence' [< от + толь 'there'] corresponds to ѿколь and ѿсєль/ѿсюль as CSU відтіль does to відкіль and відсіль, and as CSBR адтуль does to адкуль and адсюль. In IV Gröschel identifies the two forms оттолѧ and оттоль (1972, 317).

сюда (6 times, only in JU, e.g., 156b,5) 'hither, to this place' may be considered a learned, if not Slavonic, variant on the basis of final *-a*: in both CSU and CSBR the current form is сюди (but cf. Rus сюда); the occurrence of сюда in biblical passages opening a new reading offers support for such an interpretation (156b,5 and 234a,9). In PB as well as SinSlav the Ruthenian form сюды is cited, in the former under the Slavonic head word сѣмо, in the latter сюды is defined as сѣмо (which is also the form used in OB). In FS сюда is used along with other clear Slavonicisms, while it is not attested in IV (but cf. отсюдꙋ, 318). For this form, the following hierarchy seems appropriate: Ruthenian сюды—learned сюда—Slavonic сѣмо.

тогды (194 times, e.g., 39b,9) 'then, at that time' may be classified as common Ruthenian. Compare the CSU and CSBR forms, in which the pharyngeal was lost: CSU тоді, CSBR тады. The form [tohdy] is still attested in modern southwest Ukrainian (Gröschel 1972, 316–17) as well as in some Belarusian dialects (TSBM). The final vowel -ы is one indicator of the stylistic level of this form, since final -а is found in the corresponding Slavonic version; in Berynda's *Leksykon* the headword тогда is defined as тогды. Cf. CSR тогда, representing the Slavonic variant. The importance of тогды and потом in Smotryc'kyj's language may explain why тєды is so rarely used as an adverb of time.

тꙋды (392a,2) 'thither, to there' in бо тꙋды мѣлъ ити 'for thither he had to go.' The final vowel -ы (cf. тогды) and final stress indicate that the form is part of the

Ruthenian system, but it is only attested once in a biblical passage of the type that usually contains large numbers of Polish elements. This form is current in CSU and CSBR, but is not attested in IV or SinSlav; тȣды is present in SSUM (attested in a text from the year 1366) and is also found in FS, next to тȣда, тȣдє.

7.2.3 *Suffix -de.*

вєздє́ (9 times, only in JU, e.g., 36a,14: вє̑дє) 'everywhere' is found in CSR, while it is lacking in CSU and CSBR. The distribution of this form among the modern languages may be taken as an indication of the marked (= "Slavonic") status of this form; this assumption is supported by its occurrence as a head word in Berynda's *Leksykon*, and by its use (spelled вєсдє) as the Slavonic gloss for всюды in SinSlav (see всюды above). Вєздє is also present in FS.

гдє (159 times, e.g., K7b,19) 'where,' developed to CSU де and CSBR дзе after loss of initial [h] (< *g; note CSR где); the Slavonic relative form идєжє 'the place where' occurs once (K10a,24). Both forms occur in IV, and Gröschel describes the latter as "literary" (*buchsprachlich*); he is unable to determine, however, whether or not the grapheme г represents U(-R) [h] in his texts. There is no doubt about its phonetic value in MS, as has already been shown. Both гдє and the later form дє are attested in P-M (125). Note that гдє is glossed as идєжє in SinSlav. Гдє may also occasionally be interpreted as an indefinite adverbial form meaning 'somewhere,' e.g., и нє гдє индє (186b,21) 'and not somewhere else,' 'and nowhere else' (see the next entry); it is also found with the indefinite formant -колвєк in гдєколвєк 'wherever.'

индє (19 times, e.g., 51a,16; K10a,24) 'elsewhere' may be considered U-R as well as Slavonic. It is retained in CSU but has been lost in CSBR. This adverb is not mentioned in IV, but note Slavonic инȣдє 'from elsewhere' (318); it is cited in Kramko, however, as a form common in the Ruthenian period (1988, 275).

нѣгдє́ (6 times, e.g., 39a,6; only in JU) 'nowhere' [< нѣ + гдє]: the negative particle [ni-] is by this time spelled нѣ- in literary Ruthenian; the spelling ни- is not attested among adverbs in MS (cf. the marked Slavonic pronoun никто, etc.) but the reflex of *ni- ([ny]) is still found in Southwest Ukrainian dialects. The forms current in CSU and CSBR are ніде and нідзе, respectively.

овдє (2 times, only in JU, e.g., 132a,19) '(to) here' [< pronoun ов- + suffix -дє] in all likelihood represents Polish *owdzie* 'here,' but it is also attested in OCS with the same meaning. There is a departure from the original semantic expression of this adverb, however—in Polish, as in OCS, it simply refers to location 'here,' while its use in MS implies motion "to here": принєси твой палєцъ овдє "bring your finger (to) here." Kramko cites this form as current in Ruthenian documents of the sixteenth and seventeenth centuries, providing support for its interpretation as a Polonism (cf. also IV, 316); he glosses овдє in the traditional manner, as referring to location (на іншым месцы 'in another place,' дзе-небудзь 'somewhere') but one of the three examples cited also indicates motion to rather than location where: ѧк овдѣ пришолєсь 'how you came (to) here' (275). Cf. the pronoun ов- (5.2.3).

сєздє́ (145a,2) 'here' is not found in CSU or CSBR, SSUM, PB, SinSlav, or FS. This form represents a reduplication of the element *sь 'this' + *de*: *sьsьde. Compare the Russian form здесь, in which reduplication is also in evidence, except that the element *sь occurs before and after *de*. Only здє/здѣ are attested in IV (316); cf. also Slavonic здє in PB. It is difficult to assign this adverb to a specific stylistic level because of its absence from the texts of contemporary Ruthenians. The context in which it is used suggests that MS considered it to be higher style (but not Slavonic, as the presence of non-Slavonic elements in the citation show): оупевнаючи нхъ о въскресенїи Хвомъ, всталъ, мови, Гдь, нѣмашъ его сезде: ото и мѣстце где былъ положенъ (145a,1–3) 'assuring them about the resurrection of Christ, he said, the Lord arose, he is not here: there is the place where he was laid.' It is at least clear that this form should not be interpreted as a feature of Ruthenian.

7.2.4 *OtherAdverbs of Time and Place*

вон (8 times, e.g., 113a,5) 'away' is present in FS, in SSUM, as a headword in PB, as a gloss for пречъ in SinSlav, and in CSR. This form also occurs in the language of IV, but Gröschel is unable to assign it to a particular linguistic level ("Ukrainian" or Slavonic). Вон is lacking in CSU, but is present in CSBR, glossed in TSBM as 'преч.' On the basis of the data from SinSlav and PB, I would identify the form as Slavonic (the example cited here occurs in a biblical text). Gröschel's decision not to make such a determination is understandable, however, especially given the currency of this form in CSBR.

вчора́ (6 times, only in JU, e.g., 124a,26) 'yesterday' occurs in CSU and CSBR. Final stress is the norm in MS, and is attested 5 times, while penultimate stress occurs only once: compare CSU/CSBR учóра, CSP *wczoraj,* but CSR вчерá,; final stress is occasionally found in dialects, e.g., CSBR учорáсь (Turaw), and in the corresponding adjectival derivative, e.g., CSU учорáшній, CSBR учарáшні. This adverb is not cited by Gröschel. The place of stress in MS evidently reflects the native East Slavic pattern, which is in evidence in these adjectival forms. Penultimate stress in the CSU and CSBR adverb can be ascribed to the influence of Polish. Cf. also FS вчера, вчерашний.

днесь *See* сегодня below.

єще (144 times, e.g., K9a,7; 108b,12) 'still, yet.' The final stress in the majority of examples indicates that this form should be considered Ruthenian rather than Polish (which would have initial, that is penultimate, stress). Initial stress occurs 32 times, final stress 112 times.

за́вжды (166 times, e.g., K28a,19) 'always' represents the Ruthenian form, and is unchanged in the modern languages: CSU завжди, CSBR заўжды. The form is not attested in IV. The place of stress in MS suggests that this adverb can be more precisely identified as U-R in MS' language because penultimate stress is acceptable in CSU (along with final stress), whereas only final stress occurs in CSBR. Vis-à-vis завше, завжды appears on numerical grounds to be the preferred (unmarked) variant. Contextually this is not the case, however: завжды is always used in the closing formula cited above, нынѣ и завжды . . . (in *Kazan'e* as well as in JU), indicating that it is to be treated as a learned form (but not Slavonic). JU illustrates the relationship between the two: и завжды вслѣдъ мене иди (382b,10–11) 'and always follow me,' paraphrasing Christ; this is followed by an explanatory statement using завше: нежебы сегоднѧ шедши, а завтра обленила бы҃ сѧ, але завше иди замною (382b,12–13) 'that having gone [followed] today, [it is not to be] that tomorrow you should grow lazy, but always follow me.' The clear impression here is that завше is more colloquial and unmarked, a conclusion supported by SinSlav and Berynda's *Leksykon*: in both lexica завше is cited as the Ruthenian form corresponding to всегда, and завжды is not mentioned (note also the labelling of завше as "colloquial" in CSU:SUM).

завтра (3 times, only in JU, e.g., 111a,22) 'tomorrow' is common to all modern East Slavic languages; it is attested in PB, SinSlav, and FS, but not in IV. SSUM has заѹтра 'in the morning'; this spelling is also seen in PB and FS, reflecting the origins of this adverb: за + ѹтр-.

завшє (60 times, e.g., 30a,1) 'always' can with confidence be labelled a Polonism (cf. Kramko 1988, 288–89). Among the modern literary languages, завшє is found with the meaning 'always' in Polish; the form is included in SUM as a colloquial variant of literary Ukrainian завжды (see above). This adverb was widely used in Ruthenian, and is also attested in the language of P-M, SinSlav, and PB (as a gloss for всєгда); it is not mentioned with regard to the language of IV.

нѣ́кгды [nigdy] (45 times, e.g., B III,33) 'never' [< нѣ + гды] represents Polish *nigdy,* in which the digraph кг represents phonetic [g].

нынѣ (83 times, 2 times in *Kazan'e,* 81 times in JU; e.g., K7b,4) 'now' is both Ruthenian and Slavonic. This form does not occur in purely biblical contexts, but it is frequently used in JU in the formulaic phrase нынѣ и завжды и навѣки вѣкѡмъ (141a,6–7) 'now and always and forever,' at the end of a passage. This does indicate that нынѣ belongs to a higher stylistic level, but the co-occurrence of the unmarked Ruthenian form завжды (see above) in the same formula suggests that this phrase as a whole is not marked as purely "Slavonic," but rather as "learned." One orthographic convention applied to нынѣ in *Kazan'e* also points to a marked status in the system: the form is abbreviated нн҃ѣ, a convention typically applied to "God," "Jesus," etc.; we note the same pattern in SinSlav, in which нн҃ѣ is glossed as днєсь. CSU retains the form нині (cf. CSR ныне), while it is not extant in CSBR. Since this adverb is present in FS' B-R language, however, it should be identified as "common learned Ruthenian," rather than as specifically U-R.

прєчъ (1 time, 275b,29) 'away' is not present in FS or SSUM, but it is found in SinSlav and PB (equals Slavonic вон; see above). A vocalic opposition differentiates the adverb прєчъ from the preposition прочъ in MS' texts (see 8.1). While the adverb прєчъ has been lost in CSU, this form is retained in CSBR; the form of the CSR adverb, on the other hand, is прочь. Interesting in this regard is *procz* in the language of P-M: this form is used as the adverb *and* as the preposition. We might speculate that phonetic underdifferentiation of the two elements led to the loss of one of them in Russian; even in P-M we see a tendency to differentiate between them. A variant *prucz* is already in use in the adverbial function.

разъ (e.g., K11a,15) 'once' is general Slavic. Note also the noun разъ 'time, instance' (in MS, e.g., разѣ K6b,14; разы K21b,5), and in P-M, SinSlav, and PB (in the latter it is a gloss for Slavonic єдинощи).

сєгодна (31 times, only in JU, e.g., 111a,21) 'today' [< genitive of сь 'this' + genitive of 'day']; CSR сегодня, CSU сьогодні/сьогодня, CSBR сягоння/сёння (where *-h-* can > ø, and *-dn-* > *-nn-*). This adverb is clearly the norm for the expression of 'today' in MS. Once we find the old accusative днєсь [< *dьnь + sь]: хлѣбъ нашъ насꙋщный дажⷣъ намъ днєсь (474a,2) 'give us this day our daily bread.' This latter form is used by MS as a marked element, occurring with other marked Slavonic forms. It is the form used in OB. Сєгодна is not attested in IV, earlier U-R (SSUM) or FS, while днєсь is. In Gröschel's opinion the latter is to be interpreted as an element of the U(-R) vernacular, while the increased use of сьогодня/сьогодні in Ukrainian is to be explained as the result of Russian influence (1972, 303). In MS it is the exact opposite, for днєсь is only attested in a recitation of the Lord's prayer. Berynda's *Leksykon* supports this interpretation, for the Slavonic headword днє҇ is glossed as Ruthenian сєгодна. Note also SinSlav нн҇ѣ (above) which is glossed as Slavonic днєсь. One conclusion that might be drawn is that днєсь was current longer in the northern Ruthenian regions (hence IV and B-R) than in the southerly (MS and PB). Днесь is not cited in SUM (UAS has the form: 'archaic'), but is present dialectally (ESUM).

тамъ (129 times, e.g., K7b,9) 'there' is general Slavic, and must be considered Ruthenian here: compare the use of the corresponding Slavonic form тамо (K10b,2) in a biblical citation.

теды (e.g., 297a,12) 'then, subsequently,' approximate equivalent of потомъ (see above). In the great majority of cases (it occurs hundreds of times), this form functions as a conjunction, as described in chapter 8. Sometimes, however, теды is clearly used as an adverb of time meaning 'subsequently': теды . . . Іс҃ реклъ єй 'then Jesus said to her' (297a,12). In SSUM as well as in SinSlav we find теды described only as a conjunction. In the latter it is glossed as оубо 'for.' MS' form is evidently of Polish origin: the place of stress in this form is most often penultimate (i.e., Polish), but the occasional occurrence of final stress shows that this form is well adapted to the Ruthenian system. Kramko notes the widespread use of теды (alongside and sometimes in place of тогди) in B-R texts of the seventeenth century (1988, 287–88). It is not attested in IV, CSU or CSBR.

теперъ (150 times, e.g., K6a,12) 'now' is an East Slavic form: CSU тепер, CSBR цяпер, R теперь. Note, however, CSCz *teprv*, CSP *dopiero* (see Vasmer1976, 3:94).

тȣтъ (65 times, e.g., 161b,21) 'here' occurs in all the modern East Slavic languages. Note also CSP *tu, tutaj.* Gröschel describes this adverb as either Slavonic or southwest Ukrainian (1972, 314). In P-M *tu, tut, tuta, tutaka,* and *tutka* are all identified as expressing 'here'; тȣтъ is present in SinSlav, PB (as a gloss for здє), and in FS (in the latter we also find тȣ, тȣта, тȣто).

оуже *See* южъ below.

часомъ (29b,9) 'sometimes' is the instrumental singular of часъ 'time.' The adverbial use of this form is widespread, and is attested in CSU, CSBR, CSR, and CSP (both *czasem* and *czasami*). It is also found in the language of FS.

частокроть (60 times, e.g., 33b,25; K21b,17) 'frequently' [< часто 'often' + кротъ 'time'], is the Ruthenianized Polish form *częstokroć,* and is not attested in IV. Note, however, the use by IV of krot 'time' in such phrases as сто кротъ '100 times,' два кротъ 'twice' (303). Although the form as such is certainly Polish, there appears to be a connection between the place of stress and the nature of the final consonant *-t('):* when the stress is on the penultimate syllable, i.e., as in Polish, and occasionally when it is on the antepenultimate, this consonant is orthographically palatalized, ostensibly approximating the Polish palatal affricate -[ć]. When stress is on the final syllable, i.e., "Ruthenianized," the final consonant is hard. 4 of the 60 attestations occur in *Kazan'e*, and all have penultimate stress and palatalized *-t'*. Here (as in other instances) it seems the variant closest to the original Polish is the form used in this text, reflecting a more learned level of language (Polish as *Kultursprache*). Compare: часто́кроть (228b,13; K21b,17), ча́стокроть (338b,5), but частокро́т̕ (228b,16–17). Note the superscript notation, which word-finally equals back jer (it can replace front jers only at the end of a line). Note also the misspelling часто́крость (302a,6), in which the same stress-related phenomenon is observed. This spelling may be influenced by the word-formational element -ostь, but it is also tempting to see here an alternate rendering of CSP -ć [tś] as [st́]. The element крот is not found in CSU or CSBR. In Ukrainian the element крат is found in compound numerical formations such as стократный '100-fold.' On the use of крот with нле, see 7.3 below.

южъ (110 times, e.g., K3a,3) 'already' clearly represents a Polish form, based on the presence of initial *j-*. Native Ruthenian оуже is attested 125 times: 91 times with East Slavic final stress, 34 times unstressed (e.g.,

42a,8). This variant is only attested in JU, a strong indication of its status as a native Ruthenian element (versus the literary-Ruthenian/Polish южъ). Four variants are attested in IV: юже, оуже, южъ, and оужъ (321).

7.3 *Adverbs of Degree*

барзо (106 times, in *Kazan'e* and JU, e.g., K11a,16; 41a,7) 'very, much' is a Polonism: OPol *barzo*, CSP *bardzo*. In Ukrainian this form is still found in the southwestern dialects, but the preferred adverb in the literary language is дуже 'very, much' (see ESUM 1:142). This lexeme does not occur in CSBR but is attested in the northwestern dialects. At the time of Smotryc'kyj, барзо was a commonly used element in Ruthenian: it is present in SinSlav and PB (in the latter it serves as the Ruthenian definition of дзело), and it is obviously a feature of MS' language. It was very common in B-R (HSBM). Note the comparative барзѣй 'rather, sooner' in IV (Gröschel 1972, 311; see also 7.5 below). Dzendzelivs'kyj believes that the CSU dialectal form (барз, бардзо) is ultimately of Polish origin, but he leaves open the possibility that it entered the language from East Slovak. Smotryc'kyj's knowledge and use of Polish preclude such an interpretation for барзо in his language (1969, 17–18). ESBM and Leeming 1968 agree that Polish is the source of this form.

вдовоⷧ҇ (40b,26-7) 'enough, in abundance' is rare in East Slavic: of the modern languages only CSR knows this form, and it is not attested in the language of any of MS' contemporaries: HSBM lists the form as B-R, but the only source cited is JU. The presence of this adverb in CSR, as well as SinSlav's explanation of досыть as 'доволнѣ' (with the same root as вдоволъ) suggest that MS' form be assigned to the learned (Slavonic) linguistic-stylistic level.

велми (9 times, only in JU, e.g., 61b,16) 'very' may be described as common Ruthenian: this adverb is found in CSU, CSBR (in the latter it is glossed as 'надта, дужа'), CSR (described as archaic or ironic, or both), and is attested in FS, IV, and SSUM.

вє̂цє (283a,6-7) 'very' is a Polonism that is not present in FS, SinSlav, or SSUM; it does occur in PB. The form attested in MS corresponds to CSP *wielce*. Note also Old Polish *wielice* and *wieldze*.

взлишъ (2 times, only in JU, e.g., 42a,26) 'too much' can be described in the same terms as вдоволь above. It is unknown in the modern languages and in that of MS' contemporaries, but is cited in HSBM only on the basis of its presence in JU.

вмалѣ (2 times, only in JU, e.g., 327a,1) 'a little' is not uncommon in Ruthenian: it is attested in FS and is cited in HSBM. It is not extant in CSU, CSBR, or CSP, and is not found in SS, PB (as a headword), or SSUM.

внѣвєчъ (11times, in JU and *Kazan'e*, e.g., 287a,9) 'into nothing(ness),' with the verb обєрнꙋти/обєртати 'to destroy' reflects the Polish form of this adverb: CSP *wniwecz*, but CSU внівець. The latter variant is attested in SinSlav. This form is not found in IV, FS, SSUM, or CSBR.

вполъ (406b,4) '(by) half' may represent a Polonism (Pol *wpół*). It is still extant in CSBR, but is not present in CSU. Вполъ is absent from the other Ruthenian sources consulted.

вполнѣ (406b,3) 'completely, entirely' is extant in CSU and CSR, but not in CSBR or other Ruthenian sources.

всыть (46a,21) 'to satiety'(?), 'enough'(?). This adverb is not encountered in the modern languages or in the language of MS' contemporaries.

доволѣ (126a,7) 'enough' is found in CSU and CSBR (доволі and даволі, respectively); it is also current in CSP (*do woli*) with the meanings 'as much as one wants; at will, freely.' This adverb is not found in the language of MS' contemporaries.

до́сыть /до́сытъ (43 times, in *Kazan'e* and JU, e.g., K17b,15) 'enough; rather.' This lexeme was undeniably part of the Ruthenian system, and occurs in SinSlav, PB, FS, and is cited in SSUM. It is still extant in CSU and CSBR (досить and досыць, respectively), as well in dialect Russian. This form may be a borrowing from Polish (*dosyć*), but до сыти is very old (attested in OCS). ESBM takes this position, while ESUM and Vasmer do not. In MS the form is found with hard final /-t/ in JU, whereas it reflects the Polish palatal consonant by means of soft /-t'/ (2 times) in *Kazan'e*. The latter, if it represents a Polonism in MS' system, may be phonetically closer to the Polish source word because it occurs in this particular text (note other examples of the use of the Polish prestige forms in *Kazan'e*, e.g., напрод, next to наперед in JU, described in 7.2.1 above). The occurrence of this form with final back and front jer-letters is widely known in Ruthenian (cf. copious B-R examples in HSBM). The negative counterpart недоси́ть is found once (K8b,6-7); the spelling of this form reflects the coalescence of *i and *y in Ukrainian, and again has a palatalized final /-t'/. This form differs form the positive adverb in the place of stress, indicating either greater "Ruthenianization" of the form, or a reflection of the substantival source of this form: < не до сы́ти.

дочи́ста (260a,3) 'compeletely' is common in the Ruthenian period, and is cited in Kramko's description of the adverb (1988, 296-7); it does not occur in SinSlav, but is present in FS. On the basis of the place of stress in the CSU and CSBR forms, it is possible to describe this adverb more precisely as "U-R." Note CSU дочи́ста (although дочиста́ is also possible) but CSBR дачыста́.

єще may be used as an adverbial intensifier, in addition to the basic meaning "still, yet." Thus, for example, it occurs with comparatives: єще барзѣй (J393b,7) 'even more,' єще сꙋровѣй строфовати (530b,23) 'punish even more severely.' This usage of єщє (CSU ще, CSBR яшче́, CSR ещё) is characteristic of all modern East Slavic languages.

заистє (146b,22) 'indeed, certainly' is a Polonism present as a headword in SinSlav, but is lacking in IV; it is present in PB as a gloss for ꙗкѣ. Only заисто is cited in SSUM (and only once), while заистє/заисто are cited in HSBM; it is not found in CSU/CSBR, but retained in CSP *zaiste*.

звлаща (2 times, only in JU, e.g., 217b,10) 'especially, chiefly' is clearly a Polonism. It is not attested in CSU/CSBR, FS, IV, or SSUM, but does occur in SinSlav and *Aleksandryja* (Leeming 1968, 295).

илє (40 times) 'how many' is a borrowing from Polish: илє насъ єстъ (48a,25) 'how many of us there are.' This adverb may form a new compound with the element кроть 'time,' viz. илєкроть (422a,1) 'how(ever) many times' (cf. частокроть above): илєкроть . . . толкокро҃ (458a,21-23) 'how(ever) many times . . . that many times.' илє and илєкроть are both present in SinSlav; the former is not cited for the language of IV, but is found in *Aleksandryja* (Leeming 1968, 299). This adverb is not extant in CSU or CSBR. On the use of илє as a conjunction, see 8.2.

наͩто (28 times, only in JU, e.g., 29b,8) 'especially, too much' is widely used. It is current in CSU, CSBR, and CSP, and is present in SinSlav as well as SSUM. It is not mentioned by Gröschel.

на́звытъ (5 times, only in JU, e.g., 57b,19) 'too (much)' is a clear Polonism current in the Ruthenian period. It is attested in SinSlav and FS (but not in SSUM or IV); *nazbyt* is extant in CSP but is lacking in CSU and CSBR.

нємаль (8 times, in *Kazan'e* and JU, e.g., 118a,20; K17b,12) 'almost, nearly' is a Polonism (*niemal*). It is not extant in CSU or CSBR. In SinSlav нємаль is defined in Slavonic as васнь 'perhaps,' so the form is certainly not unknown in Ruthenian; нємаль is also one of the glosses for васнь in Berynda's *Leksykon*. This adverb is not attested in IV.

нѣмашъ (54 times) 'there is no' is an adverbialized form expressing the lack of something, and most likely represents Pol *nie masz,* lit. 'you (sg.) do not have': cf. *niemasz* 'nie ma' ('there is no') in Linde 1857. According to Kernyc'kyj (1967, 183) the form нимаш is not uncommon in 16c Ruthenian. Thus: личбы нѣмаⷮ (403b,6) 'without number,' lit. 'there is no number'; нѣмашъ конца (403b,25) 'there is no end'; нѣмашъ нѣ Кгрека, нѣ жида, нѣ . . . (281a,2) 'there is neither Greek, nor Jew, nor . . . .' The same form is present in Berynda's *Leksykon* as a gloss for нѣєсть (FS немать). Compare CSU нема, немає, CSBR няма, CSP *nie ma.* This form should not be considered as part of the verbal paradgim мати/мѣти (see 9.8). Next to нѣмашъ, the East Slavic form нѣтъ + gen. (< нѣєст < не єсть) 'there is no' must be considered marked. It is only found once in MS (466b,26); this form is also attested in SinSlav and FS, but is lacking in PB. Among the modern languages, нет is current only in CSR (it is cited in SUM, but is described as archaic). According to TSBM it is not present in CSBR.

нѣтъ See нѣмашъ above.

овшеки (61 times, in *Kazan'e* and JU, e.g., K11a,10) is a Polonism defined by SSP as 'completely, entirely' (5:708). It is a phonetic variant of the synonymous form *owszejki*. It conveys '(not) at all' in negative constructions: мужа овшеки не знаючи (441b,17) 'not knowing man at all' (in reference to the Virgin Mary). The large number of citations of овшеки in MS, as well as its occurrence in SinSlav and Berynda's *Leksykon*, indicate that this form was current in Ruthenian. Овшеки is not attested in IV, and is also no longer extant in CSU, CSBR, or CSP.

овшемъ (30 times, in *Kazan'e*, e.g., 34b,17) This form is a Polonism, usually a marker of the affirmative, defined as ‘quite, yes’ in CSP. Note Old Polish *owszem* ‘at least, entirely . . . ’ (Reczek 1968). Ruthenian овшємъ corresponds to CSU зовсім, CSBR зусім, and CSR совсем ‘entirely; [neg.:] (not) at all.’ In SinSlav овшємъ is glossed as и ѹбо, that is, as an affirmative adverb; compare the semantically and phonetically close form *owszym* ‘on the contrary’ for P-M, which is interpreted only in the negative sense. This adverb is not cited by Gröschel.

ѡтнюⷣ (K11a,17) ‘entirely’ is lexically marked as a Slavonic element: cf. OCS отинѫдъ ‘entirely.’ Data from Berynda support this interpretation, because Slavonic отнюдъ is present as a headword, defined as вєсма, всѧко, всѧчєски, and овшєки (see this form above); SinSlav is problematical in this regard, however: ѿнюд is also given as a headword in that lexicon, defined as Slavonic вєсма, всѧко. It appears, therefore, that this form can occur in Ruthenian, probably as a learned form. In IV the form отнюдѹжє ‘whence’ is used in a relative construction (318).

ѿчасти (K22a,3) ‘partly’ belongs to the Slavonic stylistic level: this form does not occur in CSU, CSBR, or CSP, whereas it is current in CSR. ѿчасти is apparently not identified in IV’s language, and does not occur in SinSlav or (as a headword) in *Leksykon*. It is present in FS’s language.

почасти (K22a,20) ‘partly’ is still reflected in modern CSU почасти ‘partly,’ but is not found in the other East Slavic literary languages or in Polish. This form is not cited by Gröschel as a feature of the language of IV, and is not present in any of the other Ruthenian sources consulted.

только (hundreds of attestations in *Kazan'e* and JU, e.g., 3,20; 216b,13) ‘only; so much’ may be generally characterized as East Slavic: cf. SinSlav толко, P-M толко/тѹлко, IV тол(ь)ко, CSR только ‘only’; in Berynda’s *Leksykon* толко is found as a gloss for токмо and for толма. The vast majority of examples in MS are written толко; only 6 are found with a front jer (только). In addition to только , the Polish variant *tylko* is also attested in IV (314). In CSU and CSBR this adverb is characterized by final - y/-i in place of *-o*: Ukr тільки, Br тольки; the variant толки is also found in P-M, although it is not nearly as common as толко. The construction толко . . . колко expresses 'so many/much . . . as (many/much)' in MS as well as in P-M, as it is in Slavonic (e.g., 422a,1; K25b,12-14). In CSBR this has been supplanted by стольки . . . кольки. CSU has стільки . . . скільки (cf. CSR столько . . . сколько).[3] The meaning 'so much' is in evidence in PB as well: толикоɥи is glossed 'толко ρазов.'

цѣлкѡⷨ (326a,7) 'completely, wholly' is very widely used, in East Slavic as well as West. CSU цілком, CSBR цалкам, CSP *całkiem*, but CSR целиком. In view of the wide distribution of this adverb it is rather curious that цѣлком is not attested in SS, FS, or SSUM.

7.4 *Adverbs of Manner*

вєсполъ (K2b,21) 'together, in common'; corresponds to CSP *wespół.* It is not attested in the language of IV or other contemporaries of MS. It is not unknown in sixteenth-century Ruthenian—it is found in the glossary at the end of Nimčuk et al. 1981.

---

[3] An interesting progression is in evidence from the Ruthenian model through the Belarusian and finally to the Ukrainian/Russian with specific reference to the prefixal element *s*- (plus '+' or minus '-' indicates presence or absence, respectively):

	толко	колко
Ruthenian	-	-
Belarusian	+	-
Ukrainian/Russian	+	+

вєдно́ (447b,5) 'together' is not found in any modern or Ruthenian source, but is very close in form to въєдино, cited in HSBM.

взаємъ (8 times, only in JU, e.g., 126b,19) 'lend/borrow [with verb]' may be described as belonging to the elevated style of Slavonic. Apart from MS, it is only present in PB and FS and is not extant in the modern languages.

воистиннꙋ (many times, e.g., K19a,16) 'in truth' is the Slavonic form that corresponds to Ruthenian заправды (see below). It is present as a headword in PB, as a gloss in SinSlav, and in FS.

вподивъ (530a,29) with брати: '(take) by surprise.' This form is not attested in Ruthenian or modern sources. It appears to be a new U-R form devised by the author, made up of въ + substantive подивъ. Compare CSU подив 'surprise' (but CSBR дзіва, здзіўленне).

вправдѣ (3 times, only in JU, e.g., 435b,27) 'in fact, actually' is cited in SSUM, and is currently found in CSU (вправді) and Polish (*wprawdzie*). This form may represent an early borrowing from Polish. It is not attested in IV.

впроти҃ (5 times, only in JU, e.g., 125a,7) 'on the contrary' follows the pattern of вдоволь above. It is not attested in the modern languages or in that of MS' contemporaries. HSBM does cite this form, but, once again, only on the basis of its presence in JU.

дармо *See* надаремнє (below).

даромъ *See* надаремнє (below).

заєдно (541b,16) 'together' is attested in Ruthenian at an early date (SSUM) and is still extant in CSU. It is does not occur in CSBR and other Ruthenian sources.

заправды (24 times, only in JU, e.g., 130b,7) 'indeed, in truth' is interpreted as a Polonism by Kramko (1988, 301). CSP *zaprawdę*. This form is present in SinSlav and PB, as headword and gloss for воистиннꙋ (PB въистиннꙋ), respectively, while it is absent in FS, IV, and SSUM. This distribution, as well as the presence of заправдꙋ (as well as заправды) in *Aleksandryja*

(Leeming 1968, 303) support the interpretation of the form as a Polonism. Заправды is no longer extant in CSU and CSBR.

здробна (323b,5) 'in detail'(?) is not cited in FS, SinSlav, IV, or SSUM, neither is it present in CSU, CSBR, or CSP. Kramko does list this form as a common Ruthenian adverb, however, formed according to the well-known pattern described in 7.2.1.1. Compare the Polish adjective *drobny* 'fine,' and Belorussian dialect дробна 'finely.'

злєгка (5 times, only in JU, e.g., 65a,5) 'a little (bit)' is also cited by Kramko, and is present in CSU and CSP; this form is not present in IV or CSBR.

зособна (2 times, only in JU, e.g., 193,9) 'alone, singly.' This form is especially widespread, occurring in FS, SinSlav, SSUM, Kramko, CSU and CSP; in Ukrainian and early U-R (SSUM) this form expressed "especially," but its use in MS is better understood in light of its meaning in Polish, viz. "apart." In view of the small number of adverbs of this type attested in IV, it is worth pointing out that this particular form is present in his language. We might cite this adverb as a good example of a form that shows the confluence of the Ruthenian and Polish systems.

зтрꙋдна (2 times, only in JU, e.g., 198a,26) 'with difficulty.' This form is cited by Kramko, but is not attested in FS, SinSlav, IV, or SSUM. Like здробна, зтрꙋдна is not extant in the modern literary languages.

зачимъ (89 times, only in JU, e.g.30b,25) 'why' is present in Ukrainian only as a dialect form (SUM); in the literary language the form чому is preferred. This form also is attested in MS (338a,21). Зачимъ is absent from CSBR, CSP, and the language of Smotryc'kyj's contemporaries, but can be interpreted as a feature of East Slavic (cf. Russian зачем).

инакъ (4 times, e.g., 295a,26) 'in another way' is an adverb still found in modern Polish: *tak czy inak* 'in this or some other way'; it also occurs in CSU, but is described as 'archaic' in SUM. While инакъ is not retained in CSBR, a derivative of this adverb is: інакш contains the comparative suffix -*š*- and is very close in form to the pronominal form инакшїй (see chapter 4). The form инакъ is unmarked in Ruthenian, next to Slavonic инако: the latter is given as the gloss for Ruthenian иначей in SinSlav. The form иначей is frequently used in MS, but in this study it is treated simply as one of the many morphologically comparative forms functioning as adverbs in his language (7.5). MS' data agree with Kramko's interpretation that иначей is more common than инакъ, but both are current in Ruthenian (1988, 292). The form is not found in IV, SinSlav, PB, or FS. See also онакъ below.

молчкомъ (2 times, e.g., 345a,9) 'silently, in silence' is clearly Ruthenian: cf. CSU мовчком (and мовчки), CSBR маўчком; this form is also attested in FS, but does not occur in SSUM or SinSlav.

навидо́ку (334b,9) 'apparently' is absent from all modern and Ruthenian sources consulted, with the exception of one—SBH cites this adverb as a Belorussian dialect feature. The total agreement (including place of stress) between MS' form and that cited in SBH suggests that this might be a form adopted by the author during his tenure in Vilnius.

надаль (285b,4) 'continue to . . . , keep . . . ' [with verb]. This form is a Polonism not present in the modern East Slavic languages, SinSlav, FS, or SSUM. It is still extant in modern Polish.

надаремне (20 times, in the preface to *Grammatiki* and JU, e.g., IIIb,11; 63b,20-21) 'in vain.' The frequent use of this form suggests that надаремне is well established in MS' language. This is supported by the modern languages, with attestations CSU надаремно, CSP *nadaremnie* or *nadaremno*, and CSBR даремна. This form is found in SinSlav with the same meaning. The Polonism дармо occurs twice in MS (for example,

108a,9), and is attested in IV (320) and FS. Даромъ (5 times, e.g., 431a,1) belongs to a higher style: Хс̃ . . . мовячи . . . даромъ взяли єсте, даромъ и давайте (ibid.) 'Christ . . . saying . . . in vain have you taken [and] in vain you shall give.' This interpretation is supported by the existence of CSR даром. Напрасно (2 times, e.g., 547b,25) does not occur in markedly Slavonic environments, but should also be assigned to the higher stylistic level. This form exists in Russian expressing "in vain," while it occurs (albeit rarely) in CSU meaning "suddenly" (as in OCS) and "unjustly"; the first meaning is also attested in SinSlav, suggesting that MS' use of the form is marked as "non-Ruthenian." Напрасно does not occur in CSBR.

наєдѣнѣ́ (258a,8) 'alone, privately' can only be assigned to the Slavonic linguistic/stylistic level. The variant наєдинѣ is a headword in PB, as a gloss for особне in SinSlav, and in CSR.

наоко (K14b,20) 'to be seen, for view, visibly (?)' is found as an adverb today only in Czech and Slovak, but for MS' Ruthenian it can just as easily be interpreted as a prepositional phrase used adverbially. It is not cited in IV, PB, SinSlav, or SSUM.

напрасно *See* надаремне (above).

напреко (495a,22) 'against' appears to be similar in meaning to впротивъ (above), and the presence of the element преко suggests that it should be treated as a marked form (cf. преко below and the preposition впреко in 8.1); it is not found elsewhere.

нато (28 times, only in JU, e.g., 57b,15) 'in addition, also' is structurally like надто and зато, and could therefore be classed together with them; adverbial нато is not attested in the language of MS' contemporaries or in the modern languages.

нѣ́якω (4 times, in *Kazan'e* and JU, e.g., K13b,20) 'in some way, somehow'. The place of stress differentiates this form from CSU ніякий 'no, none'; compare CSP *niejako* 'somehow, in a way,' CSBR не́як 'somehow.'

Final *-o* suggests that this is a Polonism rather than B-R; it is not cited in IV (but note ѧко, 314), SinSlav, or PB, and only the pronominal form нєѧкїй occurs in FS.

онакъ (297b,23) 'in that way' consists of the demonstrative pronominal element он- 'that' + suffix -акъ. Compare with the structurally identical form инакъ. Онакъ is not present in the Ruthenian sources consulted (e.g., SinSlav, IV), but CES онако is cited by Sreznevskij: или сицє или онако 'either this way or that way' (1955, 2:671). Онако is still found in modern literary Serbo-Croatian. The corresponding pronominal form онакий is still present in CSU (glossed as 'інший,' 'other'), although it is considered archaic by SUM. Neither adverb nor pronoun is attested in CSBR.

опѧтъ (4 times, only in JU, e.g., 103b,7) 'again' is not attested in CSU or CSBR, but was evidently widely used in the East Slavic area. It is still current in CSR, and is encountered in SinSlav, PB, FS, and SSUM (but not in IV).

поневоли (4 times, only in JU, e.g., 38a,22) 'against one's will' is common to all East Slavic languages. CSU поневолі, CSBR паняволі, CSR поневоле. It is not present in FS, SinSlav, or SSUM, but is attested in IV. Gröschel describes this form as a borrowing from Polish (1972, 30 5).

прєко (2 times, only in JU, 111b,19 and 548a,6) 'in opposition': this form is not attested in the language of other Ruthenians. Judging by its prefixal use in Berynda's *Leksykon* (прєкословиє 'спор') and its presence in modern South Slavic (e.g., Serbo-Croatian) we could describe this adverb as Slavonic; *przeko* (synonymous with MS' form) is attested in Old Polish, however, suggesting that it be identified merely as "learned." Note the following example: понєважъ вы пошлистє противъ мєнє прєко (548a,6) 'for you went against me.' Прєко here is used as a intensifying adverb, otherwise redundant in the presence of противъ.

пѣшъ (160a,6), пѣшо (244b,24) 'by/on foot.' Based on the modern languages, пѣшо can be interpreted as '(B-)R: this form is found in CSBR (пѣша) as well as in CSP (*pieszo*). Compare CSU пішки, пішком, CSR пешком; along with пѣша, the form пяшком is also present in CSBR. Пѣшъ in comparison represents a marked form (cf. OCS пѣшь), and is also attested in FS. Nowhere else is the adverb found in this form.

снать (288b,27) 'obviously, clearly' corresponds to Polish *snadź;* the final consonant in MS reflects the Polish devoicing of final consonants: as it was pronounced [snać], this had to be rendered снать in Ruthenian (cf. also the frequent Old Polish spelling *snacz,* reflecting the devoicing of final -dź). This form is also present in SinSlav, but not in SSUM, CSU, or CSBR.

сприкра (224a,10) 'disagreeably' [< preposition с 'from' + gen. sg. of the short form adjective прикр-]. This is the second most commonly found deadjectival adverbial construction in the Ruthenian period, after adverbs with the markers *-o* and *-e* (see здавна and others above); this particular form is cited in Kramko (1988, 296), but is not found in the modern languages, SSUM, SinSlav, FS, IV, or P-M.

такъ (hundreds of attestations in all three texts, e.g., K7a,2) 'thus, so, such' is general Slavic. The Slavonic variant тако occurs twice (K10a,19; K10b,3), both times in biblical passages. The combination of так + же results in an extremely common adverbial form in MS meaning 'the same way,' 'also': О чо҇ также и бж҇твенный а҇плъ Іакѡвъ наѹчаетъ на҇ (58b,3-4) 'about which also [in the same way] the holy apostle Jacob instructs us.'

тежъ (109 times, only in JU, e.g., 30b,13) 'also' is a Polonism still present in CSU (as well as in Polish), but lacking in CSBR. It is characteristic of IV, FS, PB, *Aleksandryja* (Leeming 1968, 293), and is cited in SSUM.

чомѹ *See* зачимъ (below).

четверонасобъ (393a,12) 'four times, four-fold' is not found in any primary sources; HSBM does list this form from MS' texts as the only attested example for B-R. Kramko describes the formant -nasob as evidence of Polish influence (1988, 306).

ꙗкъ (hundreds of attestations in *Kazan'e* and JU, e.g., K11a,4; 49a,27) 'as, how, like' occurs in CSU, CSBR, and CSP (but note CSR как). The Slavonic variant ꙗко(же) is attested 26 times in MS, in biblical quotations in *Kazan'e* and in JU: да ꙗкоже Хс҃ъ воста ѿ мертвыхъ такѡ . . . (K10a,18) 'and [just] as Christ arose from the dead, so . . . '; да бꙋдетъ волѧ твоѧ ꙗко на нб҃си и на замли (474a,1) 'your will be [done] on earth as it is in heaven.' The form ꙗкожъ (e.g., K18a,5) is not necessarily Slavonic, however: the vowel *-o-* can serve as a fill vowel which appears when the emphatic particle жъ is suffixed to ꙗкъ. The same is true for dozens of forms like ꙗкомъ in ꙗкомъ реклъ (e.g., K5b,8) 'as I said,' in which *-o-* is again a fill vowel, this time occurring between jak and the markers of person in past tense verbs.

ꙗкобы (162 times, e.g., 156a,12; 36a,14-15), ꙗкъбы (13 times, e.g., 239b,17) 'as, as if, somehow, approximately' do not appear to represent different stylistic levels; the former is clearly preferred in MS' texts, and occurs in opening biblical passages as well as in the explanatory texts: Справедливымъ абовѣмъ ве̂де показꙋетсѧ ꙗкобы грознымъ и срогкимъ (156a,12) 'to the just he shows himself as if [to be] threatening and harsh' (note Pol *srogi,* not Ruthenian строгий); а была година ꙗкобы шостаѧ (36a,14-15) 'and it was about the sixth hour.' The preferred form in MS is also present in FS, SSUM, SinSlav, and PB. In SinSlav ꙗкобы is glossed as 'аки,' in PB the reverse is true.

7.4.1 *Adverbial Constructions With the Preposition* по*(-)*

Eleven adverbial forms (some occurring more than once: cf. below) consisting of the preposition по with the dative singular short form adjective are attested in the language of MS. Kramko describes this construction as the third most common means of forming deadjectival adverbs (1988, 297; all individual forms noted by Kramko are found on the same page), and it is clear from MS' data that this formation was common in Ruthenian. In such constructions *po* may either occur separately from the following adjective or be written as one form. Adverbial forms in -скꙋ can express 'in language X' (as below) or 'in the manner of X people.'

побли́зꙋ (128a,1) 'close' is attested in CSU (поблизу́) and CSBR (блі́зу).

поеврейскꙋ (374b,1) 'in Hebrew.' In FS this form is attested with the ending -ски. This ending is characteristic of CSBR, while two alternative endings are possible in CSU, viz. -ськи and -ському.

поготовꙋ (72a,26) 'all the more' is general Ruthenian: this adverb is attested in IV; it is retained in CSU and CSBR with one phonetic change: final -u is lost: CSBR пагатоў, CSU поготів.

помалꙋ (4 times, e.g., 65a,6) is interesting in the context of the Ruthenian period: just one century before, this adverb expressed "soon" (e.g., in FS and SSUM). By the time of the writing of JU, however, it is used to mean "slowly," as it is today in CSU and CSBR. The meaning "little by little" is shared by these two modern languages and CSP. See по немалꙋ below.

по немалꙋ (IIIa,21-IIIb,1) 'soon' (?). The author apparently was aware of the earlier meaning of помалꙋ (above), but as this form expressed "slowly" in his language (that is, approximately the opposite of "soon," if "soon" can equal "fast") it had to be negated to retain this earlier meaning. The negated form по немалꙋ is not attested in the language of those of MS' contemporaries included in this study.

поранȣ (4 times, e.g., 135a,2) 'early' is widely attested in Ruthenian: it is cited by Kramko, and is found in FS as well as in SinSlav. CSU порано and порану are described as dialect forms in SUM.

порȣскȣ (2 times, e.g., 374b,2) 'in Ruthenian' is general Ruthenian. Its currency during the Ruthenian period is noted by Kramko, but it is also cited during the earlier period represented by SSUM; in the language of FS we find порȣски, in CSU -ськи/-ському, CSBR -скi.

пославенскȣ (IIb,20; IVa,7), пословенскȣ (3 times, e.g., 118b,16) 'in Slavonic.' The second of these is general Ruthenian (cited by Kramko), while the first represents the marked Slavonic variant; the latter is used by Smotryc'kyj in the preface to his grammar of that language. These terms are no longer current in CSU and CSBR (cf. CSU словенський 'Slovenian').

посполȣ (с) (29 times, e.g., 125b,16) 'together with' is attested in early U-R (1395 in SSUM), and is also found in FS and IV. Today this adverb is used in CSP; it is also included in SUM, labelled "colloquial," and is identified by Gröschel as a Polonism (1972, 305). Cf. the synonymous deadjectival adverbs with the formant *-e* occurring in MS' texts: сполне (с) (cf. Ukr. спільно), сполечне (с) (cf. Pol *społecznie*).

потихȣ (112b,20) 'quietly' is present in CSU, CSBR, and CSP (*po cichu*), and is cited as a common Ruthenian form by Kramko.

по жидоⷡскȣ (3 times, e.g., 147b,2-3) 'in the Jewish language' is also cited by Kramko (cf. поеврейскȣ above).

7.4.1.1 Gröschel cites two adverbs consisting of по+dative as occurring in the language of IV: he describes попростȣ and поготовȣ as "typical Ukrainian forms" (*typische ukrainische Formen*; 1972, 312). Comparison of the forms cited above allows us to make several general statements concerning this construction: first, it is not common in Ruthenian before the sixteenth-seventeenth centuries, judging by how few of these forms are cited in SSUM; second, with the exception of adverbs based on adjectives in -ский, it may be considered a native

Ruthenian formation, or at the very least as a development shared by Ruthenian and Polish (note the number of forms still found in CSR and CSBR, and more in CSU than in Polish); and, finally, the structure *po X-sku* can be treated as Polish, or at least as heavily influenced by that language, because none of these forms have remained unchanged in CSU and CSBR.

7.5.0 *The Adverbialized Comparative*

In the Ruthenian system two variants of one suffix are used adverbially: *-ěj* and *-ej*. The formant *-ěj* represents a contraction of the old comparative formant *-ěe* (*-ěje*: see Bevzenko 1978, 377), while *-ej* may be seen either as the marker of the Polish comparative or as the B-R rendering of *-ěj*.[4] The importance of *-ej* in Smotryc'ky's language is clear, accounting for 204 adverbial forms; it is nevertheless less frequently used than *-ěj*, which occurs 302 times. (Therefore the ratio of *-ěj* to *-ej* is 3 to 2). More pertinent to this discussion, however, is the number of *different* lexemes with which the two formants occur: U-R *-ěj* is more productive in MS' language, because that number is significantly larger than it is for *-ej*. All forms attested with these formants are listed below, beginning with *-ej* (in the event one lexeme occurs with both variants, both spellings are provided together). Some lexemes also occur with the superlative prefix na-, forming adverbs of the type 'most X-ly' (or, as in the case of на́перве́й, 'first of all'); such forms are supplied in the second column.

ближей (5 times)	**наближей** (1 time)
	наболей (1 time)
далей (16 times), -**ѣй** (1 time)	
должей (1 time)	
иначей (19 times)	
нижей (7 times)	
	налепшей (1 time)
обширней (1 time), -**ѣй** (2 times)	

[4] Kramko, for instance, identifies the formant simply as -ej (1988, 298). In this particular instance such an approach might be explained as "Belaruso-centric": because *ě yielded [e] in Belarusian there is no reason for a differentiation between two orthographic variants of one formant.

особливей (1 time)	
первей (75 times), -ѣй (75 times)	напервей (18 times)
порожней (2 times)	
рачей (35 times)	
(рыхлѣй [2 times])	нарыхлей (1 time), -ѣй (2 times)
рѣдшей (1 time)	
срожей (1 time)	
	натѧжей (1 time)
выш(ш)ей (11 times)	навышшей (1 time)
	нащырей (5 times)

7.5.0.1 All remaining adverbialized comparatives (30 additional lexemes) are only found with the Ruthenian formant *-ěj*:

барзѣй (99 times)/набарзѣй (8 times), беспечнѣй (1 time), быстрѣй (1 time), власнѣй (1 time), выразнѣй (3 times), значнѣй (6 times), зноснѣй (1 time), лацнѣй (6 times), латвѣй (5 times), лепѣй (1 time), милѣй (4 times), мнѣй (2 times)/намнѣй (32 times), неможнѣй (2 times), обфитѣй (1 time), оказалѣй (1 time), охотнѣй (2 times), наоздобнѣй (3 times), певнѣй (1 time), пилнѣй (1 time)/напилнѣй (1 time), покорнѣй (1 time), пожитечнѣй (2 times), принамнѣй (9 times), раднѣй (2 times), скорѣй (1 time), страшнѣй (1 time), сȣровѣй (1 time), частѣй (2 times)/начастѣй (3 times), шкодливѣй (1 time), ꙗснѣй (3 times), ꙗвнѣй (1 time).

7.5.0.2 For some lexemes the two variants clearly occur in free variation (for example, первей 75 times–первѣй 75 times), while the use of one or the other can also be lexically based: e.g., a form like барзѣй, which occurs so frequently but consistently with only one variant; or далей, which is labelled a Polonism by Gröschel (1972, 311). There is one criterion, however, that requires the use of *-ej* over *-ěj*: the presence of an alveolar hushing (š,ž) or affricate (č); this consonant can be the result of a mutation (when the stem of a form ends in a mutatable consonant, usually a velar), or the comparative formant *-š-*. Apart from далей, Gröschel only cites the form inačej as an example of *-ej*, and he describes it as a direct borrowing from Polish; *-ěj* is the rule in IV, e.g., далѣй, барзѣй (ibid.).

The fate of many of these adverbial forms in the modern languages sheds more light on this particular segment of MS' morphology. In particular, the fate of four particular forms with the ending *-ej* (ближєй, далєй, иначєй, рѣдшєй) reveals the following: the forms attested in MS are lost in CSU (cf. ближче, далі/дальше, інакше, рідше), retained in CSP (cf. *bliżej, dalej, inaczej, rzadziej*), but also retained in CSBR: бліжай, даляй, іначай, радшай. This group of adverbs cannot be simply identified as "Polonisms," then, but can also be interpreted as features of B-R.

7.5.1 *Miscellanea Comparativa*. In addition to comparative adverbs formed with the suffix *-ej*, comparatives and superlatives with the formant *-š-* (see 4.4.1) can also occur adverbially with zero-endings (therefore *-š*) and with the ending *-e* (*-še*). Comparatives are found 102 times, superlatives with na- 2 times, naj- 4 times, and pre- 1 time (these numbers have all been included in the totals cited in Chapter 4 for each type of comparative and superlative formation). The most usual ending is -# (zero): болшъ (90 times, accounting for the vast majority of these forms, e.g., 41a,12) 'greater, more greatly,' горшъ (228a,10) 'worse,' лѣпш (3 times, e.g., 155a,25) 'better,' мє/н/ш (139b,24) 'less,' вышъ (509b,19) 'higher, more highly,' as in о вышъ рєчєныхъ . . . словахъ 'about the words spoken above.' In seven examples we find *-še*: болшє (2 times, e.g., 55b,4) and вышшє (4 times, e.g., 318b,11), лѹчшє (K24a,4) 'better.' Among superlative adverbs we find only the zero-ending: наболшъ (2 times, e.g.392b,10) 'most' and наймєншъ (4 times, e.g., 245b,16) 'least.' Cf the one example of the prefix pre- in прєвышє (K26a,12) 'most high(ly).'

One adverb in *-e* not containing the formant *-š-* is Slavonic пачє (24,4) 'more' (note PB пачє: радшєй, болшєй, на̂то). The form про̂ (K11b,22) 'and so on' should be interpreted as an abbreviation of прочєє (K4a,1) 'idem.'

7.5.2 Several of the superlative formations occur with a preceding element ѧкъ and express "as X-ly as possible" (lexemes occurring in this kind of construction are included in the lists given above): ꙗкъ нащирєй (34b,27); ꙗкъ нарыхлєй (326b,20); ꙗкъ начастѣй (34b,26) 'as sincerely, quickly, often as possible.' The same construction is evident in CSU: якнайбільше 'as much as possible'; in CSBR the standard means of expressing this concept is with the modal мага: як мага больш (this is also possible in CSU, e.g., якомога більше). We find the pattern *jak* + *naj-* in CSP as well; while the presence of this feature in MS' texts is probably affected to some extent by the influence of Polish, the fact that it is retained in CSU allows for its interpretation as a shared Polish-(U-)R feature.

When the adverb is preceded by the pronominal element тым (the non-fem. instr. of то) the phrase expresses '(all) the more X-ly': тымъ рыхлѣй (67a,27) 'all the more quickly'; тымъ ıавнѣй (265b,10) 'all the more clearly.' This construction is present in East and West Slavic: CSU тим більше, CSBR тым больш 'the more,' Pol *tym gorzej* 'the worse'; cf. the same pattern in CSR, in which we find тем + comparative.

7.5.3 *Numerical adverbs.* Three adverbial forms based on ordinal numerals are also used in JU:

повторє	(3 times, e.g., 339b,12) 'secondly'; this form is present in SinSlav.
потрєтє	(339b,15) 'thirdly.'
почєтвєртє	(339b,23) 'fourthly.'

Derivatives of ordinal numerals are also identified in IV, however they are not prefixed and are characterized by long adjectival endings: вторοє, трєтєє, чєтвєртоє, etc. (319). Forms of this type are described by Kramko as belonging to an archaic tradition, in use primarily in the fourteenth-fifteenth centuries (1988, 304). The example повторє cited for MS is obviously archaic by virtue of the lexical element втор, but the construction по-X-є is still found in CSU: по-перше 'firstly,' по-друге 'secondly,' по-третє 'thirdly,' по-четверте 'fourthly.' This formation is also used in CSBR, but with the neuter long form adjectival desinence: Br. па-другое, па-трэцяе; it is therefore possible to identify the forms in MS more specifically as U-R, while those examples cited for the language of IV could also be called B-R.

7.6 *Conclusion*

As a whole, the Ruthenian category ‘adverb’ can be characterized as a morphological class that is extremely open or susceptible to the influence of Polish. In other words, in a class of forms that may be generally described as ‘lexical’ (i.e., based on whole and immutable forms rather than merely on desinences), Polish elements are plainly able to enter the system and be productive, just as ‘traditionally’ lexical elements (substantives, verbs, adjectives) are able to do. Among comparative formations, *-ěj* can be interpreted as a (Ukrainian-) Ruthenian element, while the widespread use of adverbial forms with the formant *-ej* can be explained as influenced by Polish as well as by Belarusian-Ruthenian (beyond those examples where *-ej* is required over *-ěj* by virtue of the presence of a predesinential hushing). Other adverbial formations are also of interest by virtue of their presence or absence in the CSU and/or CSBR systems.

CHAPTER EIGHT

Prepositions, Conjunctions, Particles, and Interjections

8.1 *Prepositions*

The prepositions attested in Smotryc'kyj's texts are generally the same as those used by Vyšens'kyj—they may without hesitation be classified as "Ruthenian." As was the case with adverbs, special mention of prepositions in the language of IV will only be made when particular differences between IV and MS are noted. These can include differences in form, meaning, and usage, as well as the absence of a given preposition in IV. Of the Ruthenian sources used in this book, only IV and SSUM can reliably be consulted for purposes of comparison because Didiakin-Leeming 1969, Kernyc'kyj 1967, and Bulyka et al. 1988 exclude these morphological categories from their studies. Prepositions, conjunctions, and particles may or may not be present as headwords in PB or SinSlav (they are more often lacking), while only a few are attested in P-M.

бєзъ + G — (187 times) 'without' is general Slavic: бє жадной вонтпливости 'without any doubt' (K8a,17).

въ + L — (1000+ attestations) is used to denote location: в Києвѣ (K2a,5) 'in Kyiv,' в мирѣ (K4a,6) 'in the world,' etc.; the variant во occurs before consonant clusters: во всємъ (K6b,14) 'in everything.' The same preposition occurs hundreds of times with the accusative case; this construction usually expresses "motion to/into," but is also common in time expressions: в дни тыи (K2b,26) 'in those days.' The preposition у/в occurs with the same cases and meanings in throughout East Slavic.

вє̂лє + G — (N III,32) 'according to' is attested as of the sixteenth century in U-R. Forms corresponding to вєдлє are found in modern Polish, Czech, and the southwestern Ukrainian dialects (Dzendzelivs'kyj 1969, 28). It is lacking in FS, SinSlav, IV, SSUM, and CSU and CSBR, but is present in P-M and *Aleksandryja* (Leeming 1968, 302). This form is clearly identifiable as a Polonism. See вєдлȣг below.

вєдлȣгъ + G — (317 times) 'according to' is clearly of Polish origin but functioned just as clearly as part of the living Ruthenian system: вєдлȣгъ . . . Дв́да (K3b,8) 'according to David.' The number of attestations in MS alone gives some indication of its role in that language. In contrast, вєдлȣг is only attested twice in IV, and Gröschel describes this form simply as a Polonism. It is cited as a headword in SinSlav, and is used as a gloss for по in Berynda's *Leksykon*. It does not occur in FS or SSUM. The formal and semantic properties of the pair вєдлє-вєдлȣг can be likened to the same patterns apparent in the pair подлє-подлȣг (see these forms below). See also Hruca 1976 on all of these prepositions in B-R. This preposition is no longer extant in CSU or CSBR, but is current in CSP.

вмѣсто + G — (65 times, e.g., 9a,1) 'instead' is commonly used in Ruthenian texts, but should be considered marked as a Slavonicism. This is supported by its inclusion as a headword in Berynda's *Leksykon*, as well as its use in CSR, and subsequent loss in CSU and CSBR, which have replaced this preposition with замість and замест, respectively.

внѣ + G — 'outside of' is only found 2 times and may be considered an archaic or Slavonic element in MS' language: внѣ цєркви (K11b,5) 'outside of the church.' It is unknown in CSU and CSBR, but is still found in CSR. It is listed as a headword in PB (glossed as 'звнȣтра') and is used as a gloss for на дворѣ in SinSlav. Note also FS' use внє, внѣ.

внѹтрь + G ‘inside of’ can be assigned to the “elevated” or Slavonic level along with внѣ (above). It is attested 13 times in MS: хто ѧкъ много добра в̓ теперешнѣ̂ вѣкѹ скрылъ внѹтрь себе . . . (115b,23–24) ‘he who in this life/age has hidden so much good in himself. . . .’ The Slavonic interpretation is supported by data from PB and SinSlav: внѹтрь is listed as a headword in the former, and as a gloss for внѹтрѣ in the latter. CSU has the derivative adverbial form внутрі ‘inside’ (as does CSR), but it is identified as a dialect form in SUM. In CSBR унутры exists as adverb and as preposition. The preposition внѹтрь is not attested in IV, and functions as an adverb in FS.

впередъ *See* ѹперед below.

впосредокъ + G (135a,19) ‘in the middle (of)’ is not uncommon in Ruthenian, as preposition and adverb: it is cited in HSBM, but is not attested in any of the other Ruthenian sources consulted. It is probable that Polish played a role in the maintenance of this form in Ruthenian (cf. CSP *wpośród* [adverb] and *pośród* [preposition]). Kramko cites впосредкѹ, with the locative desinence -u, as a clear Polonism (1988, 304). See also зъ посредкѹ, посредкѹ, посродкѹ.

впреко + D (3 times, only in JU, e.g., 495b,7) ‘contrary to’ is not attested in any Ruthenian sources but HSBM (in which this very example from JU is the only one cited), and does not occur in CSU or CSBR. These facts, together with the existence of вопреки + dative meaning the same thing in CSR, point to a Slavonic interpretation, possibly of Smotryc′kyj’s own invention. Compare also the adverbs преко, напреко described in chapter 7.

впротив + D (4 times, e.g., K6b,11) is identified three times in MS, in *Kazan'e* as well as in JU: Живот . . . Славы, а смерть Геенны в̓ противъ собѣ стоѧтъ (K13b,1–2) ‘the life of glory and the death of Gehenna stand opposite one another.’ This construction is marked by context as well as by the case it governs (compare против above). It is not attested in IV.

вслѣдъ + G (42 times, e.g., 62b,18) 'following, after' can be considered common Ruthenian. This form is extant as a preposition and as an adverb in all modern East Slavic languages, with the same meaning as in MS: CSU услід/вслід, CSBR услед, CSR вслед. Note шолъ вслѣдъ Х҃са (K18b,3–4) 'followed Christ.' The first element в- can be written unattached to слѣдъ (e.g., K18b,2), and Gröschel cites such spellings as an indication that the form вслѣдъ had not yet been lexicalized as a preposition (1972, 335). This orthographic practice might merely indicate MS' awareness of the origin of this preposition, viz. as a combination of the preposition въ and the substantive слѣдъ; for all intents and purposes, however, it functions as a unit in MS. This particular preposition is not cited as a headword in SinSlav or PB, and is not present in P-M.

втылъ + G (303b,18–19) 'behind (one's back)' is not found in modern East Slavic or Polish sources. Of the Ruthenian works consulted only HSBM cites this form, but it is described as an adverb rather than as a preposition (JU is not cited under this entry): а вты̑ себе абы нѣкого немѣлъ 'so that he would have no-one behind his back [when he spoke].' Smotryc'kyj's predilection for compound adverbs and prepositions beginning with the preposition въ (here + substantive тылъ) is well illustrated by this example.

дѣля + G (3 times, e.g., 275a,5) 'for.' This preposition represents the Slavonic variant of для (below), and is accordingly attested in PB as a headword; it also serves to gloss для in SinSlav, and is found in FS as well as in SSUM. Gröschel is of the opinion that дѣля could be interpreted either as a Slavonicism or as a feature of southwest Ukrainian, but its distribution in the aforementioned sources supports the interpretation of it being a Slavonicism.

дл҄ѧ + G (hundreds of attestations) 'for' is general Ruthenian, and is retained in all modern East Slavic languages: дл҄ѧ чого (K6a,5) 'for what reason.'

до + G (1000+ attestations) 'to, towards, until, before' is one of the most common prepositions in MS: до нєго (42b,19) 'to/towards him.' This preposition is current in all East Slavic languages.

зъ *See* съ/зъ below.

за + I
за + A 'behind, beyond, for': за єго помочю (K3b,10) 'for his help'; за злого осꙋжєнъ зосталъ (34a,16) 'he was/came to be condemned as an evil man'; плачтє за грѣхи свои (K6a,3) 'lament (cry for) your sins' (both constructions: hundreds of attestations). This preposition is commonly used with both cases in the modern East Slavic languages. In 4 instances we also find за + genitive meaning "during": за днїй Ірода кролѧ (459a,2) 'during the days of king Herod.' Gröschel identifies the same construction once in IV (1972, 330), and за + genitive is also present in P-M, translated as "within" a certain time period. This construction is also found in CSU and CSP. In CSBR and CSR "time during/within" is expressed by means of за + accusative, therefore the genitival construction in MS' texts might be referred to as specifically U-R/Polish. This use of за is not attested in FS or in SSUM: in the early U-R texts represented in the latter we find за + accusative for "time during/within," strongly suggesting that the Ruthenian and CSU construction arose as a direct result of contact with Polish.

зєвнꙋтр + G 'outside of' is a clear Polonism which is only found once in MS: цєркви: зєвнꙋтр которои (K20b,10) 'the Church . . . , outside of which.' In this form again note the Polish reflex of /e/ for the back jer (cf. CSP *zewnątrz; ze lzamy* under съ/зъ below). This preposition is not mentioned by Gröschel, and it is not attested in FS, SSUM, or in SinSlav. Note PB внѣ: звнꙋтра, надворѣ, кромѣ.

змєжи + G (K21a,9) 'from among' is the result of the fusion of two prepositions зъ + мєжи (see above). This combined form functions as a new preposition, as do similar forms in CSU and CSBR: CSU з-під 'from under,' з-за 'from behind,' CSBR з-пад 'from under,' etc. Such forms are also known in CSR, as well as in Polish, e.g., *spod(e)* 'from under.' This type of preposition is not discussed in Gröschel's study, and this particular preposition is found neither in CSU/CSBR, nor in the language of MS' contemporaries.

з҆ посрєдкꙋ + G (196a,8) 'from among' probably also represents a Polonism: cf. CSP *spośród;* nowhere else is the form found as it is attested in MS, but спосрєди is present in the language of FS.

къ + D (147 times) 'to, towards' is a marked element in MS' texts, versus the more common preposition до. The number of times it occurs is deceptively large, giving the impression of a form that was in common use; къ was in the process of being replaced by до, however. The contexts in which къ occurs are clearly definable, as prepositional phrases consisting of: 1) къ + personal (and other) pronouns, 2) къ + forms obviously marked as religious and/or biblical terms, and 3) къ + miscellaneous forms that clearly make up phrasal units. Examples of these categories are: к҆ нємꙋ (39 times, e.g., 42b,12) 'to/towards him,' к҆ намъ (19 times, e.g., 46b,9) 'to/towards us,' к҆ ним҆ (16 times, e.g., 212b,18) 'to/towards them'; к҆ Бг҃ꙋ (16 times, e.g., 136a,21) 'to God,' к҆ Хрⷭ҇тꙋ (237a,21) 'to Christ,' к҆ Сн҃ꙋ (278a,20) 'to the Son,' к҆ Гд҃ꙋ (337b,19) 'to the Lord'; лицємъ к҆ лицꙋ живєшъ (K8a,10–11) 'you live face to face,' один҆ к҆ дрꙋгомꙋ (4 times, e.g., 424b,3–4) 'one to another,' Ктомꙋ (2 times, e.g., K7a,17) 'in addition,' к҆ воли (11 times, e.g., 56a,23) 'to [one's] will.' In phrases such as к҆ тєбѣ (e.g., 512b,24) 'to you' the stylistic level of къ is also indicated by the form of the second singular personal pronoun: Slavonic тебѣ, as opposed to Ruthenian тобѣ. In CSU and CSBR the function of this preposition is expressed by до, whereas it is still the standard CSR preposition expressing "towards, to (a person)." The marked status of къ is confirmed by SinSlav, in which this preposition is cited as a Slavonic gloss for до. See also кꙋ below.

кромъ + G (6 times, e.g., 93b,14) 'besides, with the exception of; outside of' is a clearly Ruthenian form, corresponding to CSU крім (but note CSBR акрамя). The Slavonic variant кромѣ is only found twice, and its stylistic level is clear from the context, a biblical citation, as well as from its form: кромѣ тѣла (K13a,13) 'outside of the body.' Immediately following, this passage is translated (explained) in Ruthenian: here we find the phrase кромъ тѣла (K13a,16). The difference in levels or styles existing between *Kazan'e* and JU is apparent with regard to this preposition, for even in contexts which could be described as "biblical," in the latter we still find the Ruthenian variant кромъ (243a,15). In Berynda's *Leksykon* Slavonic кромѣ is defined as безъ 'without.' The variant окромъ is cited in SinSlav, glossed as точию, кромѣ; the latter, however, is also listed as a headword in this lexicon, glossed as оевѣнъ (кромъ is not cited in this source). Both кроме and окроме are attested in FS, while SSUM cites кромъ, кроме, and кромѣ for early U-R. In P-M кромъ is glossed 'except for,' while окромъ is glossed as 'beyond.' CSR retains the Slavonic variant, кроме.

кромѣ *See* кром above.

кꙋ + D (18 times, e.g., IIa,14) 'to, towards' is a Polonism corresponding to East Slavic/Slavonic къ: кꙋ понятїю (IIa,14) 'to/for an understanding.' This preposition is current in the three major West Slavic languages, and is still found in West Ukrainian

	dialects, e.g., под'ку мні 'come to me' (CSU іди до мене; Dzendzelivs'kyj 1969, 80).
мєждȣ	*See* below мєжи.
мєжи + I	(107 times) 'among, between' belongs to the Ruthenian stylistic level: мєжи людьми (K3a,2) 'among people.' This form of the preposition is still found as a variant of між in CSU, while only між is current in CSBR. Compare PB мєждȣ 'мєжи,' SinSlav мєжи 'мєждȣ'; both of these forms are present in FS and SSUM. With the instrumental case мєжи generally refers to location. It also occurs with the accusative case, indicating motion: насѣню ономȣ мєжи тєрнїє оупаломȣ (K12b,11) 'seed fallen among the thorns,' and и роздѣлилъ мєжи нихъ маєтность (35b,4–5) 'and he divided among them [his] property.' The form мєжи occurs in accusative constructions 22 times. The same preposition may be used with the accusative case in CSU, but CSBR attests між with the genitive. It is justified, then, to interpret this particular usage in MS as a U-R feature. Slavonic мєждȣ is found once in a biblical citation in *Kazan'e*: мєждȣ вами и Бг҃омъ (K10b,17) 'between you and God.' The Slavonic form мєждȣ is retained in CSR.
мимо + A	(16 times) 'past' is of particular interest because it is rare in East Slavic for this preposition to govern the accusative case: in CSR and CSBR it governs the genitive case, while in CSU мимо can occur with the accusative as well as with the genitive. The same possibility exists in CSP. It is possible, therefore, to identify this preposition more narrowly as U-R. Examples: мимо васъ, братїю мою (K8b,21–22) 'past you, my brethren [collective]'; мимо сєбє (154b,22) 'past [our]selves' (in which сєбє could of course be either accusative or genitive). This preposition is not attested in IV, while мимо is only attested as an adverb in FS (cf. this use of мимо in MS as well).

на + L
на + A
(hundreds of attestations) 'on, at, in; to, for' is general Slavic and expresses "place where": на небѣ (K3a,10) 'in heaven,' на земли (K3a,10–11) 'on earth.' It is equally common with the accusative case, in conjunction with which motion to or towards is expressed: на тоє мѣсцє (65a,11) 'to that place.' Both uses of на are current in CSU, CSBR, CSR, and CSP.

надъ + I
надъ + A
(hundreds of attestations) 'over, above' is general Slavic: над҆ вами (K17b,7) 'over you.' When preceding consonant clusters a fill vowel *o* can occur at the end of the preposition: надо мною (171b,6–7) 'above me.' With the instrumental case the focal point is usually the location of the action (or actor), with the accusative case motion is usually implied, even if metaphorically: на̂ мысль нашꙋ (K2b,8) 'above/ beyond our thought' (use with the accusative is as common as with the instrumental in MS). An interesting use of надъ + accusative is its use as a conjunction in the expression of comparison, also attested in IV (see 4.4.3.1). Надъ governs both cases in CSU to express these same distinctions, while it primarily occurs with the instrumental in CSBR; it can govern the accusative in that language, but this usage is limited to expressions of comparison.

напєрєдъ + G
(11a,2) 'before, in front of' is not attested in other Ruthenian sources (in SSUM, as in Polish, this form is only cited as an adverb), but is current in CSU; наперад occurs in CSBR, but it governs the dative case, not the genitive. The construction as a whole may be identified as U-R.

напротивъ + G
against, opposite' is used by Smotryc'kyj with two cases, the genitive (69 times) and the dative (15 times). The marked construction is that with the dative: 1) the dative construction is significantly rarer, 2) in *Kazan'e* only the dative is attested with напротивъ, 3) Uževič's grammar stipulates that this

preposition governs the dative (Bilodid 1970, 53a), that is, this construction represents a higher Ruthenian stylistic level. Cf. противъ Бг҃ѹ (K6b,20) 'against God,' проти҃ чл҃вка (43b,14) 'against (a) man.' Note especially the co-occurrence of the two cases in: не то҃ко противъ под҃аннмъ нашимъ, але и противъ неволникωвъ (394b,7–8) 'not only against our subjects, but also against serfs.' The use of the dative is linked to earlier patterns: in OCS противѫ occurs only with the dative, while CES противъ could occur with both cases. Both are in use with напротивѹ in FS, while противѹ is only found with the dative in PB. Similarly, in P-M the dative is used with *protyw* and *protywko*. CSU напроти, CSBR напроці, and CSR против all govern the genitive. Note CSP *naprzeciw(ko):* as "opposite, against" it governs the genitive, but when expressing "towards" (e.g., a person) it can occur with either case. CES/Slavonic tradition and Polish influence probably both played a role in maintaining the use of the dative in written Ruthenian. The place of stress is rarely marked in this form, but it does occasionally occur in final position; this might reflect the influence of Polish *(na)przeciwko,* in which suffixal -ko is disregarded and stressed penultimate i is reinterpreted as final. This preposition is not found in IV, and is listed as an adverb in SinSlav.

насередъ + G (87b,11) 'in the middle of' is present in CSU, but not in CSBR or other Ruthenian sources. Consequently, насередъ should also be described as U-R.

о + L
о + A (hundreds of attestations) 'about, concerning' is general Ruthenian. The use of о with the locative case is current in all East Slavic languages, and may be used to express "about, concerning" in all of them. This usage is now considered archaic and rare in CSU, in which it primarily occurs in such time expressions as о п'ятій годині 'at five o'clock.' The same construction is present in CSP (*o drugiej godzinie* 'at

2 o'clock') and in CSBR (а другой гадзіне), but the structure у дзве гадзіни is also possible in the latter (compare CSR в два часа 'at 2 o'clock.') The general use of the locative with о in MS' Ruthenian may be interpreted as reflecting the older CES norm, for all intents and purposes now lost in CSU. The preposition про (+ accusative) has replaced о (+ accusative) in that language. Especially interesting is the use of о + accusative, a construction that is extremely common in MS' texts. Typically we find this construction in conjunction with verbs of petitioning or trying, e.g., просити, пытати, старати сѧ: о животъ просити (K23b,8) 'to ask . . . for life'; о причинꙋ слѣпоты єго пытаютъ (167b,13) ' they ask about the reason for his blindness.' This is typical of Polish, but not of CSBR; in CSU "ask for" is expressible by means of про + accusative, but о + accusative is also acceptable (SUM). The latter construction is also attested in early U-R, for example, in 1404 in Halyč (SSUM). In a few instances, о is used with the accusative to express movement onto or against something: оударенъ о землю (97a,10) 'beaten to/against the ground.' This construction is also found in CSBR, CSR, and CSP, but is rare in CSU.

около + G (27 times, e.g., 105a,22) 'around, near' is expressed in CSU and CSBR by prepositions based on the same root кол-: CSU навколо, коло (attested in P-M, cf. CSP *koło*), CSBR каля, найкола, навокал. Ukr около and Br акола are still attested in the dialects. Около is clearly still part of MS' system, and can be identified as a general Ruthenianism. It is still attested as a literary form in U-R texts from the early eighteenth century (Bevzenko et al. 1978, 437–38). This preposition is attested in SinSlav, PB, and FS (in the last named it occurs as вокол, воокол, окол, около), but is not present in P-M or in IV. These facts indicate that около is a feature of "higher" style written Ruthenian, and therefore is marked in relation to the later elements навколо, etc. The presence of около in CSR may also be taken as an indicator of the higher stylistic level of this form. It is possible that the existence of the identical form in Polish played a role in the maintenance of Ruthenian около during the period in question.

опрочъ + G (333a,1) = прочъ (below). This preposition is common in the Ruthenian period (it is attested in SinSlav and SSUM) and is retained in CSU (опріч), CSBR (апроч), and CSP (*oprócz*). According to Brückner, however, this form was common to East and West Slavic, and should therefore not be considered a Polonism (1957, 437).

отъ (ѿ) + G (hundreds of attestations) is common to all East Slavic languages, retaining this particular shape in CSR but undergoing various changes in CSU and CSBR: CSU від attests prothetic v-, which conditioned tensing and lengthening o > [u] > [i]; CSBR ад reflects *akanne*, and in both forms the final dental stop is now voiced, as it is in Polish (cf. CSP *od*). The spelling отъ is found in MS and IV because these authors tend to adhere to traditional orthography. The spelling одъ is not uncommon in Ruthenian texts of this and earlier periods, as seen in SSUM (одъ and отъ), SinSlav, FS (also both), and P-M. This indicates that отъ probably had the phonetic value [od] in MS and IV as well. Отъ in MS can express "by" in agentive constructions: Ӏа҄ єстемъ пастыръ добрый и знаю мои, и знанъ бываю ѿ мои҄ (433b,4–5) 'I am a good shepherd and know my [sheep], and I am known by my [sheep].' This construction is not in evidence in modern literary East Slavic or Polish, and it is not cited for the language of MS' contemporaries; agentive use of отъ was typical of OCS, and is still present in older periods of East Slavic, as seen in Sreznevskij's *Materialy* (1955–56, 2:771).

передъ + I
передъ + A
(hundreds of attestations)'before, in front of' is common to all East Slavic languages. When preceding consonant clusters a fill vowel o can occur at the end of the preposition: передо мною (139a,1). This preposition is used 5 times with the accusative in MS when motion is indicated: переⷣ старосты . . . вожены будете (202a,21–22) 'you shall be brought before the elders.' Передъ is used with both cases in CSU, CSR, and the West Slavic languages, but only with the instrumental in CSBR. The variant form предъ is not uncommon in MS, occurring 18 times, all but one of which are used with the instrumental; the lone example of this form with the accusative is in вожен былъ преⷣ царѣ (K17a,20) 'he was brought before the kings' (compare with the example above). On orthographic grounds, this variant could be interpreted as reflecting either Polish *przed* or Slavonic прѣдъ. Gröschel favors the latter interpretation for the language of IV (1972, 326). In MS, however, the use of предъ is generally neutral—it therefore seems more likely to be a Polish variant rather than the B-R spelling of Slavonic прѣдъ. This variant may also appear in marked contexts, since, as noted before, MS uses Polonisms as markers of higher style: cf. преⷣ Бг҃омъ, преⷣ Гⷣемъ (76a,7; 29a,22). Note the following passage, in which East Slavic передъ is followed by предъ: поневажъ бры̑кїй естъ таковый чл҃вк переⷣ Бг҃ом, ведлугъ писма ст҃ого мовачого, нечистъ естъ преⷣ Гⷣемъ вsякъ гордосердый (29a,20–22) 'for unsightly is such a person before God, according to the holy scripture which says, impure is any arrogant [person] before the Lord.' In FS we find only предъ—approximately half of the attested forms are written with ѣ in place of е, indicating more clearly the stylistic level to which this preposition belongs in his language.

по + A
по + D
The most common usage of the three cases is with accusative. All three constructions are still found in

по + L

modern East Slavic and are well represented in early U-R (SSUM); по+ locative has for the most part replaced по+ dative in CSU and CSBR, while the latter is common in CSR and in Slavonic. По is attested 18 times with the accusative in MS, more than half of which occur in time expressions such as по весь вѣкъ (K16a,1) 'all [his] life,' по всѣ лѣта свои (K19b,21) 'all his years,' по сесь д҃е (495a,29) 'all this day,' по вси дни (409b,7) 'all the days' (here по approximately expresses 'through, during'). There are two examples of the distributional use of по: по три разы (32a,17) 'three times [each].' A few uses of по + accusative might generally be described as expressing movement to, onto, against, as in топтати . . . по змїю (43b,19–20) 'step on a snake.' This preposition is attested 42 times with the dative case, usually expressing "according to," but sometimes used in spatial constructions meaning "over, across, about": по водамъ (252b,19) 'across/about the waters,' but по серцꙋ своемꙋ (K6b,21) 'according to his heart.' The spatial application of по with the dative is relatively rare, especially in comparison with the more common occurrence of по + locative to express this same concept: по скалахъ (50b,6) 'about/over the cliffs,' по всѣхъ рꙋскихъ краинахъ (K2b,14–15) 'over all the Ruthenian lands.' Just as common is the temporal construction, expressing "after": по рожествѣ (495b,19) 'after the birth,' передъ тобою и по тобѣ (K26a,10–11) 'before you and after you,' по долгомъ засъ часѣ (292a,9) 'for after a long time,' and so on. По is attested a total of 271 times with the locative case. Comparing MS with IV, in the latter по occurs with the accusative 2 times, with the dative 32 times, and with the locative 36 times. According to Gröschel, the time at which Vyšens'kyj was writing must have been a period of competition between the dative and locative constructions, after which the locative became primary in the U-R system. He cites a lack of analytical material on which to base any other conclusion (1972, 325–26). Judging by the data compiled from MS' texts, however, the proportions in IV must be viewed either as a statistical aberration or as a reflection of the conscious use of the dative as an archaic or stylistically marked feature—they should not be seen as an accurate representation of the situation during the time of Smotryc′kyj and Vyšens′kyj. The overwhelming preference for по+ locative over по+ dative in MS is clear indication that the process of competition was for all intents and purposes already over with at this time.

поверхъ + G (250b,16) 'above' is native to East Slavic: it is cited in SSUM (but does not occur in FS or SinSlav), and is retained in CSU, CSBR, and CSR.

подъ + I
подъ + A (31 times) 'under,' e.g., поⷣ крилами (K27b,15) 'under the wings.' The occurrence of this preposition in contexts of motion (whether real or figurative) and in time expressions, that is, contexts in which the accusative case is required, is more common than the otherwise basic use of the preposition with the instrumental case. Accusative constructions are attested 57 times. Thus, for example, we see поⷣ оборонꙋ свою ... принѧти (K3b,20) 'take under one's protection'; поⷣ тотъ самый часъ (K3a,20) 'at that very time.' In CSU and CSBR, the preposition под has these same functions.

подле + genitive (2 times, e.g., 170a,11) 'beside.' According to Dzendzelivs′kyj, this preposition is attested in U-R in the sixteenth century and appears to have been common to Polish, Czech, and Slovak at that time (1969, 108). Подле is cited in SSUM, however (as early as 1389), so it evidently appeared in U-R even earlier; this form is also present in the language of FS. It is not attested in SinSlav, PB, or CSU and CSBR. It is, however, used in P-M with the same meaning as in MS. For MS as well as P-M it is best explained as a Polonism (it is extant in CSP); подлє is not mentioned by Gröschel.

подлѹгъ + G (256a,23) 'according to' is very similar to подлє in distribution: it does not occur in CSU or CSBR, but is present in Polish. It is not mentioned by Gröschel and does not occur in SinSlav or PB. It is present in SSUM and FS. MS, FS, and Polish are in complete agreement with regard to semantic usage of this form.

подчасъ + G (18 times, ony in JU, e.g., 29a,1) 'during' is not attested in the Ruthenian sources consulted, nor is it current in CSU. This preposition does occur in CSP and CSBR, however.

посєрєдъ + G (4 times) 'in the middle/midst of,' e.g., посєрєдъ морѧ (248a,1) 'in the middle of the sea.' This preposition is most likely an East Slavic (i.e., native Ruthenian) variant of a Polish form *spośród* 'in the midst of.' In addition to this East Slavic *polnoglasie* form there is a Polish and/or Slavonic variant посрєдъ (+ G) which is found twice in MS' texts, e.g., посрє̑ домѹ сєго божого (K7a,10) 'in [the midst/middle] of this house of the Lord' (cf. пєрєдъ/прєдъ above). This example clearly shows that посрєдъ is supposed to represent an educated form representing a higher level of discourse, orthographically influenced by such Polish/Ruthenian forms as прєдъ (cf. OCS посрѣдѣ). Gröschel comes to much the same conclusion with respect to спосрѣдъ (+ G) in IV (посрєдъ is not attested in the latter), identifying that form as pseudo-Slavonic (1972, 334). Посрєдъ (+ G) is used once in the same paragraph as мєжи (+ A): пало посрє̑ тє̑нѧ (319b,6) 'fell among the thorns'—пало мєжи тєрньє (319b,16–17) 'fell among the thorns.' This juxtaposition provides strong evidence of the place of посрєдъ in the system, that is, as a form characteristic of the higher or "formal" level of speech. The second statement paraphrases the first by using the clearly native Ruthenian form мєжи, and functions as an explanation of the non-native variant. Посєрєдъ is not attested in SinSlav, PB, or FS, but is cited in SSUM; this preposition is, however, current in CSU and CSBR: CSU посе́ре́д, Br. пасяро́д (in MS stress is either unmarked or final). The variant посредъ is also not attested in the language of MS' Ruthenian contemporaries, but we do find it in SSUM (as a Slavonicism) and посрѣди, посрѣдѣ, посреде, посреди in FS. In addition to посередъ, two related and synonymous forms are also attested: посредкꙋ (2 times, e.g., 132a,4) and посродкꙋ (409a,22). On the basis of the suffix -k- and desinence -u in the first form, and the vocalism in the second, both forms can be identified as Polonisms (the first is used in an introductory biblical passage).

посредъ *See* посередъ above.

посредкꙋ *See* посередъ above.

посродкꙋ *See* посередъ above.

пре + A (7 times in JU, e.g., 143b,4–6) 'through, across' is not attested in FS or SinSlav. It also is absent from CSU and CSBR. It is, however, found in SSUM and in Old Polish—in the latter it functions as a variant of *prez* (see below). It is also present in modern Slovak. It is certain, then, that пре is a West Slavic form; its presence in SSUM merely indicates that this form entered the Ruthenian system at an early date.

предъ *See* передъ above.

прежде + G 'before, earlier' is an adverb functioning as a preposition: it is clearly identifiable as Slavonic on the basis of the presence of South Slavic /žd/ instead of East Slavic /ž/. It is only identified once in MS' texts, in a biblical citation occurring in *Kazan'e*: пре҃де лѣтъ четы҃надесѧти (K13a,12–13) '14 years ago' (2 Cor 12:2–3). Прежде still functions as an adverb in CSR, but is not present in CSU or CSBR.

презъ + A (26 times) 'by, across, through' can probably be identified as a Polonism, reflecting CSP *przez*. This preposition is not cited by SUM, but is still listed in Hrinčenko's dictionary and in CSBR. It is attested in

SinSlav, FS, SSUM (прєзъ, прѣзъ), and *Aleksandryja* (Leeming 1968, 304), and occurs in PB as a gloss for чрєзъ. One can therefore confidently conclude that прєзъ was a functioning member of the Ruthenian system. Gröschel calls прєзъ a Polonism, identifying it with Polish *przez* rather than with Slavonic прєзъ (1972, 333), but this may again be somewhat too simplistic a view. It is more useful and correct to view this form as an element of "educated" or "cultured" speech in which its identity as "Polish" or "Slavonic" is necessarily lost or obscured by the phonetic shape of the form; compare прє̑ мєнє (K3b,14) 'by me' with прє̑ Ârхаг҃гла (410b,4) 'through, by means of the Archangel.'

при + L — 'at, in the presence of' is attested 106 times, e.g., з҄ сими . . . при насъ . . . мощми (K8b,19) 'with these remains in our presence.' This preposition is retained in all three modern East Slavic languages. One apparent use of при with the dative can be explained as an innovative u- locative: при озєрꙋ (303b,20) 'at/by the lake' versus the etymologically correct form in an immediately preceding biblical passage: при озєрѣ (303a,12).

противъ + G
противъ + D — (24 times, e.g., V III,126) 'against, opposite' can be equated with the same construction in CSU, viz. против/проти (+ G) (cf. also CSR против + G); in CSBR the form супрацъ + G is preferred. The same preposition is found 22 times, or almost exactly as frequently, with the dative case. Some examples of противъ + dative suggest that this construction is still marked in some way, even if not as purely Slavonic: проти҃ Бг҃ꙋ (265a,8) 'against God.' The even distribution of dative versus genitive in his texts clearly show, however, that the time of MS was a time of competition between the two constructions; compare, for example, the following in which both constructions are used: нє то̑ко противъ по̑даным нашимъ [= D], алє и противъ нєволникωвъ [= G]

(394b,7–9) ‘not only against our subjects, but also against serfs.’ IV: противъ + D, противко + G (333). The latter form is also attested in *Aleksandryja* (Leeming 1968, 297) and reflects Polish *przeciwko* ‘against’ (+ D). In P-M both forms are cited (once each) with the dative. In FS противъ (противȣ) is attested 3 times with the dative and once with the genitive. In SinSlav the headword противкȣ is glossed as Slavonic противȣ. In SSUM противъ is attested with both the genitive and the dative, although more often with the genitive. SSUM also attests противко and противкȣ (+ G and D), and противȣ (+ G and D).

прочъ + G (18 times, only in JU, e.g., O II,22) ‘besides, except for’ is not attested in FS, SinSlav, or SSUM (in which it is cited as an adverb), but is found in P-M. CSU and CSBR do not use this form, but it is known in Ukrainian dialects (SUM). On the opposition пречъ-прочъ see the entry “пречъ” in 7.2.1.

ради + G ‘for the sake of’ occurs twice postpositionally as in OCS, e.g., in васъ ради (K24a,5) ‘for your sake,’ and once prepositionally in ради имене твоего (K5a,1) ‘for the sake of your name.’ The latter construction does occur in CSU and CSR, but is not found in CSBR. The contexts in which ради is found in MS and the small number of attestations in his texts indicate that it is marked as a Slavonicism in Smotryc′kyj’s language: even the prepositional use noted above is found in a prayer opening the body of *Kazan'e*. This preposition is attested in FS, SSUM, PB, and as a Slavonic gloss for длѧ in SinSlav.

съ/зъ, со/зо, зе represent the fusion of two old prepositions, viz. съ + I and изъ + G: the result is one preposition (basic variant зъ) governing both cases. съ/зъ + G (1000+ attestations) expresses “from, out of, of,” while съ/зъ + I (hundreds of attestations) expresses “with.” The variant зъ is more frequently found in MS’ texts, съ only occurs in marked environments, usually biblical citations: ʼс тобою (K7b,7) 'with you.' Зо is common before consonant clusters, e.g., зо мною (K3a,7) 'with me,' зо всѣхъ сторѡнъ (174b,23) 'from all sides'; the variant со, like съ, is only found in marked contexts: со страстми (K18b,114) 'with passions,' со х͠ртомъ (K24a,3) 'with Christ.' Slavonic/CES изъ (= CSR) is not attested in MS. The Polonizing variant зе is also found, once in genitive and three times in instrumental constructions: зе всходꙋ (158b,13) 'from [the] rising,' зе лзами (405a,27) 'with tears.' With the exception of the last-named Polish variants, this preposition can be labelled "general Ruthenian": cf. CSU з, із (rarely зо, зі) and CSBR з, са. In early U-R the following forms are found: зъ, зо, зꙋ, зе, изе, изъ, исъ, съ (SSUM); cf. зъ, зо, изъ, изо, исъ, съ, со from the texts of FS.

скрозь + A — (4 times, only in JU, e.g., 271a,15) 'through' is encountered in FS (скрозе) and SinSlav, and is still found in CSBR. Although unknown to CSU, скрозь is still used in the dialects of that language. Cf. the Polish adverb *wskroś* 'through.'

ꙋ/оу + G — (71 times) 'at, near' is general Ruthenian: оу мене пити просишъ (156a,18) 'you ask me for [something] to drink.' In MS' texts this preposition represents only *u, not the positional variant of the preposition *vъ 'in, into.' In IV one attestation of в is an orthographic variant of /u/ (327). This also occurs in P-M. The fusion of *u and *v is in evidence quite early, e.g., in SSUM (въ, во, ве, вꙋ, вы, ꙋ, ꙋвъ, ꙋво, овъ) and in FS (ꙋ, въ, ꙋвъ, ꙋво); MS' generally traditional orthography did not allow for the reflection of this feature in the preposition, although we do find it very occasionally in other environments (see next entry and chapter 2).

оупередъ + G — (4 times, e.g., 280b,8) 'before (time)' occurs only in JU, and reflects the Ruthenian alternation /v/ ~ /u/ (see 2.1.1.8). When used with forms of the pronoun ве- 'all,' it may express 'above': оупере͠д всего (280b,8) 'above all [else],' оуперⷭ҇е всѣхъ иншиⷯ҇ (542b,2) 'above all [others],' and the like. This preposition is not attested in SSUM, FS, IV, or SinSlav, and does not occur as a headword in PB. In the modern languages вперед/уперед can be used as a preposition governing the genitive, but is more common as an adverb (SUM describes the preposition as "archaic" in CSU). On the adverb of time in the language of MS and other Ruthenians see 7.1.1.

черезъ + A (168 times) 'through; by means of' is general Ruthenian and has the same form in modern East Slavic. The place of stress is worthy of note: in all three modern languages, stress is initial, as it presumably was in MS' language; each time (4 times in all) it is used in *Kazan'e*, however, stress is final, while stress is not marked in JU (чере҇ 59b,15). Example from *Kazan'e*: чере́зъ тайнꙋ крщ҃енїѧ (K10a,13) 'through the secret of baptism.' Because of the overall Slavonic character of this latter text, final stress in черезъ must be patterned after Slavonic чрезъ (cf. PB *Leksykon*), in which there is no other vowel to carry stress.

8.2 *Conjunctions*

The "conjunction" is the most variable of categories examined to this point, and reflects the great ease with which non-East Slavic elements (of which Polonisms are the most obvious) could be used in MS' texts. Given this degree of variability, the largest sets of conjunctions expressing the same or similar meanings are grouped together.

8.2.1 "*Or*"

або (295 times) is most likely a native Ruthenian/East Slavic formation, rather than representing a borrowing from Polish. Gröschel points to final stress in CSU and CSBR as evidence of this, but in MS' texts *kamora* appears over initial a- indicating initial stress (see 2.0.4 on accentuation). In Berynda's *Leksykon* this form occurs as a gloss for или, and stress is marked on the final syllable. Its currency in the Ruthenian system is therefore undoubted. а̂бо . . . а̂бо . . . (e.g., 51a,23–24) expresses 'either . . . or . . . .' This conjunction is identified only once in *Kazan'e*, in which албо is the rule. In that text або in fact is found to occur in the same phrase as албо. Evidently або, by far the most frequently used conjunction in MS with the meaning 'or,' is felt to be too characteristic of the spoken language for frequent use in a text like *Kazan'e*. This form is attested once each in P-M and FS, and is common in early U-R (SSUM). In SinSlav або is glossed as 'зане, ꙗко.'

албо (24 times) is probably of Polish origin, a contraction of алибо. Judging by the distribution of this form in MS (especially the preference for албо over або in *Kazan'e,* e.g., K2b,5), he used it as an element of a higher style, as we have seen in other instances involving Polonisms. According to ESUM, the etymology of албо has not been satisfactorily explained (1:64), but Leeming interprets it as a Polonism (1968, 289). It is still found in western Ukrainian dialects but is not extant in CSU. SSUM and HSBM cite this form as occurring as early as the fourteenth century in U-R and B-R, respectively. Альбо is extant in CSBR, co-occurring with або. Stress in CSBR is on the final syllable, showing that this form has indeed become fully adapted to the native system, while the examples found in MS are stressed on the penultimate (i.e., initial) syllable, an indication of its Polish identity in his language. А́лбо is attested 3 times in the language of P-M, compared with only one attestation of або: this situation is similar to the distribution of албо and або in *Kazan'e*, which may be taken to mean that the level or style of language in P-M is meant to be relatively "high" (as it is in *Kazan'e*), and the Polish form албо is preferred to the native and unmarked East Slavic або. The same may be inferred from IV, in which або is found 3 times, албо/альбо a total of 37 times (340). In PB албо is one of the glosses for или (along with або and любо), while it occurs as a headword in SinSlav. Note also альбо in FS, next to або, или, либо.

или is clearly marked as a Slavonicism in Ruthenian, and only occurs once in MS' texts, in a biblical passage cited in *Kazan'e* (K2b,4). This conjunction is no longer extant in CSU and CSBR, but is retained in CSR. In contrast with MS, или is quite common in the language of IV. Gröschel is of the opinion that this conjunction should not simply be labelled as Slavonic, because its use was still widespread in fourteenth- and fifteenth-century Ruthenian (1972, 342). Data from SSUM suggest that such an assumption would be valid for this earlier period. As with да (see below), however, it seems that the use of или by Vyšens'kyj merely reflects a desire to use Slavonic elements in his written language. The inclusion of или as a headword in Berynda's *Leksykon* offers additional support for the interpretation of this conjunction as a Slavonicism: it is defined as 'або, албо, любо, хочай.' In MS или has been replaced by або, албо, and люб(о). The conjunction или does occur in one recension of P-M, but the other three conjunctions found in MS are also attested; или is also found in FS. As expected, или occurs as a Slavonic gloss for Ruthenian албо in SinSlav.

либо (5 times) is marked by its low frequency; it is not found in CSU or CSBR, in IV, PB, P-M, SinSlav, or PB (in PB it occurs neither as a headword, nor as a gloss for или). It is attested in earlier U-R and B-R, however, as reflected in FS and in SSUM, occurs in OCS, and remains in CSR. In MS it occurs only in JU, a text in which such a marked form would not be expected (if it were purely Slavonic), especially not in the unmarked contexts in which it occurs, e.g., in Бо хто ма҃є разоу҃м, або бога҃ство, або мо҃ц ѿ царѧ, або ѿ прїателѧ, либо ꙗкꙋюжъколвек в҆ собѣ силꙋ маєтъ и мꙋдрость (293b,21–23) 'For he who has reason, or riches, or power [given] from the king, or from a friend, or who has any kind of strength and wisdom in himself . . . .' Here, following several occurrences of або, it may have greater expressive force, e.g., 'or even. . . . '

люб(о) is common in Ruthenian: in SSUM only the form любо is cited, while in SinSlav one finds люб (glossed as ащє жє). In PB любо is one of the glosses for или (see above). It is not found in IV. In MS' texts люб is used 32 times, while любо is only attested three times (e.g., K6b,9). An interesting use of люб is its occurrence in juxtaposition with або and либо: слово пада҃є на слꙋхачѡвъ, которыи знайдꙋютсѧ або дорогою, або каменемъ, либо терньємъ, любъ тежъ доброю землею (322b,16–19) 'the word falls on the hearers, who are [*lit.* located] either on the road, or on stone, or on thorns, or also on good earth.' The loss of final -o in Ruthenian can be attributed to Polish influence, because Old Polish *lubo* was generally replaced by *lub* by the sixteenth century (the latter is found twice as often as the former; see SP XVI, XII:311). Although a form with final -o could have been perceived as a Slavonicism by the Ruthenian ear (cf. тако versus так, etc.), leading to a preference for the form люб, Smotryc'kyj's knowledge of Slavonic makes this unlikely. This conjunction is no longer found in CSU or CSBR; it is not unknown in the East Slavic area, however, since любо 'or' has been attested in western Russian dialects as recently as the nineteenth century (SRNG 17:237).

8.2.1.1 In tabular form, the textual distribution (of occurrences) of all conjunctions expressing "or" is as follows:

	Kazan'e	*Grammatiki*	*JU*
або	1	——	294
албо	7	2	15
или	1	——	——
либо	——	——	5
люб(о)	10 (8-#,1-о)	2 (1-#, 1-о)	24 (-#)

These data suggest the following: або is unmarked Ruthenian; албо and люб(о) are Polonisms that can be used in texts of varying stylistic levels; или is a Slavonicism; либо is not a Slavonicism or unmarked Ruthenian, but may carry greater expressive force.

8.2.2 *"But, However"*

а — (1000+ attestations) 'but, and' is common to all East Slavic languages, in which its function is primarily to accentuate contrasts, expressing "but, rather."

але — (1000+ attestations) 'but, rather' is probably of Polish origin (see Leeming 1968, 289), but has been common in Ruthenian documents from the fourteenth century (SSUM and HSBM). This conjunction is extant in CSU and CSBR, and in both languages stress falls on the final syllable. In MS' texts stress is either unmarked or occurs on the initial/penultimate syllable (i.e., as in Polish) in the great majority of cases, while final, or native Ruthenian, stress is found 8 times. Áле has clearly replaced но 'but' in MS' Ruthenian, as it has in the language of IV (341).

ано — (7 times, only in JU, e.g., 41b,26) 'but, for, that' is not present in CSU and CSBR, but is certainly well-known in the Ruthenian period. It is attested in FS and is cited in SSUM and HSBM. A corresponding form *ano* is also found in CSP, but is glossed as a particle expressing "well then, why."

вшакже — (74 times, only in JU, e.g., 36a,12) 'however' is a Polonism attested in SinSlav, PB (glossing 'обаче'),

Aleksandryja (Leeming 1968, 294), and retained only in Polish.

єднакъ (92 times, e.g., K18a,2) represents the more common of two phonetic variants for the conjunction with the meaning 'however' (i.e., [jednak] ~ [odnak]). The variant однакъ occurs 17 times (e.g., 131a,4). Compare with CSU однáк, Belarusian аднáк, Polish *jednak,* Russian однáко. Eighteen examples of єднакъ and 4 of однакъ either have initial stress or have no stress marking; 74 examples of єднакъ and 13 of однакъ have end stress, indicating active participation in the native Ruthenian system. Both forms are identified in the language of IV, and Gröschel states that Polish *jednak* could have influenced the spelling єд- in IV (1972, 31). Although однакъ is clearly the East Slavic variant with respect to the initial phoneme, here we see mixing and interaction of East Slavic and Polish in Ruthenian. The form єднакъ is attested in SinSlav as well as in Berynda's *Leksykon* (as a gloss for ѹбо); only однак(о) is attested in P-M. The forms єднако (K3a,13; 82b,4) and однако (278a,21) are not variants of єднакъ and однакъ (respectively) but express "in the same way, alike," i.e., they are adverbs formed from єдн- and одн- 'one.' Compare also єднако 'in the same way' in FS. Note the identical CSR conjunction однако 'however'; one example of однако 'however' is attested in P-M, in addition to однакъ.

лєчъ (111 times, e.g., 33a,7) 'but, however' is a Polonism that does not occur in IV. Gröschel only mentions *lecz* in connection with his discussion of the particle *le* (*le-cz, a-le*), which occurs only in West Slavic (1972, 341). All but one (in *Kazan'e*) of the attested examples in MS are found in JU. In SinSlav лєчъ is found, glossed as жє. In PB the reverse is true. This conjunction is present in FS, but is not attested in SSUM. This form clearly is a functioning member of the Ruthenian morphological system.

но (3 times) 'but' is linked to marked environments, much in the way that **или** 'or' is. As is the case with this latter conjunction, **но** is attested only in *Kazan'e*; in the overwhelming majority of cases we find **але** instead. Thus, for example, we do not find **но** in biblical environments in JU, but it does occur in *bona fide* biblical quotations in *Kazan'e:* **нектомꙋ себѣ живꙋтъ, но оумершемꙋ за них҆** (K10b,11–12) 'they do not, further, live for themselves, but for the one who died for them' (2 Cor 5:15). This conjunction is not found in P-M or SinSlav, but does occur in FS, SSUM, and is cited as a headword in PB, glossed as '**але**.'

однакъ *See* **єднакъ** above.

8.2.3 "*That*"

ижъ (635 times) is not found in CSU or CSBR, and so might be considered a Polonism—both *iż* and *iże* are found in CSP. The alternative is to explain its use in Ruthenian as an areal phenomenon supported by its presence in Polish. Gröschel favors this explanation (1972, 346–47), and the frequent attestation of **ижъ** in MS and of **иж(е)** in early Ruthenian texts support such an interpretation (cf. **иже** in SSUM and FS). The same could also be said of such conjunctions as **абовѣмъ** and **бовѣмъ**. **Иже** is present in SinSlav and **ижъ** in PB as a gloss for **заеже**. The relative pronoun **иже** (listed as a headword in Berynda's *Leksykon*) is not to be confused with this conjunction.

ꙗко (3 times) is a Slavonic element that is attested only in biblical passages cited in *Kazan'e*: **Кто вовѣститъ Аврааму, . . . ꙗко породи сн҃а во старости своей** (K2b,13–14) 'Who announces to Abraham..that she will bear a son in her old age?' This form is graphically identical to the commonly used adverbial form "as" (see 7.4).

што (60 times) 'that' is used as a conjunction as it is in CSU and CSBR today: **Вѣдаєтє абовѣмъ** ... **што ѡна єсть кꙋ понѧтю** ... **ꙗзыка чистости** (IIa,14) 'for you (should) know that it [the grammar] is for the understanding of [the] language of purity.' This use of **што** is common throughout the East Slavic languages, but note the low frequency of this conjunction relative to that of **ижъ** (635 times: see above) and **жє** (821 times: see below). The Ukrainian phonetic variant **що** is not found as a conjunction in MS.

жє (821 times) 'that' is extremely common in Ruthenian, and is widely used as of the fourteenth and fifteenth centuries (SSUM); it is a borrowing from Polish, and no longer functions as a conjunction in CSU and CSBR. This conjunction is attested only twice in IV (350). It is present in SinSlav, and for the language of P-M **жє** is only described as an emphatic particle (see 8.3 below). The distribution of the three conjunctions **жє**, **ижъ**, and **што** vis-à-vis one another is 821:635:60. The first two are no longer extant in CSU and CSBR, but are by far the most common forms in Ruthenian of 1600. The conclusion one might draw from MS' statistics is that the Polonisms were literary/educated forms that were, at least for a significant period of time, in vogue because of the level of Polish culture and the well-established use of Polish in Ruthenian society.

8.2.4 *"In Order (To, That), So That"*

абы (1000+ attestations) is clearly identifiable as "Ruthenian." Analogous forms can have the same meaning in CSU and CSBR. Final stress is occasionally marked by MS, an indication of its status as an element of the Ruthenian system. In constructions with this conjunction verbs are required to be in the past tense form, as dictated by the presence of the modal particle -**бы**-. As is the case in Polish, **абы** is frequently found with suffixed personal endings, as in абымꙿ розмовилꙿ (K7a,21–27b,3) ‘that I should speak,’ абымъ чинилъ (41b,15) ‘that I should do,’ and so forth. Gröschel calls such forms “Polonisms” (1972, 351). While Polish influence doubtless provided the impetus for wider use of such forms, the extent to which such patterns are followed indicates that this feature is to be considered “Ruthenian” and not simply a “Polonism.” As further evidence against treating this form merely as a Polonism we note its presence in early Ruthenian texts: it is amply attested in early U-R (SSUM) as well as B-R (FS and HSBM; as of the 15th century according to the latter source).

ажъбы (several occurrences, e.g., 493a,12) is attested in early U-R (SSUM) and is cited in HSBM, but is not present in the other Ruthenian sources consulted (or the modern languages); it appears to be a Ruthenianized variant of ажє́бы below.

ажє́бы (1 time: K9b,3): ажє́бы лацнѣй то, чого шꙋкаютъ, найти могли ‘so that they could more easily find that which they seek.’ Cited in SSUM and HSBM, this form is not found in PB, SinSlav, FS, IV, or P-M. It ought to be interpreted as stylistically marked; it is not current in modern East Slavic, but is in CSP (place of stress in MS reflects the Polishness of this form).

жєбы (485 times) ‘in order that, so that’ is by far the most commonly used conjunction occurring with the modal particle -бы in MS’ texts (cf. нжбы and штобы below). In this regard, the use of жєбы parallels that of жє, which is also the most common conjunction of its kind (see above). жєбы may occur alone, but is just as likely to be used with a suffixal element indicating the person(s) involved in an action: жєбысмо . . . готовили сєбє . . . (121 times, e.g., 28a,6–7) ‘in order that we prepare ourselves . . . ,’ 1pl; жєбымъ (36a,4) 1sg, etc. Most attested examples have no stress marking or have initial (here equals penultimate, or Polish) stress. Very occasionally final (Ruthenian) stress is marked in this form (see, for example, 34b,4). This conjunction is attested only twice in IV, as is the conjunction же (355). It is listed as a headword in SinSlav, and is supplied as a gloss for да in Berynda's *Leksykon*. This conjunction is current in CSP, East Slovak, and in many West Ukrainian regions (Dzendzelivs'kyj 1969, 56): in MS' texts it must be viewed as a Polonism; CSU equivalents are щоб, аби, якби, while каб is used in CSBR.

нжбы (25 times, e.g., 59a,5) is the functional equivalent of the conjunction штобы, as нжъ is of што (above); it is only attested in JU. This conjunction is not present in SinSlav, PB (as a headword), IV, or in CSU and CSBR. It is, however, extremely common in SSUM (as early as 1388), occurs in FS as нжебы, and is present in CSP. The same interpretations presented for нж(е) hold for нж(е)бы—it is either a Polonism, or the result of an areal development subsequently lost in the modern East Slavic languages.

штобы (20 times) is common in CSU and CSR (see also CES, as cited in Sreznevskij 1955–1956, 3:1579). It is not now extant in CSBR: CSU щоб (with the loss of final unstressed -и), Rus чтобы/чтоб, but CSBR каб. The purely Ukrainian variant щобы is in addition attested twice in MS (e.g., 111a,12). Gröschel does not mention the use of this conjunction by IV. It occurs in FS, and the following variants are attested in P-M: *cztoby, sztob, sztoby, szczob,* and *szczoby*. штобы is not found in SinSlav or PB, while жебы is (see above); this pattern indicates that the status of штобы in Ruthenian closely parallels that of што.

8.2.4 "*For, Since*"

абовѣмъ (313 times) may be described as a Polonism which has been lost in CSU and CSBR. Note Old Pol. *abowiem/abowim*. It is clearly part of MS' system, judging by the frequency with which this conjunction is used, even in the more conservative *Kazan'e*, for example, in нѣкоторыи абовѣмъ живота и смєрти станы . . . (K9b,14) ‘for several states of life and death . . . .’ This conjunction is common in the Ruthenian period, for it is included in SinSlav, *Aleksandryja* (Leeming 1968, 298), as well as in PB as a gloss for ибо ‘for.’[1] A Polish etymology for абовѣмъ is supported by its absence in early U-R and B-R sources (as represented, e.g., by SSUM and FS).

бо (636 times) is general Ruthenian and is retained in CSU, CSBR, and CSP (but note CSR ибо ‘for, since’); only 3 times do we find this conjunction in *Kazan'e*. A further indication of its status in the Ruthenian system is its presence in SinSlav (as well as FS) and marked absence in PB. It is generally unstressed; when stressed it does not differ in function from the unstressed form (e.g., in sentence-initial position, cf. K10b,21 and K19b,6).

бовѣмъ (604 times) is a Polonism and is no longer extant in CSU or CSBR. In Old Polish two forms of this conjunction were current, *bowiem* and *bowim* (SP XVI 2:345). Based on Smotryc'kyj’s orthographic system it appears that the latter is reflected in his Ruthenian. The Polish identity of this form is underscored by its absence in early U-R (SSUM). бовємъ is cited in HSBM, but all the datable examples come from the seventeenth century. Of the three conjunctions only бо is attested in P-M; it does not occur in FS. We note that бовѣмъ is absent in SinSlav (бо is present), бовѣмъ and бо are both lacking in PB.

понєважъ (418 times, e.g., K24b,21) is clearly a current element in the texts of MS. The fact that this conjunction is used only once in *Kazan'e* may be taken as an indication of its status in his system. This lexeme was widely used in the Ruthenian language of 1600, and is

[1] In SinSlav абовѣмъ is glossed as ‘или, ибо, бонє’; the editors state in a footnote (98) that the gloss ибо, бонє is a mistake, in place of correct либо, понє. Given the data from MS and Berynda’s *Leksykon*, however, it seems to me that the glosses provided in SinSlav are in fact correct.

given as a gloss for понеже by Berynda as well as by Zyzanij, and is present in SinSlav. It does not occur in earlier Ruthenian (as represented by FS and SSUM) and is not extant in the modern East Slavic literary languages. It is a borrowing from Polish (in which *ponieważ* is still current), a form which ultimately goes back to Czech *poněvadž* (ESSJ/P 2:574). The place of stress in many examples reflects the Polish source of this conjunction (поне́важъ: 310a,11), but in several instances, as is the case with many other conjunctions and adverbs, final stress is attested (9 times: e.g., 231b,12). поневажъ is not cited in the language of IV—only the Slavonicism понеже is identified by Gröschel (1972, 354). The same form present in FS and SSUM. In sum, frequency of occurrence is as follows:

	Kazan'e	*Gramm*	*JU*
абовѣмъ	19	1	293
бо	3	——	633
бовѣмъ	5	——	599
поневажъ	1	——	417

Абовѣмъ is clearly the least favored of the three, and belongs to a higher stylistic level. It is common in *Kazan'e* and the least common of the four within JU. The remaining three are relatively equal in stature, vis-à-vis each other in JU (with поневажъ the least common of the three) and distributionally in JU versus *Kazan'e.*

8.2.5 The remaining conjunctions can be listed without further subdivisions. Although one might make a case for creating certain subcategories, for example, for the expression of "if," secondary meanings can be present in some of the conjunctions that preclude their inclusion in such specific subcategories.

ажъ 'up to, until' is historically derived from а + же, with subsequent loss of the unstressed final vowel (ESUM

I:51). This conjunction is not to be confused with ажє (see below). ажъ is very common in MS, and is found 131 times in JU and *Kazan'e*. The distribution of this form in his texts can be described as occurring in two distinct patterns, with prepositions following it (nominal constructions) and without such prepositions (verbal constructions). Verbal constructions: ажъ выслꙋханъ бꙋдєшъ (298b,14) 'until you are [will be] heard out'; ажъ прїйдєтъ (459b,12) 'until he comes.' Nominal constructions: ажъ до скончєнѧ свѣта (518b,20) 'until the end of the world'; ажъ до крови працовали (513a,5) 'they worked until blood [until they bled]'; ажъ до розѣлєнѧ [*sic*] дши и дха (K24b,3) '(up) to the division of the soul and the spirit' (Heb 4:12). The preposition по can also occur with ажъ, expressing 'up to (and including),' as for example in: ажъ по сєй часъ (469b,115) 'up until this time.' Ажъ can occur with other conjunctions: ажъ поки рєкоу (463b,4) 'until I speak/have spoken' (see поки below). The use of ажъ in MS is parallelled by its occurrence in P-M, in which we find the combinations ажъ до, ажъ въ, ажъ на, and ажъ за, all of which in some manner express "as far as, until." ажъ is listed in SinSlav without a following preposition or conjunction, but ажъ поки is a gloss for доньдєжє in Berynda's *Leksykon*. It is lacking in FS. The conjunction аж is extant in CSU and CSBR. In SUM and TSBM ажъ by itself is termed a "conjunction" and is differentiated from ажъ + preposition-conjunction, which is labelled a "particle." In HSBM we find examples of ажъ поки and ажъ до cited under ажъ "conjunction," while ажъ до is also cited as an example of ажъ "particle." This vacillation indicates that the division between "conjunction" and "particle" is not so clear-cut in this instance, possibly suggesting that ажъ до and ажъ поки should be considered "complex" or "compound" conjunctions. Gröschel considers it a Polonism (1972, 342), as does Leeming (1968, 289).

ажє (6 times, e.g., K7a,19) ‘if’ is found in *Kazan'e* and once in JU (492a,9). It is no longer extant in CSU and CSBR and is not attested in PB, SinSlav, FS, IV, or PM. It is cited in earlier Ruthenian texts (SSUM and HSBM). ажє can be described as a marked form in MS’ texts, representing a stylistic level characteristic primarily of texts such as *Kazan'e*, e.g. ажє ꙗснѣй рєкꙋ (K3b,17–18) ‘if I speak more clearly.’

ачъ ‘although, if only’ occurs 4 times (e.g., K7b,5; 163a,7) and is attested in U-R and B-R from the fourteenth century, according to SSUM and HSBM. Ачъ has been lost as a conjunction in CSU and CSBR, but it still occurs in CSP. Gröschel makes no mention of this conjunction in IV. It is present in SinSlav. The presence of *acz* in Polish indicates that the influence of this language was responsible for its use in Ruthenian. Widespread attestations in Ruthenian over two centuries do suggest, however, that ачъ functioned as a full member of the Ruthenian system. See ачколвєкъ below.

ачколвєкъ ‘although’ is a Polonism, and is identified 33 times in MS’ language (e.g., 106b,26), while the native Ruthenian form ачколи (SSUM) is not attested. ачколвєкъ is also attested in SinSlav, PB (as a gloss for оубо), and *Aleksandryja* (Leeming 1968, 293). The forms ачкольвє and ачколи are found in FS. ачколвєкъ is not present in IV. See ачъ above.

ащє is a Slavonic conjunction which corresponds to Ruthenian Гды (see below), and consequently is attested only 13 times, all examples of which occur in *Kazan'e*. Note the following example, which is used in a biblical citation: Правєдник ащє постигнєтъ скончатисѧ (K9a,12; Wisdom of Solomon 4:7) ‘if/when a just man has to die.’ Further evidence of the marked status of this form in Ruthenian is its presence as a headword in Berynda’s *Leksykon*, glossed as єсли, бы, Ґды бы. Similarly, Ruthenian єсли is glossed as аще in SinSlav. In spite of the status of аще in Ruthenian, however, variants of this conjunction are still found in Ukrainian dialects: ащ, ащби, ащеби (cf. CES аче 'if'; see ESUM I:100). This form is not attested in CSBR; the phonetically very similar forms аще, ащы are attested in the dialects of that language, but these are variants of яще 'still, yet.'

Ґды (826 times: 1 time *Grammatiki*, 29 times *Kazan'e*, 796 times JU) 'if, when' is the unmarked Ruthenian counterpart of Slavonic аще; the clearest illustration of the status of these two conjunctions is the use of the former in an explanation of a biblical passage containing the latter: Праведникъ аще постигнетъ скончатися . . . (K9a,12) = Справедливый чл҃вкъ, Ґды ємꙋ прїйдетъ оумерети . . . (K9a,13) 'A just man, when/if he has to die . . . .' Although it was borrowed from Polish and was not retained by CSU and CSBR, Ґды is clearly a vital part of the system. Orthographically JU differs from Smotryc'kyj's other writings: in *Grammatiki* and *Kazan'e* the new grapheme Ґ is used for the voiced velar stop [g], while the old digraph кг is the norm in JU (cf. the same older spelling convention кгды/кгдыжъ in IV; 348; see also 2.1.1.1). The spelling кды is used twice in JU, an indication that the grapheme к here can represent voiced [g] by assimilating voice from the following voiced stop /d/; this spelling is also attested in SSUM. The suffix -жъ can be appended to this conjunction, expressing "as, since" (< Polish *gdyż*), for instance in 239a,16. Ґды often occurs with the suffixed particle -бы, in which case the new form is still used to mean 'if' or 'when,' and is used in modal constructions (e.g., in 422b,9).

да 'and; that . . . might' is rare in CSU, found more often in the dialects (if it occurs in the latter at all it is probably the result of Russian influence). It is not extant in CSBR. In MS' texts it occurs 3 times meaning "and," e.g., да ꙗкѡже воста Хс҃ . . . (K10a,18; Rom 6:3–4) 'and as Christ arose. . . . ' It means 'that . . . might' 5 times, e.g., in Хс҃ за вся оумре, да живꙋщїи . . . (K10b,11; 2 Cor 5:15) 'Christ died for all, that the living might . . . .' These citations show that да was marked as a Slavonic element in MS' language (this is especially evident in the environment of such Slavonic morphological forms as the aorists and the participle, etc.). Indicative of this is also the fact that да is not attested in JU. Note also the presence of да as a headword in PB (glossed as жебы), and as a gloss for жебы in SinSlav. In IV this conjunction is found much more frequently. Because да may still be used in colloquial and dialectal Ukrainian, Gröschel believes that it is impossible to label it as either Ruthenian or as Slavonic (1972, 398–99). Vyšensʹkyj's general proclivity for the use of Slavonicisms would seem to argue for its identification as Slavonic, however, rather than as a dialect feature of Ukrainian. This conjunction is extremely common in P-M, but the high style of many of its passages (and co-occurrence with other marked elements such as the preposition къ) support such an interpretation (see passages in Struminsky 1984, 24).

єжели (3 times, only in JU, e.g., 284a,21) 'if' belongs to the Slavonic level. It occurs in SinSlav as a gloss for Ruthenian єсли (see next entry).

єсли (594 times) 'if' [< *jest'* + *li*] is general Ruthenian, and is found in all modern East Slavic languages. Gröschel agrees with Humecʹka that єсли entered Russian from Polish via Ukrainian (1972, 353). The many attestations of єстли, єстьли, єсли in 15th-century U-R tend to support Humecʹka's view (SSUM). 549 times єсли has final stress in Smotrycʹkyj's texts, indicating its status as a full member of the native Ruthenian system, rather than merely reflecting Polish *jeśli*. In the remaining 45 forms stress is either unmarked or marked on the initial syllable. It is possible that such forms (especially with initial stress) indicate participation in a different, marked, stylistic level, and is intended to come across as more elevated: most of these examples are found in the biblical passages which begin each new section in JU, for instance in **Рєклъ Гдь; єсли вы ѿпꙋскаєтє чл҃вкѡмъ грѣхи ихъ, ѿпꙋститъ и вамъ ѻ҃цъ вашъ нбсный** (55a,1–2) 'The Lord said: If you forgive people their sins, your Lord shall forgive also you.'

зась (356 times) 'whereas, whereupon, for' is a Polonism not retained in the modern East Slavic literary languages, but one that is generally current in 16th–17th-century Ruthenian. Note the presence of this conjunction in SinSlav, PB, and *Aleksandryja,* but its absence from FS and SSUM. It is found in *Kazan'e* as well as in JU. From the former we can cite **смєрть зась грѣха, єстъ** . . . (K10b,12) 'whereas [a] death of sin is . . . '; from the latter **грѣшныхъ зась дꙋшѣ** (227a,20) 'for the souls of sinners . . . .' These two examples indicate that the general status of this conjunction in Ruthenian is that of an element characteristic of learned speech and the written language. Gröschel lists **зась** as an adverb in his study of IV (1972, 315).

и (thousands of attestations) 'and' is by far the most common conjunction found in MS' texts. In addition to "and" **и** may express "also," e.g., in **знаєтє и вы, православныи** (K19b,18) 'do you also know, Orthodox [Christians]'; it is a linking element, not one that implies a contrast (cf. "**а**" above). Its use as a particle is discussed in 8.3 below.

илє (K18a,16; 25a,1) 'inasmuch as.' This form is an adverb of degree which can occasionally be used as a conjunction. When used with the preposition **до** 'to' **илє** may express "with regard to, as far as X is concerned": **илє до смєрти цноты** (K18a,16) 'with regard to a life of virtue.' This conjunction is present in SinSlav ('**єлико, єлмаі**') and is found as a gloss for the

Slavonic adverb "how much" as well as for the conjunction "for, inasmuch" in PB. It is not found in IV, nor in earlier sources represented by SSUM and FS. These data, in addition to the absence of нлє in CSU or CSBR and its presence in CSP, argue persuasively for its interpretation as a Polonism that was current in the Ruthenian period.

коли — 'when'; in addition to its role as an adverb of time, коли can rarely also function as a conjunction, for example 47a,6–7.

нѣжъ, нѣжли — (91 times and 29 times, respectively) 'than' are both used in expressions of comparison. The latter has initial stress 28 times and final stress once. Both forms found in MS are current in 17c. Ruthenian—both are cited as glosses for нєжє, нєжєли in Berynda's *Leksykon*. нѣжли is found as a headword in SinSlav, нижли occurs in FS, while *niż* is present in P-M. In an example from JU, нѣжли is used in a paraphrased biblical passage and is clearly unmarked: лацнѣйшаѧ єстъ речъ велбѹдѹ скрозь игланоє оѹшко пройти, нѣжли богатомѹ в҆ цр҃тво бж҃єє войти (383a,28–383b,1) 'it is an easier matter for a camel to pass through the eye of a needle, than for a rich man to enter the kingdom of God.' Gröschel states that нижли is the form which occurs in documents written in Ruthenian that is close to the vernacular, while нижєли (not attested in MS) is a Polonism (1972, 343). The SSP cites almost exclusively *niżli* for Old Polish, a form that is attested from the end of the fourteenth century (5:281–84). SSUM cites the same from the early (but primarily mid to late) fifteenth century, the earliest attestations of which come from regions under strong Polish influence (such as Galicia, L'viv; 2:47). *Niż* is also widely attested in Old Polish (and is current in CSP), while SSUM does not cite this as a conjunction used to express "than." It is still current in CSU but is found neither in CSBR nor in CSR. All indications noted above point to a Polish source for нѣжъ/нѣжли. The Slavonic variant нєжєли is not attested in MS.

нѣмъ (4 times) 'by the time when, before the time when' corresponds most closely to Polish *nim/zanim.* This conjunction is cited as a Ukrainian dialect form in SUM, but it is not retained in CSBR. Нѣмъ is not mentioned by Gröschel, and is not found in SinSlav, P-M, FS, or SSUM. Example: Пєрє̑тымъ абовѣ̑, нѣмъ Сн҃ъ Бж҃ий чл҃вкомъ сталсѧ (109b,11–12) 'for beforehand, before [the time when] the Son of God became man . . . .'

поки (37 times, e.g., K24a,15) 'now, for the present, while' can be considered general Ruthenian, and appears to have arisen as an areal phenomenon: this conjunction is current in CSU (поки), CSBR (покі, described in TSBM as a dialect form) and CSP (*póki*). Final -a differentiates CSR пока from these forms. Bevzenko et al. indicate that поки came into Ukrainian from "староукраïнська мова" (1978, 462), an assertion that still allows for an areal interpretation, while Leeming identifies it as a Polonism (1968, 296). The distribution of this conjunction in Ruthenian texts and the modern languages suggests that it is not simply a borrowing. Gröschel does not cite поки for the language of IV, and it is not attested in P-M. It occurs in SinSlav and *Aleksandryja*, and is attested in earlier texts as well (FS and SSUM, fifteenth century). In Berynda's *Leksykon* дондєжє is glossed as 'ажъ покинѣ' The use of поки with the conjunction ажъ is described above.

покꙋль (2 times, e.g., 408b,13) 'while' is synonymous with поки (above), and is composed of the prefix по- and the adverbial root *koli (cf. отколь, отєюль, etc. in chapter 7). Just as поки is found with the conjunction ажъ, ажъ покꙋль 'until' also occurs in MS. The conjunction покꙋль is cited in SSUM, in SinSlav given as an equivalent of поки, and as a gloss for доколѣ in PB. Note also FS, in which it is used only as an adverb. This conjunction is not attested in IV. CSU покіль (described in SUM as "colloquial") and CSBR покуль/пакуль can function either as a conjunction or as the adverb "in the meantime".

прєто (356 times) 'therefore, consequently' is a Polonism (cf. Polish *przeto*) widely used in Ruthenian. It is identified in SinSlav and *Aleksandryja* (Leeming 1968, 296). Прото is cited as a gloss for тѣмъ in Berynda's *Leksykon*, and is present in FS as well as in SSUM. Прєто and прото occur in IV, but these forms are described by Gröschel as adverbs (1972, 315).

притомъ (7 times, only in JU, e.g., in 143a,21) 'in addition' can only be described as general Slavic; it is not attested in the language of MS' contemporaries, but does occur in CSR and CSBR (прытым).

тєды (hundreds of attestations, e.g., K10a,8) 'then' is Polish *tedy:* очи тєды вѣрнѣйшїи сѹтъ свѣдкѡвє нѣжъ слѹхъ (171b,25–26) 'eyes, then, are more reliable witnesses than rumor.' Cf. the native East Slavic forms in CSU (тоді) and CSBR (тады) with the same meaning. In addition to the majority of cases without stress marking or with penultimate (i.e., Polish) stress, a few forms do occur with final (i.e., Ruthenian) stress. The form тєды is also attested as an adverbial form (meaning "then") in chapter 7. An especially interesting example of the conjunction тєды occurs in juxtaposition to the Ruthenian adverb тогды 'then': Ꙗкъ тєды тогды потѡпъ былъ ѿ водъ, так тєпє҃ потѡпъ дрѹгїй ѿ грѣхѡвъ (484a,5–7) 'Just as, then, at that time the flood was [one] of water, now [it is a] flood of sins.' This conjunction is not attested in IV or FS, but it is present in SinSlav ('оубо') and in PB (as a gloss for оубой). Тєды entered the Ruthenian system early; it is attested in a text dating from 1413 (SSUM).

оубо (4 times) 'therefore' is a Slavonic element found in biblical citations in Smotryc'kyj's language: спогрєбохо҃сѧ оубо ємѹ крщєнїємъ во смрть (K10a,17–18; Rom 6:4) 'we were buried therefore with him [*lit.* 'to him'] by baptism into death.' This conjunction is not attested in JU. It does occur as a headword in PB, and as a gloss for тєды in SinSlav. Оүбо is cited as a particle in the language of FS, but is not present in SSUM.

хоть, хотѧ, хотѧй, хотѧжъ, хочъ, хоча

are used in MS' texts to express 'although.' Compare CSU хоч, хоча, CSBR хоць, хаця, CSR хоть, хотя. All of these can be treated as part of the Ruthenian system: хоть (48 times), хотѧ (18 times), хотѧй (5 times) are clearly East Slavic, while хочъ (2 times) and хоча (1 time; 63a,9) may be treated as pure Ukrainianisms. Of note is that the form хотѧй should sometimes, given context, be interpreted as хотѧ and a following и 'and'—this shows the graphemic representation of a phonetic process also known in CSU and CSBR, that is, the tendency for the vowel [i] to become a glide [j] when preceded by a word-final vowel. However word-final -/j/ clearly can be part of this conjunction. This is shown, among other places, in the phrase хотѧй и (202a,9), where the conjunction и is a separate element. Хотѧжъ (30 times) corresponds to Polish *chociaż,* but final stress in this form (for example, K5a,11) follows the pattern of хотѧ. In IV Gröschel identifies Ukrainian хочъ (5 times) and one example of хоть. He labels both forms as "ukrainisch-volkssprachlich" (1972, 345). P-M exhibits as many variants as MS, if not exactly the same ones: *chocz* (i.e., хочъ), *choczay* (i.e., хочай, not attested in MS), *chot'* (i.e., хоть), *chotia* (i.e., хотѧ), *chotiay* (i.e., хотѧй), *chotiaz* (i.e., хотѧжъ); the variant хоча is not found in P-M. Хоть is listed in SinSlav as a headword, and—based on CSBR, CSR, and MS—should be interpreted as generally East Slavic and unmarked. However, хотѧ̀ and хоча are both given as glosses for хоть, suggesting that both are Slavonic. Their interpretation as "Slavonic" or "un-Ruthenian" cannot be accepted for the following three reasons: First, neither is found as a headword in Berynda's *Leksykon*. Second, хотѧй is cited in that work as a

Ruthenian gloss for Slavonic оубо аще. Third, хотѧй, хоть, and хочъ occur in the same source as Ruthenian glosses for аще же. None of these forms is attested in FS, while only хотѧ (and the variants хотѣ, хоте) are cited in SSUM. One must conclude that all of the forms attested in MS should be treated as current elements of Ruthenian.

8.3 *Particles*

аза (50 times, e.g., 298a,8) 'interrogative particle,' including the suffixed forms азали and азажъ (e.g., K23a,19). Although this particle might be treated as a Polonism, it is certainly common in Ruthenian. In addition to MS, it is found in SinSlav and in PB. In the latter азажъ and азали (as well as ли, see below) are given as glosses for еда. It is not mentioned by Gröschel, however. One indication of the role of Polish in the spread of аза is its absence in FS and SSUM. Азажъ and азали are well represented in HSBM, but all of the examples cited are attested in 17th-century and very late 16th-century texts. Leeming treats азажъ as a Polonism (it is attested in *Aleksandryja*; 1968, 298). Example: аза не видиш што чинѧтъ (298a,8–9) 'do you not see what they are doing?' Structurally the forms азажъ and азали represent the combination of the interrogative аза (< а + за) + emphatic particle -жъ and interrogative particle -ли, respectively. The latter may be described as redundantly or twice marked as an interrogative element. Note that the variant и зали (191a,21) occurs one time in an introductory biblical passage, another indication of the Polish identity of this set of particles. The graphic separation of и from зали indicates an awareness of the origin of its constituent parts, but they still function as a unit. These forms are not included in SUM or TSBM, but азаж is found in ESBM, suggesting that this particle is still used in Belarusian, even if not in the literary language.

анѣ 'nor, neither, and not, not even' (< а + нѣ) is very common in MS' texts, and occurs with a preceding or following negative particle нѣ, не (see below), or by other negative expressions such as нѣчого (e.g., K18b,19; 34a,10–11). The construction анѣ . . . анѣ expresses 'neither . . . nor': А сꙋдїею справедливымъ, ѿ самъ єстъ правдивый Бгъ, который анѣ свѣ҃дка потребꙋетъ, анѣ инстикгатора, анѣ доводѡвъ (48b,3–5) 'And as a just judge, he himself is the just God, who needs neither witness, nor accuser, nor proof.' The origin of this particle in Ruthenian is to be explained either as a borrowing from Polish or as the result of a West Slavic/Ruthenian areal development—it is extant in all West Slavic languages, CSU, and CSBR, but is not attested in CSR. Rudnic'kyj (EDUL 1:25) and ESUM (1:73) mention neither possibility, stating merely that ани is the result of the combination of the conjunction а and the negative particle ни (see also ESSJ/P 2:56–59).

бы (e.g., 53b,11) is the general Slavic conditional particle (cf. its presence in conjunctions above): it requires the presence of an l-preterite verb form. Personal endings may occur with this particle, for instance бымъ (1sg), бысь (2sg), бысмо (1pl), бысте (2pl); such forms, which are not uncommon in MS' texts, are best interpreted as a reflection of this feature of Polish morphology, rather than as an archaism in Smo-tryc'kyj's language.

да (2 times) 'let, may' represents the Slavonic stylistic level; this particle is used once each in *Kazan'e* and JU as a hortative or 3rd person imperative particle: да бꙋдетъ воля твоя ꙗко на нбси и на земли (474a,1) 'let your will be [done] as it is in heaven on earth' (from the Lord's Prayer). This use of да is found in PB, FS, and as a gloss for Ruthenian жебы in SinSlav, but it is not present in P-M.

же, жъ 'emphatic particle' is usually suffixed to the form which is being emphasized: наштож҃ (K23a,18) 'for what,' тамже (K23b,9) 'in that [very] place'; this particle can be identified as general Slavic.

за 'too' (2 times, e.g., 300b,4): не завелико 'not too large.' This clearly is a Polonism—it is rare in Ruthenian, being absent in SSUM, FS, SinSlav, and PB, and now is productive only in CSP. That this use of за is not unknown in the present-day Ukrainian-Belarusian regions is shown by the CSU, and especially by the CSBR, forms used to express "too": CSU занадто (< за 'beyond' + над + то), CSBR занадта, задужа, залішне; it also appears to be productive in southwest Ukrainian dialects, e.g., зарано 'too early,' запізно 'too late,' завеликий 'too big' (Žylko 1966, 188). The use of за to express "too" is not mentioned by Gröschel.

и can occur as an emphatic particle in addition to its primary function as a conjunction: бы добре ѧ ѡтомъ и молчалъ (K16a,3–4) 'it would be better for me to be silent about that.'

наветъ (2 times, only in JU, e.g., 41a,12) 'even' is not found in other Ruthenian sources, although it entered the system (probably from Polish *nawet*) and was retained in CSU: навіть; TSBM does not cite this as a CSBR form.

не 'not' is the general Slavic particle of negation.

нехай (150 times) 'let' is the Ruthenian counterpart to Slavonic да in 3rd person imperative-hortative constructions: бꙋкварь . . . до выꙋченѧ подаванъ нехай бꙋдетъ (IIIb,12–18) 'let a primer be given for study.' Compare CSU нехай, CSBR няхай, CSP *niech(aj)*, CSCz *necht'*, CSSl *nech* (but SSl *neka*): these forms suggest that the form *nech-* may be a common development embracing West Slavic and Ruthenian. This particle is attested in P-M, FS, SSUM, SinSlav, and PB (under да in *Leksykon*).

нѣ is the general Slavic particle used to express 'nor, neither' in constructions of negation, and it occurs in conjunction with some other particle of negation:

не . . . нѣ (e.g., 55a,14), не . . . нѣ . . . анѣ (e.g., 444b,16–17); нѣ . . . нѣ expresses 'neither . . . nor' (e.g., K17b,21–18,1). The relative status of не . . . нѣ . . . анѣ vis-à-vis one another is well illustrated in a passage containing all three particles: не о золото, нѣ о серебро, не о покармъ, анѣ о одѣже проситъ (388a,15–16) 'asks not for gold, neither for silver, not for food, not even for clothing.' This particle is rarely spelled ни in JU, twice in *Kazan'e* (K13a,21); context in JU does not dictate that this element should be written in the etymological ("Slavonic") manner, whereas it does in *Kazan'e*: both examples are used in one biblical citation.

ось 'demonstrative particle' is found once in MS (K11a,20). It is retained in CSU and CSBR, in the latter with prothetic в-: вось (compare CSR вот 'here is'). This particle does not occur in IV or SinSlav, but is found in P-M (glossed as "look") and in FS.

ото (114 times) 'demonstrative particle; here is' is clearly common in MS' language: this form is still found in CSU (ото́) CSBR (with loss of final unstressed -o: от, defined as вось in TSBM), and Polish (*oto*). Gröschel describes ото as common East Slavic (1972, 363); initial stress in MS indicates either Polish influence, or possibly a feature of B-R. The use of this particle is illustrated by its use in the translation of a biblical passage: ото баранокъ Бжїй который беретъ грѣхи всего свѣта (482a,22–23) 'this is the lamb of God which takes the sins of the whole world.' The immediate lexical indicator of the level of ото in this particular context is the use of баранокъ 'lamb' instead of Slavonic агнецъ.

оужъ (201b,19) 'emphatic particle' is known in this form in CSR, but the corresponding CSBR and CSU forms are formally identical to the adverb, ужо́ and уже́, respectively (cf. CSR уже́). The form оужь is attested in SSUM, but it is described as the adverb 'already.'

чи (20 times, e.g., 150a,24) 'interrogative particle' may be regarded as common Ruthenian: it is native to the East Slavic languages, and is still current in CSU (чи), while the corresponding form is ці in CSBR. In Gröschel's opinion the use of *czy* in Polish merely had the effect of supporting its continued use in the Ruthenian language. Of interest is the occurrence of the form ци (now CSBR ці) in SinSlav and in PB as a gloss for єда. This suggests that this form was quite widespread during the Ruthenian period and чи in MS' language can therefore be interpreted as a specifically U-R variant. In P-M *czy* is only cited as the conjunction "or."

чили (8 times, e.g., 191a,23) 'interrogative particle' represents a twice marked form similar to азали cited above: both чи and ли function as interrogative particles in their own right. This particle is extant in CSP (*czyli*), but is not found in CSU or CSBR. Although it is not found in SinSlav or IV, this form does occur in FS. Note that the example cited occurs in a biblical passage in JU, where such Polonisms are often concentrated.

8.4 *Interjections*

Few interjections are attested in Smotryc'kyj's texts: two of the four listed below are widespread among Slavic and other languages (о and аг), while the other two might be interpreted as specifically Slavic.

агъ (e.g., 511b,23) 'oh!' introduces a negative statement or thought: агъ нєстєйты (sic) 'oh unfortunately . . . '; агъ пастырєвє Ізраилєвы (436a,8) 'oh pastors of Israel.' This interjection is interesting from the orthographic standpoint, because [h] is represented by the grapheme г.

ѡ (e.g., 83b,27) 'oh!' occurs in a vocative function with personal names or lexemes referring to human or divine beings: ѡ Книжникѡвє и фарисєѡвє 'oh scribes and Pharisees!' The interjection o is only written by means of the omega, and consequently remains graphically differentiated from the preposition o.

олє (2 times, e.g., 532b,19) might be interpreted as a mild interjection used to focus attention on the following subject, as it is used in some Ukrainian dialects: оле, дай мі покуй! 'hey, leave me alone!'; it is probably not to be associated with the homophonous *ole* of CES, which functioned as a conjunction (Dzendzelivs'kyj 1969, 161).

оувы (e.g., 511a,15) 'alas!' is negative, introducing a lament of some sort. This form is present in SinSlav as a gloss for **бѣда**, and as a headword in PB glossed as **бѣда ми**! 'alas!' or 'woe is me!' The Slavonic character of this form in Ruthenian is supported by its absence in CSU and CSBR.

CHAPTER NINE

The Verb

The verbal system of the Ruthenian period differs little from the CSU and CSBR systems. The features of written Ruthenian that are no longer current in the modern literary languages primarily are Polonisms. As in the modern languages, tense and aspect are interconnected: imperfective verbs have three basic tenses (past, present, future), while perfective verbs strictly speaking have two (past and future). A number of compound tenses are present in MS' system: the compound imperfective future used by MS is still the norm in the modern languages, while various compound past tenses, inherited from CES and influenced by Polish, are not. Verbal aspect and aspectual derivation in MS are essentially identical to CSU and CSBR, and are not addressed in this analysis. Purely syntactic questions are likewise not treated. For the placement of the enclitic particle or suffix -ѥѧ, the marker of reflexive/intransitive verbs, see chapter 5.

9.1 *The Infinitive*

The marker of the infinitive in MS' texts is uniformly -ти and -чи. The former was general Slavic and represented the norm for Ruthenian. The latter occurs with velar stems (-*či* < *-gti/-kti), and was the CES form, as well. Examples include: взѧти (K2b,12) 'take,' спасти (147a,7) 'save,' слышати (K6a,2) 'hear,' брати (147b,19) 'take'; речи (K12b,6) 'say, speak' (< *rek-ti), оустеречи сѧ (147a,1) 'keep, preserve,' and so on. The Slavonic reflex of this mutation (for East Slavic, šč) does not occur in MS. CSU retained -*ty* (< *-ti) as the standard infinitive marker in (for example, читати 'read'), while in CSR and CSBR final unstressed /i/ of *-ti was lost, yielding palatalized -*t′* (читать 'read') and -*c′* < -*t′* (чытаць 'read'), respectively. In velar stems in CSU the original velar is reintroduced in the environment of the infinitive marker: ректи 'speak,' устерегти 'retain,' могти 'be able.' In CSBR, on the other hand, the mutated infinitive marker -чы is retained but the original velar is also reintroduced: берагчы 'keep,' магчы 'be able,' пекчы 'bake.' In MS the marker -ти can be identified as "traditional-CES/U-R" (in B-R *-t'* is not infrequently attested in the 16c), -чи only as "traditional-CES." The forms of the infinitive attested in IV are the same as those found in MS, except that the Slavonic reflex -щи < *kti/gti does occur alongside the native East Slavic reflex (206). The forms of the infinitive found in the language of PB are the same as those found in MS (e.g., оутечи, 94), but headwords in his *Leksykon* are marked as Slavonicisms: рещи 'speak, say.'

9.1.1 Anomalous verbs (from the old "athematic" verbs) attested in the infinitive include быти (e.g., K16a,16) 'be,' мѣти (e.g., 255a,1) 'have,' вѣдѣти (e.g., K10a,6) 'know,' єсти (29b,22) 'eat' (primarily with intial є-, but occasionally with expected ѣ: see 9.6.3), ѿдати (e.g., IIIb,10) 'give up.' CSU 'to be' is бути (but dialectal быти, ESUM 1:188), in CSBR by быць < быти. MS' быти therefore is traditional CES (and possibly B-R). On *měj-* versus *maj-* see 9.8 below. The verb имати is attested only 6 times in Smotryc'kyj's texts, five examples of which are found in *Kazan'e*, specifically in biblical citations. The verb вѣдѣти is also marked in this way, and consequently also occurs in a purely biblical passage: Вонже аще день снѣсте, ѿ ѿ [*sic*] плода древа, єже вѣдѣти добро и зло, смертїю оумрете (K10a,6–7) 'if on that day you eat of the fruit of the tree that knows good and evil, you shall surely die.' In JU the verbal stem -вѣдѣ- is found only in the verb оповѣдѣти. In other environments "to know" is expressed by вѣдати (e.g., K11b,8), which is cited as an archaic and dialectal form in SUM, and by знати (e.g., K19b,7). The former is still current in CSBR (ведаць), while the latter is found in all three East Slavic languages: CSU знати, CSBR знаць, Rus знать. Athematic infinitives attested in IV include быти, имѣти and мѣти, ѥсти, отповѣдѣти and "Ukrainian" отповести (206–207). For the language of PB only быти and дати are cited (94).

9.2 *The Non-Past Paradigms*

The term "non-past" is used here to combine the forms of the imperfective present tense and the perfective future because the morphemes of person and number are identical and are not tied to the expression of one or another tense. The conjugational system can be described in traditional terms as consisting of two conjugational types ("I" and "II"), depending on which connecting vowel occurs between the stem and the desinence: *-e-* for conjugation I (čitaj-e-), *-i-* for conjugation II (mov-i-), in all persons but the first singular and the third plural. The verbal desinences of the non-past are given below in tabular form, and sample verbs are provided for both conjugations. Fortunately an entire paradigm is available for conjugation I, viz. жити 'to live.' For conjugation II we must rely instead on several different verbs to construct the paradigm. Desinences in parentheses by and large represent rare forms or anomalies, and are discussed in the pertinent sections below.

		I Conjugation	II Conjugation
Singular	1. -u (-m)	жив-ꙋ	мов-л-ю
		(K18b,10)	(K25b,7)
	2.—	жив-ѥшъ	прос-нишъ
		(K8a,11)	(156a,16)
	3. -t (-t')	жив-ѥтъ	мов-нтъ
		(K10a,5)	(K10a,16)
Plural	1. -mo (-m, -my)	жив-ѥмъ	оупокор-нмо
		(K10b,7)1	(35a,1)
	2. -te	жив-ѥте	люб-ните
		(K10b,20)	(308b,4)
	3. -t (-t')	жив-ꙋтъ	мов-ѧтъ
		(K12b,6)	(K19b,16)

Conjugation I in addition includes such verbs as чекай- (K25b,20) 'wait,' потребꙋй- (K10a,21) 'demand,' зов- (132b,15) 'call,' мог- (A III,113) 'be able.' Such verbs are clearly differentiated in modern studies according to the particular stem-type of each verb, in addition to being classifed as conjugation I verbs. Conjugation II includes such verbs as послыша- (K16b,11) 'hear,' выполни- (547b,2) 'fulfill,' видѣ- (K8a,12) 'see,' among others.

9.2.1 The following observations are based on the entire MS corpus of these verbs:

9.2.1.1 *First Person Singular*. Next to standard *-u* (прошȣ [K8b,11] 'ask,' сплю [K13a,6] 'sleep,' розȣмѣю [K9a,6] 'understand,' etc.) the desinence *-mъ* appears in forms from the old athematic verbal paradigm (which is the same as the anomalous paradigm in the new system): имамъ (K24a,3) 'I have,' вѣм҃ (K13a,12) 'I know,' and дамъ (e.g., 156b,1) 'I shall give.' The first two of these forms occur in biblical citations, in *Kazan'e*; in unmarked contexts in *Kazan'e*, and the rule in JU, we find маю (K7a,6) and вѣдаю (K22a,2), respectively. The lone example of the verb имати in JU is conjugated not as an anomalous verb but according to a normalized pattern, thus we find имȣ (132a,16) used in an introductory biblical passage. The context in which it occurs is marked in comparison with the body of the explanation which follows, but, as is the norm in these passages in JU, it is not a purely Slavonic citation. The form дам is still the norm in all of the East Slavic languages as the first person form of the perfective verb 'to give': CSU дати, CSBR даць, CSR дать. The 1sg оповѣмъ (367a,8) is also attested in MS, but this is likely a Polonism (Pol *opowiedzieć,* 1sg *opowiem* 'tell, relate'); оповѣсти (infinitive) is cited once in SSUM (1499).

In II declension labial stems MS forms contain epenthetic -l- in the 1sg, as inherited from CES and found in CSU and CSBR (for example, мовлю, as above). Other II declension verbs with predesinential mutable consonants exhibit the expected East Slavic mutations (d > ž, t > č, z > ž, s > š). [1]

9.2.1.2 *Second Person Singular*. The marker of this form is *-šъ:* видишъ (K8a,12) 'see,' рȣшаешъся (K25b,10) 'move, stir,' among others. The morpheme *-s'* is also attested in the non-past conjugation,

---

[1] Horbatsch has identified several 1sg verb forms in the text of *Grammatiki* as peculiar to certain Ukrainian dialects: 1) forms of the type *hnězdju, doždju, slezju,* without stem-final consonant mutations, are described as Southeast, South Podilljan, and Pokuttja Ukrainian; and 2) *hrimju, dymju, lomju, molvju, spju* (among others), without epenthetic *-l,* are identified as being strictly Pokuttja Ukrainian forms (1974, vii). Such forms are not reflected in *Kazan'e,* the preface to *Grammatiki,* or in JU.

but only in connection with the verb 'to be' (єстесь: see 9.2.2 below). Several forms from the old athematic conjugation are attested, all based on verb (-)дати 'give': мнѣ дай сегодня, а Бг҃у даси завтра (95b,1–2) 'give to me today, and to God thou shalt give tomorrow,' все штоко̂век продаси роздай (382a,24) 'all that you will [would] sell, give away.'

9.2.2.3 *Third Person Singular*. In MS' texts the desinence is hard *-tъ*: мовитъ (K10a,24) 'say,' хочетъ (K3a,11) 'want,' даетъ (K9b,19) 'give,' маетъ (383b,12) 'have,' among others. The 3sg non-past desinence is hard *-t* in modern southwest Ukrainian and CSR (Ukr. dialect ходит, CSR ходит) as it was in Slavonic. In CSU and east Ukrainian a palatalized *-t'* is present in verbs of the II conjugation (ходить). A palatalized *-t'* also was present in B-R (cf. носить in FS), which later mutated to /c'/ in CSBR (ходзіць). Verbs of the I conjugation have a zero-ending in CSU and CSBR, however, the zero-ending is not attested in MS. Palatalized *-t'* is found in anomalous (athematic) verbs: дасть (52a,8) 'give,' здасть ся (177a,13) 'seem,' подасть (155b,27) 'offer,' имать (K13b,5) 'have,' вѣсть (K13a,14) 'know,' єсть (K14a,2) 'be.' Of these, имать and вѣсть are found in biblical passages cited in *Kazan'e*. The form єсть is found only 4 times with a palatalized *-t'*, each time in *Kazan'e*. This verb form otherwise occurs with hard final *-t*, in *Kazan'e* (56 times) as well as in JU (hundreds). The frequent occurrence of the latter in all contextual environments is evidence of the unmarked status of *-t*. Third singular forms with palatalized *-t'* are consequently archaisms (they were the norm in CES) and/or Slavonicisms. In either case, such forms are marked in Smotryc'kyj's language and do not reflect a feature of his own language. 3sg оповѣстъ (K2b,15), with hard *-t*, is therefore unmarked next to вѣсть. An exception to the rule is the athematic form дасть 'give' which was and is current in the spoken language. The construction здастмися (K2a,12) 'it seems to me' can be treated as a Polonism, since the whole reflects the Polish phrase *zda mi się* 'it seems to me'—native Ruthenian здастъ replaces Polish *zda* in the construction.

A 3sg minimal pair in MS is єстъ 'be' and єсть 'eat' (e.g., 220a,16): only the softness or hardness of the final consonant determines what the form expresses (without taking context into consideration). The CSU and CSBR forms corresponding to these two examples differ in their vocalism, but they have palatalized *-t':* CSU їсть 'eat,' єсть 'be' (the latter is rare); CSBR єсць 'eat,' ёсць 'be.'

9.2.1.3 *First Person Plural*. Three desinences (*-mo, -mъ, -my*) are attested in MS, of which *-mo* is the rule. In *Kazan'e -mo* occurs 14 times, *-mъ* only 7 times. All of the latter are found in biblical quotations and are thus marked: ходимъ (K10a,19) 'walk, go,' живемъ (K10b,7; 8; 8) 'live,' оумираемъ (K10b,8) 'die.' This desinence occurs only 3 times in JU, while there are hundreds of examples of *-mo*: бѹдемъ (58a,2) 'be' (in a reference to a biblical passage), прїймѹемъ (481b,22) 'accept,' невонтпимъ (67a,18) 'not doubt' (clearly a Polonism; note the reflection of the Polish nasal vowel). Compare forms with *-mo* from JU: зовемо (132b,15) 'call,' хочемо (31a,25) 'want,' впадемо (39b,16) 'fall into,' подамо (125a,7) 'give,' ѿдамо (125a,4) 'give back,' among others. The Polish desinence *-my* is found twice in MS in the verb "to be" (see 9.2.2 below).

In the early Ruthenian period (before the sixteenth century) the predominant desinence was *-mъ* inherited from CES; the desinence *-mo* came to be more widely used in the sixteenth century, but *-mъ* was still the rule in U-R (except in texts from the Galician region, see Kernyc'kyj 1967, 191–92). The former supplanted the latter in U-R, such that *-mo* is the norm in CSU, while *-m* is standard in CSBR. Southwest Belarusian dialects alone commonly have *-mo* (Bulyka et al. 1979, 247–48). Although A. I. Žurawski claims that both desinences regularly occur in B-R documents from the early seventeenth century, his examples of texts where *-mo* was the norm are Smotryc'kyj's *Kazan'e* and JU (in Bulyka et al. 1988, 179). Note statistics compiled by Bulyka et al. (1990) concerning these desinences in the texts of FS: *-m* 57.8%, *-mi* 31.2%, *-mo* 11%. The first plural forms in MS are certainly U-R rather than B-R.

9.2.1.4 *Third Person Plural*. In Smotryc'kyj's system unpalatalized [t] is the norm: хотѧтъ (K9a,17) 'want,' идѹтъ (K13b,9) 'go,' чекаютъ (K23b,9) 'wait.' Note also the 3pl of the old athematic verb дати 'give': дадѹ́т (393a,21). In CSU and CSBR the 3pl desinence is similar to that of the 3sg (II conjugation). In CSU it is characterized by palatalized *-t'* (читають 'read') and in CSBR this form again reflects cekanne (чытаюць: *c'* < *t'*). Hard *-t* is still found in southwest Ukrainian dialects. With the exception of anomalous сꙋть (3pl of "to be": see 9.2.2 below), a palatalized *-t'* is not evident in MS' verbal system.

9.2.2 *Excursus on* byti *'to be.'* The anomalous verb *byti* 'to be' is worthy of special study because it has been almost entirely lost in the East Slavic literary languages, while it still functions with a complete paradigm in other Slavic languages, notably in Polish. In CSU and CSBR only a shortened form of the 3sg remains: CSU є (rarely єсть: cf. CSR есть), CSBR ёсць. In these languages the past and future tenses are expressed by full morphological paradigms based on the root буд-/би-/бу-.

In Smotryc'kyj's texts the infinitive is the inherited form быти; in CSU the standard form is бути (by analogy to буд-), while бити is still attested in the Ukrainian dialects (ESUM 1:188). The infinitives in CSR and CSBR are based on the CS/CES original: CSBR быць, Rus быть. The present tense paradigm as reflected in MS' texts is comprised of the following forms. Compare MS' forms (column 1) with the Slavonic paradigm in the body of *Grammatiki* (column 2):

	MS	Slavonic (*Grammatiki*)
1	єстємъ (93 times), єсми (4 times)	єсмь
2	єстєсь (33 times), єси (15 times)	єси
3	єстъ (hundreds)	єсть
1	єстєсмо (54 times), єсмо (15 times), єсмы (2 times)	єсмы
2	єстє (27 times), єстєстє (2 times)	єстє
3	сꙋть (the rule; occasionally сꙋтъ)	сꙋть

9.2.2.1 The use of particular forms, specifically єстъ, єстє, and сꙋть, represents a continuation of the CES pattern for this verb, perhaps in the latter stages of their currency in the Ruthenian system; as for the rest, it is possible to identify єстємъ, єстєсь, and єстєстє as essentially pure Polonisms which were widely used in 16th- to 17th-century Ruthenian texts.

9.2.2.2 єстємъ is listed as a headword in SinSlav, glossed as єсмъ, and it also occurs as a gloss for єсмь in Berynda's *Leksykon*. It is not cited in early U-R (SSUM), a strong indication of the role of Polish in its introduction to Ruthenian. єсми (450a,11) is very common in early U-R (see SSUM *sub* быти) but is clearly uncommon as a copula for MS: 1 time versus 3 times as perfect auxiliary (see 9.3.4 below).

9.2.2.3 єстєсь is attested in 16th-century U-R next to the form єсь (i.e., єсь), which represents a shortened variant of the earlier 2sg form єси (Kernyc'kyj 1967, 183). єси reflects the athematic 2sg, and is the marked variant functioning in MS' texts as a Slavonicism. This interpretation is supported by evidence from SSUM: the use of єси as a copula is decreasing already in early U-R, and is more commonly found in conjunction with other verbal forms (for example, in the formation of the perfect; see 9.3.4 below).

9.2.2.4 Note єстъ versus єсть (with soft final -t'), with the latter in the body of *Grammatiki.*

9.2.2.5 єстє is the rule in the 2pl in MS, as it was in 16th-century U-R. In MS' texts it is found with initial stress 6 times, with final (that is, Ruthenian) stress 21 times, as is also found in *Grammatiki*. This form is Ruthenian and/or Slavonic. єстєстє (corresponds to Pol *jesteście*) occurs only twice. It is evident from its occurrence in an introductory biblical passage in JU that its status as a pure Polonism elevates it to the level of an "educated-literary" element in the text.

9.2.2.6 сꙋть 3pl is common in MS' Ruthenian period, as it is in early Ruthenian.

9.2.2.7 The first person plural includes three variants: єстєсмо, єсмо, єсмы. Of these, єсмы is clearly marked as belonging to an elevated style. This form is attested only twice, both times in biblical passages in *Kazan'e*. Although єсмы is widely attested in 16c U-R texts, and is still found in some present-day dialect areas bordering on Poland (Kernyc'kyj 1967, 193), Smotryc'kyj's textual evidence and the paradigm in *Grammatiki* indicate that this form is perceived and used by that writer as a marked (archaic) feature. єсмо exhibits the Ruthenian

1pl desinence -мо. It can be used as a predicative copula, as in єсмо добры (224b,1) 'we are good,' повинни єсмо (7 times, e.g., 73b,12–13) 'we are obliged,' and in the construction of the perfect tense, for example прибыли єсмо (7 times, e.g., 55a,18) 'we have arrived.' The basic 1pl form of 'to be' in his language, however, is єстесмо, a blending of Polish *jesteś-(my)* and Ruthenian -мо. It is found 54 times, in *Kazan'e* (3 times) as well as in JU (51 times). It was common in the 16th century (Kernyc'kyj 1967, 194), and is not present in early U-R (as reflected in SSUM). єстесмо can only used be as a predicative copula in Smotryc'kyj's system.

9.2.2.8 The examples of this paradigm cited in Bevzenko et al. provide a valuable insight into the way such forms are viewed by some linguists: єсмь, єсми, єси, єсь, єсмо, єсмы, єсми, єсте, сѹть (1978, 316). Three forms missing from this list are єстемъ, єстесь, and єстесмо. These forms are clearly functioning as active members of the Ruthenian system, but their identity as "Polonisms" prevents their inclusion in this particular historical morphology of Ukrainian. All of the forms given in MS *Grammatiki* as "Slavonic" are represented in the list of forms in Bevzenko et al. (1978), however: єсмь, єси, єстъ, єсмы, єсте, сѹть. For the period in question such forms as єстемъ ought not to be disregarded, whether or not they are Polonisms.

9.2.3 *The Non-Past.* It is possible to characterize this component of MS' morphology as U-R, but such a characterization relies almost entirely on the evidence of the first person plural desinence *-mo*. The existence of this same morpheme in modern southwest Belarusian suggests, however, that the non-past is pan-Ruthenian. What is clear with regard to Smotryc'kyj is that data from his texts appear to contradict Kernyc'kyj's statements describing the gradual emergence of *-mo* in place of *-m* in the Ruthenian language of 1600. According to Kernyc'kyj, the only region in which *-mo* is dominant in the sixteenth century is Galicia (1967, 198). Because Smotryc'kyj cannot be described as a Galician we must assume that the displacement of *-m* by *-mo* took place at different rates in different regions. The few examples of *-m* in the 1pl are to be interpreted as archaic CES or as Slavonicisms (with the exception of невонтпимъ, which is a Polonism), rather than as features of B-R.

There are only a few noticeable differences between the non-past of MS on the one hand and of PB and IV on the other. The 1sg is essentially the same in all three. In the 2sg Gröschel identifies more examples of forms with the Slavonic desinence *-ši* than he does of Ruthenian *-š* (118:102; 1972, 208), while the latter is more common in PB (96). No examples of Slavonic *-ši* are identified in MS.

In the language of all three Ruthenians, the unpalatalized desinence *-t* is preponderant in the 3sg. The palatalized variant is found only in three athematic verbs in PB (97), which parallels the situation in MS. Three instances of *-t'* are identified in IV (e.g., **глаголєть**), and Gröschel also finds several zero-ending forms (e.g., **пишє**) which in his opinion may reflect either a Ukrainian dialect feature or Polish influence (1972, 209). Based on MS, IV, and PB, it is clear that hard *-t* is the basic 3sg (and 3pl) marker. Evidence from their Ruthenian texts does not agree with Bevzenko's (et al.) assertion that *-t'* predominates everywhere except in texts from Moldavian territory, while *-t* and *-t'* may co-occur in texts from Dniester, Galician, Moldavian, Polish, and Lithuanian regions (1978, 314–15); in other words, with the exception of Moldavia, *-t* is not supposed to predominate. According to Žurawski, however, hard *-t* is widespread at the end of the sixteenth century (1988, 177). Modern dialect material also shows that this desinence is widely used: Marčuk cites the presence of this ending in North and (far) West Ukrainian (1969, 174–76). DABM shows that 3sg *-t* is found in Southwest and Northeast Belarusian (map #153), especially in *jest* 'is,' which is widely attested in the West-Central and Southwest dialects (map #163), while 3pl *-t* is also attested in Southwest Belarusian and along the southern border between Belarus and Ukraine (maps #156 and #160). Although palatalized *-t'* is clearly attested in U-R and B-R works predating Smotryc'kyj, we must conclude that *-t* still represents the norm for non-athematic verbs. It is a feature of various Ruthenian variants rather than an artificially standardized archaism.

The relative distribution of 1pl desinences *-mo* and *-m* is almost identical in IV and PB. In IV the ratio is 30:17 (209–210), in PB it is 20:14 (100), or not quite 2:1 in both. Although the proportion is closer to 100:1 in MS, this can be ascribed to the style used in JU, in which the reader (the priest) constantly uses inclusive language to involve the congregation. In *Kazan'e* the distribution is identical to that of PB and IV, or 2:1 (14:7). Gröschel describes the ending *-m* as either southwest

Ukrainian or Slavonic, but he does not mention whether this desinence is used in biblical passages. As in MS, the 2pl desinence is regularly *-te* in IV and PB, and in the 3pl *-t* is the rule (as in the 3sg: above); 3pl *-t'* is identified only once in IV (210), while it occurs regularly among the athematic verbs and once in the form мовѧть in PB (101).

9.3 *The Preterite*

The 16th- to 17th-century Ruthenian preterite tense reflects the processes of simplification characteristic of the developments in the East Slavic preterite as a whole. The system of tenses which CES had inherited from Common Slavic was forced to change by the existence of a strong aspectual system. In practice, this means that a number of tense formations were simply lost. By the time of Meletij Smotryc'kyj, the l-preterite (9.3.3) predominated; although other, obsolete, tenses were still used in texts, they were clearly marked and unproductive. Still other tense forms are attested in sufficient numbers that they cannot be described as relics of a dead system. Since these are not present in CSU or CSBR, they must be examined in light of dialect evidence and the influence of Polish, as well as by comparison with the language of other, contemporary, Ruthenians.

9.3.1 *The Aorist*. The aorist was no longer in use in spoken Ruthenian of the 17th century. In MS' texts this is reflected by the scarcity of such forms, as well as by the marked contexts in which aorists are attested—most of which are found in *Kazan'e*. The 29 aorists in this text all occur in biblical quotations. The only forms used are the 3sg (22 times), 1pl (3 times), and 3pl (3 times). Examples include: 3sg разꙋмѣ (K2b,4) 'understand,' воста (K10a,18) 'arise,' пи (K13a,21) 'drink,' даде (K10a,22) 'give,' бысть (K2b,4) 'be (perf.),' бѣ (K13a,21) 'be (imperf.),' and приближисѧ (K5b,20) '(has) approached,' 1pl крестихо̑сѧ (K10a,17) 'baptize,' спогребохо̑сѧ (K10a,17) 'bury,' 3pl ведоша (K13a,20) 'lead,' взыйдоша (K13b,7) 'go up,' and распѧша (K18b,13) 'crucify.' In contrast, only two aorists are attested in JU: рече (47a,10) 'say,' in an introductory biblical context, and ѧде (511a,11) 'eat,' in the context of a biblical tale but used in the body of the text.

9.3.2 *The Imperfect.* The imperfect tense was lost in the East Slavic dialects even earlier than the aorist (Avanesov and Ivanov 1982, 80). Consequently, the imperfect is all but absent from MS' texts. Two such forms are attested in *Kazan'e*, and both occur in biblical citations: таашеса (K2b,22) 'hide oneself' 3sg, and видаше (K13a,20) 'see,' the latter East Slavic in form. The imperfect is not represented in JU.

In CES the third person desinence *-t'* could be appended to the 3sg and 3pl forms of the imperfect (e.g., ведашеть, бахуть). Three relics of this formation can be identified in MS, but in this case the desinence occurs with third person l-preterites: былоть (194a,26) 'was.' In the following it is appended to preceding elements (similar to patterns involving personal endings in the l-preterite discussed in 9.3.3 below), once in a modal construction: болшуюТь оученикωве смѣлость мѣли (301a,6) 'the disciples had greater courage,' доброеть бы то занеСте было (146b,22) 'it would indeed have been good.' This construction is not present in IV, and is not mentioned with regard to PB.

9.3.3 *The "l"-preterite.* The predominant preterite forms by the 16th–17th centuries are traditionally referred to as "l-participles": these were originally participial forms in CS ("resultative" participles) which were used together with auxiliaries in the formation of such tenses as the perfect and pluperfect (below). In the modern standard East Slavic languages this is the only preterite form used, and it occurs without auxiliaries. In MS' texts the l-preterite is the basic, unmarked, preterite form. It occurs thousands of times. As an originally participial form, the l-preterite can sometimes occur with adjectival desinences. These forms are examined in 9.7.2.

9.3.3.1 Unlike CSU and CSBR, in which the past tense morphemes in the singular express only gender and number, and in the plural express only number, in MS the l-preterite is regularly combined with personal endings in the first and second persons singular and plural; these markers of person have their origin in the auxiliary verb "to be." In the following table the attested forms in MS are compared with those of CSP, CSU, and CSBR:

	MS	CSP	CSU	CSBR
1sg	-lem (220x; -lam 2x)	-łem, -łam	-v, -la, -lo	-w, -la, -ló (´-la)
2sg	-les′ (82x)	-łeś, -łaś	-v, -la, -lo	-w, -la, -ló (´-la)
3sg	-l, -la, -lo	-ł, -ła, -ło	-v, -la, -lo	-w, -la, -ló (´-la)
1pl	-lismo (231x)	-liśmy, -łyśmy	-ly	-li
2pl	-liste (90x)	-liście, -łyście	-ly	-li
3pl	-li, -ly (non-masc.)	-li, -ły (non-virile)	-ly	-li

Examples include: слꙋжилъ (K7a,9) 'he served,' приходили (K13a,8) 'they arrived,' реклемъ (K6a,20; 61a,5) 'I said,' згрѣшилемъ (35b,15) 'I sinned,' таиламсѧ (K2b,25) 'I hid myself,' оучинилисмо (34b,8) 'we did,' пришлисмо (47a,9) 'we arrived,' далесь (36a,4) 'you gave,' зосталесь (K8b,4) 'you remained,' далисте (47a,3) 'you gave,' among others.

9.3.3.2 All desinences are found in both *Kazan'e* and JU with the exception of *-ste*, which is only attested in JU. Since they are used in both texts, they cannot be interpreted as representing a particular stylistic level. Polish influence certainly contributed to the widespread use of these personal forms in Ruthenian: they are still the norm in CSP, and are occasionally found in the southwest Ukrainian dialects (Kernyc′kyj 1967, 216; Žylko 1966, 186–87). Bevzenko et al. state that the ending *-smy* was more common than *-smo* as a marker of the 1pl, as a result of Polish influence; in MS, however, only the latter is found. The 1sg desinence *-am* can only be identified as a Polish feature, since that language differentiates the masculine and feminine genders in the singular preterite personal endings (see table above). As expected in vocalic stems (for example, *bači-*), *-l* is appended to the stem-final vowel in 3d sg masc. forms. This also generally is the case in consonantal stems (for example, *nes-*), although no longer true in true in the modern ESl languages. Compare MS реклъ (31a,8) with CSU мiг < *mog-lъ. 'he said.' As in the modern languages, however, a few instances in JU reflect the fact that this *-l* was probably no longer pronounced: зажогъ (362a,20) 'lit, burned,' оумолкъ (278a,7) 'fell silent,' погребъ (485b,27) 'buried,' оумеръ (45a,6) 'died.'

9.3.3.3 A striking characteristic of the personal endings is their frequent tendency to occur separately from the main verb, and to be suffixed to some other element preceding that verb. This feature is also characteristic of CSP and southwest Ukrainian, and has been noted in others studies of Ruthenian (see Bevzenko et al. 1978, 325; Bulyka et al. 1990; 233, Žuraŭski 1988, 190–91). The "Polish" identity of this pattern is supported by its frequent occurrence in the opening biblical passages in JU, in which a higher concentration of Polish elements has already been noted. Thus, for example, we find:

> што҇ тєды мовй҇ (175b,22) '(this is) what I then said'
> ꙗкомъ рєклъ (51a,20) 'as I said'
> тысь мнѣ . . . нє далъ (44b,15–16) 'you did not give to me'
> чогось нє взѧлъ (241a,6) 'which you did not take'
> колисмо тѧ видѣли (47a,8) 'when we saw you . . . '
> колижєсмо тѧ видѣли (47a,6–7) '(for) when we saw you' (more emphatic than the preceding example)
> которыхєсь ми далъ (189a,30) '(of) which you gave to me'
> абысмосѧ . . . стали (35a,23) 'in order that we might become'; cf. абысь . . . (55a,9)
> штобысмо могли (52a,19) 'so that we would be able to'
> жєбымъсѧ . . . ѹвєсєлй҇ (36a,4–5) 'so that I might celebrate'

As these examples show, the elements to which personal endings can be appended are pronouns, adverbs, and conjunctions. This phenomenon is especially common with conjunctions: for example, абысмо is attested 203 times in JU (once абысмы: 211a,22), while жєбысмо is found 121 times in the same text. The third example shows that the personal element can occur at quite some distance from the main verb, while чогось may be taken as a warning not to interpret every pronominal form with the suffix -sь as an indefinite pronoun (compare чогось "something," chapter 5)—here it is the marker of the 2sg in conjunction with the following verb.

9.3.3.4 It is clear from the above that the use of personal endings with the l-preterite should be considered part of the Ruthenian system, not merely as a "Polonism." Such use also is common in PB, and Didiakin-Leeming treats the endings as productive elements (1969, 102–104).

Gröschel does as well, and treats such forms as мовилеми as "southwest Ukrainian" (1972, 230).

9.3.3.5 *-лы versus -ли: Morphological GenderMarking*. In the 3pl of l-preterite verbs "masculine" and "non-masculine" are generally distinguished in MS' texts (*Kazan'e* as well as JU) by means of the desinences -ли, -лы, respectively. This feature is not characteristic of CSU and CSBR, but may have been influenced by the Polish distinction "virile–non-virile" using the same desinences (*czytali–czytały*). Compare the following:

1. знаете и вы . . . которынестеся томꙋ присмотрѣли . . . (K19b,18–19) 'and you know, you who observed that . . . '
   But:
2. алеся и томꙋ наши очи барзо добре присмотрѣлы . . . (K20a,2–3) ' . . . but also that our eyes observed well'
3. жебы праца наша и старанїе внѣвеч марне не пошлы (34b,4–5) 'so that our work and effort have not been in vain [*lit.* 'go into nothingness']'
4. и рекли оученикѡве єго (112b,1) 'and his disciples said'
5. и великїи мѣста оупадокъ ѿнеслы (29a,24) 'and large cities were ruined'
6. мнѡгїи . . . пожиткꙋ не ѿнесли (59a,3–4) 'many (people) . . . took away [got] no benefit'
7. . . . справы цнотливыи пожиткꙋ оучинити не моглы (59a,5–6) 'worthy deeds could not [result in] benefit'

One particular passage illustrates this feature by the use of many *-ly* preterite plurals in reference to the two Marys on Easter. It also reveals that this feature is a general tendency but not an absolute rule, as an occasional *-li* variant appears where one expects *-ly*. Thus: кꙋпилы, пришлы, обачилы, оустрашилы ся, реклы, ся боялы, but смотрѣли (142a,18–31); шлы, намазалы, чекалы (143b,25–27), and so on throughout the discussion of the tale.

This tendency is also seen in other environments, for example, in the spellings повинни єсмо (73b,12–13) 'we must, are obliged,' повинни были (34b,8) '[they] were obliged,' which consistently refer to masculine beings (cf. older Polish *powinni jesteśmy* 'we are obliged, must'). It is unclear to what extent this practice is characteristic of the language of other Ruthenian texts, and more comparative research will be needed to make such a determination.

9.3.4 *The Perfect.* The perfect is a compound tense formed by combining the l-preterite form with the present tense of быти 'to be.' In the Ruthenian of Smotryc'kyj's day this compound preterite is still widely used in the first and second persons (singular as well as plural), unless a personal pronoun is present. In general the copula is absent in the third person (Bevzenko et al., 325.). The following forms of the copula are used in the formation of the perfect in MS: 1sg ѥсми, 2sg ѥси, 1pl ѥсмо, and 2pl ѥсте. As noted earlier, the plural forms ѥсмо and ѥсте are also used as present tense copulas, while the singular forms ѥсми and ѥси are not. The Polish and/or Ruthenian dialect forms ѥстемъ, ѥстесь, ѥстесмо, and ѥстесте are not used as auxiliaries in the formation of the perfect. Compare the following examples:

1sg привє̑ ѥсми сына своєго до тебє (97a,2–3) 'I have brought my son to you' (in an opening biblical passage)
2sg посадилъ ѥси, мови҃, грѣшникѡвъ, а они сѧ оукорєнили (45b,10–11) 'you have planted, he says, sinners, and they have taken root' (in a paraphrased biblical context in the body of the text)
1pl Бо ѥслибы и весь законъ выполнили ѥсмо . . . (34b,5–6) 'for if we have/had fulfilled the whole law . . . '
2pl мнѣсте оучинили (47a,12) ' . . . you have done for me' (in an opening biblical passage)

The context in which all of these forms are found clearly indicate that they are considered to belong to a higher style. The last example cited occurs in a passage full of such perfects alongside personal forms of the l-preterite; thus: . . . нє ввєли ѥстє мєнє: нагъ, и нє приѡдѣлистє мєнє (47a,16–17) 'you did not take [lead] me in; [I was] naked, and you did not clothe me.' This indicates that the difference between the two formations is not clear-cut: the latter is the preferred method of indicating person in the preterite, however, the former is a stylistic marker only. The perfect is not present in *Kazan'e*, while it occurs 134 times in JU.

9.3.5 *The Pluperfect.* The pluperfect tense is structurally similar to the perfect, in that it is comprised of the l-preterite and the auxiliary verb *byti*. In the pluperfect, however, the verb "to be" is also in the form of an l-preterite. (In CES the auxiliary was in the form of an aorist or imperfect form.) The attestations of the pluperfect in *Kazan'e* are relatively few in number (10 times) which we can attribute to the style in which this document is written—there is little narrative language in the sermon. Of the 10 forms used, 3 are 1sg пр҃есѧвзалемъ былъ (e.g., K5b,7) 'I had undertaken'; there is one 2sg на которꙋюсь ма былъ выслалъ (K7b,8– 9) 'you had sent out'; the remaining forms are 3sg, e.g., былъ приходилъ (K21b,21–22) 'he had come.' In JU, on the other hand, there is a total of 175 pluperfect constructions, the vast majority of which are third person, singular as well as plural: были перешли (29b,14) 'they had crossed,' ꙋмеръ былъ (36a,9) 'he had died'; an occasional 1pl form also occurs, e.g., былесмо . . . хотѣли (56b,25–26) 'we had wanted.'

The pluperfect was clearly still in use in the 16th-century Ruthenian, especially in narrative language, as well as in B-R administrative ("дзелавы") documents. The markers of person which were used with the simple l-preterite (see above) are also used with the pluperfect. In CSU the pluperfect is occasionally used, but it has generally been replaced by the simple past (l-preterite). This compound tense is still evident, however, in the southwest Ukrainian dialects (Kernyc'kyj 1967, 223) and to some extent in Belarusian (Bulyka et al. 1979, 226). Many of the pluperfect forms in JU are found in introductory biblical passages, reflecting the higher style to which the pluperfect belongs in Ruthenian. These are *not* East Slavic archaisms, but a reflection of the "Polishness" of the pluperfect in Smotryc'kyj's system (cf. CSP *czytałem był/byłem czytał* 'I had read'). This is plausible given the large number of Polonisms used in these passages, but also because of the occurrence of this tense with peculiarly Polish lexemes. One particular example from *Kazan'e* is seen in пр҃есѧвзалемъ былъ, in which the base form is the Polish verb *przedsięwziąć,* rendered предсѧвзати in Ruthenian. MS' texts are in stark contrast with PB, in which the imperfect is only found in (biblical) "citations." Didiakin-Leeming counts these forms as archaisms (1969, 106). The situation is similar in the case of IV, in whose texts this tense is identified only once.

Gröschel likewise considers it an archaism. The difference between MS on the one hand, and PB-IV on the other, must be attributed to the different level of Polish influence in the language of their texts.

9.4 *The Future*. Perfective non-past forms have future meaning in Ruthenian, as they do in the modern East Slavic languages: посльшите (K16b,11) 'you will hear,' ѹмрете (K10a,7) 'you will die,' оживемо (113b,18) 'we will come [back] to life,' пойдешъ (117b,21) 'you will go,' among others. The future tense of imperfective verbs consists of the future tense of *byti* plus the infinitive: видѣти бѹдетъ (K24a,15) 'he/she will see,' хвалити бѹдемо (K28a,18) 'we shall praise,' квитнѹти бѹдетъ (287b,16) '[it] will flower/bloom,' among others. This construction is the norm in all three East Slavic languages as well: CSU буду ходити 'I will walk,' CSBR буду хадзіць, CSR буду ходить. The Ruthenian (and CSU-CSBR) formation consisting of the infinitive + the personal suffixes *-mu*, *-meš*, etc. is not attested in MS' texts. Two instances of the Slavonic future construction *imati* + infinitive occur in *Kazan'e*, both times in the same biblical quotation: аще, мовитъ, поплоти живете, имате ѹмрѣти (K10b,20; see also K12a,14: Rom 6:13) 'if, he says, you live by the flesh, you shall die.' Two other occurrences of this Slavonic verb express "to have" (see K13b,5; K24a,4).

The imperfective future in IV is the same as in MS: *budu* + infinitive is the rule, while *imam* + infinitive occurs only in a biblical citation. In addition, however, Gröschel cites 7 examples of the Slavonic construction *xoščulxoču* + infinitive, all of which occur in religious contexts (1972, 231–36). *Budu* + infinitive is also the rule in PB, but two examples of the modern alternative formation are identified by Didiakin-Leeming, e.g., диспѹтоватиме[т] (1969, 106).

9.5 *The Conditional*

The conditional mood is expressed in MS' texts by means of the particle *by* + the l-preterite. This is the norm in the Ruthenian language of the day, as it is in the modern East Slavic languages. The contracted form *b* is used in all three modern languages, but is not attested in MS. It is, however, found in FS and P-M. The particle by can be appended to the end of the verb in question (sometimes orthographically separate, as with бы . . . молчал [K16a,3–4] 'he [should] remain silent'), or appended to another form preceding the verb: оутонꙋлъбы былъ (252a,9) 'he would have drowned,' признальıбы (K21b,9) 'they would admit,' Гдыбы сѧ комꙋ . . . дало (K11a,20) 'if someone were allowed to . . . .' As in the formation of the l-preterite, personal endings often occur in the conditional attached to the particle *by:* моглбымъ (K14b,11) 'I would be able.' Gröschel describes a similar conditional system in the language of IV—the primary difference between MS and IV is the extensive use in the latter of *by* plus copula (быеси, быесмоли, быестели), *by* plus copula reflex (быстели), or simply *by* plus l-preterite desinences (according to gender and number: see Gröschel's table, 1972, 237). The construction *by* plus l-preterite is also identified in the language of PB.

Note that numerous conjunctions incorporate the particle *-by*. These naturally also constitute conditional constructions: абы, ижбы, штоби, жебы (see 8.3). All of these conjunctions, as dictated by the particle *-by*, require the presence of an l-preterite verbal form. Two of these in particular, абы and жебы, are commonly found with markers of person: абымъ . . . ѡбѧснилъ (K14b,18–20) 'so that I [should] explain,' абысмо . . . полнили (52a,17–18) 'in order that we fulfill . . . ,' жебысмо . . . готовили себе (28a,6–7) 'so that we [should] prepare ourselves . . . ,' and so forth. Constructions of the type "абымъ + l-preterite" are also attested in IV, which Gröschel refers to as a Polonism (1972, 237.). The construction абы + l-preterite is found once in PB (109–110).

9.6 *The Imperative.*

9.6.1 *The Second Person Singular*. The marker of the 2sg imperative is either -*#* (zero) or -*i:* ховай (K28a,9) 'keep, preserve,' надари (K27b,3) 'give good counsel,' єжъ, пїй (354a,8) 'eat, drink,' сѧдь (177b,21) 'sit down,' принеси (132a,19) 'bring,' обачъ (ibid.) 'look at,' допꙋсти (224a,8) 'let,' не плачъ (315b,1) 'do not cry,' змилꙋйсѧ (386a,19) 'have mercy.' All forms with final *-i* occurs have desinential stress.

Six forms can be identified as Slavonicisms in *Kazan'e*, on the basis of form or context, or both. Note, for example, напра́ви (K12a,6) 'direct,' which is is Slavonic rather than Ruthenian because it is root-stressed, in which case we would expect *naprávь as in CSU направ/CSBR направў. In the case of помозими (K5a,1) 'help me,' it is the mutation of *g ([h]) > z that marks this imperative as Slavonic, as well as context (the use of the enclitic dative pronoun *mi*). In защичаже (K27b,14) 'protect, defend,' used in a supplication in which Smotryc'kyj asks for God's protection, it is the reflex *šč* < *tj that serves to identify it as a Slavonicism. As for Slavonicisms in JU, only даждъ (474a,2) 'give' is marked as such by the reflex *žd* < *dj and by context (the Lord's Prayer): хлѣбъ нашъ насущный даждъ намъ днесь 'give us this day our daily bread.'

9.6.2 *The Third Persons Singular and Plural*. In the Ruthenian period there was no longer a desinential marker of the 3sg and 3pl imperative. Consequently they are expressed analytically, by means of the the particle нехай 'let' (CSU нехай, CSBR няхай) plus 3sg or 3pl non-past form. The construction нехай plus non-past is the rule in MS' texts and it occurs 150 times in all three texts: нехайся . . . полнит (K24a,10) 'let . . . be filled.' The unmarked status of this particle in his system is especially clear from its use in biblical contexts as well as in unmarked environments: нехай будетъ имя гсне блсвено на вѣки (K7a,1–2) 'may the name of the Lord be blessed for ever.' Slavonic да + non-past is attested three times, twice in *Kazan'e*: да некогда ѿступитъ . . . (K20a,4) 'may [the Lord] never depart'; да ѡстятъся (ibid.) 'let them be consecrated, consecrate themselves': Ex 19:22; and once in JU, in the Lord's Prayer: да будетъ воля твоя яко на нбси и на земли (474a,1) 'thy will be [*lit.,* 'let be'] on earth as it is in heaven' (cf. даждъ above).

The relative frequency of нехай and да is reversed in IV: the latter occurs 17 times in the singular, while native нехай is found only 9 times. The archaic desinence -*i* occurs twice in chapter headings (241–42). In the 3pl да and нехай occur 3 times and 4 times, respectively (244). The 3sg imperative occurs 3 times with нехай and нехъ in PB, the latter probably representing Polish *niech* (108). The 3pl apparently occurs a few times in PB, but no examples are cited (107).

9.6.3 *The First Person Plural*. The 1pl imperative is the most commonly found imperative form identified in JU (hundreds of attestations), and therefore in all of Smotryc'kyj's texts. In addition to explaining the Gospels, the purpose of JU is to exhort the congregation to act, believe, and live according to the Holy Writ—Žuraŭski also notes this characteristic of JU (1988, 222). Inasmuch as *Kazan'e* is a funeral sermon, the 1pl imperative is used relatively infrequently (5 times).

The 1pl imperative is formed by appending the Ruthenian 1pl marker *-mo* (compare with the non-past above) to the form of the 2sg imperative: мовмо (126b,20) 'let us speak,' ѥтарайможѧ (33b,21) 'let us try,' зненави̂мо (34a,13) 'let us hate'; жалꙋймо (K26b,16) 'let us lament,' радꙋймоѥѧ (K26b,11) 'let us rejoice,' покажѣмо (35a,10; 14) 'let us show,' задрижѣмо (210a,19) 'let us hold on (to),' ꙋбойможъѥѧ (210a,18) 'let us be afraid,' наꙋчѣмоѥѧ (34a,25–26) 'let us learn,' ѣжмо (35b,24) 'let us eat,' and so on. Only once is the Slavonic variant *-m* attested, in a reference to the biblical commandment 'honor thy mother and thy father': чтѣм ѿца и маткꙋ (273a,8) 'let us honor [our] mother and father.' Several lines later this very verb is used with the Ruthenian desinence *-mo* also in reference to the same commandment, but paraphrased in such a manner that it is more "distant" from the original commandment: Родичѡвъ ѥвоихъ . . . чтѣмо (273a,24) 'let us honor our parents.'

It was common in the early Ruthenian period for the 1pl and 2pl desinences *-ěm-* and *-ěte* from verbs of the (traditional) classes I and II to supplant *-im-* and *-ite* (respectively) in classes III and IV. The desinences *-ěm-* and *-ěte* thus predominate in the 16th century, and can be interpreted as reflecting phonetic [im-] and [ite] in U-R, [em] and [ete/ece] in B-R (Kernyc'kyj 1967, 248). In PB, alongside 6 Ruthenian forms (*-mo*/*-ěmo*) 2 forms are identified with the marker *-mъ* (108). IV uses *-m* 7 times, *-mo* 5 times, and *nexaj* + *-mo* 2 times (p. 243).

9.6.4 *The Second Person Plural*. The marker of the 2pl imperative is the same as for the non-past: *-te*. As with the 1pl, this desinence is appended to the 2sg form of the imperative: жалꙋйтѥ (K6a,3) 'lament,' проѥѣтѥ (K23a,16) 'ask,' живѣтѥ (26a,4) 'live.' Forms of this person are not interpretable as Slavonicisms on the basis of morphology alone, and must be marked lexically, phonologically, and/or contextually: внийдѣтѥ . . . в҆ радоѥть Гд҃а ѥвоѥгѡ (K26b,3) 'enter . . . into the joy of your Lord'; раѥтѣтѥѥѧ, и множитѥѥѧ, и наполнѧйтѥ з҃ѥлю . . . (K10a,3–4) 'grow, and multiply, and fill the earth.' Both of these examples are used in biblical citations. There are no evident differences between the forms of the 2pl imperative of MS, IV, and PB.

9.7 *The Participles*. There are four participles used in MS' texts: present active, past active, present passive, and past passive. Occasionally a participial form of one type or another was already frozen as an adjectival form in the Ruthenian period (this is often the case in CSU and CSBR). Instances of such a change in morphological class are pointed out in the pertinent sections below.

9.7.1 *Present Active Participle*. The native East Slavic marker of the present active participle is *-č-* (-ч-), while the corresponding Slavonic formant is *-šč-* (-щ-), rarely *-ę(j)* (-ѧ[й]). The native variant is attested hundreds of times, while the marked variant *-šč-* occurs only 62 times. Both occur in all texts: всевѣдаючїй (K8a,13–14) 'all knowing' Nsgm, мовѧчого (K20a,11) 'speaking' Gsg non-fem, живѹчеи (K8b,11) 'living' Gsgf, горѧщемъ (K13b,16) 'burning' Lsg non-fem, исходѧщаго (186a,5) 'coming [from]' Gsg non-fem. Note the presence in the latter of the morphological indicator of the marked status, the Slavonic variant of the Gsg non-fem adjectival desinence (treated in chapter 4). The number of attested Slavonicisms is artificially high, however, because 52 of the 62 are forms of one and the same lexeme: животворѧщїй, *lit.* 'life-creating.' The difference between *Kazan'e* and JU is especially telling—only 42 examples are found in the latter, of which 41 are forms of животворѧщїй (исходѧщаго is the other: Žuraŭski states that животворѧщїй is the only such form found in JU [1988, 237]). The 20 participles attested in *Kazan'e* (11 of which are forms of животворѧщїй) are therefore proportionally a much larger number than the 42 forms found in JU. The short form is attested 3 times with Slavonic desinences, all in *Kazan'e*: гл҃ющи (K2b,22) 'saying' Nsgf, Luke 1:24; ведѹще (K13a,20) 'leading' Npl, Acts 9:8; and правѧщѹ (K4a,7) Asgf 'ruling/governing.' The last form is used in a prayer closing the preface to MS' sermon. One example from JU worthy of note: приистѹпѣмо до ... животворѧчого Гд҃ (318b,19–20) 'let us go to ... [our] life-creating Lord' Gsg non-fem. In this form, significantly, the native participial formant and case form occur with the marked verbal lexeme.

The archaic Slavonic formant *-ęj* (-ѧй) (in OCS *-ęi*) is historically the nominative singular non-feminine long form. This formant is attested 3 times in MS, all in *Kazan'e*, while the corresponding short form -ę (-ѧ) is attested only once, also in *Kazan'e*. All four of these participles are used in biblical quotations: видѧ (K13a,21) 'seeing,' видѧй (K13b,4) 'seeing,' вѣрѹѧй (K13b,4) 'believing,' and воинствѹѧй (K20a,11–12) 'fighting.'

In CSU and CSBR the present active participle is not commonly used, and is replaced for the most part by relative clauses. Such participles can be used adjectivally in the modern languages, and this is also the case in MS, e.g., горѧчїй 'hot' and всемогѹчїй 'omnipotent.' Participles are frequently used in IV and PB as well. Forms of the present active occur in IV 345 times (both short and long; 248); in the latter approximately 450 examples are found in the nominative singular masculine alone, while very few short forms are identified (79–81).

9.7.2 *Past Active Participle*. Two markers of the past active participle are attested in MS' texts: *-(v)š-* and *-l-*. 1) In vocalic stems (*uhodi-*, etc.) the full suffix *-vš-* is found, in consonantal stems (*moh-*, *voskres-*, etc.) it is simplified to *-š-*. In glide stems (*čitaj-*) the full suffix *-vš-* is retained and the glide is deleted. 2) The marker *-l-* is that of the "l-participle" from which the l-preterite is formed (9.3.3 above). Of the two formations, the l-participle is by far the more common in MS as a whole, as it is in the individual texts. In *Kazan'e*, for instance, *-(v)š-* is attested 8 times, whereas *-l-* is found 16 times. In JU the former is attested only 10 times, while the latter is extremely common (and therefore unmarked). Examples include: мѣвшихъ (K2b,17) '[which/who] had' Gpl, оумершемѹ (10a,12; 2 Cor 5:15) '[who] died' Dsg non-fem, пришедшого (388b,2) '[who] arrived' Gsg non-fem. Two short forms are used in *Kazan'e:* бывша (K13a,14) 'being' Gsg non-fem, and оумершѹ (K26b,12) 'dying' Dsg non-fem, the latter in a dative absolute construction. оумерлѹю (K11b,4) '[who] died, deceased' Asgf, ѡтеклыи (K17b,5) 'streaming [with]' Npl, зболѣлого (100b,16) '[who] fell ill' Gsg non-fem, зболѣлыхъ (82a,15) '[who] fell ill' Gpl non-fem, оумерлого (100b,11) 'who died' Gsg non-fem, among others.

These data reflect patterns of usage already prevalent in Ruthenian in the 16th century (Kernyc'kyj 257–58 and Žuraŭski 1988, 242). In MS' texts this participle is clearly no longer productive, and is used only in marked environments such as biblical citations and other similar contexts. This participle has been lost as a productive verbal category in

CSU (the old CES and OCS long forms no longer occur at all, except in poetry and lexicalized expressions), while the long forms are very rarely encountered in CSBR. This is the reverse of the situation in CSR, in which the category of the past active participle, once again under the influence of Slavonic, is not only retained but is commonly used in the literary language. The l-participle has survived in several ways in CSU and CSBR: first, as a purely participial form in a limited number of verbs;[2] or, the forms have been reanalyzed as adjectives, a tendency that can be seen in MS as well (for example, "who fell ill" becomes "ill"); and, finally, as the preterite *par excellence*. The past active participle is significantly more common in IV—there are 193 attestations of the past actives, short forms as well as long, the majority of which (145) are short. These data are in keeping with the generally more common use of Slavonicisms/archaisms in his texts (see Gröschel's tables, 1972, 249 and 265). In this respect the language of PB is closer to that of MS: only approximately 20 forms are identified by Didiakin-Leeming, of which half are forms of the l-participle (1969, 81).

9.7.3 *Present Passive Participle*. The present passive participle is relatively common in MS' texts: short and long forms are attested 130 times in MS. Short forms are less common and are, as a rule, limited to marked contexts. Five of the 7 present passives in *Kazan'e* are short forms. In that text 6 of the 7 attested participles are forms of the same verb: вѣдом҃ (K17a,8) 'known' Nsgm short form, вѣдома (K17a,9) Nsgf, вѣдомымъ (K8a,12) Isg non-fem (compare CSU adjective відомий 'known,' CSBR вядоми). The seventh form is непоколебимѡ (K17a,19) 'steadfastly,' functioning as an adverb. Examples from JU: Іс҃ зовемый Хс҃ (451a,26) 'Jesus [who is] called the Christ' Nsgm, хвалимого (498b,22) 'praised' Gsg non-fem, называемый (429a,1) '[that is] called' Nsgm, посылаемъ єстъ (427a,22) 'he is [the one who is] sent' Nsgm, and so on. As these latter examples illustrate, the tendency is for present passives to be used adjectivally. The distinction

2 This appears to be more characteristic of Ukrainian than of Belarusian: cf. CSU минулий 'past,' described as the past active participle of минути (secondarily as a participle used as an adjective) in SUM, and CSBR мінулы 'past,' not described as belonging to one or the other morphological class in TSBM (and therefore leading one to assume that it is an adjective).

between true verbal (participial) use, as in посылаємъ єстъ, and adjectival, as in называемый, is contextually determinable.

The present passive is comparatively rare in IV: 40 forms are attested, of which 8 are short and 32 are long (273–74). Their number is remarkably similar in the language of PB, in which 6 short forms are cited (all found in religious contexts), while long forms number approximately 30 (82–83). Data from the language of all three Ruthenians clearly show that the present passive participle was losing its role as a viable verbal category during the Ruthenian period. As suggested by this fact, this form is no longer present in CSU and CSBR, and although it is still formed in CSR, it is the least used of all participles. Only adjectivalized remnants remain, such as CSU любимий, CSBR любімы, CSR любимый 'favorite.'

9.7.4 *Past Passive Participle*. The past passive participle is the most frequently used participial form in Smotryc'kyj's texts. Two formants *-t-* and *-n-* (in the suffixes *-n-*, *-en-*, *-nn-* <*-n-* + adjectival **-ьn-*, *-enn-*) are used to form the past passives. The formant *-n-* is found a total of 2904 times, and *-t-* 260 times, producing an approximate ratio of 11:1. Their distribution among stem-types does not differ from that of CES. The small number of *-t-* forms is dictated by its occurrence with unproductive monosyllabic roots, for example, stem-types *-ij-* (e.g., otkryj-) and *-ja-* (old nasal stems: *vzę-*, *-klę-*); *-en(n)-* occurs with i-stems (*ljubi-*), consonant stems such as *-k-* (*rek-*), *-s-* (*nes-*); *-n(n)-* with *aj*-stems (*čitaj-*, with loss of *-j-*), *-ava-* (*dava-*), *-ova-* (*najdova-*), *-a-* (*skaza-*), and irregular verbs with a vocalic stem in the past (*da-*).

Examples with *-t-* include: оное цр҇ство в дꙋши и҆х єстъ закрито (115b,3) *lit.* 'that kingdom in their soul is closed' Nsgn short form; а ꙗкъ ѿ проклѧтыхъ и негодны҆х, лице свое ѿ них ѿвернетъ (49b,5–6) 'and [just] as from the damned and unworthy he will turn his face away from them.' The latter is also attested in *Kazan'e:* проклѧтое (K27a,19) 'damned.' In the Ruthenian period, as it is in the modern East Slavic languages, these past passive participles were already particularly liable to reanalyzation as adjectives. At the very least, such forms were able to function as adjectives while also functioning as participles.

9.7.4.1 Among past passive participles with the formant *-n(n)-* there appears to be an opposition of sorts between *-(e)n-* (2717 times) and

-(*e*)*nn*- (187 times). Here and in the following discussion "n" includes -*n*- as well as -*en*-, while "nn" includes -*nn*- and-*enn*-, since they are functionally equivalent. The distribution of past passives in -*n*- versus -*nn*- is similar in *Kazan'e* and JU, differing in degree rather than in substance: in the former their distribution is 135 versus 19 (or a ratio of 7:1), in the latter 2582 versus 168 (or a ratio of 15:1). The substantial favoring of -*n*- over -*nn*- indicates that the former reflects a feature that is more part of the Ruthenian system than the latter. In CSU and CSBR only -*n*- is found, while -*nn*- is preserved in CSR. As seen in other morphological categories, the difference between the two sets of texts is largely one of style: forms with -*n*- are favored in both, but a larger proportion of past passives in *Kazan'e* has -*nn*- because of the formal and archaic style of language in that document. Many of the lexemes found with this formant are Slavonic or are used in environments requiring marking of this kind. The formant -*nn*- was an East Slavic innovation not present in OCS or in CES (Ivanov 1983, 365). (U-)R often used the shorter formant -*n*-, which presumably reflects the influence of the spoken language. Kernycʹkyj points out that -*nn*- is common in sixteenth-century texts written in the Galician regions (1967, 262). It appears, then, that the longer formant -*nn*- never took root in the Ruthenian regions to begin with; this formant was consequently used as a marker of higher style.

9.7.4.2 *Examples*. -*nn*-: прєбл҃гословєнн- (e.g., K23b,13) 'most blessed,' нєрȣкотворєнн- (K23a,9–10) 'not wrought by [human] hands,' оѵготованн- (K26b,2) 'prepared' (the last two in biblical quotations), нєсказанн- (96a,23) 'untold,' возлюблєнн- (174a,14) 'beloved,' рождєнн- (185b,24) 'born.' Some of these forms are lexically Slavonic (прєбл҃гословєнн-, нєрȣкотворєнн-) while others are phonologically marked (жд in рождєнн-). -*n*-: освобожєн- (43b,17) 'liberated, freed,' рєчєного (33b,13) '[that which was] said,' дан- (K14a,10) 'given,' найдован- (K14a,16) 'found,' осȣжєн- (30b,2) 'condemned,' and the like. In addition to the stylistic marking of one formant over the other, there is also lexical-syntactic differentiation between the two variants: in some cases the form with -*nn*- is clearly adjectival, while the corresponding form with -*n*- is more likely to retain its role as a participle. Thus: нєсказанныи оѵтѣхи (96a,23) 'untold joys,' возлюблєнныи братїє (174a,14) 'beloved brethren,' свѧщєнного крещенїа (42a,18–19) '[of the] holy baptism,' данны҇ дарѡмъ (110b,17) *lit.* 'given gifts' Dpl, зготованноє длѧ ва҇ црство (47a,2) 'the kingdom prepared for you,' but животъ . . . ѿ Бг҃а намъ даный (K14a,10) 'a life . . . [which is] given to us from/by God,' а длѧ того и осꙋженымъ сталъ сѧ (30b,2) 'for that he was condemned,' в огонь, длѧ дїавола и ангелѡвъ зготованый (53a,18–19) 'into the fire, [which was] prepared for the devil and his angels,' смерть Цноты маетъ быти найдована (K14a,16) 'a death of virtue must be found.' The syntactic role of the latter forms (-*n*-) is reflected by their use in predicate complements, especially when the short forms of these are used (participles with -*nn*- have no short forms). There are, however, also instances in which both formants can occur with no obvious differences in function or stylistic marking, as in ведлꙋгъ реченого (33b,13) 'according to [what has been] said,' and ведлꙋ҇г реченного (43b,21–22). Both can occur in the same phrase, such as речъ єстъ оувелбенаѧ и оублагословеннаѧ (469b,4) 'is an adored and blessed thing.' Here the two participles are syntactically equivalent (but note the marked status of the second lexeme, which may or may not play a role in requiring -*nn*-). A strict division between the two kinds of past passive participles purely on syntactic grounds is impossible given such vacillations.

9.7.4.3 The aspect of these participial forms deserves note, as well. In MS' texts past passive participles can be formed from imperfective as well as from imperfective verbs, as they could in CES (Avanesov and Ivanov 1982, 372). This is the Ruthenian norm, and is still characteristic of CSU. In CSBR and CSR, on the other hand, the past passive participle is, as a rule, limited to perfective verbs. Compare the following imperfectives: прошеный (343a,4) 'asked,' даванъ (194a,21) 'given,' звани (369a,18) 'called,' читаное єѵ҃лїе (327b,24–25) 'the Gospel [which was] read.' The viability of these imperfectives is occasionally clear from context: три разы . . . дава҇н былъ 'was given three times' (repetition); звани бывши жидовскїи кнѧжата 'they were called Jewish princes,' reflecting a definition (and thus constant). The occurrence of both imperfective and perfective past passive participles from the same verb together in one sentence illustrates the difference in meaning: дѧкꙋимо . . . Бг҃ꙋ за всѣ єго дары . . . даныи и даваныи

(403a,12–15) 'let us thank God for all his gifts . . . [which had been] given and [were] being given.'

9.7.4.4 In sum: 1) the formant *-n-* is unmarked and vastly outnumbers *-nn-*; 2) *-nn-* is common in marked lexemes (Slavonicisms) and marked contexts; 3) there is a reanalysis of forms with *-nn-* (participle > adjective) and this process does not have to be limited to Slavonicisms; 4) past passives with the formant *-n-* can be formed from imperfective as well as from perfective verbs; and 5) these are tendencies and not rules.

9.7.4.5 In the language of IV the past passive participles with *-n(n)-* also are the most commonly found forms, occurring 260 times as opposed to 31 examples of participles with the formant *-t-*. Gröschel attests 94 short forms (1972, 280, 289). PB yields a large number of these participles, with long forms outnumbering short forms by 400:30 (or 13:1; 82–84).

9.7.5 *Adverbialized Participles: The Gerunds.* The forms of the gerund are invariable in MS' system, and both are extremely common (1000+ attestations of each); the markers are present *-či,* past *-(v)ši.* Compare with CSU/CSBR *-čy, -(v)šy.* The same forms are found in IV (248–49).

9.7.5.1 Examples of the present gerund include: хотѧчи (K3a,21) 'wanting,' оумираючи (K18a,17) 'dying,' бл҃вѧчи (K10a,3) 'blessing,' идꙋчи (35b,27) 'going,' живꙋчи (35b,7) 'living,' говорѧчи (165b,24) 'saying, speaking,' among others. Final stress is characteristic of CSU and CSBR gerunds, and this feature is also found in the marked form бл҃вѧчи́. Note the place of stress in гово́рѧчи, which is reflected by CSU/CSBR stem *hovóry-/havóry-*.

9.7.5.2 Examples of the past gerund include: оуслышавши (K3a,6) 'hearing,' взѧвши (K8b,13) 'taking,' живши (K15a,19) 'living,' пришєдши (K13a,18) 'coming,' бывши (369a,18) 'being,' etc. The formation that this gerund follows is the same as that of the past active participle (see 9.7.2 above), and the place of stress is dictated by the place of stress in the preterite; the final vowel is never stressed.

9.8 *Excursus on* mĕti-mati. The verb "to have" has been mentioned in the contexts of the infinitive and the non-past, with special attention paid to the Slavonic verb имати. In Ruthenian there was no one verb which corresponded to this Slavonic lexeme: two verbs are used to express "to have" in the Ruthenian period (and therefore in Smotryc'kyj's texts), viz. мѣти and *мати. In CSU and CSBR the verb "to have" is мати and мець, respectively. Thus, both were in use in the Ruthenian system, and the modern languages generalized different variants. CSR generalized the more archaic from иметь, similar to CSBR but retaining initial i-. Judging by such reference works as SSUM, it would appear that мѣти and мати were in head-to-head competition in the 14th and 15th centuries. Data from MS' texts indicate that the competition between them had given way to a strict division by the beginning of the 17th century.

9.8.1 мѣти is attested 434 times, while *мати (infinitive not attested) is found 616 times in Smotryc'kyj's texts. Compare the following distribution of forms:

	*мати	мѣти
Present Tense:	x	
Preterite Tense:		x
Infinitive:		x
Imperative:		x
Pres. Act. Part.:	x	
Past Act. Part.:		x

This division of forms is strictly adhered to. Compare the following examples, especially the juxtaposition of forms in the second set:

мѣй (270b,4) Imperative
маешъ (156a,21) 2sg
мѣлемъ (505b,15) Preterite 1sg
мѣти (255a,1) Infinitive
маючихъ (277a,6) Present Active Participle Gpl

не маючихъ и мѣти не могꙋчихъ (277a,6) ‘not having and being unable to have’
мѣлемъ и завжды маю (187b,6–7) ‘I had and always have’
мѣти мѣли (310b,21) ‘had to have’
Што теды сегоднѧ маемо, а завтра можемо не мѣти (542b,24–25) ‘what, then, we have today, and tomorrow may not have.’

9.8.2 The forms and distribution above suggest the following: zero- and consonantal desinences occur with *mĕj*- (in the presence of a consonant -*j*- is deleted), vocalic desinences with *maj*-. Coincidentally, the distribution of the two roots is characteristic of an aspectual pair, with мати functioning as the imperfective and мѣти as the perfective. Although this appears to hold up in most instances, one example in particular contradicts such an interpretation: єсли боудете мѣти вѣрꙋ (255a,1) ‘if you will have faith.’ Forms of the present paradigm of мѣти are common in Old Ruthenian, as represented by SSUM (имѣю alongside маю). In FS, earlier than MS but no longer really “Old” Ruthenian, we find мети, имати, имевати, and имети. The second form is Slavonic, the rest are based on the stem *(i)mej-,* that is to say, there is already a preference for *-mej-* in the language of this Belarusian-Ruthenian. In the systems of Smotryc'kyj’s contemporaries, we find the same distribution as in MS, that is, only мати in the present tense (e.g., SinSlav, PB), мѣти in the past tense (мѣлемъ: SinSlav).

9.8.3 The use of these two verbs with infinitives expresses the modal “to have to,” as in CSU and CSBR: ꙗкъ в̓ писмѣ с҃томъ найдꙋемо и читаемо, та҃к вѣрити маемо (195b,8–9) ‘as we find and read in the holy scripture, so must we believe’; cf also мѣти мѣли (310b,21) ‘had to have.’ It is possible that a future meaning is also present in some of the attested constructions: день сꙋдны̏, однакꙋю помстꙋ мае҃ оучинити зко҃дого зневѣ҃цы и пышного (30b,27–31a,1) ‘judgement day will/must take identical vengeance on every insulter and haughty [person]’; ꙗ єстемъ той, который прїйти мѣлемъ (505b,14–15) ‘I am the one who had to come’ or better ‘who was to come.’ This possible use of мати/мѣти with the infinitive ought to receive further attention in future studies.

CHAPTER TEN

Afterword

10.0 A reader of Smotryc'kyj's texts notes, first of all, that the lexicon is generally East Slavic, characterized by a substantial admixture of Polish elements. This admixture is common to all three texts, but, as described in chapter 1, it is higher in some passages than in others. A closer analysis of MS' Ruthenian, moreover, reveals that this language can be described more specifically as *phonologically* "Ukrainian-Ruthenian." However, while such a determination may also be justified with regard to morphology, the presence of occasional Belarusian-Ruthenian features requires a more tempered approach.

The morphological component of this language must be examined as a set of two categories: flectional and non-flectional elements. In categories characterized by flectional endings we can speak only of "general Ruthenian." At the same time individual elements in particular categories may be labelled "U-R" or "B-R," as a whole they may not. MS' non-flectional morphology (e.g., the adverb, conjunction) also reflects features of U-R, B-R, CES, or Slavonic, or both CES and Slavonic. But the major factor separating the two sets of categories is the very substantial Polish component in the second: the "lexical" characteristics of this morphological component encourage the borrowing and use of Polonisms, whereas bound morphemes are unlikely to be adopted. The following discussion highlights those elements that may be identified as U-R or B-R in flectional morphology (others as Common Ruthenian). Slavonicisms are extrasystemic and have no bearing on the description of the Smotryc'kyj Variant of Ruthenian (readers interested in the presence of particular morphological Slavonicisms are encouraged to refer to the relevant chapters). Because of their high visibility in non-flectional categories, Polonisms are identified in this component of MS' language. Slavonicisms are included when they stand in clear oppostion to semantically identical Ruthenian/Polish forms.

10.1 *Flectional Morphology*

10.1.1 *The Substantive*. Some forms in Smotryc'kyj's texts might be interpreted as Ukrainianisms on the basis of the phonological analysis (e.g., D/L *-ě* (-ѣ) = [i]), whereas others do not require phonological interpretation. Among the latter we can count forms of the II declension masculine paradigm: Dsg *-ovi/-evi*, Lsg *-u,* Vsg *-u,* all of which are present in CSU but not in CSBR. Note that the vacillation between Gsg *-a* and *-u* described among II declension masculines still exists to some extent in CSU, but is more prevalent in CSBR. From the III declension feminine note U-R Asg матєръ (CSU матір, but CSBR маці). Three plural forms are worthy of note as possible reflections of U-R dialect features: Lpl *-ox* (hard stems; cf. modern West Ukrainian), Gpl *-ij* and Lpl *-ex* (soft stems; cf. modern Southwest Ukrainian). One other may be interpreted as U-R: Gpl поль (CSU піль, but CSBR палёў).

10.1.2 *The Adjective*. Several features can be identified more specifically as U-R: 1) Gsgf -ои, compare with CSU -oї; the B-R variant -оє (< *-oě) is found only once (оустaвичноє ростꙋсты, cited in 2.1.2.1 and in chapter 4; see also 10.1.3 below), compare with CSBR - ой/-ое. This spelling is often attested in the language of Vyšens'kyj and is interpreted by Gröschel as a feature of North Ukrainian (or as orthographically B-R). The latter solution appears to be preferable in this instance: when specific Ukrainian dialect evidence is found, it is usually southwest Ukrainian. One example is not evidence of a B-R morphological feature in his language, but it certainly can be ascribed to the influence of B-R tradition. 2) Lsg non-fem -омъ, as *-om > [im] in modern Southwest Ukrainian: compare CSU -ому and CSBR -ым.

10.1.3 *The Pronoun*. Several individual features might be described as U-R: 1) initial *n-* is present in the oblique cases of the 3sg/3pl personal pronoun in MS and in CSU, whereas it is not in CSBR; 2) as in the adjective, Lsg томъ corresponds to CSU тім (next to тому) rather than to CSBR тым; and 3) щ о can only be described as "Ukrainian" (compare to CSBR што). There are also several features that can be interpreted as B-R: 1) the relative pronoun который corresponds to CSBR каторы rather than to CSU котрий (the latter is amply attested in the language of MS' contemporaries), although its function as a relative may be characterized as U-R (in CSBR it is only found as an interrogative); 2) the use of the prefixal particle *ni-* as a marker of indefiniteness is retained in CSBR but not in CSU; 3) жадный 'none' may be B-R or Polish, but when considered together with кождый 'every,' the former interpretation is preferable. Thus, MS жадный, кождый are reflected by CSBR жадны, кожды, while CSU attests жодний, кождий, and CSP *żaden, każdy*.

10.1.4 *The Numeral*. If the grapheme ѡ represents [u] then for the G-L of "two" both [dvox] (U-R) and [dvux] (B-R) are present in MS' texts. These are more likely mere spelling variants for [dvox]. For the G of "three" only трѡхъ is present, analogical to двѡхъ. In CSBR this form is трох, in CSU трьох, thus the hard [r] may reflect the B-R variant. Other forms; пѧтма 'five' (instrumental) is clearly U-R (CSU п'ятьма but Br. пяццю). The collective тридцатеро 'thirty' may be patterned on CSP *trzydzieścioro,* but this form is present in SUM (its occurrence in CSBR is not precluded, but the absence of such larger collective forms in TSBM seems to indicate that they are a rarity in that language). According to Kernycʹkyj чотырдесѧтъ 'forty' is limited to Galicia in 16c U-R, while Bulyka et al. show that it is common in B-R. This allows the form in MS' language to be identified with some certainty as a B-R feature.

10.1.5 *The Verb*. This morphological class is comparable to the other inflected classes reflected in Smotrycʹkyj's language in that it generally represents a solidly "pre-Ukrainian-Belarusian" category. No one feature in MS' verbal system can be pointed to as unambiguously "Belarusian." The exclusive use of the 1pl non-past desinence *-mo* in unmarked environments might be pointed to as U-R, but this morpheme is also found in Southwest Belarusian. On the other hand, the frequent formation of past passive participles from imperfective verbs can be cited as one specifically U-R verbal feature present in his language. In addition, the exclusive use of мати, маю in the present tense (not мѣти, *мѣю) can be interpreted as U-R, since CSBR uses the latter and B-R authors such as FS show a preference for мѣю, and so forth.

One striking aspect of the verbal system is the importance of the Polish morphological component. 1) The active use of the present tense forms of 'to be,' viz. єстемъ, єстесь, єстесмо, and єстесте (1sg, 2sg,

1pl, 2pl, respectively) cannot be interpreted as a chance occurrence. It makes more sense to explain it as compensation for a void in the system: the living language was in the process of losing (or had already lost) the marked 1sg, 2sg, 1pl, and 2pl forms, so speakers adopted the available Polish forms in their place to restore systemic equilibrium. These forms are retained in modern Southwest Ukrainian. In other words, a full present tense paradigm is still found in this variant, whereas CSU/CSBR are characterized by the use of only the unmarked 3sg form. The system keeps either the entire set of forms, then, or just one representative unmarked form (as is also the case in CSR). 2) The personal endings *-emъ*, etc., were probably suffixed to the l-participle under the influence of Polish, again because the native system had lost the overt markers of person in the copula and auxiliary verb "to be." The use of these endings in modern Southwest Ukrainian is certainly supported by the proximity of this region to Polish linguistic territory. 3) The opposition masculine—non-masculine in 3pl preterite verb forms must be considered in light of the Polish distinction virile—non-virile. More research will be required to determine how widespread this phenomenon is in the Ruthenian period.

10.2 *Non-Flectional Morphology*

10.2.1 *The Adverb*. 1) The majority of adverbial forms (MS где, ꙗкъ, etc., including many Polish borrowings) are still current in CSU as well as in CSBR. Adverbs with the comparative formant *-ěj* belong here as well. 2) U-R forms include: иногды (CSU іноді), почасти (CSU почасти), допо́зна and дочи́ста (on the basis of place of stress), вправдѣ, заєдно, одаль, внѣвечъ, тежъ, вполнѣ, зачим, and оподалъ (a dialect form). The superlative construction ꙗкнай plus comparative is CSU but not CSBR (cf. CSBR якмага + comparative). Numerical adverbs of the type потрєте, почєтвєрте can be identified as U-R on the basis of the final *-e* (compare the corresponding use of the long form adjectival neuter ending in CSBR). 3) B-R elements include: подчасъ, пѣшо, звнꙋтра (? compare CSBR знутры), пречъ, навидокꙋ (dialect), внꙋтръ. Prefixal (stressed) *ně-*: нѣ́коли is still found in CSBR as well as in CSU, but only in the former is не́калі used as an indefinite adverb, as in MS' texts. The comparative formant *-ej* (probably originally influenced by Polish) is today widely found in CSBR adverbs, whereas this is not the case in CSU. 4) In 15 instances adverbs of Polish origin were commonly used in Ruthenian (attested in such sources as SinSlav and PB) but then lost to CSU and CSBR: барзо, велце, вєсполъ, вкоротце, вполъ, врыхлѣ, вспакъ, завше, заправды, звлаща, иле, надалъ, назбытъ, натыхмѣстъ, немаль, нѣгды, овшеки, овшемъ, оттамтолъ, передтымъ, снать, теды, частокроть, южъ. The adverb овде, otherwise identifiable with Polish *ówdzie,* may represent an innovation by referring to motion to rather than location in a particular place. If other examples of this specific use of овде are found in Ruthenian texts then it may be considered a Polonism current in Ruthenian but lost in later stages of the language. Note that many forms consisting of *po* + dative of adjective, *z* + genitive of adjective, have not been retained by CSU/CSBR, as is the case with the 15 examples cited above, while others have (здавна, зпочаткȣ, зверхȣ).

10.2.2 *The Preposition*. Slavonic or "higher style" adverbs were not separately listed above, but prepositions are because most of the prepositions classified as "Slavonic" or "higher style" stand in direct opposition to corresponding unmarked Ruthenian prepositions. 1) Common Ruthenian prepositions retained in CSU and CSBR (not necessarily always in the literary languages) include: безъ, въ, вслѣдъ, длѧ, до, за, мимо, на, надъ, напротивъ (+ G), о, около, опрочъ, отъ, передъ, по (+ L), подъ, посередъ, поверхъ, при, зъ/съ, сквозь, ȣ, черезъ. On the basis of its presence in Hrinčenko's dictionary of Ukrainian, one can include презъ here as well (it is still present in CSBR). 2) U-R forms include: кромъ (CSBR акрамя), межи, передъ (+ A), противъ (+ G), прочъ, напередъ (+ G), насередъ. 3) B-R forms include: подчасъ and втылъ (only in MS and several examples cited in HSBM). 4) Polonisms include: ведле, ведлȣгъ, кȣ, подле, подлȣгъ, пре. 5) Extrasystemic Polonisms include: зевнȣтръ, зпосредкȣ, посредкȣ, впосредокъ, посродкȣ. These do not appear to have been widely used in the Ruthenian period, although the root *-sred-/-srod-* was clearly productive. 6) Slavonicisms and/or "high style" prepositions: вмѣсто, внѣ, внȣтрь, впреко, дѣлѧ, къ, кромѣ, междȣ, напротивъ (+ D), по (+ D), прежде, противъ (+ D), ради. 7) змежи 'from among' may have been devised by the author himself, reflected in the pattern of such prepositions as CSU з-під/CSBR з-пад 'from under.'

10.2.3 *The Conjunction*. 1) Conjunctions retained in CSU and CSBR are а, або, абы, албо, алє, аж, бо, єслн, и, коли, однакъ, поки, покȣль, тєды, што. 2) U-R examples include: надъ in comparative constructions ('than'), нѣжъ, нѣмъ, хочъ/хоча, щобы. Were it not for the fact that this final form occurs in present-day Ukrainian dialects, this form would represent our only example of an extrasystemic Polonism. 3) The variants хоть and хотѧ are present in CSBR but not in CSU; зато and притомъ are slightly different in form, but occur in CSBR: затое and прытым. 4) Polish conjunctions play an extremely important role in the Ruthenian system, outnumbering Common Ruthenian forms: абовѣмъ, ачъ (although this could be more precisely identified as "early Ruthenian"), ачколвєкъ, ано, бовѣмъ, вшакже, Гды, єднак, илє, жє, жєбы, зась, ижъ, ыжбы, лєчъ, люб(о), нѣжли, понєважъ, прєто, хотѧжъ. 5) There is one extrasystemic Polonism: єно. 6) Slavonicisms include: аще, ажє, да, єжєли, или, либо, но, ȣбо, ѧко.

10.2.4 *The Particle*. In comparison with the conjunction, the particle reflects a generally higher representation of forms retained in CSU and CSBR, in absolute numbers as well as in proportion to Polonisms lost after the Ruthenian period. There are very small U-R, B-R, as well as Slavonic components, and no extrasystemic Polonisms. 1) Forms retained in CSU and CSBR are анѣ, бы, жє, за (in the construction што за), и, нє, нєхай, нѣ, ось. 2) U-R forms include: чи (cf. CSBR ці) and навєтъ. 3) One particle may be considered B-R by virtue of the place of stress: compare MS óто, CSU ото́, but CSBR от (final unstressed -o was lost in this Belarusian form). It is also possible that MS óто reflects the corresponding Polish form. The other particle that may be identified as B-R is азажъ. 4) Polonisms lost after the Ruthenian period include аза, чили, за (used to express "too"). The last element cited is not present in either literary language as a productive element (although it is productive in Western Ukrainian). Only remnants of this use of за remain in the modern literary languages, and in fact more remnants are found in CSBR than in CSU (we would be overreaching, however, if we went so far as to say that this constitutes a B-R form. 5) The lone Slavonic example is да 'let.'

10.3 *A Final Word*.

A study of Smotryc'kyj's morphology in comparison with that of Berynda and Vyšens'kyj based only on the preface to *Grammatiki* and *Kazan'e* (Pugh 1990) came to the conclusion that Smotryc'kyj's system lay somewhere between the other two: Vyšens'kyj's was the most conservative and Slavonic, while Berynda's appeared to be the closest to the vernacular. As it happens, this conclusion was a function of the stylistic level of Smotryc'kyj's language, which was dictated by the identity of the texts themselves. After analyzing the volumes of linguistic information present in JU, it is now apparent that Smotryc'kyj's system is virtually indistinguishable from Berynda's: JU was meant to be a vehicle by which the priest could communicate with his congregation, and its language is accordingly much closer to the vernacular than that of *Kazan'e*, a funeral sermon.

This difference in register is first of all reflected in the function of Slavonic in the texts: in all of Smotryc'kyj's Ruthenian writings (as in Ruthenian generally) Slavonic forms were used in marked contexts such as biblical citations, therefore such elements are proportionately much more common in *Kazan'e* than they are in JU. Although Slavonicisms can occur in JU, they are comparatively rare: limited contexts in which they are common include the Lord's Prayer, a prayer presumably known to all and therefore universally understood, individual lexemes (ρаспѧтїе 'crucifixion') and chapter headings (*perv-* 'first,' not *perš-*; *vtor-* 'second,' not *druh-*; etc.). Occasionally an archaic element is used very subtly and does not always come across as a Slavonicism as such: cf. єсли хто прагнетъ нехай прїйдетъ ко мнѣ (192a,8) 'if someone thirsts let him come to me' versus єсли хто прагнетъ нехай прїйдетъ до мене (192a,13). The second "explains" the first, which does not appear to be in need of explanation: two specifically Ruthenian elements (хто, нехай) occur in both sentences, and the only difference between them is the use of the marked preposition *k* (+ dative) in place of Ruthenian *do* (+ genitive). With a limited role for Slavonic in JU, a central problem for the translator was his need for a way to convey particular passages in a higher, more prestigious, style of language. A solution presented itself in the form of Polish: whereas the marking structure of *Kazan'e* is essentially Slavonic is marked (+) and Ruthenian [East Slavic with Polonisms] is unmarked

(-), the marking structure of JU is a function of higher versus lower concentrations of Polonisms. Every reading in this collection begins with the recounting of a biblical story, followed by an explication of that same story. The biblical passage, which would have been Slavonic in *Kazan'e*, is still Ruthenian, but contains a higher concentration of Polish elements (lexical as well as morphological). Thus, for example, in biblical readings we find the verb цаловалъ (35b,19) 'he kissed' (< CSP *całować*), цалѹю ночъ (303a,18–19) 'all night' (< CSP *cały*), and оукрыжованого 'the one who was crucified' in an introductory biblical passage (142a,26). In order to set apart these readings from their explication, the corresponding CES forms can appear in the course of the explanatory narrative: цѣлѹетъ (42b,26) 'kisses,' роспѧтого (142b,21) 'the one who was crucifed.' The higher stylistic level (Polish) can also be reflected in place of stress: єщє́ is treated as an unmarked Ruthenian form (final stress) while є́щє (with Polish penultimate stress) often occurs in a biblical reading.

This pattern is significant socially as well as linguistically: the priest/reader is presenting a biblical passage to an Orthodox congregation and Polish is the vehicle for the transmission of the prestige factor, because 1) the language of a biblical passage must be non-Ruthenian to be prestigious and 2) he wants it to be understood, but the people do not understand Slavonic, whereas they presumably understand Polish. Smotryc'kyj may well have believed in the theoretical equality of Slavonic and Latin, of Ruthenian and Polish in their respective societies (returning to Frick 1985); the very fact that he used Polish in JU the way he did, however, indicates that he saw Polish as the language of a higher culture, and therefore one which enjoyed prestige in Ruthenian society. In order of relative stylistic marking, Slavonic occupies the highest position (the Lord's Prayer could only be recited in that language), followed by Polish, and then by Ruthenian. The line between "Polish" and "Ruthenian" is of course a fuzzy one— since "Ruthenian" contains a large number of systemic Polonisms.

An overall characterization of Smotryc'kyj's language must emphasize the common "Ukrainian-Belarusian" nature of the system: most of the forms in all morphological classes studied are still present in both modern languages. The Smotryc'kyj Variant is certainly "Ruthenian" *par excellence*, for there is general (and often specific) agreement between his language and that of his Ruthenian contemporaries, Berynda, Vyšens'kyj, *Sinonima Slavenorosskaja*, and even Skaryna. Occasionally individual forms can be identified as purely U-R or B-R by virtue of their presence in one or the other modern system. In terms of the morphological system as a whole, it reflects a slightly larger number of U-R forms than B-R; this fact, together with the phonological evidence presented in chapter 2, might lead one to characterization of his Ruthenian as U-R rather than as B-R. The presence of a significant number of clear B-R features cannot be dismissed on statistical grounds, however, and the temptation to label Smotryc'kyj's language as a whole as U-R ought to be avoided. In short, I see this language as a regional (certainly not *national*) variant of a supradialectal literary system. It is especially important in this context not to dismiss "Polonisms" as "un-Ruthenian," given the great influence that that language had on the development of modern Ukrainian and Belarusian. Telling in this respect are the non-inflectional morphological categories: Leeming shows that a large percentage of Polish conjunctions and prepositions used in *Aleksandryja*, 44.44% and 37.55% (respectively), are retained in both CSU and CSBR (1968, 311).

The analysis of the literary Ruthenian language of Smotryc'kyj's texts therefore leads to the following conclusions: First, the language is characterized by a high level of variation, which is both lexical and grammatical. Second, it foreshadows both CSU and CSBR, without necessarily being "pre-Ukrainian" or "pre-Belarusian" alone, and thus reflects much that is still characteristic of both present-day languages. In sum, it is not an artificial literary system, it is not divorced from the living language of the Ruthenian lands, and may be said to represent a learned variant of the Ruthenian Vernacular Standard.

Works Cited

Ambrosiani, Per. 1991. *On Church Slavonic Accentuation: The Accentuation of a Russian Church Slavonic Gospel Manuscript from the Fifteenth Century*. Stockholm. [= Stockholm Slavic Studies 21.]

Andersen, Henning. 1969. "Indo-European Voicing Sandhi in Ukrainian." *Scando-Slavica* 15: 157–69.

Andrusyshen, C. H. comp. 1955. *Ukrainian-English Dictionary*. Toronto. [4th Printing, 1990.]

Aničenka, U. V. 1969. *Belaruska-ŭkrainskija pis'mova-moŭnyja suvjazi*. Minsk.

————. 1977, 1984. *Sloŭnik movy Skaryny*. Vols. 1 and 2. Minsk.

————. 1982. "Vyvučnne mjascovaj raznavidnasci knižnaslavjanskaj movy ŭ hramatycy M. Smatryckaha." In *Sxidno-slov'jans'ki hramatyky XVI–XVII st. Materialy sympoziumu*. Ed. I. P. Čepiha et al., pp. 122–27. Kyiv.

Avanesov, Ruben Ivanovič, ed. 1961. *Xrėstamatyja pa historyi belaruskaj movy*. Častka peršaja. Minsk.

————, and V. V. Ivanov, eds. 1982. *Istoričeskaja grammatika russkogo jazyka. Morfologija. Glagol*. Moscow.

Bacenko, K. S. 1982. "'Hramatyka' M. Smotryc'koho i tohočasne ukrajins'ke narodne movlennja." In *Sxidno-slov'jans'ki hramatyky XVI–XVII st. Materialy sympoziumu*. Ed. I. P. Čepiha et al., pp. 155–58. Kyiv.

Baxan'koŭ, A. Ju., et al. eds. 1970. *Histaryčnaja leksikalohija belaruskaj movy*. Minsk.

Bevzenko, Stepan Pylypovyč, et al. 1978. *Istorija ukrajins'koji movy. Morfolohija*. Kyiv.

Bilodid, Ivan Kostjantynovyč, et al. 1970. *Hramatyka slov'jans'ka I. Uževiča. Prymitky*. Kyiv.

Blinava, Evelina, and Je. Mjacel'skaja. 1980. 2nd ed. *Belaruskaja Dyjalektalohija*. Minsk.

Bogusławski, Andrzej. 1966. *Semantyczne pojęcie liczebnika i jego morfologia w języku rosyjskim*. Wrocław. [=Monografie sławistyczne, 10].

Borisenko, V.V., et al. eds. 1977. *Istorija beloruskoj dooktjabrskoj literatury*. Minsk.

Brückner, Aleksander. 1957. *Słownik Etymologiczny Języka Polskiego*. Warsaw.

Bulaxovs'kyj, Leonid Avsenevič. 1956. *Pytannja poxodžennja ukrajins'koji movy*. Kyiv.

Bulyka, Aljaksandr Mikalaevič, et al. 1979. *Histaryčnaja marfalohija belaruskaj movy*. Minsk.

————. 1988. *Mova belaruskaj pis'mennasci XIV–XVIII stst*. Minsk

————. 1990. *Mova vydannjaŭ Francyska Skaryny*. Minsk.

Čemeritsij et al. eds. 1977. *Istorija beloruskoj dooktjabrskoj literatury*. Minsk.

DABM: *Dyjalektalahičny atlas belaruskaj movy*. 1963. Ed. Ruben Ivanovič Avanesov. Minsk.

De Bray, Reginald G. A. 1980. *Guide to the East Slavonic Languages*. Columbus, Ohio.

Didiakin-Leeming, Monica. 1969. *Fleksja ukraińska w leksykonie Pamby Beryndy*. Wrocław. [=Monografie Sławistyczne, 16].

Diels, Paul. 1963. *Altkirchenslavische Grammatik I/II. Mit einer Auswahl von Texten und einem Wörterbuch*. Heidelberg.

Dingley, J. 1972. "The Two Versions of the Gramatyka Slovenskaja of Ivan Uževič." *The Journal of Byelorussian Studies* 2 (4): 369–84.

Dolenko, Mitrofan Terentevič, et al. 1987. 3rd ed. *Sučasna ukrajins'ka mova*. Kyiv.

Dzendzelivs'kyj, Iosif Alekseevič. 1969. *Ukrajins'ko-zaxidnoslov'jans'ki leksyčni paraleli*. Kyiv.

EDUL: *See* Rudnyc'kyj 1966– .

Entwistle, William James, and W. A. Morison. 1949. *Russian and the Slavonic Languages*. London.

ESBM: *Ėtymalahičny sloŭnik belaruskaj movy*. 1978–. Ed. Viktor Vladzimiravič Martynaŭ. Minsk.

ESSJ/M: *Ètimologičeskij slovar' slavjanskix jazykov*. 1974–. Ed. Oleg Nikolaevič Trubačev. Moscow.

ESSJ/P: *Etymologický Slovník Slovanských Jazyků*. 1973. Vol. 1. 1980. Vol 2. Ed. František Kopečný et al. Prague.

ESUM: *Etymolohičnyj slovnyk ukrajins'koji movy*. 1982–. Ed. Oleksandr Savyč Mel'nyčuk et al. Kyiv.

Filin, Fedot Petrovič. 1972. *Proisxoždenie russkogo, ukrainskogo, i belorusskogo jazykov*. Leningrad.

Flier, Michael S. 1983. "The Alternation l-v in East Slavic." In *American Contributions to the Ninth International Congress of Slavists. Vol. 1, Linguistics*. Ed. M. S. Flier, pp. 99–118. Columbus, Ohio.

Frick, David A. 1983. *Meletius Smotricky and the Ruthenian Question in the Age of Counter-Reformation*. (Ph.D. Dissertation, Yale University).

————. 1985. "Kazanie Melecjusza Smotryckiego z lat 1620/21: wersje ruska i polska." *Studia z Filologii Polskiej i Słowiańskiej* 23: 153–61.

————. 1985. "Meletij Smotryc'kyj and the Ruthenian Language Question." *Harvard Ukrainian Studies* 9 (1/2): 25–52.

Goldblatt, Harvey. 1991. "On the Language Beliefs of Ivan Vyšens'kyj and the Counter-Reformation." *Harvard Ukrainian Studies* 15 (1/2): 7–34.

Grimsted, Patricia. 1981. *Archives and Manuscript Repositories in the USSR. Estonia, Latvia, Lithuania, and Belorussia*. Princeton.

Gröschel, Bernhard. 1972. *Die Sprache Ivan Vyšens'kyj's, Untersuchungen und Materialien zur historischen Grammatik des Ukrainischen, Slavistische Forschungen 13*. Köln.

GSPS: *Grammatiki Slavenskija Pravilnoe Syntagma*: see Nimčuk 1979.

Harvard Library of Early Ukrainian Literature. Texts. Cambridge, Mass., 1987. Vol. 1, *Collected Works of Meletij Smotryc'kyj*. With an Introduction by David A. Frick. Vol. 2, *The Jevanhelije učitelnoe of Meletij Smotryc'kyj*. With an Introduction by David A. Frick.

HSBM: Histaryčny sloŭnik belaruskaj movy. 1982– . Ed. Arkadzij Josifavič Žuraŭskij et al. Minsk.

Holovaščuk, S. I., et al. 1975. *Orfohrafičnyj slovnyk ukrajins'koji movy*. Kyiv.

Horbatsch, Oleksa. 1964. *Die Vier Ausgaben der kirchenslavischen Grammatik M. Smotryc'kyj's*. Wiesbaden. [=Frankfurter Abhandlungen zur Slavistik 7.]

————, ed. 1974. *Hrammatiki Slavenskija Pravilnoe Syntagma, Jevje 1619, Kirchenslavische Grammatik (Erstausgabe)*. Frankfurt.

Hrinčenko, Boris. 1907–1909. *Slovar' ukrajins'koji movy*. 4 vols. Kyiv.

Hruca, A. P. 1976. "Prynazoŭniki podle, podlug", v"podlug", vedle, vedlug u starabelaruskaj move XIV–XVIII stst.." *Belaruskaja linhvistyka* 10: 64–70.

Humec'ka, L. 1962. "Fonetyčni substytuciji v staroukrajins'kyx zapožyčennjax z pol'skoji movy." In *Doslidžennja i materialy z ukrajins'koji movy*, pp. 53–61. Kyiv.

————. 1963. "Morfematyčni substytuciji v najdavnišyx ukrajins'kyx zapožyčennjax z pol'skoji movy." *Pytannja slov'jans'koho movoznavstva/Voprosy slavianskogo jazykoznanija* (L'viv) 9: 52–56.

————. 1969. "K istorii ukrainsko-pol'skix jazykovyx svjazej." *Issledovanija po pol'skomu jazyku. Sbornik statej.* Ed. Zoja Nikolaevna Strekalova, pp. 219–28. Moscow.

————. 1971. "Zametki ob ukrainsko-zapadnoslavjanskix leksičeskix svjazjax drevnego perioda." In *Problemy istorii i dialektologii slavjanskix jazykov*. Ed. Fedot Petrovič Filin, pp. 113–18. Moscow.

Hurski, Mikalai Ivanovič. 1962. *Paraŭnal'naja hramatyka ruskaj i belaruskaj moŭ. Fanetyka i Marfalohija.* Minsk.

Isačenko, Alexander V. 1983. *Geschichte der russischen Sprache. 1. Band: Von den Anfängen bis zum Ende des 17. Jahrhunderts.* Heidelberg.

Ivanov, Vsevolod Vjačeslavovič. 1983. *Istoričeskaja grammatika russkogo jazyka*. 2nd ed. Moscow.

————. 1990. *Istoričeskaja grammatika russkogo jazyka*. 3rd ed. Moscow.

Jankowski, F. 1974. *Histaryčnaja hramatyka belaruskaj movy. 1. Uvodziny. Fanetyka.* Minsk.

————. 1977. *Histaryčnaja hramatyka belaruskaj movy. 2 Marfalohija.* Minsk. [2nd ed., 1983; 3rd ed., 1989. Minsk.]

Jaremenko, Porfirij Kyryllovyč. 1986. *Meletij Smotryc'kyj. Žyttja i tvorčist'.* Kyiv.

Karaś, Mieczysław and A. Karasiowa. 1969. *Mariana z Jaślik. Dykcjonarz słowiańsko-polski z roku 1641.* Wrocław.

Karaulov, Iurij Nikolaevič, ed. 1985. *Vostočnyje slavjane. Jazyki, istorija, kul'tura.* Moscow.

Karskij, Evfimij. 1926. *Geschichte der weissrussischen Volksdichtung und Literatur.* Berlin and Leipzig.

Kedajtene, E. I. 1985. "Variantnost' form imen suščestvitel'nyx mužskogo roda jedinstvennogo čisla v jazyke pamjatnikov polemičeskoj literatury jugo-zapadnoj rusi XVI–XVII vv." In Karaulov 1985, pp. 130–35.

Kernyc'kyj, I. M. 1967. *Systema slovozminy v ukrajins'kij movi*. Kyiv.

Klemensiewicz, Zenon. 1974. *Historia języka polskiego*. Warsaw.

————. 1981. T. Lehr-Spławiński, and S. Urbańczyk. *Gramatyka historyczna języka polskiego*. Warsaw.

Kramko, Ivan Ihnatavič. "Ličebnik" and "Prysloŭje," in Bulyka et al., 1988, pp. 127–144 and 272–308.

Krivickij, A. A., et al. 1978. 2nd ed. *Belorusskij jazyk dlja nebelorusov*. Minsk.

————. 1982-87. *Turaŭski sloŭnik*. Vols. 1–5. Minsk.

Kuraszkiewicz, Władysław. 1963. *Zarys dialektologii wschodniosłowiańskiej*. Warsaw.

Leeming, Henry. 1968. "Polonisms in a 17th-Century Ruthenian Text." *The Slavonic and East European Review* 46 (107) July: 282–314.

————. 1976. *Rola języka polskiego w rozwoju leksyki rosyjskiej do roku 1696. Wyrazy pochodzenia łacińskiego i romańskiego*. Wrocław.

Lehr-Spławiński, Tadeusz. 1978. *Język polski. Pochodzenie, powstanie, rozwój*. Warsaw.

Łesiów, M. 1963. "Rola cerkiewizmów i polonizmów w ukraińskim języku pisanym XVII w." *Z polskich studiów sławistycznych. ser.* 2, 1: 341–50.

Linde, M. Samuel Bogumił. 1854–1860. *Słownik języka polskiego*. 6 vols. 2nd ed. L'viv.

Lunt, Horace Gray. 1959. *Old Church Slavonic Grammar*. 2nd ed. The Hague.

————. 1970. *Concise Dictionary of Old Russian (11th–17th Centuries)*. Munich.

Mackevič Ju. F., et al. 1979-1986. *Sloŭnik belaruskix havorak paŭnočnazaxodnjaj belarusi i jaje pahraničča*. Vols 1-5. Minsk.

Mańczak, Witold. 1965. *Polska fonetyka i morfologia historyczna*. Łódź.

Marčuk, N. J. "Formy 3–ji osoby teperišn'oho času v ukrajins'kyx hovorax." In Žylko, et al. 1969, pp. 168–77.

Martel, Antoine. 1938. *La langue polonaise dans les pays ruthènes. Ukraine et Russie Blanche 1569–1667*. Lille.

Maslov, S. 1907. "Kazan'e Meletija Smotrickago na čestnyj pogreb o. Leontija Karpoviča." *Čtenie v istoričeskom obščestve Nestora-letopisca* (Kyiv) 20: 101–119.

McMillin, Arnold.. 1980. "Belorussian." In *The Slavic Literary Languages: Formation and Development*. Ed. A. M. Schenker and E. Stankiewicz, pp. 105–117. New Haven.

Meillet, Antoine. 1934. 2nd ed. *Le Slave Commun*. Paris.

Nimčuk, V.V. 1961. *Leksykon slovenoros'kyj Pamvy Beryndy*. Kyiv.

————. 1964. *Leskis Lavrentija Zizanija. Synonima slavenorosskaja*. Kyiv.

————, comp. and ed. 1979. *M. Smotryc'kyj. Hramatyka*. Kyiv. [Facsimile edition with analytical text by Nimčuk.]

————. 1980. *Staroukrajins'ka leksykohrafija v jiji zv'jazkax z rosijs'koju ta bilorus'koju*. Kyiv.

———— et al., 1981. *Dilova mova Volyni i Naddniprjanščyny XVII st.* Kyiv.

OB: *Ostrožskaja Biblija*. 1988. Ed. I. V. Dergačeva. (Facsimile edition.) Moscow-Leningrad.

Ohijeńko, Ivan. 1931. "Wpływ języka polskiego na ukraiński w XIV–XV w." In *Pamiętnik zjazdu naukowego im. J. Kochanowskiego*, pp. 131–41. Cracow.

Oxford Russian-English Dictionary (ORED). 1972. Gen. ed. Boris O.Unbegaun. Oxford.

Pljušč, Pavlo Pavlovyč. 1971. *Istorija ukrajins'koji literaturnoji movy*. Kyiv.

Pritsak, Omeljan. 1981. *The Origin of Rus', Vol. 1: Old Scandinavian Sources Other Than the Sagas*. Cambridge, Mass.

Prokošina, Ekaterina Sergeevna. 1966. *Meletij Smotryc'kyj*. Minsk.

Pugh, Stefan M. 1984. *The Language of Meletij Smotryc'kyj: a Linguistic Analysis*. (Ph.D. Dissertation, The University of North Carolina at Chapel Hill.)

————. 1985. "The Ruthenian Language of Meletij Smotryc'kyj: Phonology." *Harvard Ukrainian Studies* 9 (1/2) June: 53–60.

————. 1986. "Leksyka polska i litera jat' w Kazaniu Melecjusza Smotryckiego." *Język Polski* 61 (1–2) January-April: 98–100.

———. 1987. "Omega in East Slavonic Orthographic Tradition," *The Slavonic and East European Review* 65 (1) January: 1–12.

———. 1990. "A Contrastive Study of Ruthenian Morphology: Smotryc'kyj, Berynda, Vyšens'kyj." T*he Slavonic and East European Review* 68 (2) April: 201–216.

Reczek, Stefan. 1968. *Podręczny słownik dawnej polszczyzny*. Wrocław.

Richhardt, Rosemarie. 1957. *Polnische Lehnwörter im Ukrainischen*. Wiesbaden.

Rothe, Hans. 1976–1977. *Die älteste ostslavische Kunstdichtung 1575–1647*. 2 vols. Giessen. [=Bausteine zur Geschichte der Literatur bei den Slawen. no. 7.]

Rudnyc'kyj, Jaroslav B. 1966– . *An Etymological Dictionary of the Ukrainian Language*. 2nd, revised ed. Winnipeg.

Rusanivs'kyj, Vitalij Makarovyč. 1982. "Sxidnoslov'jans'kyj komponent u 'Hramatyci' M. Smotryc'koho." In *Sxidno-slov'jans'ki hramatyky XVI–XVII st. Materialy sympoziumu*. Ed. I. P. Čepiha et al., pp. 116–22. Kyiv.

Sadnik, Linda and R. Aitzetmüller. 1955. *Handwörterbuch zu den altkirchenslavischen Texten*. Heidelberg.

Samijlenko, S. P. 1964. *Narysy z istoryčnoji morfolohoji ukrajins'koji movy*. Kyiv.

———. 1970. *Narysy z istoryčnoji morfolohoji ukrajins'koji movy*. Časť 2-a. Kyiv.

Samilov, Michael. 1964. *The Phoneme Jat' in Slavic*. The Hague.

Šamjakin, Ivan X., ed. 1988. *Francysk Skaryna i jaho čas. Ėncyklapedyčny davednik*. Minsk.

SBH: *Sloŭnik belaruskix havorak paŭnocna-zaxodnjaj Belarusi i jaje pahraničča*. 1982. Ed. Ju. F. Mackevič et al. Vol. 3. Minsk.

Schenker, Alexander M. and E. Stankiewicz, eds. 1980. *The Slavic Literary Languages: Formation and Development*. New Haven.

Šerex, Jurij. [George Shevelov.] 1953. "Problems in the Formation of Belorussian." Supplement to *Word* 9 (Dec).

———. 1958. *Reader in the History of the Eastern Slavic Languages*. New York.

Shevelov, George. 1979. A Historical Phonology of the Ukrainian Language. Heidelberg.

————. 1991. *In and Around Kiev*. Heidelberg.

SP XVI: *Słownik polszczyzny XVI Wieku*. 1966– . Wrocław.

SRNG: *Slovar' russkix narodnyx govorov*. 1965– . Moscow.

Sreznevskij, Izmail Ivanovič. 1955–56. *Materialy dlja slovarja drevnerusskago jazyka*. 3 vols. Graz.

SSH: *Sxidno-slov'jans'ki hramatyky XVI–XVII st. Materialy sympoziumu*. 1982. Kyiv.

SSP: *Słownik staropolski*. 1953– . Warsaw.

SSUM: *Slovnyk staroukrajins'koji movy XIV–XV st*. 1977–78. Kyiv.

Struminsky, Bohdan. A. 1984. *Pseudo-Meleško. A Ukrainian Apocryphal Parliamentary Speech of 1615–1618: A Study*. Cambridge, Mass.

SUM: *Slovnyk ukrajins'koji movy. 1970–80*. 11 vols. Ed. I. K. Bilodid, et al. Kyiv.

Svjažynski, U. M. 1988. "Prymetnik," and "Zajmennik." In Bulyka et al. 1988, pp. 101–126 and 145–69.

Sysyn, Frank E. 1986a. "The Cultural, Social and Political Context of Ukrainian History-Writing: 1620–1690." *Europa Orientalis* 5: 285–310.

————. 1986b. "Concepts of Nationhood in Ukrainian History-Writing, 1620–1690" *Harvard Ukrainian Studies*10 (3/4): 393–423.

Szober, Stansisław. 1969. *Słownik poprawnej polszczyzny*. 7th ed. Warsaw.

Taszycki, Witold. 1969. *Wybór tekstów staropolskich XVI–XVIII wieku*. Warsaw.

Timberlake, Alan. 1978. "K istorii zadnenebnyx fonem v severnoslavjanskix jazykax." In *American Contributions to the 8th International Congress of Slavists*. Vol. 1. Ed. Henryk Birnbaum, pp. 699–726. Columbus.

TSBM: *Tlumačal'ny sloŭnik belaruskaj movy*. 1977–84. Minsk.

UAS: *See* Andrusyshen 1955 (1990).

Urbańczyk, Stansisław. 1968. "O staropolskim przedrostku na-/naj-." In *Szkice z dziejów języka polskiego*, pp. 328–31. Warsaw.

Uspenskij, Boris Andreevič. 1983. "Diglossija i dvujazyčie v istorii russkogo literaturnogo jazyka." *International Journal of Slavic Linguistics and Poetics* 27: 81–126.

————. 1987. *Istorija russkogo literaturnogo jazyka (XI–XVII vv.)*. Munich.

Vaillant, André. 1950. *Grammaire Comparée des Langues Slaves*. vol. 1. Lyon.

————. 1958. *Grammaire Comparée des Langues Slaves*. vol. 2 (pts. 1 and 2). Lyon.

Vasmer, Max. 1976. *Russisches etymologisches Wörterbuch*. 3 vols. Heidelberg.

Vynnyk, V. O., et al., 1983. *Istorija ukrajins'koji movy. Leksyka i frazeolohija*. Kyiv.

Weinreich, Uriel. 1953. *Languages in Contact. Findings and Problems*. New York.

Wexler, Paul A. 1977. *Historical Phonology of the Belorussian Language*. Heidelberg.

Witkowski, Wiesław. 1969. *Język utworów Joannicjusza Galatowskiego na tle języka pismiennictwa ukraińskiego XVII wieku*. Cracow. [=Prace językoznawcze. Zeszyt 25.]

Xudaš, M. L. 1960. "Sposterežennja nad leksyčnymy polonizmamy v ukrajins'kij movi kincja XVI–počatku XVII st." *Doslidžennja i materialy z ukrajins'koji movy* (Kyiv) 3: 121–39.

Zilyns'kyj, Ivan. 1979. *A Phonetic Description of the Ukrainian Language*. Cambridge, Mass.

Žovtobrjux, Mykhailo Andrijovyč, et al. 1979. *Istorija ukrajins'koji movy.* Fonetyka. Kyiv.

————. 1980. Istoryčna hramatyka ukrajins'koji movy. Kyiv.

Žuraŭski, A. I. 1988. "Dzejasloŭ." In Bulyka et al. 1988, pp. 170–271.

Žylko, Fedot Trokhymovyč. 1966. *Narysy z dialektolohiji ukrajins'koji movy*. 2nd ed. Kyiv.

————, et al. 1969. *Ukrajins'ka dialektna morfolohija*. Kyiv.

Žytec'kyj, Pavlo Ihnatevyč. 1889. Očerk literaturnoj istorii malorusskogo narečija v XVII veke. S priloženiem slovarja knižnoj malorusskoj reči po rukopisu XVII veka. Kyiv.

Index

Ukrainian Research Institute
Harvard University

TITLES RELATING TO THE UNION OF BREST AND STUDIES OF THAT PERIOD

Gudziak, Borys. *Crisis and Reform: The Kievan Metropolitanate, the Patriarchate of Constantinople, and the Genesis of the Union of Brest.* Harvard Series in Ukrainian Studies. Forthcoming. Hardcover, ISBN 0-916458-74-1; Paperback, ISBN 0-916458-80-6.

Frick, David A. *Meletij Smotryc'kyj.* Harvard Series in Ukrainian Studies. Hardcover, ISBN 0-916458-55-5; Softcover, ISBN 0-916458-60-1.

Krevza, Lev. *Defense of Church Unity* (1617) and Zaxarija Kopystens'kyj *Palinodija or Book of Defense of the Holy Apostolic Eastern Catholic Church and Holy Patriarchs* (1620–1623). Trans. and comp. with foreword by Bohdan Strumiński. Ed. Roman Koropeckyj and Dana Miller, with William Veder. Harvard Library of Early Ukrainian Literature, English-language translations, vol. 3. Hardcover. Part 1 (Introduction and Translation) ISBN 0-916458-29-6 1995; part 2 (Sources and Indices) ISBN 0-916458-53-9.

The Collected Works of Meletij Smotryc'kyj. Introduction by David A. Frick. Harvard Library of Early Ukrainian Literature, Texts and Facsimiles, vol. I. Hardcover, ISBN 0-916458-20-2.

The Jevanhelije učytelnoje *of Meletij Smotryc'kyj.* Introduction by David A. Frick. Harvard Library of Early Ukrainian Literature, Texts and Facsimiles, vol. II. Hardcover, ISBN 0-916458-21-0.

Lev Krevza's Obrona iednosci cerkiewney *and Zaxarija Kopystens'kyj's* Palinodija. Introduction by Omeljan Pritsak and Bohdan Struminsky. Harvard Library of Early Ukrainian Literature, Texts and Facsimiles, vol. III. Hardcover, ISBN 0-916458-22-9.

Sysyn, Frank. *Between Poland and the Ukraine: The Dilemma of Adam Kysil, 1600–1653.* Harvard Series in Ukrainian Studies. Hardcover, ISBN 0-916458-08-3.

Struminsky, Bohdan. *Pseudo-Meleško: A Ukrainian Apocryphal Speech of 1615–1618.* Harvard Series in Ukrainian Studies. Hardcover, ISBN 0-916458-11-3.

For further information on ordering or for Institute publications catalogues:

Ukrainian Research Institute, Harvard University
Publications Office
1583 Massachusetts Ave.
Cambridge, MA 02138
tel. 617-495-3692 / fax 617-495-8097

Text: Typeset at the Ukrainian Research Institute in 11 pt DCTimes (Latin) and Sophia (Cyrillic), developed by Adrian Hewryk, and 14 pt Chasoslov (PaleoCyrillic), developed and copyrighted by Louis Rosenblum, except for the supplemental Ruthenian characters Г and ʼ, which were developed at the URI. Information about these fonts may be obtained from the Publications Office (address on facing page). Printed in the USA by BookCrafters, Inc.
Cover Design: URI Publications office.
Map: Adrian Hewryk and Robert De Lossa.